Ice Age Trail Guidebook

2020 – 2022 EDITION

More than 100 Detailed Segment-by-Segment Descriptions and Maps to Help You Connect with the Ice Age National Scenic Trail

*A Publication of the
Ice Age Trail Alliance*

© 2020 by Ice Age Trail Alliance.
First edition. All rights reserved.
ISBN 978-0-578-58111-8.

No part of this work may be reproduced or transmitted in any form by any means, electronic or mechanical, including photocopying and recording or any information storage-and-retrieval system, without the written permission of the Ice Age Trail Alliance, PO Box 128, 2110 Main St., Cross Plains, WI 53528; info@iceagetrail.org.

Information in this book will change. Efforts were made to make it as accurate, timely and useful as possible. For the most current information contact the Ice Age Trail Alliance, **iceagetrail.org**, **800-227-0046**.

All illustrations used with permission or in public domain.

Cover photo: Stone staircase along the Devil's Lake Segment, Sauk County. Photo by Cameron Gillie of **ThePinholeThing.com** and **AroundWisco.com**.

Back cover photos:

- Top: Gibraltar Rock Segment, Southern Columbia County. Photo by Amy Bayer.
- Middle: Harwood Lakes Segment, Chippewa County. Photo by Dave Caliebe.
- Bottom: Kewaskum Segment, Washington County. Photo by Amy Bayer.

Cover design by Sue Knopf.

Interior design by Sue Knopf.

Cartography by Mapping Specialists Limited (**mappingspecialists.com**), Fitchburg, WI.

Printed by Versa Press, Inc. (**versapress.com**), East Peoria, IL.

Dedicated to the thousands of volunteers who have contributed their time and effort to the Ice Age Trail for more than 60 years.

Hike Locator

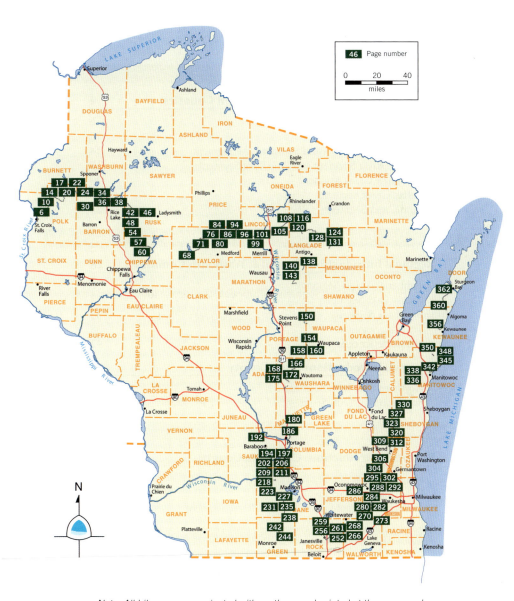

Note: All hike maps are oriented with north up and printed at the same scale.

Contents

Acknowledgments	viii
Introduction	x
Background Information	xi
Hiking the Ice Age Trail	xvi
Using the Ice Age Trail Guidebook	xxvii

Regional Map: Polk & Burnett Counties — 3

Regional Introduction: Polk & Burnett Counties — 4

St. Croix Falls Segment	6
Gandy Dancer Segment	10
Trade River Segment and Straight Lake Segment	14
Straight River Segment and Pine Lake Segment	17
McKenzie Creek Segment	20
Indian Creek Segment	22
Sand Creek Segment	24

Regional Map: Barron, Washburn & Rusk Counties — 27

Regional Introduction: Barron & Washburn Counties — 28

Timberland Hills Segment	30
Grassy Lake Segment	34
Bear Lake Segment	36
Tuscobia Segment	38
Hemlock Creek Segment	42

Regional Introduction: Rusk County — 44

Northern Blue Hills Segment	46
Southern Blue Hills Segment	48

Regional Map: Chippewa County — 51

Regional Introduction: Chippewa County — 52

Chippewa Moraine Segment	54
Harwood Lakes Segment	57
Firth Lake Segment and Chippewa River Segment	60

Regional Map: Taylor County — 65

Regional Introduction: Taylor County — 66

Lake Eleven Segment	68
Jerry Lake Segment	71
Mondeaux Esker Segment	76
Pine Line Segment and East Lake Segment	80
Rib Lake Segment	84
Wood Lake Segment	86

Regional Map: Lincoln County — 91

Regional Introduction: Lincoln County — 92

Timberland Wilderness Segment — 94
Camp 27 Segment and Newwood Segment — 96
Averill-Kelly Creek Wilderness Segment — 99
Turtle Rock Segment and Grandfather Falls Segment — 101
Underdown Segment and Alta Junction Segment — 105
Harrison Hills Segment — 108

Regional Map: Langlade County — 113

Regional Introduction: Langlade County — 114

Parrish Hills Segment — 116
Highland Lakes Segment — 120
Summit Moraine Segment — 124
Lumbercamp Segment — 128
Kettlebowl Segment — 131

Regional Map: Marathon County — 135

Regional Introduction: Marathon County — 136

Plover River Segment — 138
Dells of the Eau Claire Segment and Thornapple Creek Segment — 140
Ringle Segment — 143

Regional Map: Portage & Waupaca Counties — 147

Regional Introduction: Portage & Waupaca Counties — 148

New Hope-Iola Ski Hill Segment — 150
Skunk and Foster Lakes Segment and Waupaca River Segment — 154
Hartman Creek Segment — 158
Emmons Creek Segment — 160

Regional Map: Waushara & Marquette Counties — 163

Regional Introduction: Waushara County — 164

Deerfield Segment — 166
Bohn Lake Segment and Greenwood Segment — 168
Mecan River Segment — 172
Wedde Creek Segment and Chaffee Creek Segment — 175

Regional Introduction: Marquette County — 178

John Muir Park Segment — 180

Regional Map: Sauk & Columbia Counties — 183

Regional Introduction: Northern Columbia County — 184

Portage Canal Segment — 186

Regional Introduction: Sauk County — 190

Baraboo Segment — 192
Sauk Point Segment — 194
Devil's Lake Segment — 197
Merrimac Segment — 202

Regional Introduction: Southern Columbia County — 204

Gibraltar Rock Segment — 206
Fern Glen Segment and City of Lodi Segment — 209
Eastern Lodi Marsh Segment and Lodi Marsh Segment — 211

Regional Map: Dane & Green Counties — 215

Regional Introduction: Dane County — 216

Springfield Hill Segment and Indian Lake Segment — 218
Table Bluff Segment — 221
Cross Plains Segment — 223
Valley View Segment and Madison Segment — 227
Verona Segment — 231
Montrose Segment — 235
Brooklyn Wildlife Segment — 238

Regional Introduction: Green County — 240

Monticello Segment — 242
Albany Segment — 244

Regional Map: Rock, Walworth & Jefferson Counties — 249

Regional Introduction: Rock County — 250

Arbor Ridge Segment and Devil's Staircase Segment — 252
Janesville Segment — 256
Janesville to Milton Segment — 259
Milton Segment and Storrs Lake Segment — 261

Regional Introduction: Walworth & Jefferson Counties — 264

Clover Valley Segment — 266
Whitewater Lake Segment — 268
Blackhawk Segment — 270
Blue Spring Lake Segment — 273

Regional Map: Waukesha County — 277

Regional Introduction: Waukesha County — 278

Stony Ridge Segment — 280
Eagle Segment — 282
Scuppernong Segment — 284
Waterville Segment — 286
Lapham Peak Segment and Delafield Segment — 288
Hartland Segment — 292
Merton Segment and Monches Segment — 295

Regional Map: Washington County	299

Regional Introduction: Washington County	**300**
Loew Lake Segment	302
Holy Hill Segment	304
Pike Lake Segment, Slinger Segment and Cedar Lakes Segment	306
West Bend Segment and Southern Kewaskum Segment	309
Kewaskum Segment and Milwaukee River Segment (Washington County)	312

Regional Map: Fond du Lac & Sheboygan Counties	317

Regional Introduction: Fond du Lac & Sheboygan Counties	**318**
Milwaukee River Segment (Fond du Lac County)	320
Parnell Segment	323
Greenbush Segment	327
LaBudde Creek Segment	330

Regional Map: Manitowoc County	333

Regional Introduction: Manitowoc County	**334**
Walla Hi Segment	336
City of Manitowoc Segment	338
Dunes Segment and City of Two Rivers Segment	342
Point Beach Segment	345
Mishicot Segment and East Twin River Segment	348
Tisch Mills Segment	350

Regional Map: Kewaunee & Door Counties	353

Regional Introduction: Kewaunee & Door Counties	**354**
Kewaunee River Segment	356
Forestville Segment	360
Sturgeon Bay Segment	362
Glossary	368
Bibliography	372
Useful Addresses & Phone Numbers	373
Segment Names Index	374
Places of Interest Index	378
Key to Map Symbols	382
Key to Segment Snapshot Symbols	383
Hike Locator	384

Acknowledgments

Without the contributions of the following individuals publication of this book would not have been possible.

Volunteer Field Editors

As with most Ice Age Trail Alliance projects, publication of this book relied on the contributions of volunteers. The following individuals served as Field Editors, hiking segments of the Trail and checking drafts of this book for accuracy:

Ed Abell, Kristin Abell, Chris Arndt, Mary Atkinson, Mike Awve, Mark Balhorn, Diane Balmer, Brian Bednarek, Don Behm, Candace Beine, Don Berg, Emmy Berning, Max Bigler, Tim Bigler, Heather Brinkman, Dustin Brockway, Sarah Brundidge, Emily Butler, Karin Cairns, Debby Capener, Betty Carmichael, Barb Ceder, Sarah Christiaansen, Rick Coelho, Barb Converse, Jerome Converse, Anna DeMers, Ben Dohlby, Jeff Dohlby, Shelly Dohlby, Jason Dorgan, Lisa Dretske, Wesley Duberstein, Betsy Duginski, Christi Ehler, Jill Ellinwood, Jessica Featherstone, Scott Finger, Carl Fisher, Gary Foster, Brian Frain, Barb Frey, Jay Gasser, Mark Graczykowski, Dave Gramling, Julia Gray, Amelia Gregor, Jen Gregor, Mary Gronlund, Kari Hagenow, Ed Hahn, Tim Hahn, Marlys Hamberger, Diane Harp, Gary Hegeman, Melissa Hegeman, Sandy Hegeman, Ginny Henkel, Lee Henkel, Dave Henning, Glenda Henning, Patti Herman, Blake Higley, Caley Hildebrand, Margo Hoile, Amy Holzwart, Jim Holzwart, Craig Houghton, Andy Jacobson, Dennis James, Wayne Janik, Brad Javorsky and Rachel Javorsky Family, Maia Reck Johnson, Stacy Kaiser, Eileen Kaminski, Kathy Kehl, Alyson, Sevie Kenny, Kenyon, Brian Klawikowski, Eli Klawikowski, Sara Klawikowski, Sue Knopf, Becky Kohl, Milo Kohl, Erin Koth, Diana Kraus, Kevin Kuhlmann, Jim Lange, Lynn Larson, Chris LaVesser, Holly LaVesser, Bob Littlejohn, Kerry Lynch, Ed Madere, Crystal Martzall, Kim Stepien and Andrew Maulbetsch Family, Patty McCormick, Steve Meurett, Nicole Mosta, Cary Mullen, Tess Mulrooney, Bonnie Nommensen, Dave Nommensen, Lou Ann Novak, Wendy Ochs, Rob Olson, Amy Onofrey, Kyle Orlando, Joanna Parlee, Randy Parlee, Lindsey Peterson, LuAnn Peterson, Maria Pietz, Abby Plambeck, Thomas Podbesek, Carol Prchal, Sarah Probasco, Eric Rogers, Lisa Rondini, Dan Rosin, James Runge, Robert Rusch, Jeff Saatkamp, Jo-An Sabonjian, Robert Sabonjian, Heidi Schertz, Magen Schliesman, Jessica Schrimpf and John Schrimpf Family, Regina Schurman, Nancy Schuster, Tony Schuster, Jim Servi, Beth Shimmyo, Brent Sieling, Mary Smaby, Mike Smaby, Madeline Soleski, Eric Sorvari, Fred Stadler, Galen Steig, Geoff Streator, Jenn Streator, Robyn Swanson, Craig Tauscher, Kaitlin Thompson, Jenny Thorsen, Ed Tucker, Mark Ulrich, Lysianne Unruh, Jeremy Vechinski, Maria Verbrugge, Barb Voigt, Rachel Vorlander, Lila Waldman, Dale Walsh, Staci Walsh, Buddy Watford, Anne Weiss, Beth Whitaker, Andy Whitney, Erika Wittekind, Janet Wood.

Ice Age Trail Alliance Chapter Leaders

Volunteers who lead the Ice Age Trail Alliance's 19 chapters offered valuable input to field editors and the IATA's Editing Team through personal insights along with book review assistance from fellow chapter members:

Jenny Addis, Gerald Anderson, Daniel Brereton, Debby Capener, Butch Clendenning, Barb Converse, Dean Dversdall, Gary Ertl, Joanna Fanney, Lloyd Godell, Cheryl Gorsuch, Scot Harvey, Bob Held, Anne Helsley-Marchbanks, Ruby Jaecks, Dennis James, Joe Jopek, Steve Kaiser, Sevie Kenyon, Debbie Krogwold, James Luebke, Donna and Neal Meier, Buzz Meyer, Fred and Marilynn Nash, Melinda and Brian Nelson, Bonnie Nommensen, Gail Piotrowski, Carol Prchal, Julie Schneider, Richard Smith and Andrew Whitney.

Editing Team

Publication of the *Ice Age Trail Guidebook* was coordinated by the Ice Age Trail Alliance's Editing Team:

Sharon Dziengel, volunteer
Gary Hegeman, volunteer
Sandy Hegeman, volunteer
Sue Knopf, volunteer
Robert Root, volunteer
Tiffany Stram, IATA staff
Lysianne Unruh, IATA staff

The Editing Team extends a special thank you to:

- David Mickelson, for sharing his vast expertise relating to glacial geology.
- All IATA staff members for support and a wide variety of contributions throughout the revisions of the Ice Age Trail Alliance's three hiker resources: the Ice Age Trail Guidebook, Atlas, and Databook.
- Evelyn Swatkowski, IATA intern, who gave a special assist to the maps in both the Guidebook and Atlas.
- Those whose valuable contributions blazed the Trail in the writing and editing of past editions:
    Andrew Hanson III, volunteer (and former IATA staff member)
    Matt Kauffmann (former IATA staff member)
    Eric Sherman, IATA staff

In Memory of Sharon Bloodgood (1939–2020)
Her spirit was inspirational and contagious. A long-time supporter of the Ice Age Trail Alliance and advocate of the Ice Age National Scenic Trail, Sharon wore many hats: dedicated volunteer, board member and past board president, Thousand-Miler, and champion of the Ice Age Trail Guidebook, a collaborative effort between staff and volunteers.

Introduction

The Ice Age National Scenic Trail, one of only eleven such trails in the country, is a thousand-mile footpath that immerses users in the fascinating, world-renowned Ice Age features of Wisconsin. The Trail offers a little something for everyone. Long stretches of uninterrupted tread through quiet Northwoods forests meet the demands of backpackers looking for a multiday adventure away from it all. Closer to home, the Trail weaves in and around more populous areas, such as West Bend, Janesville and St. Croix Falls, satisfying those seeking a brief, after-dinner jaunt to recharge life's batteries with plenty of fresh air. For the scientific-minded, the story behind the kames, drumlins, eskers and erratics seen along the Trail invites a lifetime of investigation, while for the artistic crowd, there are innumerable spots, both quiet and grand, that will inspire the author to pick up her pen and the artist to grab his sketchpad or camera. And, perhaps most importantly, the Ice Age Trail provides an outlet for those who like to give as well as receive, with volunteer opportunities to match most any talent.

Given the Ice Age Trail's broad appeal, a critical task for the Ice Age Trail Alliance (IATA), the nonprofit volunteer- and member-based organization that works to create, support and protect the Trail, is to make sure people can find it! The two most common questions received by staff at the IATA main office are "Where can I find the Trail?" and "What will I see when I get there?" We here at the IATA are proud to say that this book will provide the answers to those two questions and just about any other head-scratcher related to hiking the Ice Age Trail.

No matter how you approach the Ice Age Trail, please keep in mind that it is a work in progress and there is still much to be done. If these books are helpful and you find yourself having one enjoyable Ice Age Trail adventure after another, consider joining the effort to maintain what we've built so far, complete what we haven't and protect the Trail for future generations. Please visit **iceagetrail.org** or give us a call (**800-227-0046**) to discover how you can provide financial support (through an IATA membership) or "sweat equity" (through volunteer effort) to enable others, both present and future, to enjoy the remarkable Ice Age National Scenic Trail.

Background Information

Ice Age Trail Landscapes

Through the eons, the landscapes along the Ice Age Trail have been shifted, shaped and eroded by wind, sedimentation, hardening of molten rock and the movement of water and glacial ice. The Trail showcases the dramatic effects of continental glaciers.

Colossal ice sheets repeatedly gripped the Earth during the Ice Age of the past two million years. Ice sheets are the largest glaciers, and unless you travel to Greenland or Antarctica, it may be hard to imagine their immensity. They can be two miles thick and stretch for more than 1,000 miles. The modern glaciers found at some of America's national parks are mountain glaciers—mere rivers of ice. Ice Age ice sheets were like oceans of ice with lobes along their margins similar to gulfs or bays.

Glaciers scrape, sculpt, carry and drop materials of all sizes, from tiny particles of clay to huge boulders. During the last period of the Ice Age, more than a third of the Earth's land was impacted. Some materials were deposited directly by the ice while others were transported by the meltwater that flowed over and away from the ice sheets. Glaciers and their meltwater piled material into particular landforms that we call moraines, drumlins, kames and eskers.

The Ice Age Trail is one of the best places to witness many of the landforms created by continental glaciation. The most recent period of the Ice Age, which slowly ended about 10,000 years ago, is known as the Wisconsin Glaciation.

Most of the landforms of the Ice Age Trail were created near the end of the Wisconsin Glaciation. Some features are much older. Along eastern segments of the Trail are occasional outcrops of 400-million-year-old dolomite. The bedrock at Dells of the Eau Claire and Grandfather Falls is approximately 1.8 billion years old.

Rounded boulders scattered along the Trail (sometimes piled in fencerows by farmers) were likely carried by glaciers from sources far to the north. These are known as erratics. Some erratics were carried from as far away as Canada. Rocks that look like and come from local bedrock are not erratics.

As you hike the Ice Age Trail, look for evidence of past glaciation. Take the time to speculate how far an erratic traveled to reach its resting place. Guess how large the block of ice was that created a kettle. Envision a torrent of sand-laden meltwater gushing through a valley. Imagine a thousand feet of glacial ice above a kame.

There are stories in the land...

Glacial Lobes

This is an illustration of the glacial lobes during the Late Wisconsin Glaciation. All but the southwestern corner of Wisconsin was glaciated. The last glaciation was not as extensive as some that had preceded it. Arrows indicate the direction of ice flow.

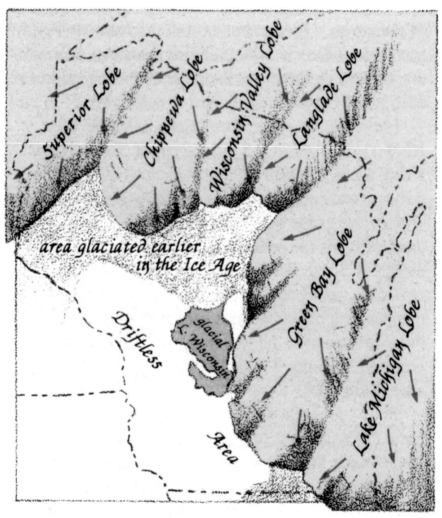

Image from The Ice Age Geology of Devil's Lake State Park, John W. Attig et al., Wisconsin Geological and Natural History Survey, 1990.

Ice Age Trail Elevation Chart

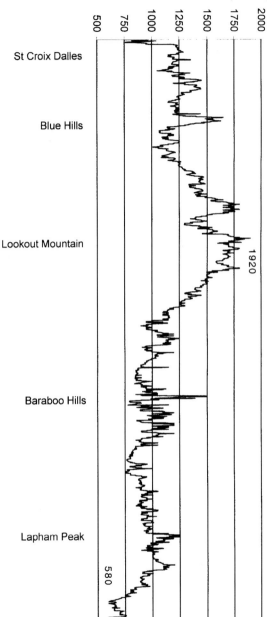

The topography along most of the Ice Age Trail is gently rolling, although some sections, like the Baraboo Hills (Sauk County) and Harrison Hills (Langlade and Lincoln counties), have steep climbs and descents. The highest point along the Trail is Lookout Mountain (1,920 feet) in Lincoln County. The lowest point, 580 feet, is along the shore of Lake Michigan in Manitowoc, Kewaunee and Door counties.

The Ice Age Trail Alliance

The Ice Age Trail Alliance is a nonprofit volunteer- and member-based organization whose mission is to create, support and protect a thousand-mile foot trail tracing Ice Age formations across Wisconsin. Established in 1958 (and then known as the Ice Age Park & Trail Foundation), the IATA has more than 3,000 members across the nation. Working cooperatively with the Wisconsin Department of Natural Resources (DNR), National Park Service, local governments, businesses and private landowners, the IATA works to protect, promote, build and maintain the many segments of the Ice Age National Scenic Trail.

Check out **iceagetrail.org** for an in-depth look at the organization. You can also get more information by calling or writing:

Ice Age Trail Alliance
PO Box 128, 2110 Main Street
Cross Plains, WI 53528
800-227-0046 • info@iceagetrail.org

Supporting the Ice Age Trail

Become a Member of the Ice Age Trail Alliance
As a member of the IATA, your dues will provide critical support for Ice Age Trail volunteer activities, trailway protection and land stewardship. As a member, you'll receive:

- A subscription to the IATA's newsletter, *Mammoth Tales*, with features on new Ice Age Trail segments, chapter events, land acquisitions, trailbuilding activities and more.
- Discounts on Ice Age Trail merchandise.
- Membership (and voting privileges) in your local volunteer chapter and invitations to participate in chapter hikes, Trail improvement events and social activities.
- An invitation to the IATA Annual Conference and voting privileges at the Membership Meeting and other special events.

To support the Ice Age Trail through an IATA membership, please visit **iceagetrail.org** or call us at **800-227-0046**.

Become a Volunteer
In addition to supporting the Ice Age Trail through an IATA membership, you can also support the Trail by becoming a volunteer. Because the Trail is built and maintained almost exclusively by volunteers, they are the heart, soul, hands and backbone of the Ice Age Trail. New faces are always welcome and no experience is necessary!

CHAPTER EVENTS

With 19 IATA volunteer chapters organized throughout Wisconsin, if you live near the Trail there is an opportunity to get involved right in your own backyard. Chapters are active throughout the year, organizing activities such as Trail construction, maintenance, hikes, campouts, land stewardship, promotion and education. Check the IATA website (**iceagetrail.org**) for chapter contact information and a calendar of events.

MOBILE SKILLS CREW PROGRAM

In addition to the local events at the chapter level, the IATA also organizes statewide trailbuilding projects each year through its Mobile Skills Crew (MSC) program. Whether you are a seasoned trail builder or just starting to learn about the Trail, MSC events offer a great opportunity for all types of volunteers to give back to the outdoors, visit new landscapes and make new friends. Volunteers at MSC events work hard, earn a sound education in trailbuilding and, perhaps most important, have fun!

Though the goal of the MSC program is to educate and empower volunteers on methods of building high quality, sustainable trail, no previous background in trail construction is needed to participate. Those who just want to check out what Ice Age Trail volunteering is all about are welcome to lend a hand at any time during an event. Further, other help is welcome in many areas, including food preparation, community outreach, publicity, administration and entertainment.

Check out **iceagetrail.org** for more information about the Mobile Skills Crew program and a calendar of events.

As shown in these before, during and after photos, Ice Age Trail volunteers skillfully opened up the landscape for hikers to enjoy. More help is always needed…join us for some of the most rewarding volunteer work around!

Hiking the Ice Age Trail

Property Types

The Ice Age National Scenic Trail is uniformly marked with yellow blazes. However, as a "partnership" project, the land ownership and management for the Ice Age Trail are anything but consistent. The Trail crosses a wide variety of property types, including private land and lands owned and managed by municipal, county, state and federal agencies. Generally speaking, lands open to public access are shown on the maps in this book with green shading, while those not open to general public access are shown in beige.

From a hiker's perspective, the experience of navigating the Trail doesn't change substantially when passing over varying land types, with a few key exceptions related to private lands. Hikers should be mindful of these points to help ensure the continued good relations with private landowners that are so critical to the Ice Age Trail.

- While hiking a portion of the Trail crossing private lands, hikers must stay on the Trail. Sticking to the Trail tread is a general recommendation for the entire Trail but a **requirement** on private lands.
- Portions crossing private lands may be closed during some hunting seasons. See p. xxiii for more information on hunting.

The patchwork of land management also yields different regulations for camping, hiking with pets, parking and so on. Because blanket statements for a particular aspect of hiking on a particular property type can be difficult to formulate, this book attempts to identify both "rules of thumb" and instances where there are eºeptions to the rule.

Trail Signage

Yellow blazes are the official indicator used to mark the Trail route. They are painted or plastic 2-by-6-inch vertical rectangles placed on trees and posts along the Trail. Other shapes of yellow blazes may be found along the Trail, but these are being phased out and replaced by the standard 2-by-6-inch blaze.

- **Blue blazes** indicate a spur or access trail.
- **White blazes** indicate a loop trail—one that leaves the Ice Age NST and later returns to it.
- **Directional arrows or offset double blazes** indicate sharp Trail turns. The directional arrows are yellow on a brown 4-by 4-inch plastic sign and can be found on posts. The offset blazes are painted on trees and are arranged as shown at right.

Directional Arrows and Offset Double Blazes

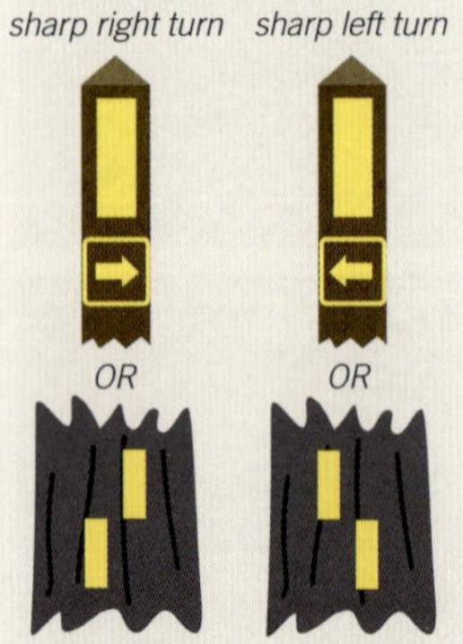

sharp right turn   sharp left turn

OR   OR

For offset double blazes, the top blaze indicates the turn direction.

The Trail route in some state and county parks shares existing park trails and may have no blazes. For an additional navigational aid in these cases, consult local park maps.

GPS Waypoints

Global Positioning System (GPS) waypoints listed in the Guidebook text and on the Atlas maps highlight glacial, natural or historical landmarks along the Ice Age Trail. In addition, some waypoints identify critical navigational points such as Trail junctions, stream crossings and Trail access points difficult to see or find from the road.

GPS waypoint references appear in the text in parentheses containing the county's two-letter abbreviation followed by a number. For example: (**DK1**) indicates Door and Kewaunee counties Waypoint 1. Because new waypoints are added each year, waypoints may not be in numerical order.

The GPS coordinates for each waypoint are available for download to GPS devices from the Ice Age Trail Alliance's website, **iceagetrail.org**. Also available for download from the IATA website is an Excel file with waypoint coordinates and descriptions.

Trail Conditions

Trail conditions change constantly. Nature and animals impact the Trail as much as humans do. Some parts of the Trail are better maintained than others. Volunteers do their best to maintain the Trail, but storm damage or vandalism can occur any time of the year. Some segments are well maintained and easy to follow, while others may become overgrown or more difficult to follow due to recent logging, storms or beaver activity.

Not all streams or creeks have bridges, especially in remote areas. Some waterways require fords or crossing on beaver dams. Use caution at all water crossings without a structure. The easiest and safest place to cross may not necessarily be where the Trail meets the waterway.

As trailway protection and volunteer trail-building progress, the Ice Age Trail evolves toward completion. The Trail route changes regularly. Some of these changes are small, such as a slight relocation to take a more sustainable route. Other changes are more dramatic, such as when a new segment is opened following the acquisition of a large property. For Trail updates and conditions, visit the Hiker Resources page at **iceagetrail.org,** where there is a link to a listing of reported Trail conditions. This is where hikers and volunteers alike can report conditions like a flooded path, downed trees, or other damage along the Trail.

On the website, you will also find a list of Ice Age Trail Alliance chapter coordinators. Mike Rotter, an Ice Age Trail "Thousand-Miler," provided this helpful advice on communicating with chapter coordinators about Trail conditions:

- Call the coordinator before hiking in a chapter's territory for information and advice. The coordinators can often provide the most up-to-date Trail conditions (including news about logging in the area and suggested alternate routes). They can also tell you if others are hiking at this time.

- Call the chapter coordinator after hiking with information about Trail conditions you encountered. Tell them the good things you saw and experienced along with your thoughts on where improvements could be made.

Seasonal Variation

Each moment of the year has its own beauty.
RALPH WALDO EMERSON

The Ice Age Trail can be enjoyed in all four seasons and provides a fresh perspective for the hiker with each passing month.

During spring, the land comes alive with a wide variety of wildflowers and migrating birds. Seasonal rains and winter snowmelt can result in wet areas along some sections of the Trail and can raise river water levels. Hikers should be extremely cautious when fording rivers and streams.

The warm temperatures of summer encourage hikers to reward themselves with a refreshing dip in one of the many lakes or rivers along the Ice Age Trail's route. Wildflowers continue to bloom, especially in the many finely restored prairies through which the Trail passes. May and June represent the onset of tick, mosquito and black fly seasons, though in many years these pests become less of a bother by August. Ripened blackberries, raspberries, blueberries and thimbleberries encourage the hiker to slow his or her pace and enjoy a trailside treat.

There is no better way to enjoy Wisconsin's fall colors than by trekking the Ice Age Trail. The state's many hardwood forests provide a visually stunning array of hues for the hiker to enjoy. During late fall, hunters take to the woods, and hikers should check for Trail closures or special considerations before heading out. Refer to p. xxiii for more information on hunting and the Ice Age Trail.

The Ice Age Trail provides a cure for cabin fever during winter, with ample opportunities for snowshoeing and cross-country skiing along the Trail. The leafless landscape offers views of the Trail's famous glacial topography, enabling the user to better witness the legacy of the Ice Age.

Dogs on the Trail

The best practice, when hiking with dog(s) on the Ice Age Trail, is that the dog(s) be leashed (8-foot maximum length) and under control at all times. This is for the safety and comfort of all who use the Trail. A leashed dog will not unnecessarily startle other hikers or wildlife. This is also for the safety of the dog, especially in areas where hunting and trapping are allowed near the Trail corridor.

Dogs may be unleashed when they are being used for hunting purposes in areas that are open to hunting during an established season. Check with the individual DNR property (e.g. state park, forest, wildlife area) for more information.

Safety

Personal safety is a concern when one ventures to unfamiliar places. Always use common sense and take precautions. It is best to not hike alone. Do not be lulled into a false sense of security, even with a partner or a group. Two or more can be just as vulnerable as one. The following are some suggestions:

- Leave an itinerary of your trip with family and friends.
- Stay in contact with home or friends on longer hikes. Call from towns to update them on your location.

- When parking at Trail access areas, secure your vehicle. Do not leave anything of value in plain sight.
- Carry a cell phone, but realize it may not work in remote sections of the Trail.
- Avoid camping within half a mile of road crossings.
- Do not tell strangers where you are headed or plan to camp.
- If you run into a suspicious person, consider moving on to another location.
- Always trust your instincts.

If you are a victim of crime or witness a crime, report the incident to the police or local sheriff's department and notify the IATA. Call **911** for emergencies.

Be prepared for natural dangers. Hiking anywhere for any length of time, including day hikes, can expose you to dehydration, hypothermia, heat exhaustion, contaminated water, lightning, dangerous water crossings, rabies, insect-borne diseases and poison ivy. To steer clear of these hazards, read and learn about backcountry travel and safety before you go. Knowledge, experience and common sense are your best tools. Be prepared with a map, compass, appropriate weather gear, water, light, matches, first aid kit, signal whistle and food, even for day hikes.

Special Concern: Tickborne Illnesses

Tickborne diseases typically first cause flu-like symptoms and usually can be treated with antibiotics if caught early. Untreated, they may cause serious health problems, including death in rare cases.

Lyme disease is caused by bacteria that are transmitted to humans by the bite of infected deer ticks. The deer tick, at its largest, is only about half the size of the common wood tick—about the size of a pinhead or speck of black pepper. Symptoms may include a characteristic "bull's-eye" rash and flu-like symptoms such as fever, malaise, fatigue, headache, muscle aches and joint aches. Infrequently, Lyme disease may have long-term severe, chronic and disabling effects, but it is rarely, if ever, fatal.

Ehrlichiosis is also caused by bacteria transmitted by certain species of ticks. Symptoms generally include fever, headache, malaise and muscle aches. Other signs and symptoms may include nausea, vomiting, diarrhea, cough, joint pains, confusion and occasionally a rash, particularly in children. Ehrlichiosis can be a severe illness, especially if untreated, and as many as half of all patients require hospitalization. It can be fatal.

Ticks are typically most active in Wisconsin from May to September, but taking preventive measures year-round is wise. The following precautions can reduce the risk of acquiring these and other possible tick- and mosquito-related infections.

- Wear shoes, high socks, long pants with cuffs tucked into socks and a long-sleeved shirt with shirttails tucked in to keep ticks off your skin and on the outside of clothing.
- Light-colored clothing will make ticks easier to find.
- Insect repellents containing 0.5% permethrin (applied to clothing only, not skin, and allowed to dry) or 20–30% DEET have been shown to be effective in repelling deer ticks. If such products are used, follow the manufacturer's directions on the label. A useful search tool to help you choose the right prod-

uct for you is at **epa.gov/insect-repellents**.
- Walk in the center of mowed trails to avoid brushing up against vegetation.
- Avoid hiking at dusk and dawn, when mosquitoes are most active.
- Conduct thorough "tick checks" on yourself and your children after spending time outdoors, inspecting all parts of your body carefully, and take a shower as soon as possible afterwards.
- Tumble dry your clothes on high heat for 10 minutes to kill any ticks that might come in on your clothes.
- Treat dogs for ticks. Dogs are very susceptible to tick bites and to some tickborne diseases. They may also bring ticks into your home. Talk to your veterinarian about the best tick prevention products for your dog and other pets.

Prompt removal of ticks can drastically reduce the chance of disease transmission. If a tick is found, remove it by grasping it as close to the skin as possible with a narrow-bladed tweezers. Pull straight out slowly and firmly until the tick lets go. After removing it, thoroughly wash the site with soap and water or rubbing alcohol. Apply an over-the-counter antibiotic cream like Neosporin or Bacitracin. Save the tick in a jar or plastic bag and make a note of the day you removed it. If you develop any flu-like symptoms, fever or rash over the next thirty days, visit your doctor for any necessary follow-up care and treatment. Tell your doctor when and where you may have come into contact with the tick.

For more information on tickborne diseases, visit:
cdc.gov/ticks/diseases
dhs.wisconsin.gov/communicable
mcevbd.wisc.edu/ticks

Camping

Camping opportunities along the Ice Age Trail vary greatly and are not set at regular intervals. The locations of developed campgrounds, camping shelters, walk-in campsites and dispersed camping areas are identified in the *Ice Age Trail Guidebook*, Databook and Atlas maps. Most areas of the Trail allow camping in designated campgrounds only. A complete list of camping opportunities on or near the Trail or suggested connecting routes is available on the IATA website. Primitive camping is allowed in scattered areas along the northern tier of Ice Age Trail counties, where the Trail passes through national and county forest lands, from the Trail's western terminus east through Langlade County. Camp at least 200 feet from roads, trails, streams, rivers, lakes, ponds and wetlands, and follow Leave No Trace principles (see p. xxi) to minimize vegetation loss, erosion and wildlife disturbance. The *Ice Age Trail Guidebook* and Atlas maps show primitive camping areas with a green speckled pattern.

Note the following special camping situations:

- Campsites in Wisconsin Department of Natural Resources (DNR) state park or state forest campgrounds (including those at group camps) must be reserved by calling **888-947-2757** or **800-274-7275 (TTY)** or online at **wisconsin.goingtocamp.com.** For complete state park and state forest camping information, go to **dnr.wi.gov/topic/parks/**.

- All state campgrounds along or near the Trail or connecting routes have a limited number of nonreservable campsites that can be claimed only by showing up at the campground. They are generally available weekdays, but they fill up fast Friday through Sunday in summer and fall.
- Long-distance hikers should make a reasonable effort to secure campsite reservations. However, at DNR-managed campgrounds, there is a "safety net." According to the Wisconsin DNR *Recreation Area Operations Handbook (#25051): Non-motorized Camper Accommodations*, long-distance hikers in need of a campsite will not be turned away at a "full" campground. Long-distance campers are still encouraged to make camping reservations whenever possible. This policy is only for DNR-managed campgrounds; it does not apply at, for example, county-managed or U.S. Forest Service–managed campgrounds.
- The Northern and Southern Units of the Kettle Moraine State Forest (KMSF) have nine backcountry camping shelters along the Ice Age Trail. Reservations are required and only one group per site per night is permitted. Reservations can be made by calling **888-947-2757** or online at **wisconsin.goingtocamp.com** and often need to be made weeks in advance. When searching, choose the "campsite" tab, the "backpack" radio button and the appropriate KMSF unit to help you locate a shelter.
- A few areas of the Trail provide primitive walk-in campsites, which are listed in the Guidebook and Databook and shown on Ice Age Trail Atlas maps. Some areas may require hikers to check in at a visitor center or park office before using a campsite.
- The IATA has established Dispersed Camping Areas (DCAs) specifically for long-distance, multiday Ice Age Trail hikers. DCAs are not "campgrounds" or even "campsites" in the traditional sense. Typically, they are not much more than a cleared area where hikers may legally camp for a night within sight of a DCA-marked post. DCAs are listed in the Guidebook and Databook and shown on Ice Age Trail Atlas maps.

Leave No Trace Ethics

You are encouraged to get out and enjoy the gifts the Ice Age has left us. To preserve and protect the natural beauty of Wisconsin, low impact camping and "leave no trace" ethics should be followed. The purpose of these guidelines is to help decrease the impact of humans on the Trail.

- Plan ahead and be prepared. Call for Trail conditions, carry maps, know the regulations of the area and plan or reserve your overnight camping.
- Remember to carry out what you carried in, including all garbage and leftover food. Repackage food to minimize waste. Leave the natural environment better than you found it. Inspect your campsite and rest areas for trash or spilled food before leaving.
- Leave only footsteps. Take only photos. Do not pick flowers or plants or remove bark from trees.
- Preserve the past. Observe and do not disturb or take historical artifacts such

- as arrowheads, historical or cultural structures, rock walls or sensitive natural resources. Do not build structures or furniture or dig trenches.
- Travel and camp on durable surfaces. Durable surfaces include established trails and campsites, rock, gravel, dry grasses or snow.
- Stay on the Trail at all times. Do not cut switchbacks. Walk single file in the middle of the Trail, even when it is wet or muddy.
- Be considerate of other hikers. Let nature prevail. Avoid loud voices and noises. Be courteous and yield to other users on the Trail.
- Limit groups to 20 on day hikes and 10 for overnight trips.
- Where primitive camping is permitted, camp off trail, at least 200 feet from lakes and waterways and out of sight of developed areas. Good campsites are found, not made. Altering a site is not necessary.
- Make low impact fires at existing fire rings only and use only downed wood. Drown out fires thoroughly before breaking camp. Never leave a fire unattended. Campfires can cause lasting impact to the backcountry. Use a portable stove for cooking instead of a campfire.
- Dispose of human waste properly. Dig a 6-inch-deep cat hole at least 200 feet from trails or water. Cover and disguise the cat hole when finished. Pack out toilet paper and feminine hygiene products.
- Avoid using soap within 200 feet of any waterway. Sand makes an excellent scrubber. Use biodegradable soap and scatter strained dirty dishwater at least 200 feet from any waterway.
- Respect wildlife. Observe wild animals from a distance. Do not follow or approach them. Do not damage their habitat. Never bait or feed wild animals. Feeding wildlife damages their health, alters natural behaviors and exposes them to predators and other dangers.
- Store food and trash securely to avoid rodents or bears. Do not eat in or around your sleeping area. Hang your food properly in bear country. This has generally been considered to be the northern region of the state; however, the black bear population is expanding. To gain an accurate understanding, go to **dnr.wi.gov/topic/hunt/bearpop.html**.
- Some Ice Age Trail segments intersect or use cross-country ski trails that are groomed in winter. Proper hiking etiquette asks for winter hikers and snowshoe users to walk well to the side of the groomed ski trails.
- Respect private property. The Trail relies heavily on support of private landowners. Respect their rights. Stay on the Trail at all times. The Trail often crosses private property to get to public or IATA land. Do not camp on or vandalize private land. It is a privilege to access the Trail through private landowners' property.

For more on Leave No Trace ethics, visit **LNT.org** or call the Leave No Trace Center for Outdoor Ethics at **800-332-4100**.

Hunting

Many public and private lands along the Ice Age Trail are open to hunting during a variety of hunting seasons. Hikers should keep the following in mind during the state's major hunting seasons:

Hunting Season Dates and What to Wear

The Wisconsin Department of Natural Resources annually sets season dates for a wide range of game species. The most popular hunting seasons include deer (bow and gun), turkey, small game and waterfowl. Season dates vary from year to year and in different locations around the state. Get the most updated information on the Wisconsin Department of Natural Resources' Season Dates page (**dnr.wi.gov/topic/hunt/dates.html**).

The nine-day gun deer-hunting season is in late November. This is the most popular hunting season and the one during which Ice Age Trail hikers are most likely to see their hiking options limited.

For your safety, consider this time of year "Blaze Orange Season"—wear blaze orange (or other bright colors) from October through March when you are on the Trail. If you hike with a pet, you may want to make sure "Fido" is wearing blaze orange, too.

Hiking on Private Lands during Hunting Season

The private landowners who generously serve as Ice Age Trail hosts may close the portion of the Ice Age Trail that runs through their property during hunting season. This is most common during the nine-day gun deer season, but closures can be in place during other seasons as well.

"Private Land" signs are placed at any point where the Ice Age Trail enters private land, most often at a road crossing. Landowners and/or Ice Age Trail Alliance volunteers also often place "Segment Closed" signs (with dates of the closure) at Trail access points.

Respect signs that announce a closed portion of Trail and be cognizant when you pass "Private Land" signs. This will help ensure the continued good relations with private landowners that are so critical to the Ice Age Trail.

In advance of your hike, consider calling the chapter coordinator or the IATA office (**800-227-0046**) for details on sections of the Trail that are closed. Visit **iceagetrail.org** to find chapter coordinator contact information.

Hiking on Public Lands during Hunting Season

Just about all segments of the Ice Age Trail that cross public lands remain open for hiking during hunting season, including the Chequamegon-Nicolet National Forest, state and county forests and state parks.

Wisconsin Act 168 allows hunting in most state parks and State Ice Age Trail Areas (SIATAs) from Nov. 15 to Dec. 15 and from April 1 to the Tuesday nearest May 3.

In these locations, no hunting or trapping is allowed within 100 yards of the Ice Age Trail. Note that this rule does not apply to other trails in state parks.

Visit the Wisconsin DNR's Hunting and Trapping in State Parks page (**dnr.wi.gov/topic/parks/hunt**) for more information and for hunting and trapping maps for each state park and SIATA.

Invasive Species Impact

Each year IATA volunteers and partners exert great effort combating invasive or non-native plant species such as buckthorn, garlic mustard, honeysuckle and others along the Ice Age Trail corridor and throughout the state. Without these efforts, the non-native plants, animals and pathogens can displace native species, disrupt ecosystems and curtail recreational activities. Invasive species can spread rapidly and aggressively because they lack predators and competitors. Controlling invasive species is difficult and getting rid of them is often impossible.

Anyone who spends time in the outdoors is a potential vector of undesirable plant material. To minimize the introduction and spread of invasive species, hikers should:

- Minimize disturbance by staying on the Trail and if possible staying out of heavily infested areas entirely.
- Before and after a hike on the Trail, inspect and clean clothing, footwear and gear. Make sure that your gear, especially your footwear, is clear of plant materials. Remove and discard any plant material or soil in the garbage. Use boot brushes where available, or bring your own brush to scrape off dirt.
- Firewood can harbor many kinds of invasive pests and diseases that are harmful to Wisconsin's trees in both forest and urban settings. Follow the DNR regulations on firewood, which prohibit bringing firewood onto any DNR properties from more than 10 miles away or from outside of Wisconsin.
- Be a proactive land steward. If a new patch of invasives is discovered, please let the IATA staff know. Do not attempt to remove it on your own, as much of the Trail is on private lands.

For more information visit **dnr.wi.gov/topic/invasives.**

Recommended Resources

The Ice Age Trail Alliance's website, **iceagetrail.org**, includes Trail navigation information as well as updates on current Trail conditions and route changes. As the Ice Age Trail route evolves continually from year to year as volunteers build new segments and upgrade existing ones, this is a great resource to consult to learn how the Trail has changed relative to the information presented in this book.

The volunteers who head up the 19 Ice Age Trail Alliance chapters are passionate about helping people get out and enjoy the Trail. Contact information for chapter leaders is available on the IATA's website. Hikers are urged to get in touch with these folks (especially ahead of longer hikes and/or those in remote areas) to get a clear picture of the state of the Trail in a particular area. Chapter leaders are volunteers with busy lives outside of the Trail; therefore, hikers should be ready to wait a few days for a response to inquiries. Hikers who strike out with email are urged to try calling instead. Those who hit a dead end should call the IATA main office to see if another chapter leader in the area is available to answer questions.

The *Ice Age Trail Atlas* has more than 100 color hiking maps of the Trail route, including not only established Ice Age Trail segments but also unofficial connecting routes. Each Atlas page is 8.5 by 11 inches; those who like a little more contextual information for the area around the Ice Age Trail route may appreciate these maps.

The Atlas also includes a gazetteer that describes many place names along the Trail. To order the Atlas, visit **iceagetrail.org** or call the IATA at **800-227-0046**.

DeLorme's *Wisconsin Atlas and Gazetteer* also offers a larger view of the surrounding area along the Ice Age Trail and access to it.

Long-distance hikers will want to check out the *Ice Age Trail Databook*. The book has highly detailed mileage breakdowns for hundreds of access points along the entire thousand-mile Ice Age Trail route. It also includes in-depth resupply and town service info. For more info visit **iceagetrail.org** or call the IATA at **800-227-0046**.

Plan your hike from your smartphone. Guthook Guides for iOS and Android feature GPS-enabled maps of the Ice Age Trail, hundreds of waypoints along or near the Trail, including all of our ColdCaches, satellite imagery and more. Whether you're backpacking or in search of IATA's ColdCaches, this app will help you plan your trip and check your location on the Trail. No mobile or internet service is required to use it after the initial setup. The app, built through a collaboration between the IATA and the creators of Guthook Guides, is available via the iTunes Store and Google Play.

Those looking for highly detailed descriptions of the glacial processes that shaped the Wisconsin landscape and the Ice Age Trail landforms left behind will want to get a copy of *Geology of the Ice Age National Scenic Trail*, by David M. Mickelson et al. Copies of this book, published by UW Press, are for sale through the Ice Age Trail Alliance. Copies are also likely available through your local library or its interlibrary loan service.

Hikers are urged to contact tourism boards listed in this book for county road maps and local points of interest beyond the Ice Age Trail.

The ColdCache Award Program

New and experienced users of GPS technology may be interested in the IATA ColdCache award program. ColdCaching is a family-friendly activity that provides the opportunity to experience the thrill of a treasure hunt, learn important navigational skills and develop an appreciation for Wisconsin's fascinating Ice Age history. The concept of Ice Age Trail ColdCaching is based on the popular activities of geocaching and earthcaching. Participants seek out natural features along the Ice Age Trail, identify the landmark, record the GPS coordinates and leave only footprints on the landscape. The ColdCache program awards patches based on the number of identified ColdCaches logged in. For more information and to download the award program log, go to **iceagetrail.org** or email **coldcache@iceagetrail.org**.

Chapter and Thousand-Miler Certificates

Many Ice Age Trail Alliance volunteer chapters have programs that acknowledge hikers who have completed all Ice Age Trail miles and connecting routes in their territory. The hiking programs are listed by chapter, from west to east, followed by the name of their hiking award program. More information about these programs can be found at **iceagetrail.org** or by contacting the local chapter.

- Indianhead Chapter—Traprock Trekkers
- Superior Lobe Chapter—Superior Lobetrotters
- Baraboo Hills/Heritage Chapter and Lodi Valley Chapter—Glacial Drifters

- Dane County Chapter—Dane Drifters
- Rock County Chapter—Walk Across Rock County
- Walworth/Jefferson County Chapter—Kettle Trekkers
- Waukesha/Milwaukee County Chapter—Walk the Wauk
- Washington/Ozaukee County Chapter—Meander the Mid-Moraine
- Lakeshore Chapter—Hall of Kamers

The IATA recognizes anyone who reports having hiked the entire Trail and completes a recognition application as a "Thousand-Miler." The IATA policy operates on the honor system, assuming anyone who applies for recognition has hiked all 1,000+ miles between Interstate State Park and Potawatomi State Park. To qualify, it is necessary to have hiked all current Ice Age Trail segments and connected all Trail segments by walking the connecting route of your choice. Not considered are issues of speed, length of time from start to finish, sequence, direction or whether or not one carries a pack. Visit **iceagetrail.org** to obtain a Thousand-Miler application.

Two friends and dog Charlie on the Gandy Dancer Segment.

Using the Ice Trail Guidebook

This book is broken down by region, county and then Ice Age Trail segment.

Each region, made up of a county or group of adjacent counties the Trail crosses, is introduced with a map that shows the approximate location of each segment relative to major roads and municipalities.

Each county section is introduced with a page that includes a general description of the landscape in that area. It may also include an introduction to the native tribes who inhabited the region and/or an overview of known pioneer activity.

Each county section also includes information on the Ice Age Trail Alliance volunteer chapter that is active in the county.

The description for each Ice Age Trail segment in this book includes the following elements.

SEGMENT SNAPSHOT

The snapshot for each segment starts with distance. Distance in some cases includes not only established Ice Age Trail, marked with yellow blazes, but also portions of "connecting route" (CR), unmarked sections not officially part of the Ice Age Trail that typically follow quiet country roads. *Disclaimer: Roads on connecting routes, while legally open to pedestrians, may not have been designed for safe use by pedestrians (in contrast to Ice Age Trail segments). By identifying these routes, neither the Ice Age Trail Alliance, National Park Service, Wisconsin Department of Natural Resources nor the local governmental body are implying any guarantee about their safety or suitability for Ice Age Trail hikers.*

After distance, the snapshot includes a one- or two-sentence general description of the segment that describes the hiking experience.

From there, the snapshot uses a variety of icons and accompanying notes to describe "need to know" information about the segment. **A key to these symbols is found on p. 383.**

This symbol provides a general idea of how much elevation change (and physical challenge) there is on the segment. The range is 1 (mostly flat) through 5 (very hilly). A higher number may be the result of one very steep climb or the accumulation of many shorter climbs over the full length of a segment.

This symbol provides a general idea of how challenging the segment may be to a hiker. The range is 1 (not rugged) through 5 (very rugged). The number takes into account Ice Age Trail signage, maintenance and/or layout challenges; water hazards or crossings; remoteness and presence of logging activities. Users of this book should recognize that these numbers may mean different things to hikers of different abilities and expectations. Generally speaking, though, anyone hiking a segment with a higher ruggedness rating should be prepared for a challenging and perhaps difficult adventure.

This symbol indicates that a pump or spigot with potable water is available on or near the segment. Hikers should assume that these water sources are unavailable early fall through late spring.

💧 Of special interest to long-distance hikers, this symbol indicates the presence of a natural source from which hikers may draw water for filtration/chemical treatment.

🚱 This symbol provides an important "heads up" that hikers should plan on packing plenty of drinking water before arriving at the segment, as no source of water is available in the area.

🥾⛺ Of interest to backpackers, this symbol indicates that the segment has walk-in camping options that are further defined by map symbols. **A map symbol key is on p. 382.** In terms of walk-in camping, four map symbols are used:

⛺ This symbol indicates a walk-in campsite developed for backpackers. These sites have varying levels of development but typically include a flat spot to pitch a tent and a fire ring.

⋯ This pattern of shading on the maps indicates areas where hikers may practice Leave No Trace primitive camping (see p. xxi for details on Leave No Trace). These areas are found scattered along only the northern tier of the of counties the Ice Age Trail passes through, from the Trail's Western Terminus east through Langlade County.

🅳🅲🅰 This symbol denotes a Dispersed Camping Area (DCA). To help increase camping opportunities for Ice Age Trail long-distance, multiday hikers, the Ice Age Trail Alliance and its partners are working to establish DCAs, especially in areas (i.e., the southern two-thirds of the Trail) where convenient camping options are otherwise limited for long-distance, multiday hikers. DCAs are not "campgrounds" or even "campsites" in the traditional sense; instead, they are typically nothing more than a cleared area where hikers may legally camp for a night. Use of DCAs is restricted to those on multi-night long-distance hikes.

🛖 This symbol shows the location of trailside shelters that are available for camping. For those shelters in the Northern and Southern Units of the Kettle Moraine State Forest on the southeastern leg of the Trail reservations are required and only one group per site per night is permitted. Reservations can be made only by calling **888-947-2757** or **wisconsin.goingtocamp.com** and often need to be made weeks in advance.

🚗⛺ This symbol indicates that a traditional "car-camping" campground is located on or within a few miles of the segment. Reservations and/or a fee are often required at these campgrounds.

🎪 For those interested in having some relaxing meal or social time before or after a hike, this symbol indicates that a picnic area is available on or near the segment.

🧒 Bring the kids! For those looking for something fun to do with children before or after hitting the Trail, this symbol indicates that child-friendly amenities like playgrounds and/or swim areas are available on or near the segment.

🚻 This symbol indicates that a toilet is available on or near the segment. Amenities vary (from a pit toilet to a heated restroom with running water) and hikers should assume that these facilities will be closed early fall through late spring.

🌐 This symbol indicates the segment has one or more ColdCache sites. ColdCaching is a family-friendly activity that develops an appreciation for Wisconsin's fascinating Ice Age history (see page xxv). For more information and to download the award program log, go to **iceagetrail.org** or email **coldcache@iceagetrail.org**.

🚫🔫 For those who are uncomfortable hiking in the presence of hunting, this symbol indicates that hikers will not have any interaction with hunting on the full length of a particular segment. Most of these segments are in urban areas and may include long stretches of multiuse paths, sidewalks and/or roads.

🚶 This symbol indicates that the segment crosses private land and portions or the full segment may be closed to hikers during hunting season(s). The Ice Age Trail relies on the generosity of private landowners. Respect these Trail closures at all times. **By hiking a closed portion of the Trail, one irresponsible hiker can jeopardize the future of an entire Ice Age Trail segment.**

See p. xxii for more information on hunting and the Ice Age Trail.

🐕 This symbol indicates that when hiking with dog(s) on the Ice Age Trail, the dog should be leashed (8-foot maximum length) and under control at all times.

🐕! This symbol indicates that, in addition to the above statement, there are additional regulations for hiking with dogs on a particular segment. In some areas, dogs are prohibited entirely; in others they must be leashed by law, especially during sensitive times of the year, i.e., bird nesting season April through July.

〰️ This symbol indicates that portions of the segment overlap biking, snowmobiling or groomed cross-country ski trails or roads and/or sidewalks. The message behind this symbol is twofold: (i) hikers can expect to see non-hikers during the hike and (ii) the segment may include wide paths or roads that may not conform to the traditional idea of a hiking path.

⤳ This symbol indicates that other hiking trails (spurs, loops or lollipops) are present off the main segment route. The message behind this symbol is twofold: (i) hikers should pay close attention to Trail signage to stay on the main segment route and (ii) those looking for additional miles to explore on foot may have opportunities **from** this segment.

♿ For those using a wheelchair or similar device, this symbol identifies segments that may have portions suitable for wheelchair use. The list of segments flagged with this symbol is not exhaustive and does not attempt to identify segments meeting legally defined criteria of "accessible." Those seeking more specific accessibility information for a particular segment should contact the Ice Age Trail Alliance (**800-227-0046, info@iceagetrail.org**).

Using the Ice Age Trail Guidebook

TRAIL ACCESS AND PARKING

This section includes driving directions to the Trail access points at the start and end of each hike. Also included is a description of the parking on or near the segment(s). Hikers failing to park legally may jeopardize the relationships and agreements the Ice Age Trail Alliance and its chapters have in place with public partners and private landowners and may be ticketed by local law enforcement.

Parking Area (indicated by a 🅿 icon on the maps) denotes a space where cars can be parked legally and fully off the road. There is quite a wide range within this category, from "a grassy, open space" to a full-fledged paved parking lot.

Roadside Parking (no accompanying map icon) denotes an area where cars may be parked along a road but still within relatively close contact with road traffic. Those uncomfortable with parking in these areas should seek out the nearest Parking Area instead.

Additional considerations for parking:

- A Wisconsin State Parks day pass or annual sticker is required when parking at any state park or state forest parking area.
- If parking overnight, park in a Parking Area only and avoid roadside parking. Some parking areas are more suitable than others; in all cases, hikers should notify the county sheriff's department with overnight parking dates and location. Parking areas not open to overnight parking are noted for each segment.
- Those feeling uncomfortable with the parking situation on a particular segment may want to try contacting the Ice Age Trail Alliance volunteer chapter leader for that area. Chapter leader contact information is available at **iceagetrail.org** or from the IATA main office, **800-227-0046**. In some cases, chapter leaders may be able to find a volunteer in the area who will generously donate time, vehicle usage and fuel costs to help you with a shuttle to and/or from the Trail access. Those benefiting from this type of help are strongly encouraged to provide a generous gratuity to the volunteer.

THE HIKE

This section describes significant geological, historical and natural information about the area and provides hikers with turn-by-turn directions for areas where the Ice Age Trail route is not immediately evident based on Trail signage. GPS waypoints are included in this section for all waypoints except those at the start and end of each segment. The waypoints are listed in parentheses and in bold type, e.g., (**MN2**). See p. xvii and **iceagetrail.org** for more information on waypoints.

POINTS OF INTEREST

Some segments include an additional listing for an attraction on or near the Trail route that would be an interesting side trip for hikers.

AREA SERVICES

This section includes nearby amenities (e.g., restaurants, grocery stores, lodging, medical services) that hikers may find helpful. Note that medical services is a broad term that may range from clinics to fully staffed hospitals. The Inns and B&Bs listed are part of the IATA's INN Style program. They have teamed up with the Ice Age Trail Alliance to offer hikers access to first-rate hospitality and accommodations. See **iceagetrail.org** for more information on the INN Style program.

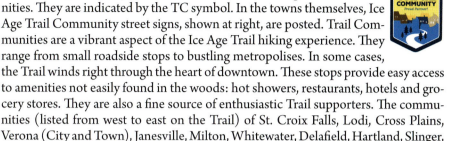

Some towns that the Ice Age Trail goes directly through and that have a partnership with the IATA are called Ice Age Trail Communities. They are indicated by the TC symbol. In the towns themselves, Ice Age Trail Community street signs, shown at right, are posted. Trail Communities are a vibrant aspect of the Ice Age Trail hiking experience. They range from small roadside stops to bustling metropolises. In some cases, the Trail winds right through the heart of downtown. These stops provide easy access to amenities not easily found in the woods: hot showers, restaurants, hotels and grocery stores. They are also a fine source of enthusiastic Trail supporters. The communities (listed from west to east on the Trail) of St. Croix Falls, Lodi, Cross Plains, Verona (City and Town), Janesville, Milton, Whitewater, Delafield, Hartland, Slinger, West Bend and Manitowoc–Two Rivers eagerly signed up for the special designation of Trail Community. It is a way for them to show their support for the Trail and to recognize Trail users as important players in their local economies.

Make sure you mention you are a user of the Trail when you shop or stay overnight. Help confirm this connection between your hike along the Trail and dollars you spend in a Trail Community. See **iceagetrail.org** for more information.

SEGMENT MAP

For each segment a map from the Ice Age Trail Alliance's popular *Ice Age Trail Atlas* is included. The map includes a green dot corresponding to the start of the segment as described in "THE HIKE" section and and a red dot corresponding to the end. Info boxes on the map point the way to the next segment in either direction; brief driving directions are included for those segments separated by a connecting route of less than 5 miles.

GPS waypoint symbols are included on the map for all waypoints except those at the start and end of each segment. See page xvii for more information on waypoints.

A map symbol key is located on p. 382.

There are things you cannot control on the Trail: the weather, the mud, the rises and falls. One must learn to accept it.

DAVID WHITE (AKA "FOODWALKER"), ICE AGE TRAIL THOUSAND-MILER

Using the Ice Age Trail Guidebook

Simply letting your mind rest as your legs do the work is like taking a mini-vacation.

So what are you waiting for? Go take a walk and invite a friend or a child to go with you. It may be the most important thing you can do for them—and for yourself.

SHARON BLOODGOOD (AKA "TRIPALONG"), ICE AGE TRAIL THOUSAND-MILER

Fall color as backdrop highlights large knobs of basalt bedrock on the Trade River Segment.

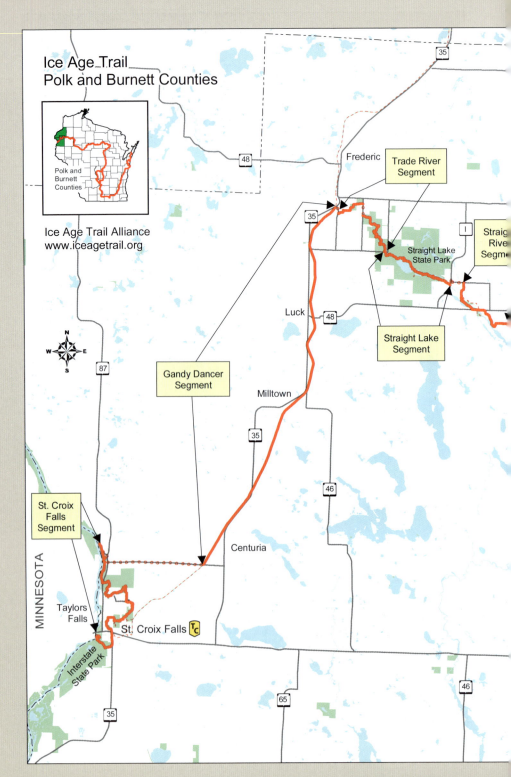

Polk & Burnett Counties

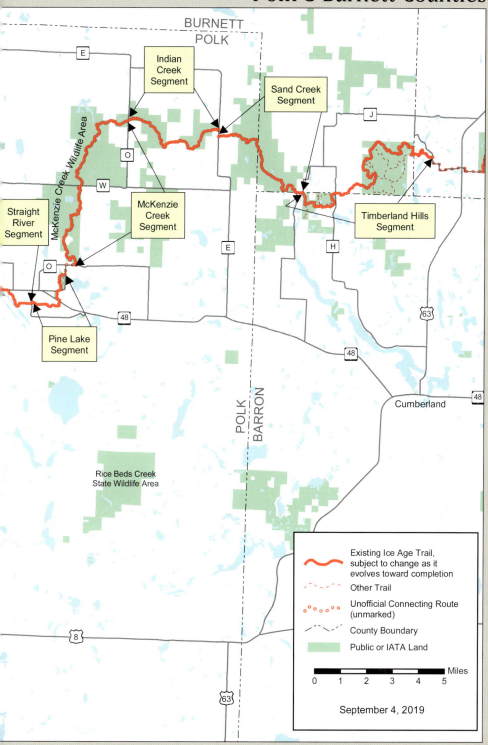

Polk & Burnett Counties

Atlas Maps 1f–6f; Databook pages 1–6
Total miles: 65.7 (Trail 58.5; Connecting Route 7.2)

The Superior and Des Moines lobes largely shaped Polk and Burnett counties. First, the Superior Lobe came from the northeast. Later, the Des Moines Lobe moved south through Minnesota and the Grantsburg Sublobe branched northeastward into the St. Croix Falls area, through the present-day towns of Atlas, Cushing and Grantsburg. The Superior Lobe had numerous ice margin positions where eskers and ridges of glacial till and boulders were deposited.

Most of the Ice Age Trail through Polk County is confined to the hilly and forested moraines. The exception is on the Gandy Dancer State Trail from Centuria to Milltown. Here the Trail is on a glacial outwash plain along some of Polk County's best cropland.

The Ice Age Trail's western terminus overlooks the St. Croix River in Interstate State Park. Glacial potholes are featured trailside with the Trail's terminus perched above the riverway and the Dalles of the St. Croix gorge. The park is Wisconsin's oldest state park, established in 1900, as well as an Ice Age National Scientific Reserve unit with an interpretive center containing educational displays about the Ice Age. Nearby St. Croix Falls is an Ice Age Trail Community. Polk County is also home to one of Wisconsin's newest state parks, Straight Lake State Park, designated in 2004. Due north of Straight Lake State Park, in Burnett County, Forts Folle Avoine Historical Park maintains two reconstructed fur posts and a Living History Ojibwe Village site.

Much of the Trail covers remote areas of the county. Finding water can be a problem during the summer. Logging in the county forest and private lands occurs regularly and can make it a challenge to locate Trail blazes. Take your time, pay close attention to blazes and carry a map and compass.

Primitive camping is allowed on Polk and Burnett County Forest land. Please camp at least 200 feet from trails and waterways. Burnett County officials request that campers call in advance for permission. Polk County also has three Dispersed Camping Areas (DCAs).

CHAPTER INFORMATION

The Indianhead Chapter hosts numerous hikes, work outings and presentations by glacial geologists throughout the year. The chapter's "Traprock Trekkers" program rewards hikers who hike all the Ice Age Trail miles in the chapter's territory. Upon completion, Trekkers receive a certificate, an attractive patch and, of course, memories to last a lifetime. Contact the chapter for details.

COUNTY INFORMATION

Burnett County Department of Tourism and Information: 715-349-5999 or 800-788-3164, burnettcountyfun.com

Burnett County Forest and Parks Department: 715-349-2157; call for primitive camping permission, burnettcounty.com

Polk County Visitor Information Center: In St. Croix Falls, on the Ice Age Trail, at the intersection of STH-35 and USH-8; 715-483-1410 or 800-222-7655, polkcountytourism.com

A hiker in the dappled light of the Straight Lake Segment.

St. Croix Falls Segment (Atlas Map 1f; Databook page 2)

SNAPSHOT

9.0 miles: Ice Age Trail Western Terminus in Interstate State Park to River Rd.

This segment highlights several outstanding features including the Dalles of St. Croix River, Hospital Esker and Riegel Park.

 At the Ice Age Trail Interpretive Center and other locations in Interstate State Park, the Polk County Tourist Information Center and Lions Park.

 From the St. Croix River, Big Rock Creek and other small streams/creeks. Do not take water from Mindy Creek as the headwaters are at the site of an old landfill.

 Walk-in campsite in the St. Croix National Scenic Riverway.

 Interstate SP campgrounds and campgrounds in nearby Taylors Falls, MN (see Area Services).

 At Interstate SP and Lions Park.

 At Interstate SP (incl. Interpretive Center), Polk County Tourist Info Center, Lions Park and St. Croix National Scenic Riverway campsite.

 Five ColdCache sites on segment.

 By law, dogs must be leashed in Interstate SP.

 Portions overlap bike trails, ski trails, roads and sidewalks.

 Interstate SP and the Wert Family Nature Center have a network of trails; Riegel Park and Ray Zillmer Park each have white-blazed loop trails.

 Portions of this segment may be suitable for those using wheelchairs or similar devices.

TRAIL ACCESS AND PARKING

Ice Age Trail Western Terminus in Interstate State Park: From St. Croix Falls at the intersection of USH-8 and STH-35, take STH-35 south for 0.6 mi. Turn right, enter Interstate State Park and follow park roads 1.5 mi to the Pothole Trail parking area. A brief walk clockwise on the Pothole Trail leads to the western terminus marker.

River Rd.: From St. Croix Falls at USH-8 and STH-87, take STH-87 north for 3.0 mi. At River Rd. turn left and go northwest 0.5 mi to the Trail access. Roadside parking.

Additional Parking: (i) Interpretive Center and other parking areas in Interstate State Park. (ii) Polk County Visitor Information Center at STH-35 and USH-8. (iii) East Georgia St. parking area near its intersection with Vincent St. (iv) Riegel Park on Louisiana St. A spur trail leads to the Ice Age Trail. (v) Oregon St. Roadside parking. (vi) Ray Zillmer Park on Day Rd. (vii) Wert Family Nature Preserve on the east side of STH-87. (viii) Lions Park on STH-87.

THE HIKE

The St. Croix River valley that hikers pass through on this segment was formed when the glacial lobe in the area retreated. Meltwater created Glacial Lake Duluth. Then giant floods drained the lake and cut the valley through billion-year-old volcanic basalt bedrock.

Access to the Ice Age Trail's western terminus is via Interstate State Park's Pothole Trail, a loop trail that was built shortly after the park was created in 1900 and is one of Wisconsin's oldest recreational footpaths. From the Pothole Trail parking area, hikers can reach the Ice Age Trail's western terminus either by trekking on the northern non-Ice Age Trail portion of the loop or along the Ice Age Trail

southern portion of the loop. The glacial potholes and Dalles of St. Croix River highlighted on the Pothole Trail were formed when torrential glacial meltwater scoured the riverside bedrock cliffs with rock and silt in a drilling-type motion. The potholes vary in size and depth, with one 16 feet deep and 3 feet wide. Additional larger potholes are located in Minnesota's Interstate State Park on the other side of the St. Croix River.

Upon reaching the Ice Age Trail's western terminus, hikers will find the official terminus marker (similar to the marker found at the Trail's eastern terminus in Potawatomi State Park, Door County) affixed to a large glacial erratic on a basalt cliff overlooking the 100-foot-deep gorge of the Dalles of the St. Croix River. From just below the terminus marker, looking upriver, one can see the famous rock face of the "Ol' Man of the Dalles." Looking downriver, one can see a basalt rock protrusion that was hard enough to redirect the roaring outflow of the prehistoric lake and river, making a rare 90 degree turn in the river. This protrusion was the site of the world's largest log jam in 1886. It took three months to dynamite the river clear for log traffic coming from the logging forests to the saw mills.

From the segment starting point at the western terminus, hikers will head back to the Pothole Trail parking area on the southern portion of the loop, cross Park Road and head southwest and then southeast on the state park's Horizon Rock Trail. The segment ascends steeply, passing a stone shelter near a rock-ledge overlook (**BP26**) with views of the river as it makes its way toward the Ice Age Interpretive Center. At the center, hikers can pick up a map for detailed information on the park's trails and facilities.

From the Interpretive Center, the segment briefly shares the northern portion of the Skyline Nature Trail loop then departs the nature trail by heading eastward toward the state park entrance road. The segment then links up with a paved bike path and turns north along STH-35, quickly leaving (**BP25**) Interstate State Park

Polk & Burnett Counties

and soon passing the Polk County Tourist Information Center, located across STH-35 just south of the STH-35/USH-8 junction.

After crossing USH-8 the segment ascends the Hospital Esker (**BP24**). From here hikers can enjoy excellent views of the city of St. Croix Falls and the glacial lake plain left behind by the drained Glacial Lake Duluth.

The segment descends the esker to the hospital parking area on State Street and continues north on Roosevelt Street, then turns east on Kentucky Street. The segment leaves Kentucky Street and continues east then southeast up a bluff into a wooded area, then connects with a paved city bike path heading east, where it passes through the school grounds.

From here, the segment enters another wooded area, intersects Blanding Woods Road and then enters the city-managed Florence Baker Riegel Memorial Park. The segment makes its way northeast through the park passing over rock outcroppings and basalt knobs. Shortly before reaching Louisiana Street the segment intersects a blue-blazed spur trail that leads west to the Louisiana Street parking area. The segment soon intersects a white-blazed trail that explores other areas of Riegel Park.

Crossing Louisiana Street, the Trail climbs to the top of a ridge and meanders through the woods as it gradually descends to an opening and the intersection of Oregon Street and Sunrise Road. The segment briefly follows Oregon Street to the left and then turns right and crosses through open fields between two fence lines. The segment eventually reenters the woods and crosses into Ray Zillmer Park.

The segment winds through Zillmer Park crossing exposed rock outcroppings, basalt knobs and surface bedrock. The Trail comes to a large rock outcropping, curves around to the right side of the outcropping and reaches a junction (**BP44**) with a white-blazed loop trail. A short trek on the loop trail leads to a sign identifying the rock outcropping as Zillmer Point. At the highest point on the outcropping there are two Leopold benches with long views of the St. Croix Falls river valley. The segment continues its journey through Zillmer Park, intersecting the western end of the white-blazed loop trail and reaching the Zillmer Park parking area on Day Road.

The segment briefly follows Day Road to the left then turns to the right and crosses a 26-foot-long footbridge. Look carefully at the bridge's limestone landing (**BP22**) closest to Day Road; when the limestone is wet, two 6-inch nautilus fossils appear. The segment continues west through woods and goes downhill along boulder-strewn Mindy Creek, named after a Native American woman from the Bad River Band of the Ojibwe who was the last of the Native Americans to live and work by the St. Croix River in the area.

After leaving Mindy Creek, the segment heads north as it continues to descend toward the STH-87 Trail access through the Wert Family Nature Preserve. The segment crosses STH-87 (dangerous road crossing) and passes through part of Lions Park, then turns north and takes hikers to the scenic shoreline of the St. Croix River. There are several social trails ("unofficial" trails created by meandering hikers) in the area; hikers should pay close attention to signage and stay close to the riverbank.

Heading north, hikers will soon come across a shoreline walk-in campsite

(**BP20**). The campsite is part of the St. Croix National Scenic Riverway and is available on a first come, first served basis. After passing the campsite, the segment reaches bridgeless Big Rock Creek (**BP19**), which hikers can usually cross on steppingstones but may have to ford in high water. Once across the creek, hikers will continue north along the St. Croix River and cross two small streams that may result in wet feet. From here the segment quickly reaches its terminus at River Road.

Mobile Skills Crew project site, 2005, 2014

AREA SERVICES

Interstate State Park: Camping. On Trail (715-483-3747, dnr.wi.gov/topic/parks/name/interstate; reservations: 888-947-2757, wisconsin.goingtocamp.com).

St. Croix Falls: Restaurant, grocery store, convenience store, general shopping, lodging, camping, library, medical service. On Trail. Most services in downtown on Washington St., USH-8 and STH-35. Camping at Minnesota Interstate State Park (Taylors Falls, MN, 651-465-5711, dnr.state.mn.us/state_parks/interstate; reservations: 866-857-2757 or see website) and at Camp Waub-O-Jeeg (Taylors Falls, 651-465-3500, tfcamping.com). For area info, contact the Falls Chamber of Commerce (715-483-3580, fallschamber.org) or the Polk County Tourist Information Center (715-483-1410, polkcountytourism.com).

St. Croix National Scenic Riverway Visitor Center: Walk-in campsite. On Trail (St. Croix Falls, WI, 715-483-3284, or 715-483-2279, NPS.gov/sacn).

A hiker keeps feet dry traversing a boardwalk along the St. Croix Falls Segment.

Gandy Dancer Segment (Atlas Maps 1f, 2f, 3f; Databook pages 2–3)

SNAPSHOT

15.5 miles (15.1 IAT, 0.3 CR): 160th Ave. to 150th St.

 This segment follows the multiuse Gandy Dancer State Trail (GDST) on a level, crushed-rock surface.

 At village parks in Centuria and Milltown and near Luck at Big Butternut Lake Park.

 From the Trade River and a few intermittent streams/creeks.

 At a Dispersed Camping Area in Centuria.

At nearby Big Butternut Lake Park in Luck, 1.0 mi east of the Trail (see Area Services).

 By law, dogs must be leashed on the GDST.

 Segment overlaps the GDST and also includes a short roadwalk. The GDST is open to biking and snowmobiling.

 The GDST continues both north and south.

 Portions of this segment may be suitable for those using wheelchairs or similar devices.

TRAIL ACCESS AND PARKING

160th Ave.: From Centuria at the intersection of 8th St. and STH-35, take STH-35 south 0.5 mi. At 160th Ave. turn right and go west 0.9 mi to the Ice Age Trail/Gandy Dancer State Trail (GDST) access. No parking. Instead, park at the GDST parking area in Centuria at the intersection of Polk Ave. and 4th St.

150th St.: From Frederic on STH-35/48, take STH-35/48 south 2.0 mi. At 150th St. turn left and continue south 0.3 mi to the parking area.

Additional Parking: GDST trailheads in the towns of Luck and Milltown.

THE HIKE

From 160th Avenue, this segment heads northeast along the Gandy Dancer State Trail (GDST). The 98-mile, multiuse GDST crosses the Wisconsin–Minnesota border twice on its way from St. Croix Falls to Superior. The crushed limestone–surfaced trail was converted from the abandoned Soo Line railway. The name "Gandy Dancer" was chosen to honor the men who built and maintained railroad tracks. "Gandy dancers" used tools manufactured by the Gandy Manufacturing Company and, while

4.5-mi CR to St. Croix Falls Segment. West on 160th Ave., north on STH-87, north on River Rd.

working, followed songlike calls and melodies that helped synchronize the swinging of tools and the movement of feet as they "danced" to the next rails. The GDST connects with the North Country National Scenic Trail south of the city of Superior.

The segment takes hikers through three small towns: Centuria, Milltown and Luck. Founded at the turn of the 20th century, Centuria has a rest stop along the segment with restrooms and vending machines. This log-sided structure is fully enclosed, affording all-weather protection for the hiker. North of the rest stop, the segment passes a Dispersed Camping Area (DCA) (**BP45**), for long-distance, multiday hikers, on the west side of the Trail. Between Centuria and Milltown, the segment crosses from the west side of STH-35 to the east side. In Milltown, there is a picnic area with restrooms at the intersection of Milltown Avenue and STH-35. Milltown services are located on Main Street two blocks west of the segment. In Luck, hikers will find picnic tables at the segment's intersection with STH-48. Luck was a stopover for travelers between Clam Falls, WI, and Taylors Falls, MN. Travelers felt that if they made it here by nightfall they were "luck"-y.

Between towns, the segment is largely sheltered on both sides by trees. While the GDST does get used by bikers and snowmobilers, a hiker may walk for long stretches without encountering others.

The segment departs from the GDST where the GDST crosses STH-35/48 about 5 miles north of Luck. The segment follows an access path along the highway to 150th Street, where it heads south on an unblazed connecting route for 0.3 miles to the segment's terminus.

Polk & Burnett Counties

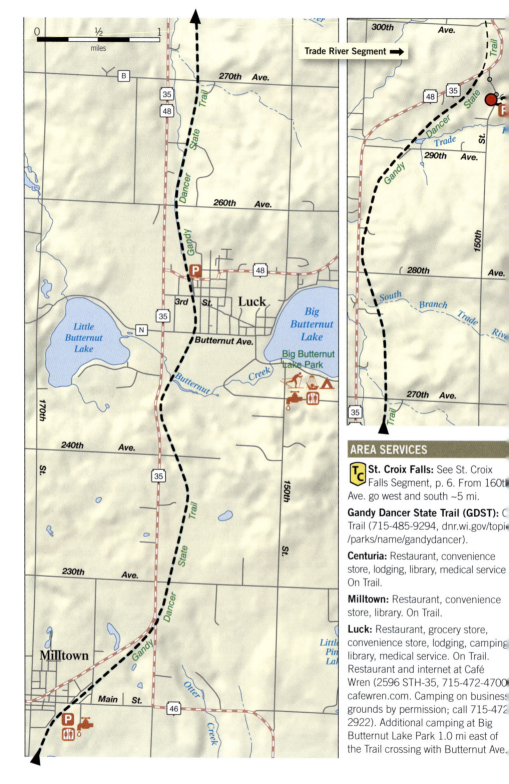

AREA SERVICES

St. Croix Falls: See St. Croix Falls Segment, p. 6. From 160th Ave. go west and south ~5 mi.

Gandy Dancer State Trail (GDST): C Trail (715-485-9294, dnr.wi.gov/topi /parks/name/gandydancer).

Centuria: Restaurant, convenience store, lodging, library, medical service On Trail.

Milltown: Restaurant, convenience store, library. On Trail.

Luck: Restaurant, grocery store, convenience store, lodging, camping library, medical service. On Trail. Restaurant and internet at Café Wren (2596 STH-35, 715-472-4700 cafewren.com. Camping on business grounds by permission; call 715-472 2922). Additional camping at Big Butternut Lake Park 1.0 mi east of the Trail crossing with Butternut Ave.

Restaurant and lodging at Luck Country Inn and Oakwood Café (STH-35 and STH-48, 715-472-2000 or 800-544-7396, luckcountryinn.com).

Frederic: Restaurant, convenience store, camping, library, medical service. From the GDST near 150th St. go 1.5 mi north on GDST or STH-35.

Siren: Restaurant, lodging. From the GDST near 150th St. go ~12 mi north on STH-35. Lodging at Best Western Motel (715-349-7800) and The Lodge at Crooked Lake (715-349-2500).

A not-so-shy turtle poses for the camera on the Gandy Dancer Segment.

Polk & Burnett Counties

Trade River Segment and Straight Lake Segment (Atlas Map 3f; Databook pages 3–4)

SNAPSHOT

Trade River Segment—4.3 miles (3.9 IAT, 0.4 CR): 150th St. to 280th Ave.

Straight Lake Segment—3.6 miles: 280th Ave. to 100th St. (CTH-I)

▲2 🥾 The **Trade River Segment** highlights the Trade River and its headwaters area, which hikers will explore on serpentine boardwalks.

 From the Trade River and headwaters wetlands.

 At Coon Lake Park in Frederic, ~2 mi north of the Trail.

 Two ColdCache sites on segment.

 Portion of the segment crossing private land between 150th St. and the SIATA property east of 140th St. is closed during gun deer season.

 Dogs should be leashed (8-ft max) and under control at all times.

 Segment includes connecting route roadwalk. Portions overlap cross-country ski trails and logging/forest roads.

Trade River Ski Trail network.

▲4 🥾 The dramatic **Straight Lake Segment** highlights wild Straight Lake State Park (SLSP) and beautiful, pristine Straight Lake.

 From Straight Lake, Rainbow Lake and the Straight River.

 At SLSP

 At several walk-in campsites 🏕 in SLSP and at two Dispersed Camping Areas 🏕.

 Portion of segment crossing private land between the eastern boundary of SLSP and CTH-I is closed during gun deer season.

 Dogs should be leashed (8-ft max) and under control at all times.

 SLSP trail network and access roads and a blue-blazed spur trail (**BP39**) to the two DCAs.

TRAIL ACCESS AND PARKING

150th St.: From Frederic on STH-35/48, take STH-35/48 south 2.0 mi. At 150th St. turn left and continue south 0.3 mi to the parking area.

100th St. (CTH-I): From Luck at the intersection of STH-35 and STH-48, take STH-48 east 5.2 mi. At 110th St. (CTH-I) (becomes 100th St. (CTH-I)) turn left and go north 0.9 mi to the parking area on the west (left) side of the road.

Additional Parking: (i) 140th St. parking area. (ii) 280th Ave. parking area on the south side of the road. (ii) 120th St. Straight Lake State Park (SLSP) parking area 0.1 mi north of the intersection of 120th St. and 270th Ave.

THE HIKE

Prominent features in this area are knobs of basalt bedrock. During the pre-Cambrian era, 1.1 billion years ago, the Earth's crust split across part of the North American continent. Known as the midcontinent rift, the split extended from Kansas to Lake Superior. Huge volumes of molten lava flowed to the surface and cooled, forming the basalt bedrock seen here. For most of that distance the basalt is beneath sedimentary rock, but from St. Croix Falls to Lake Superior outcroppings of exposed bedrock can be found.

The **Trade River Segment** begins at 150th Street at the parking area for the Trade River Ski Area, which offers 4 km of groomed ski trails in winter. The segment briefly overlaps the ski trail route; those hiking here in winter should hike well off to the side of the groomed trail.

When the segment reaches 140th Street, hikers should turn right and head south for 0.4 miles along the unmarked connecting route before departing 140th Street and continuing eastward on the off-road portion of the segment. Here, the segment passes through a prairie, along the Trade River and through a wooded area. A notable waypoint is the big basalt rock (**BP17**) dropped here by the Superior Lobe.

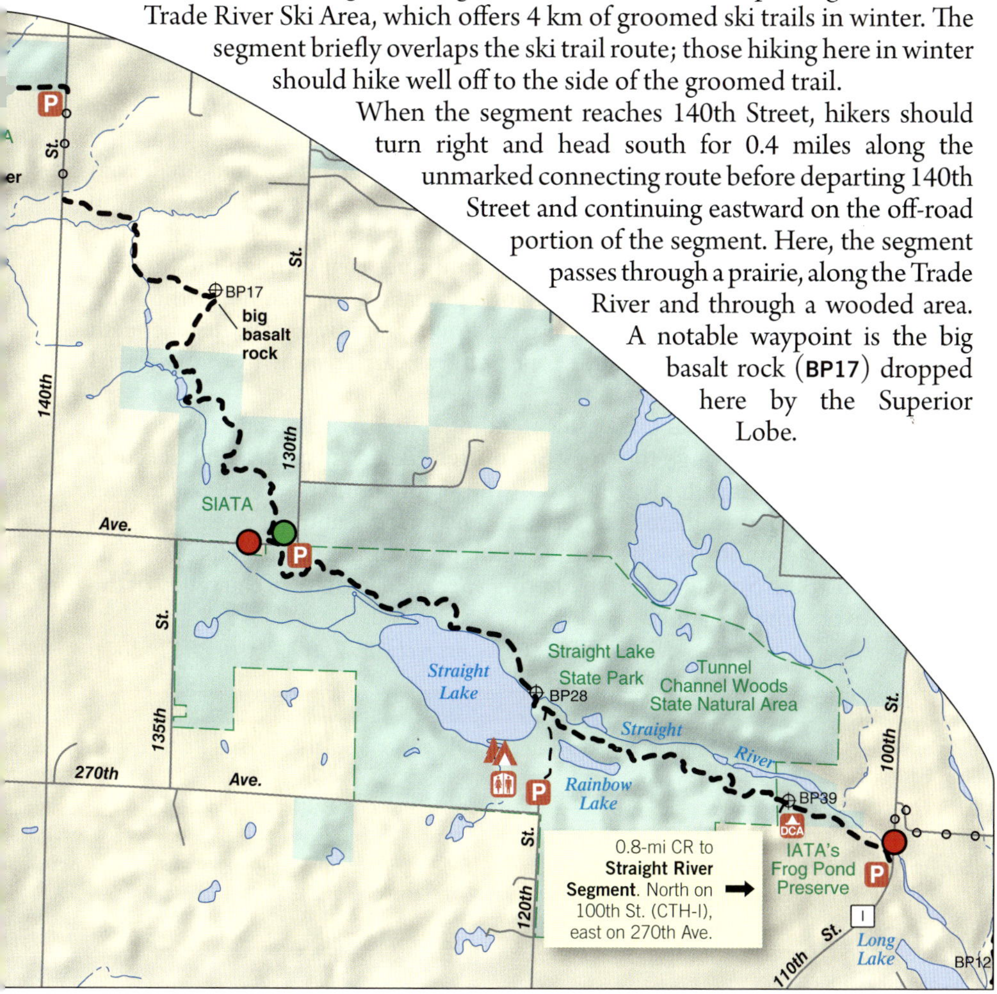

Polk & Burnett Counties

Because of impermeable bedrock, for the last half mile before the segment's endpoint on 280th Avenue the route has to navigate wetlands (and accompanying beaver dams) that make up the headwaters of the Trade River. The segment design incorporates the uniqueness of the terrain, saturating the hiker's senses by meandering next to, around and over some of the bedrock and serendipitously coursing above the perpetually wet ground on an elevated serpentine boardwalk.

Mobile Skills Crew project site, 2010, 2011, 2016

The **Straight Lake Segment** travels through the heart of 3,000-acre Straight Lake State Park (SLSP), which contains the headwaters of two river systems: the Straight River draining southeast and the Trade River draining northwest. The landscape is hummocky with outcroppings of basalt bedrock. Because the bedrock is close to the surface, the terrain contains numerous ephemeral ponds, perched wetlands and marshes.

The park exists in a transition zone between two vegetative communities: the northern hardwood forest and the prairie forest. One finds an intermingling of species from both communities and here many plants and animals tighten northern and southern limits. The extensive block of oak forest approaches old-growth status. Black bear, red fox, river otter, gray tree frog, leopard frog and four-toed salamander are common. *Note: The DNR bans all glass containers in SLSP.*

From its starting point on 280th Avenue the segment makes its way past the north shore of 107-acre Straight Lake, a shallow drainage lake with a small dam (**BP28**) at its outlet to the Straight River. Shortly after crossing the dam the Trail intersects an access road that leads to SLSP parking areas, other park facilities and the park's main entrance. The segment continues east through the Straight River tunnel channel, the finest example of a glacial tunnel channel in the Midwest. During the Ice Age, a subglacial river flowed rapidly as it exited beneath the receding glacier. The sediment it collected was carried away from the glacial margin, leaving the channel intact.

The segment passes near the eastern end of Rainbow Lake, and glimpses of the lake can be seen through the trees. Soon after hikers will cross a unique, curving boardwalk. Shortly after leaving SLSP, the segment intersects (**BP39**) a blue-blazed spur trail that leads to two separate Dispersed Camping Areas (DCAs) for long-distance, multiday hikers. The segment continues to make its way to its endpoint on 100th Street (CTH-I), offering spectacular views of the valley of the Straight River tunnel channel

Mobile Skills Crew project site, 2009, 2010, 2011, 2016

AREA SERVICES

Frederic: See Gandy Dancer Segment, p. 10. From 150th St. go north 1.5 mi. Also see Trail Access and Parking directions, above.

Oak Forest Retreat Center: Lodging (715-327-4500, oakforestcenter.org). Call before visiting. Limited availability.

Straight Lake State Park (SLSP): Camping. On Trail. (715-431-0724, dnr.wi.gov/topic /parks/name/straightlake/; ten walk-in campsites available; reservations: 888-947-2757, wisconsin .goingtocamp.com).

Luck: See Gandy Dancer Segment, p. 10. From 120th St. Trail access go west ~5 mi. Also see Trail Access and Parking directions, above.

Straight River Segment and Pine Lake Segment (Atlas Maps 3f, 4f; Databook page 4)

SNAPSHOT

Straight River Segment—3.4 miles: 270th Ave. to Round Lake Rd.

Pine Lake Segment—2.9 miles: Round Lake Rd. to 70th St.

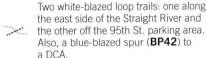 *The Straight River Segment highlights the Straight River tunnel channel and includes an enjoyable loop trail.*

 From the Straight River and Long Lake.

 At Dispersed Camping Areas on Long Lake and east of 95th St.

 The segment is closed during gun deer season.

 Dogs should be leashed (8-ft max) and under control at all times.

Portions overlap a snowmobile trail, STH-48, a private gravel driveway and some logging/forest roads.

Two white-blazed loop trails: one along the east side of the Straight River and the other off the 95th St. parking area. Also, a blue-blazed spur (**BP42**) to a DCA.

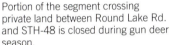 *The Pine Lake Segment is rich in variety, highlighting glacial remnants, restored prairies and hummocky woodlands.*

 No reliable sources of water.

 Portion of the segment crossing private land between Round Lake Rd. and STH-48 is closed during gun deer season.

 Dogs should be leashed (8-ft max) and under control at all times.

 Portions overlap snowmobile trails, logging/forest roads and 260th Ave.

 A white-blazed loop trail crossing a debris field.

TRAIL ACCESS AND PARKING

270th Ave.: From Luck at the intersection of STH-35 and STH-48, take STH-48 east for 5.2 mi. At 110th St. (CTH-I) (becomes 100th St. (CTH-I)) turn left and go north 1.3 mi. At 270th Ave. turn right and go east 0.6 mi to the Trail access. Roadside parking.

70th St.: *From Cumberland* at the intersection of STH-48 and STH-63, take STH-48 west 15.7 mi. At 260th Ave. turn right and go east 0.7 mi. At 70th St. turn left and go north 0.7 mi to the parking area on the west side of the road. *From Frederic* at the intersection of STH-35 and CTH-W, take CTH-W east 9.0 mi. At 60th St. (CTH-O) turn right and go south 3.0 mi and follow CTH-O to the west on 270th St. for 0.9 mi. At 70th St. turn left and go south 0.3 mi to the parking area on the west side of the road.

Additional Parking: IATA Straight River Preserve parking area (**BP14**) on 95th St.

THE HIKE

The **Straight River Segment** starts out by heading south from 270th Avenue, passing through a dry kettle as it makes its way toward the Straight River tunnel channel. Dropping down from the rim of the tunnel channel the segment intersects (**BP12**) a white-blazed loop trail. A side trip on the white-blazed trail leads to an enormous white pine on private land and then continues along the east side of the Straight River to STH-48. The white-blazed trail is at river level and therefore offers excellent bird viewing opportunities of eagles and nesting

Polk & Burnett Counties

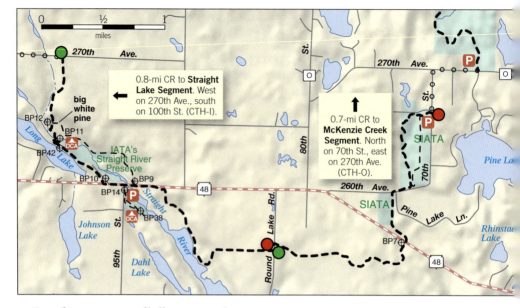

Canadian geese, sandhill cranes and trumpeter swans.

From the intersection with the white-blazed trail the segment continues south, going up and down a small kame, crossing the Straight River and switchbacking up an esker (**BP11**) that separates the Straight River and Long Lake. Shortly after reaching the top of the esker, the segment reaches a junction (**BP42**) with a blue-blazed spur trail that leads to a Dispersed Camping Area (DCA) on Long Lake for long-distance, multiday hikers.

The segment continues a short distance southeast on the esker above the shore of Long Lake before reaching a private gravel drive and several private cabins. From here, hikers can see both the Straight River to the east and Long Lake to the west. The segment follows the gravel drive southeast to its intersection (**BP10**) with STH-48.

At the intersection of the private drive and STH-48, hikers should head east for 0.3 miles along the southern shoulder of STH-48. In the process, the route intersects 95th Street. Hikers can walk a short distance south on 95th Street to a parking area (**BP14**) for the IATA's Straight River Preserve, which has a white blazed loop trail leading to a wooded hilltop known as "Moh's Mountain" and a DCA (**BP38**) for long-distance, multiday hikers.

Back on STH-48, the segment crosses the wide Straight River, where a hiker may see otters and water birds, and intersects (**BP9**) on the north side of STH-48 the southern access to the white-blazed loop trail encountered earlier in the segment. Shortly, the segment departs from STH-48 and heads southeast through a pine plantation back toward the shore of the Straight River. The route hugs the shore of the river for nearly half a mile before turning east, climbing a hill and traversing along field edges to the segment's endpoint on Round Lake Road.

The **Pine Lake Segment** continues east from Round Lake Road, passing mostly through wooded areas and a recently logged area, on its way to STH-48. After 0.5 miles, the segment reaches a gated cattle field. Hikers may enter the field through

18   Ice Age Trail Guidebook 2020 – 2022 Edition

the gate if it is unlocked (please make sure to close the gate) or by using fence stiles on the adjoining fences. Once in the field, the Trail hugs the forest edge before heading east into the forest over another fence stile. From here, the segment occasionally shares a snowmobile trail; hikers should pay close attention to blazes and directional arrows on posts.

Upon reaching STH-48 (**BP7**), hikers should cross with caution and continue on the segment as it bends to the northwest and then north along a field edge to 260th Avenue. The segment turns right and heads east for 0.2 miles on 260th Avenue before going off-road and heading north again.

The portion of the segment between 260th Avenue and its endpoint on 70th Street crosses land that is a veritable glacial dumping ground, with hilly, open fields, restored prairie areas and hummocky woods that highlight many glacial features. Shortly after the segment leaves 260th Avenue, it intersects a white-blazed loop trail that offers a side trip to explore these many glacial features in greater depth.

AREA SERVICES

Frederic: See Gandy Dancer Segment, p. 10. From 270th Ave. Trail access go north ~10 mi. Also see Trail Access and Parking directions, above.

Luck: See Gandy Dancer Segment, p. 10. From STH-48 Trail access go west ~7 mi. Also see Trail Access and Parking directions, above.

Cumberland: See Grassy Lake Segment, p. 34. From 70th St. Trail access go east ~17 mi. Also see Trail Access and Parking directions, above.

Snowshoeing on the Straight Lake Segment.

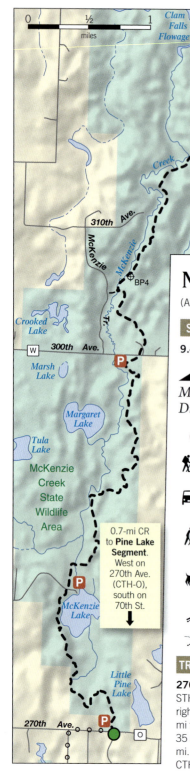

McKenzie Creek Segment

(Atlas Maps 4f, 5f; Databook page 5)

SNAPSHOT

9.4 miles: 270th Ave. (CTH-O) to 50th St. (CTH-O)

This wild and scenic segment highlights the McKenzie Creek tunnel channel and McKenzie and Dinger kettle lakes.

 From McKenzie Creek, the Clam River, Dinger Lake, McKenzie Lake and other smaller streams/creeks.

 County forest land west of CTH-O only. Primitive camping is not permitted in the State Wildlife Area.

 In Clam Falls, ~2 mi north of the 60th St. parking area.

 Portion of segment crossing private land between 60th St. parking area and 50th St. (CTH-O) is closed during gun deer season.

 Dogs should be leashed (8-ft max) and under control at all times. **By law, dogs must be leashed April 15 to July 31 in the State Wildlife Area.**

 Portions overlap snowmobile trails and logging/forest roads.

Intersects a few side trails.

TRAIL ACCESS AND PARKING

270th Ave. (CTH-O): *From Cumberland* at the intersection of STH-48 and STH-63, take STH-48 west 10.0 mi. At 40th St. turn right and go north 2.0 mi. At 270th Ave. turn left and go west 2.5 mi to the parking area. *From Frederic* at the intersection of STH-35 and 300th Ave. (CTH-W), take 300th Ave. (CTH-W) east 9.0 mi. At 60th St. (CTH-O) turn right and go south 3.0 mi and follow CTH-O to the west on 270th St. for 0.6 mi to the parking area.

50th St. (CTH-O): *From Cumberland* at the intersection of STH-48 and USH-63, take STH-48 west for 8.0 mi. At 10th St. (CTH-E) turn right and go north, west then north 4.7 mi. *Note: When CTH-E turns west then north, it becomes 15th St.* At 300th Ave. (CTH-W) turn left and go west 4.0 mi. At 50th St. (CTH-O) turn right and go north 2.5 mi to the parking area on the west side of the road. *From Frederic* at the intersection of STH-35 and 300th Ave. (CTH-W), take 300th Ave. (CTH-W) east 10.0 mi. At 50th St. (CTH-O) turn left and go north 2.5 mi to parking area on the west side of the road.

Additional Parking: (i) 280th Ave. at McKenzie Lake boat launch parking area. (ii) 300th Ave. (CTH-W) parking area. (iii) 60th St. Clam River parking area.

THE HIKE

The segment highlights the steep and hilly topography of the 5,497 acre McKenzie Creek State Wildlife Area. Established in 1945, the wildlife area provides watershed protection and access to four trout streams and six lakes. Often growing near the lakes and in bog areas are tamarack, alder and black spruce, with occasional white spruce and balsam fir. Seasonally, frogs are abundant. The remainder of the forest is mostly red oak, aspen and pine, with some maple, ironwood, basswood, hickory and elm. The forest is reestablishing after years of logging and fire. Growing beneath the forest canopy is a wide variety of ferns, wildflowers like yellow lady's slipper, wild geranium, Solomon's seal and trillium, and an assortment of fungi along with wild strawberries and raspberries.

From 270th Avenue (CTH-O), the segment heads north, enters a northern hardwood forest and follows a logging road down a slope. Soon the Trail leaves the logging road and heads right to a single-track trail that follows the ups and downs of the kettle topography in this area. After passing a Leopold bench overlooking an ephemeral wetland hikers will climb a slope to catch a first glimpse at McKenzie Lake through the woods.

Continuing through forest and meadow, the Trail skirts the shore of spring-fed McKenzie Lake and crosses a gravel road leading to a boat ramp. The serene, undeveloped kettle lake is a prime example of an end product of the glacial activity in the area.

North of McKenzie Lake, the segment cuts through an area of towering white pines, crosses McKenzie Creek and then climbs a ridge overlooking the creek. Hikers may notice a change in species as the segment covers rolling topography, sticking mostly to a ridge. This area is also home to undeveloped Margaret Lake and Tula Lake, which are accessible from a trail west of where the segment crosses 300th Avenue (CTH-W).

North of 300th Avenue (CTH-W), the segment joins a sandy logging road through an older logging harvest area. Hikers should pay close attention to signage as the Trail intersects other logging roads and a few side trails. The segment soon meets McKenzie Creek again and follows the creek north as it winds along McKenzie Creek's tunnel channel (**BP4**), a pristine Class I trout stream with a naturally sustaining wild trout population. The segment passes another Leopold bench on top of a hummock with great views of the creek below and the valley of the tunnel channel.

Eventually, the Trail crosses a small tributary of McKenzie Creek on a wooden bridge and climbs out of the tunnel channel. The segment then drops down to lower elevations as it passes along the west shoreline of Dinger Lake, one of many remote kettle lakes in the area. As the segment curves around to the north of the lake, hikers pass another Leopold bench offering views across the lake. The segment continues through forest and shortly crosses the scenic Clam River, a Class III trout stream, on a long boardwalk and bridge, just before reaching the 60th Street Trail access and parking area.

From the Clam River parking area, hikers climb a hill and follow a wide snowmobile trail. Near a tributary of the Clam River, the segment route leaves the snowmobile trail and continues on well-marked and maintained single-track trail through northern hardwood forest. Here the Trail crosses a section of private lands and then enters a State Ice Age Trail Area (SIATA). The segment crosses another small ephemeral stream shortly before reaching its terminus on 50th Street (CTH-O).

AREA SERVICES

Frederic: See Gandy Dancer Segment, p. 10. From 300th Ave. (CTH-W) Trail access go west ~13 mi. Also see Trail Access and Parking directions, above.

Cumberland: See Grassy Lake Segment, p. 34. From 300th Ave. (CTH-W) Trail access go east and south ~20 mi. Also see Trail Access and Parking directions, above.

Clam Falls: Restaurant, camping. From the Clam River Trail access on 60th St. go north ~2 mi. Camping at Moody's Wildwoods Campground (628 335th Ave., 715-653-2306) and Clam Falls Campground (642 335th Ave., 715-653-2617).

Indian Creek Segment (Atlas Map 5f; Databook page 5)

SNAPSHOT

5.4 miles: 50th St. (CTH-O) to 15th St. (CTH-E)

 This segment explores rolling, remote Polk County Forest lands.

 From the headwaters of Indian Creek (**BP31**) and other small intermittent streams/creeks.

 Portion of the segment crossing private land west of 30th St. is closed during gun deer season.

 Primitive camping on county forest lands.

 Dogs should be leashed (8-ft max) and under control at all times.

 Portions overlap snowmobile trails and logging/forest roads.

TRAIL ACCESS AND PARKING

50th St. (CTH-O): *From Cumberland* at the intersection of STH-48 and USH-63, take STH-48 west for 8.0 mi. At 10th St. (CTH-E) turn right and go north, west then north 4.7 mi. *Note: When CTH-E turns west then north, it becomes 15th St.* At 300th Ave. (CTH-W) turn left and go west 4.0 mi. At 50th St. (CTH-O) turn right and go north 2.5 mi to the parking area on the west side of the road. *From Frederic* at the intersection of STH-35 and 300th Ave. (CTH-W), take 300th Ave. (CTH-W) east 10.0 mi. At 50th St. (CTH-O) turn left and go north 2.5 mi to the parking area on the west side of the road.

15th St. (CTH-E): *From Cumberland* at the intersection of STH-48 and USH-63, take STH-48 west for 8.0 mi. At 10th St. (CTH-E) turn right and go north, west then north 7.4 mi to parking area on west side of the road. *Note: When CTH-E turns west then north, it becomes 15th St. From Frederic* at the intersection of STH-35 and 300th Ave. (CTH-W), take 300th Ave. (CTH-W) east 14.0 mi. At 10th St. (CTH-E) turn left and go north, west, then north 2.7 mi to parking area on west side of the road. *Note: When CTH-E turns west then north, it becomes 15th St.*

Additional Parking: 30th St. Trail access. Parking area on the east side of the road.

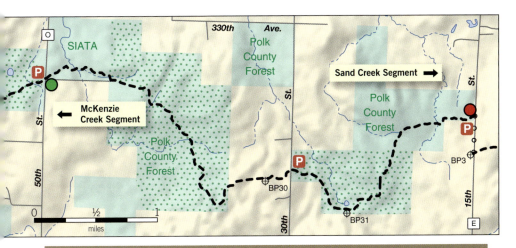

THE HIKE

The segment passes through thickly forested and hummocky areas of a State Ice Age Trail Area, Polk County Forest and private land. The majority of the segment is on public land and the forest is mostly managed for larger stands of hardwoods by select cutting.

The segment heads east from 50th Street (CTH-O) through mostly softwood lowlands, crossing numerous creek beds on generally level terrain. This portion of the Trail can be wet in spring and during rainy weather. Thick berry bushes, many with edible berries, are common in late summer.

The segment then travels through a high-relief hummocky area created when sand and gravel, carried by under-the-ice rivers and streams, were left behind after the ice sheets melted. These hummocks will challenge hikers with steep climbs and descents and provide nice views of the surrounding forest. Shortly before reaching 30th Avenue, a Leopold bench (**BP30**) sits on top of a hummock.

Crossing 30th Street marks the approximate midpoint and the start of a trek through more open woods and a few rocky creek beds. A short climb up a ridge puts the segment above a small picturesque lily-filled lake (**BP31**), the headwaters of Indian Creek. Herons and other waterfowl can be spotted from the forested ridge as the Trail winds north and east. Hikers may spot deer, grouse, various other birds and signs of black bear.

The final mile of the segment consists of narrow hand-carved trail, a short bridge crossing and an open meadow dotted with young white pines, as the segment makes its way to its terminus on 15th Street (CTH-E).

AREA SERVICES

Frederic: See Gandy Dancer Segment, p. 10. From 50th St. (CTH-O) Trail access go north and west 12.5 mi. Also see Trail Access and Parking directions, above.

Cumberland: See Grassy Lake Segment, p. 34. From 15th St. (CTH-E) Trail access go south and east ~15.5 mi. Also see Trail Access and Parking directions, above.

Clam Falls: See McKenzie Creek Segment, p. 20. From 50th St. (CTH-O) Trail access go north and west ~3 mi.

Sand Creek Segment (Atlas Maps 5f, 6f; Databook pages 5–6)

SNAPSHOT

6.0 miles (5.7 IAT, 0.3 CR): 15th St. (CTH-E) Northern Trail Access to Lake 32 Rd.

 This remote and beautifully wooded segment highlights the Sand Creek tunnel channel while exploring county forest lands and frequently sharing logging roads.

- From Sand Creek and some smaller streams/creeks and wetland areas.
- Primitive camping on county forest lands.
- The portion of the segment crossing private land between 15th St. (CTH-E) and Polk County Forest boundary is closed during gun deer season.
- Dogs should be leashed (8-ft max) and under control at all times.
- Segment includes a short connecting route roadwalk. Small portions overlap snowmobile trails and gravel/dirt roads; a significant portion overlaps logging roads.

TRAIL ACCESS AND PARKING

15th St. (CTH-E) Northern Trail Access: *From Frederic* at the intersection of STH-35 and 300th Ave. (CTH-W), take 300th Ave. (CTH-W) east 14.0 mi. At 10th St. (CTH-E) turn left and go north, west, then north 2.7 mi to parking area on west side of the road. *From Cumberland* at the intersection of STH-48 and USH-63, take STH-48 west for 8.0 mi. At 10th St. (CTH-E) turn right and go north, west then north for 7.4 mi to a parking area on the west side of the road. *Note: When CTH-E turns west then north, it becomes 15th St.*

Lake 32 Rd.: *From Frederic* at the intersection of STH-35 and 300th Ave (CTH-W), take 300th Ave. (CTH-W) east 14.0 mi. At 10th St. (CTH-E) turn right and go south 1.0 mi. At 290th St. turn left and go east 1.0 mi. At Polk Barron St. turn left and go north 0.5 mi. At 29½ Ave., turn right and go east 1.5 mi. At 1½ St. turn left and go north 0.5 mi. At 30th Ave. turn right and go east 0.2 mi to junction with Lake 32 Rd. and the parking area on the corner. *From Cumberland* at the intersection of STH-48 and USH-63, take STH-48 west for 5.0 mi. At 2nd St. turn right and go north 1.6 mi. At 26th Ave. turn left and go west 1.0 mi. At 1st St. turn right and go north 1.5 mi. At 27½ Ave. turn right and go east 0.5 mi. At 1½ St. turn left and go north 2.5 mi. At 30th Ave. turn right and go east 0.2 mi to the junction with Lake 32 Rd. and the parking area on the corner.

THE HIKE

Starting from the 15th Street (CTH-E) northern Trail access and parking area, hikers should walk 0.3 miles south to the point (**BP3**) where the segment heads off road. From here the segment makes its way east over private land for the first half mile before entering Polk County Forest lands. The segment bends to the southeast and follows the Sand Creek tunnel channel over hummocky sand and gravel. Sand Creek flows southeast through the bottom of the tunnel channel in a valley that extends to the town of Cumberland and includes several large lakes.

At a point just southeast of the Polk/Burnett county line, the segment reaches a bridge over Sand Creek (**BP2**). The bridge is a favorite resting and gathering spot for hikers. The creek has a wide variety of fish including largemouth bass, smallmouth bass and walleye. Shortly after the creek crossing, the segment hooks up with a dirt forest road as it makes its way south and then southeast. The segment turns left off the road and meanders along on old logging roads through the

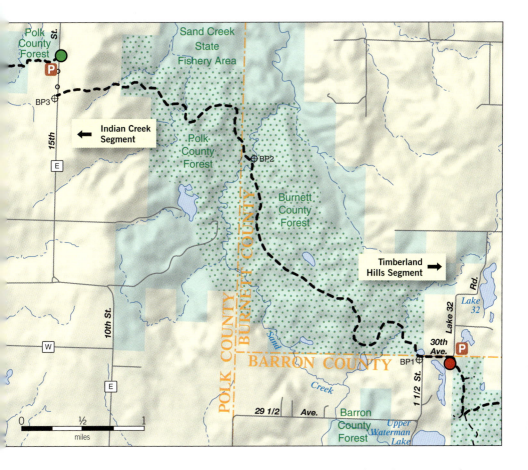

woods. Hikers should pay close attention to signage as these logging roads can become overgrown.

The segment crosses in front of an old overgrown beaver dam that is in poor repair. The Trail in this area may be wet or flooded in spring or during rainy periods. The segment passes along the south side of a wetland before reaching the intersection (**BP1**) of 1½ Street and 30th Avenue. Hikers should continue east on 30th Avenue to the segment's endpoint at the 30th Avenue and Lake 32 Road intersection.

AREA SERVICES

Frederic: See Gandy Dancer Segment, p. 10. From 15th St. (CTH-E) Trail access go north and west ~18 mi.

Cumberland: See Grassy Lake Segment, p. 34. From Lake 32 Rd. Trail access go east 12.3 mi. Also see Trail Access and Parking directions, above.

We spend millions to go fast; let's spend a little to go slow.
RAYMOND T. ZILLMER, FOUNDER, ICE AGE TRAIL ALLIANCE

Barron, Washburn, & Rusk Counties

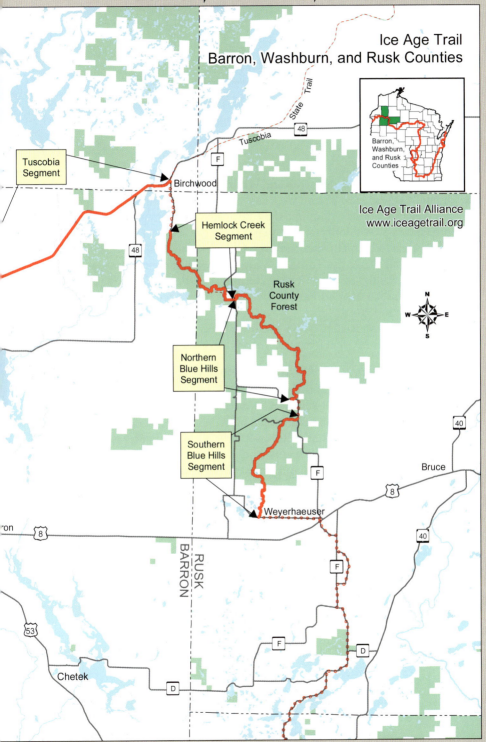

Barron & Washburn Counties

Atlas Maps 6f–10f; Databook pages 7–11
Total miles: 53.6 (Trail 43.0; Connecting Route 10.6)

The Ice Age Trail route in Barron and Washburn counties winds through three different landscapes. To the west and north is the Superior Lobe end moraine, a lake-studded zone dominated by steep kettle topography. To the east are the Blue Hills, a 1.6-billion-year-old quartzite range. Between the two is an outwash plain created by meltwater from the Chippewa and Superior glacial lobes. The Ice Age Trail shares the Tuscobia State Trail, a multiuse rail-trail, across the outwash plain. Southeast of the western terminus of the Tuscobia Segment, Barron County's Indian Mound Park is the site of twelve remaining mounds of a former fifty-mound group.

Primitive camping is allowed on Washburn and Barron County Forest land. Please camp at least 200 feet from trails and waterways.

CHAPTER INFORMATION

The Superior Lobe Chapter was formed in 2001 and meets regularly at the University of Wisconsin-Barron County in Rice Lake. The chapter maintains area Ice Age Trail segments and sponsors seasonal hikes, including snowshoe hikes, bird walks and the Woolly Mammoth Classic Run/Walk. The chapter also offers the "Superior Lobetrotter" award to hikers who preregister and complete all Ice Age Trail segments from Lake 32 Rd. in Burnett County to CTH-F in Rusk County. Contact the chapter for details.

COUNTY INFORMATION

Barron County Visitor Information: 715-637-6871, barroncountywi.gov
Barron County Forest and Recreation Department: 715-537-6295
Washburn County Forest Department: 715-635-4490, co.washburn.wi.us

Along the Hemlock Creek Segment, this tree was likely a Native American trail marker.

Timberland Hills Segment (Atlas Map 6f; Databook page 8)

SNAPSHOT

10.9 miles: Lake 32 Rd. to Leach Lake Rd.

This segment mostly follows ski and snowshoe trails on hilly terrain through the Timberland West and Timberland ski areas, passing some scenic small lakes and wetland areas along the way.

 From some small lakes and small intermittent streams/creeks.

 Primitive camping on county forest lands.

Two portables available near the crossings of CTH-H and Boyd Ln.

 Portions of segment crossing private land (i) east of the end of the gravel road to Timberland Hills ski area western boundary and (ii) east of the Timberland Hills ski area eastern boundary to Leach Lake Rd. are closed during gun deer season.

 Dogs should be leashed (8-ft max) and under control at all times. **Dogs should stay off portions that overlap groomed ski trails in winter.**

Small portions overlap logging/forest roads and a gravel road. Large portions overlap ski and snowshoe trails. Hike to the side of groomed ski trails in winter. Ski-area trails are open to horseback riding during the non-ski season.

 Ski/snowshoe network trails are open to hiking.

TRAIL ACCESS AND PARKING

Lake 32 Rd.: From Cumberland at the intersection of STH-48 and USH-63, take USH-48 west for 5.0 mi. At 2nd St. turn right and go north 1.6 mi. At 26th Ave. turn left and go west 1.0 mi. At 1st St. turn right and go north 1.5 mi. At 27½ Ave. turn right and go east 0.5 mi. At 1½ St. turn left and go north 2.5 mi. At 30th Ave. turn right and go east 0.2 mi to the junction with Lake 32 Rd. and the parking area on the corner.

Leach Lake Rd.: From Cumberland at the intersection of STH-48 and USH-63, take USH-63 north for 8.3 mi. At Brickyard Rd. turn left and go west 0.9 mi. At Leach Lake Rd. turn right and go north then west then north 0.7 mi to the Trail access (look for yellow arrow). Roadside parking.

Additional Parking: (i) 3rd St. (CTH-H) Timberland West ski area parking area on the west side of the road. (ii) Boyd Ln. Timberland Hills ski area main parking area.

THE HIKE

This segment traverses hummocky topography of the Superior Lobe's St. Croix Moraine. From its starting point on Lake 32 Road, the segment heads south on the Waterman Lakes Snowshoe Trail through a recent selectively logged area on a logging road and then east on a narrower snowshoe trail. The segment weaves through mixed hardwood forests and crosses an old beaver dam (**BW15**) between two wetlands. The Trail then transitions to the wide grassy path of the Timberland West ski trails.

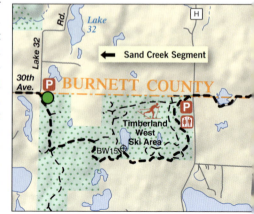

The segment crosses CTH-H (about 500 feet north of the Timberland West parking area) and continues east on a gravel road for about a quarter mile where the road ends at two driveways. The Trail leaves the road and follows the southern edge of an open field before heading northeast across the field and reentering the woods. The segment enters Burnett County Forest lands at a signed junction (**BW14**) and connects with the wide, mowed trails of the Timberland Hills ski area. There are several intersecting ski trails; hikers should pay close attention to and look for yellow blazes and Ice Age Trail directional arrows. This portion of Trail through the ski area is quite hilly, often steep and may have wet areas at the bottoms of the hills. The segment continues about a mile north to the ski area's main parking lot and winter warming hut off Boyd Lane.

The segment generally continues north then east from Boyd Lane through a fine stand of white pine and over a bridge. From this point to a spot just northwest of Offers Lake, the segment ascends and descends frequently as it goes in and out of two tunnel channels, one of which flowed from the area of the present-day South Fork of the Clam River and the other from Leach Lake.

Reaching the east side of the ski area the segment leaves the ski trail (**BW13**) to follow a narrow track alongside some wetlands and beaver ponds. The segment passes a Leopold bench (**BW17**) overlooking a scenic pond and then goes through a blueberry patch and down a steep hill to intersect a grassy road (**BW12**) near a log fish carving.

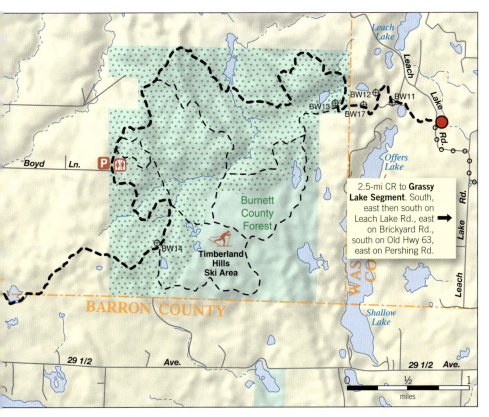

From here the segment follows grassy roads for about a quarter mile. Hikers should pay close attention to signage as there are intersecting roads and a right turn. The Trail abruptly leaves the grassy road to the left (**BW11**) and enters a brushy area (site of a clearcut), skirts the shoreline of a pond and climbs the side of a steep ravine. The segment then meanders a short distance through the woods to its terminus on Leach Lake Road.

AREA SERVICES

Timberland Hills and Timberland West ski areas: Lodging, camping. On Trail. (1821 Boyd Rd., Barronett, winter trail conditions: 715-822-3727, timberlandhills.com); Rental lodging at Burnett County Camper Cabin. Accessible by foot. (Rental reservations through Airbnb link: burnettcounty.com/index.aspx?NID=1148). Camping (primitive) on Burnett County Forest land.

Barronett: See Grassy Lake Segment, p. 34. From Leach Lake Rd. Trail access go south ~2.5 mi.

Cumberland: See Grassy Lake Segment, p. 34. From Leach Lake Rd. Trail access go south ~10 mi. Also see Trail Access and Parking directions, above.

Shell Lake: See Grassy Lake Segment, p. 34. From Leach Lake Rd. Trail access go north ~8.5 mi.

Pinch us and say it's real. It was a wonder to hear birds continuously sing, and for animals to give us a glimpse of their daily activity. Trumpeter swans, what a treasure to witness the successful reintroduction of this once nearly extinct bird to our state. Osprey, with nests on highline poles, soar high displaying their majestic manner. Loons so serene, coveys of partridges drumming and thrusting forward in surprise, turkeys strutting while taking their sweet ol' time. Woodpeckers that drummed incredible holes into trees, leaving wood chips piled high on the ground. Frogs croaking their mating calls. Fat toads, feasting on the gazillion mosquitoes, while almost being trodden on. Even a baby mink that Jane nearly stepped on. When David arrived, the mother was on standby, ready to pounce and protect her charge from "imminent danger." The bear we startled while breaking the crest of a knoll; that burly animal was enormous. Thankfully, we must have looked pretty scary too, as it quickly lumbered away. We spotted fox, coyote, wolf, fleeting deer, and beavers enjoying ownership of small lakes.

JANE AND DAVID LECOUNT, ICE AGE TRAIL THOUSAND-MILERS

A boardwalk across the marsh protects fragile habitat along the Bear Lake Segment.

Grassy Lake Segment (Atlas Map 7f; Databook pages 8–9)

SNAPSHOT

8.5 miles: Pershing Rd. to 30th Ave.

 *This remote segment crossing through Washburn County Forest is almost entirely on logging roads and features several small and scenic beaver-inhabited lakes.*

	From several small lakes, streams/creeks and other wetland areas.		Dogs should be leashed (8-ft max) and under control at all times.
	At nearby private campground ▲ (see Area Services for Sarona).		Nearly the full segment is on logging/forest roads, portions of which are open to snowmobiling. A portion overlaps primitive Shingle Camp Rd., which is open to cars and ATVs.
	Primitive camping on county forest lands.		

TRAIL ACCESS AND PARKING

Pershing Rd.: From Cumberland at the intersection of STH-48 and USH-63 take USH-63 north for 8.3 mi. At Brickyard Rd. turn right and go east 0.1 mi. At Old Hwy. 63 (unsigned) turn right and go south 0.1 mi. At Pershing Rd. (unsigned) turn left and go east 0.7 mi just past W8661 Pershing Rd. to the Trail access parking area.

30th Ave.: From Haugen at the intersection of CTH-SS and CTH-V, take CTH-V (3rd St.) west 0.5 mi. Curve south on CTH-V (now 18th St.) and go 0.7 mi. Join 27th Ave. where CTH-V curves west and follow it west 1.7 mi. When CTH-V curves south, continue west on 27th Ave. for another 0.3 mi. At 16th St. turn right and go north 4.0 mi joining 13¾ St. (Shallow Lake Rd.). At 30th Ave. turn left and go west 0.1 mi to the parking area on the north side of the road.

Additional Parking: Lehman Lake Rd. parking area.

THE HIKE

Like the Timberland Hills Segment, the Grassy Lake Segment continues through hummocky topography of the Superior Lobe's St. Croix Moraine and skirts beaver-inhabited lakes and wetlands. Hikers should pay close attention to signage and the map while navigating through this segment as Ice Age Trail signage can be knocked down by animals or concealed by foliage. A significant portion of the segment may be wet or flooded during rainy periods so appropriate gear for wet travel is recommended.

From its starting point on Pershing Road the segment heads north around a gate and soon passes near the west side of Grassy Lake (**BW9**). From here the segment heads north and then east to Lehman Lake Road through generally forested terrain and past some small lakes and wetlands.

East of Lehman Lake Road the segment enters the Washburn County Forest Welsh

Lake Unit. For the first 0.6 miles the segment shares the route with primitive Shingle Camp Road; this portion of the segment is open to car and ATV traffic. After 0.6 miles, the segment leaves Shingle Camp Road and follows a logging road to the right and up a hill. At the next logging road junction, the segment turns to the left and soon reaches another junction where the segment makes a sharp left. From here the Trail intersects (**BW8**) an old forest road where the logging road ends and turns left on the forest road. After another 0.2 miles the segment makes a hard right and continues southeast on old grassy forest roads and logging roads.

The segment makes its way to its terminus on 30th Avenue through more wetland areas and some hummocky terrain. Hikers will encounter several low-lying washouts of varying sizes that may have standing water. No footbridges exist on the segment. Some washouts can be easily stepped over while others may produce wet feet.

AREA SERVICES

Barronett: Restaurant, grocery store, convenience store. From Pershing Rd. Trail access go west 0.7 mi. At Old Hwy 63 turn right and go north 0.1 mi. At Brickyard Rd. turn left and go west 0.1 mi. At USH-63 turn left and go south 1.5 mi.

Cumberland: Restaurant, grocery store, convenience store, lodging, camping, library, medical service. From Pershing Rd. Trail access go west and south ~9 mi. Also see Trail Access and Parking directions, above. Area information from Cumberland Chamber of Commerce (715-822-3378, cumberland-wisconsin.com).

Shell Lake: Restaurant, grocery store, convenience store, lodging, camping, library, medical service. From Pershing Rd. Trail access go west and north ~8 mi.

Sarona: See Bear Lake Segment, p. 36. From 30th Ave. Trail access go north ~8 mi.

Haugen: See Bear Lake Segment, p. 36. From 30th Ave. Trail access go south and east 7.3 mi. Also see Trail Access and Parking directions, above.

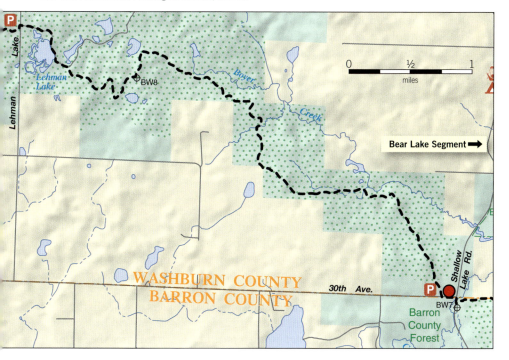

Bear Lake Segment (Atlas Map 8f; Databook page 9)

SNAPSHOT

5.4 miles: 30th Ave. to 16th St. (CTH-VV)

This segment crosses hummocky terrain and highlights several lakes and scenic wetlands.

 From Crooked Lake and other small lakes, intermittent streams/creeks and wetland areas.

 Primitive camping on county forest lands.

 At two nearby private campgrounds (see Area Services).

 Dogs should be leashed (8-ft max) and under control at all times.

 Small portions overlap a bike trail, gravel roads and logging/forest roads.

 Scout camp trail network.

TRAIL ACCESS AND PARKING

30th Ave.: From Haugen at the intersection of CTH-SS and CTH-V, take CTH-V (3rd St.) west 0.5 mi. Curve south on CTH-V (now 18th St.) and go 0.7 mi. Join 27th Ave. where CTH-V curves west and follow it west 1.7 mi. When CTH-V curves south, continue west on 27th Ave. for another 0.3 mi. At 16th St. turn right and go north 4.0 mi joining 13¾ St. and becoming Shallow Lake Rd. At 30th Ave. turn left and go west 0.1 mi to the parking area on the north side of the road.

16th St. (CTH-VV): From Haugen at the intersection of CTH-SS and CTH-V (3rd St.), take CTH-V west 0.2 mi. At Norvin Ave. turn right and go north 0.2 mi. At 5th St. (CTH-VV), which first becomes 28th Ave. and then becomes 16th St., turn left and go west then north 2.7 mi. Roadside parking.

THE HIKE

This segment continues from the Grassy Lake Segment through hummocky topography of the Superior Lobe's St. Croix Moraine, the outer edge of which is about 1.5 miles southeast of the segment's endpoint on 16th Street (CTH-VV).

From its starting point on 30th Avenue the segment heads east on the road for 0.1 miles to an intersection with Barron County's 13¾ - 16th Street (a road whose name changes to Shallow Lake Road a short distance north, at the Barron/Washburn county line). The segment route turns south at the intersection and follows 13¾ - 16th Street (a Rustic Road) for 0.1 miles to a point (**BW7**) where the segment leaves the road and continues east through a mix of forest and marsh on Barron County Forest land. Hikers may catch a glimpse of Bear Lake through the woods in the distance to the east as they cross the hummocky terrain, especially when leaves are off the trees.

As the segment nears the southern shore of Crooked Lake hikers will pass two benches overlooking the lake. The segment then leaves Barron County Forest land and enters the Boy Scouts' L.E. Phillips Scout Reservation. The segment soon crosses a cattail-lined wetland on a 16-foot puncheon and 190-foot boardwalk (**BW6**). This portion of the segment is a haven for northern waterfowl and dragonflies and often features a nightly chorus of frogs.

Heading south from Crooked Lake and Round Lake hikers may see in the trees one of the camp's framed platform tent areas. *Note: Please stay on Trail crossing through the Scout property and do not use their facilities.* From this area the segment

continues east and then northeast, passing the camp's Bass Lake beach before reaching the segment endpoint on 16th Street (CTH-VV).

Mobile Skills Crew project site, 2003

AREA SERVICES

Barronett: See Grassy Lake Segment, p. 34. From the 30th Ave. Trail access go west ~6 mi.

Sarona: Camping. From the 30th Ave. Trail access, take Shallow Lake Rd. north 2.2 mi to White Tail Ridge Campground and RV Park, which has 6 tent sites (N753 Shallow Lake Rd., 715-469-3309, whitetailridgecampground.com).

Haugen: Restaurant, grocery store, camping. From 16th St. (CTH-VV) go east and south 2.9 mi. Camping at Shady Rest Campground (2883 17¾ St., 715-234-7339, ricelakewis.com/listing/shady-rest-campground/).

Rice Lake: See Tuscobia Segment, p. 38. From the 16th St. (CTH-VV) Trail access go east and south ~11 mi.

I'm an adventurer and I wanted to see more of Wisconsin. I was enthralled by every inch of Wisconsin I hadn't seen before. Until you go walk it, you don't know it.

SANDY THORPE, ICE AGE TRAIL THOUSAND-MILER

Tuscobia Segment (Atlas Maps 8f, 9f, 10f; Databook pages 9–10)

SNAPSHOT

11.2 miles: CTH-SS to Featherstone Rd. at Loch Lomond Rd. (28¾ St.)

This segment, featuring glacial erratics, several small kettle lakes, views across an outwash plain and a tunnel channel, follows the multiuse Tuscobia State Trail (TST) and a short portion of the historic Blueberry Line railway.

 At the Brill baseball field and park.

 From several small lakes, the Brill River and other small intermittent streams/creeks.

 At Chain Lake/Twin Lake walk-in campsite.

 At nearby Waldo Carlson County Park, Doolittle Park and private campgrounds (see Area Services).

 At Waldo Carlson County Park.

 At the CTH-SS parking area, the Brill baseball field and park and Waldo Carlson County Park.

 Three ColdCache sites on segment.

 By law, dogs must be leashed while hiking on the TST.

 Portions of the TST are open to biking, horseback riding, ATVs and snowmobiling.

 The western end of the segment intersects the Wild Rivers State Trail. The TST continues east from Balsam Lake Rd. A blue-blazed spur trail leads from the eastern end of the segment to the western edge of Birchwood.

 Portions of this segment may be suitable for those using wheelchairs or similar devices.

TRAIL ACCESS AND PARKING

CTH-SS: From Rice Lake at the intersection of STH-48 and CTH-SS, take CTH-SS north 4.5 mi. A large parking area for the Tuscobia State Trail, with a kiosk and restrooms, is on the right side of the road.

Ice Age Trail Guidebook 2020 – 2022 Edition

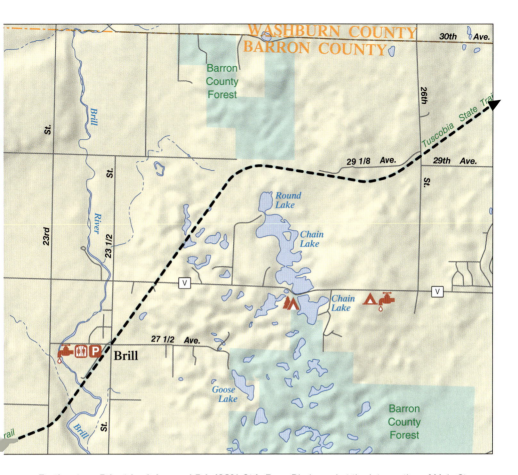

Featherstone Rd. at Loch Lomond Rd. (28¾ St.): From Birchwood at the intersection of Main St. and STH-48, take STH-48 west 1.0 mi. At Loch Lomond Rd. (28¾ St.) turn left and go south 0.1 mi to the intersection with gravel Featherstone Rd. Roadside parking.

Additional Parking: (i) 21st St. parking area. (ii) Town of Brill parking area. (iii) 26th St. Roadside. (iv) Big Fish Wayside parking area in Birchwood. Located on STH-48 at Vance St., 1.0 mi east of Loch Lomond Rd. (28¾ St.).

THE HIKE

This segment follows a portion of the 74-mile Tuscobia State Trail (TST), which in 1966 became the second abandoned rail line in the state to be converted for recreational use. During its rail days the route was called the Omaha Line and at its peak operation, one passenger, one freight and 11 logging trains traveled each way—a total of 26 trains passing a given point every day. When the line was abandoned in 1965 after years of decline in the railroad and logging industries, the corridor land was to be parceled out to farmers. Hulda Hilfiker, a local resident, was instrumental in persuading neighbors and the State of Wisconsin to convert the railroad grade to a recreational trail. The portion of the Ice Age Trail that shares the TST is open to walking, bicycling, horseback riding and snowmobiling in winter. A short section on the bridge crossing the Red Cedar

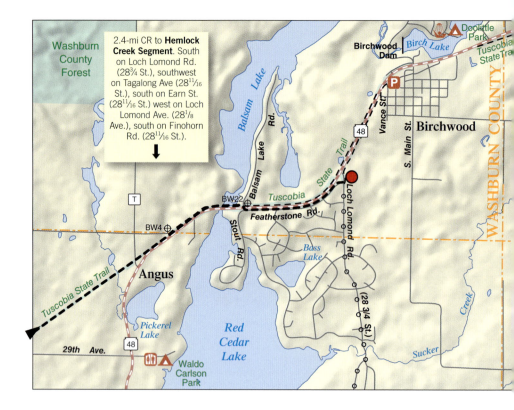

Narrows and the eastern approach to the bridge is open to ATVs.

Between the segment's western terminus on CTH-SS and the town of Brill, the segment links the terminal moraines of the Superior and Chippewa lobes as it crosses their outwash plain. The segment maintains a level grade with one exception: an area about a mile east of CTH-SS where the segment dips into a valley and crosses scenic Tuscobia Creek flowing south into Tuscobia Lake.

Upon reaching Brill, the segment crosses onto the Chippewa Moraine. Between Brill and Angus the segment passes numerous erratics and several small kettle lakes.

Soon after crossing CTH-T the segment enters Washburn County (**BW4**), where ATV use is allowed on the TST; caution is advised. The segment parallels the ATV portion of the TST until joining it at the bridge over "The Narrows" connecting Balsam Lake and Red Cedar Lake, which are part of a tunnel channel of the Chippewa Moraine. A bench overlooks Balsam Lake on the north side of the TST.

The segment departs from the TST at Balsam Lake Road and heads south across STH-48. Hikers should use caution when crossing the highway. From here the segment turns east and follows part of the historic Blueberry Line railway, paralleling Featherstone Road and STH-48.

The Blueberry Line and similar smaller rail lines were important links between communities and the rest of the world at the turn of the 20th century. Everything was brought in or shipped out by rail, and most people traveled by rail. Eventually rail travel gave way to the automobile, and the Blueberry Line ceased passenger service to Birchwood in 1936. Part of the rail bed was refurbished and converted to a foot-travel-only path in 2011.

The segment ends at Featherstone Drive at Loch Lomond Road (28¾ Street). A blue-blazed spur trail continues northeast to the western edge of Birchwood. This spur ends at the "Big Fish Wayside" parking area, where IATA volunteers and workers from local Dobiehill Timber engineered a 14th-century-style timber-framed structure that acts as a depot for hikers arriving at or departing from Birchwood.

Mobile Skills Crew project site, 2011, 2016

POINTS OF INTEREST

Indian Mounds Park: From the western terminus of the Tuscobia Segment, take CTH-SS 4.2 mi southeast to Rice Lake, turn east on North St. and merge onto Lakeshore Dr. (1015 Lakeshore Dr., Rice Lake).

Twelve conical mounds remain of a former 51-mound group, open to public foot traffic. A historical sign 100 yd farther south marks the location of the Bayfield Indian Trail.

AREA SERVICES

Tuscobia State Trail (TST): On Trail. (715-274-5123, dnr.wi.gov/topic/parks/name/tuscobia).

Haugen: See Bear Lake Segment, p. 36. From the CTH-SS Trail access go ~2.5 mi north on CTH-SS.

Rice Lake: Restaurant, grocery store, convenience store, general shopping, lodging, camping, library, medical service. From the CTH-SS Trail access go 4.5 mi south on CTH-SS. Area info from the Rice Lake Area Chamber of Commerce (715-234-2126 or 877-234-2126, ricelakechamber.org).

Brill: On Trail.

Chain Lake/Twin Lake Walk-in Campsite: From the Trail crossing with CTH-V (28th Ave.), go east 1.2 mi on CTH-V. Walk-in campsite (0.1 mi south); first come, first served. No facilities. (parks.co.barron.wi.us/parks/camping/chain_laketwin_lake_primitive).

Mikana: Restaurant, grocery store, lodging, camping. From the crossing at CTH-T go 3.0 mi south on CTH-T/STH-48. Lodging at Mikana Marine & Resort (715-234-3008). Camping at Waldo Carlson Park & Campground (715-354-3353 or 715-537-6295, parks.co.barron.wi.us/parks/camping/waldo_carlson_park/).

Birchwood: Restaurant, grocery store, convenience store, lodging, camping. From Loch Lomond Rd. (28¾ St.) and STH-48 go 1.0 mi northeast on STH-48. INN Style program lodging at Cobblestone B&B (715-354-3494, cobblestonebedandbreakfast.com) and Tagalong Golf Resort & Conference Center (715-354-3458, tagalonggolf.com). Other lodging at the Birchwood Motel (715-354-7706, birchwoodmotelwi.com). Camping at Doolittle Park & Campground (715-354-3300, birchwoodvillagewi.com/doolittle-park/), K & C Country Air Campground (715-354-7301), Birch Lakes RV Park (715-651-2961, birchlakesrvpark.com) and Featherstone RV Campground (715-354-3610, featherstonervpark.com). Area info available from the Birchwood Area Chamber of Commerce (birchwoodwi.com).

One of my favorite moments was in the Northern Blue Hills segment when we crossed the beaver dam. I was overwhelmed with amazement and thought: If it wasn't for our goal of becoming a Thousand-Miler, I would have never done something like this.

DAWN THAYER, ICE AGE TRAIL THOUSAND-MILER

Hemlock Creek Segment (Atlas Map 10f; Databook pages 10–11)

SNAPSHOT

7.0 miles: Finohorn Rd. (28¹¹⁄₁₆ St.) to S. Bucks Lake Rd. at CTH-F

 This scenic segment through rolling county forest highlights the western edge of the Blue Hills and a loop around Hemlock Creek.

At the Murphy Flowage Picnic Area and Murphy Flowage Campground.

From Pigeon and Hemlock creeks and a few small intermittent streams and lakes/wetland areas.

 Primitive camping on county forest lands.

 At Murphy Flowage Campground and at Rusk County Remote Campsite 6 (see Area Services).

 Dogs should be leashed (8-ft max) and under control at all times.

 Small portions overlap a snowshoe trail and logging/forest roads.

 A blue-blazed spur trail and a white-blazed loop south of Hemlock Creek.

TRAIL ACCESS AND PARKING

Finohorn Rd. (28¹¹⁄₁₆ St.): From Birchwood at the intersection of Main St. and STH-48, take STH-48 west 1.0 mi. At Loch Lomond Rd. (28¾ St.) turn left and go south then west 2.5 mi. At Finohorn Rd. (28¹¹⁄₁₆ St.) turn left and go south 0.1 mi to the Trail access. Roadside parking.

S. Bucks Lake Rd. at CTH-F: From Birchwood at the intersection of Main St. and STH-48, take STH-48 east 2.3 mi. At CTH-F turn right and go south 8.5 mi to S. Bucks Lake Rd. Roadside parking on S. Bucks Lake Rd.

Additional Parking: (i) Bolger Rd. (25½ Ave.) parking area, 1.2 mi west of CTH-F. (ii) Murphy Flowage Picnic Area 0.5 mi north of S. Bucks Lake Rd. on the west side of CTH-F. Follow access road around to the picnic area.

THE HIKE

From its starting point on Finohorn Road (28¹¹⁄₁₆ Street) the segment heads south and quickly crosses Pigeon Creek. It continues over flat terrain and in about 0.9 mi intersects a blue-blazed spur trail that leads south to E. Lake Shore Drive. A little farther on, the segment passes an abandoned blue heron rookery (**BW3**), now home to nesting osprey.

South of the rookery the segment reaches a boardwalk; hikers should use caution when passing through this area and will likely come out with wet feet. An alternative is to walk on top of a beaver dam that parallels the segment.

As the segment makes its way to Bolger Road, it ascends into Barron quartzite hills, the first taste of the Blue Hills highlighted on segments farther east in Rusk County. Hikers should watch carefully for signage in this area as the route intersects many grassy logging roads.

Now in Rusk County, south of Bolger Road the segment drops steeply toward Hemlock Creek. Along the way the Trail passes some small, quickly flowing creeks. After paralleling Hemlock Creek for half a mile the segment reaches a junction (**BW2**) with a white-blazed trail that highlights the southern side of the creek.

From the junction with the white-blazed loop, the main segment continues east along the north side of Hemlock Creek with several trailside benches pre-

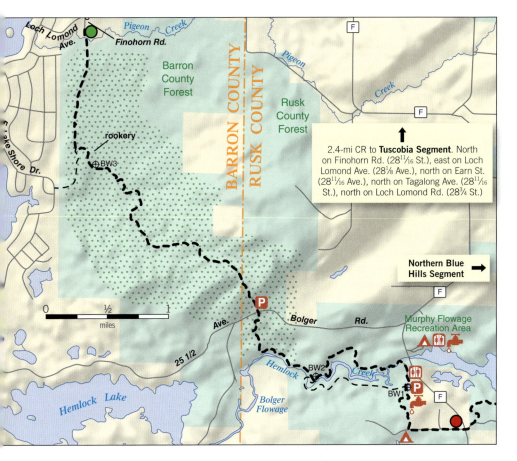

senting scenic views of the wetland below. The segment crosses the creek on an abandoned road bridge and enters the Murphy Flowage Picnic Area.

The segment continues south through a forested area, then reaches a primitive road and turns left. In 0.1 miles the Trail intersects another forest road that heads southwest 0.1 miles to the Rusk County Remote Campsite 6. The segment continues to follow the main primitive road east to its terminus on CTH-F.

Mobile Skills Crew project site, 2007, 2008, 2013, 2014, 2016

AREA SERVICES

Birchwood: See Tuscobia Segment, p. 38. From the Finohorn Rd. ($28^{11}/_{16}$ St.) Trail access go north then east 3.6 mi. Also see Trail Access and Parking directions, above.

Murphy Flowage Recreation Area: Camping. On Trail. Picnic area is on the west side of CTH-F on the Trail route. The campground is on the east side of CTH-F, 1.0 mi north of S. Bucks Lake Rd. Rusk County Forestry Deptartment (715-532-2113, RuskCounty.org/department/ forestry /camping-information).

Rusk County Remote Campsite 6: Camping. From S. Bucks Lake Rd. at CTH-F Trail access go west 0.4 mi on primitive road (recommend 4WD). At "Y" junction, go southwest 0.1 mi on another primitive dirt road to campsite. For more information contact Rusk County Forestry Department (715-532-2113, RuskCounty.org/department/forestry/camping-information). A very remote site established for hunter use. No facilities.

Barron & Washburn Counties

Rusk County

Atlas Maps 10f–14f; Databook pages 7, 12–13
Total miles: 33.7 (Trail 16.9; Connecting Route 16.8)

Two distinct landscapes dominate the Ice Age Trail route through Rusk County. In the northern half of the county are the Blue Hills, once a mountain range of quartzite bedrock older than the Appalachian Mountains and most of the Rocky Mountains. The 1.6-billion-year-old quartzite peaks wore down over time. The Chippewa Lobe, flowing south and southwest, came to a halt as it reached the Blue Hills. It left a legacy of scattered lakes that offer an enticing habitat for an abundance of wildlife. Seen in the county forest have been whitetail deer, wolf, black bear and on rare occasion moose, who travel from as far away as Michigan's Upper Peninsula. The southern half of Rusk County is a land of lakes, which extends into Chippewa County.

On Rusk County Forest land, primitive camping is permitted at least 200 feet from trails and waterways.

CHAPTER INFORMATION

The Blue Hills Chapter formed in 1992 after the Rusk County Chapter, formed in 1975, reorganized. Most of the Ice Age Trail through this area was designed and built in the late 1970s and early 1980s by Adam Cahow, a professor at the University of Wisconsin-Eau Claire. The chapter members continue his pioneer trailblazing with ongoing Trail maintenance projects and construction of new Trail routes.

COUNTY INFORMATION

Rusk County Tourism (and Visitor Center): 800-535-7875, ruskcountywi.com

Rusk County Forestry and Parks Information: 715-532-2113, ruskcounty.org

Small ponds are plentiful; a rustic boardwalk offers dry passage along the Northern Blue Hills Segment.

Rusk County

Northern Blue Hills Segment (Atlas Map 11f; Databook page 12)

SNAPSHOT

9.6 miles: S. Bucks Lake Rd. at CTH-F to CTH-F Southern Trail Access

 This remote and rugged segment crossing through the Blue Hills features a number of scenic stream crossings and several beautiful wetland areas.

At the nearby Murphy Flowage Picnic Area and Murphy Flowage Campground.

From Devils Creek and other small streams/creeks and lakes/wetland areas.

 Primitive camping on county forest lands.

 At Murphy Flowage Campground, Audie Flowage-Perch Lake Recreation Area and Rusk County Remote Campsite 6 (see Area Services).

 Dogs should be leashed (8-ft max) and under control at all times.

 Portions overlap logging/forest roads and gravel S. Bucks Lake Rd.

 A blue-blazed spur trail to Stout Rd. parking area.

TRAIL ACCESS AND PARKING

S. Bucks Lake Rd. at CTH-F: From Birchwood at the intersection of Main St. and STH-48, take STH-48 east 2.3 mi. At CTH-F turn right and go south 8.5 mi. Roadside parking on S. Bucks Lake Rd.

CTH-F Southern Trail Access: From Weyerhaeuser on USH-8 take CTH-F north then west 6.6 mi. Roadside parking.

Additional Parking: (i) Murphy Flowage Picnic Area 0.5 mi north of S. Bucks Lake Rd. on the west side of CTH-F. Follow access road around to the picnic area. (ii) Bucks Lake Rd. where the Trail goes off-road (**RU8**). Roadside parking. (iii) Stout Rd. Trail access parking area (**RU6**) 2.2 mi north of CTH-F. From the parking area, follow the blue-blazed trail 0.3 mi to the Ice Age Trail.

THE HIKE

The segment starts at the intersection of South Bucks Lake Road and CTH-F. Hikers should head east on South Bucks Lake Road 0.1 mile where the segment leaves the road and heads north into woods. The segment courses through the woods over rolling terrain on rocky tread and makes its way to another intersection with South Bucks Lake Road. Shortly before reaching the road, hikers can catch glimpses of the Murphy Flowage through the trees from a boardwalk.

Reaching South Bucks Lake Road, the segment turns left and follows the road for 0.1 mile then goes off-road (**RU8**) to the south. The segment traverses low-relief hummocky terrain through a mixed hardwood forest mostly on logging/forest roads passing several small ponds. Hikers should pay close attention to Trail signage at intersecting logging/forest roads. This area shows evidence of extensive beaver activity and the Trail skirts close to and offers views of large beaver lodges. Shortly before reaching the blue-blazed spur trail to the Stout Road parking area, the segment crosses over a large active beaver dam. The tread across the dam is uneven and slippery, so hikers should use caution when crossing the dam.

Reaching the wide, grassy road/spur trail to the Stout Road parking area, the segment continues southward through rolling, hummocky glacial topography in a mix of hardwood forest. During periods of heavy rain, portions of the Trail may become

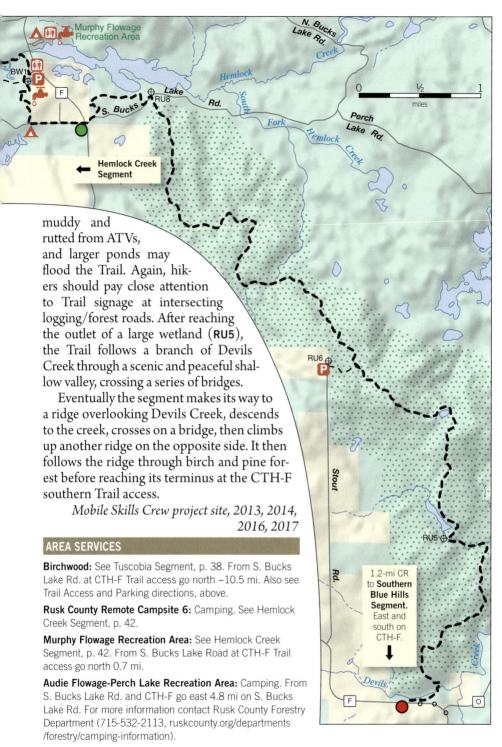

muddy and rutted from ATVs, and larger ponds may flood the Trail. Again, hikers should pay close attention to Trail signage at intersecting logging/forest roads. After reaching the outlet of a large wetland (**RU5**), the Trail follows a branch of Devils Creek through a scenic and peaceful shallow valley, crossing a series of bridges.

Eventually the segment makes its way to a ridge overlooking Devils Creek, descends to the creek, crosses on a bridge, then climbs up another ridge on the opposite side. It then follows the ridge through birch and pine forest before reaching its terminus at the CTH-F southern Trail access.

Mobile Skills Crew project site, 2013, 2014, 2016, 2017

AREA SERVICES

Birchwood: See Tuscobia Segment, p. 38. From S. Bucks Lake Rd. at CTH-F Trail access go north ~10.5 mi. Also see Trail Access and Parking directions, above.

Rusk County Remote Campsite 6: Camping. See Hemlock Creek Segment, p. 42.

Murphy Flowage Recreation Area: See Hemlock Creek Segment, p. 42. From S. Bucks Lake Road at CTH-F Trail access go north 0.7 mi.

Audie Flowage-Perch Lake Recreation Area: Camping. From S. Bucks Lake Rd. and CTH-F go east 4.8 mi on S. Bucks Lake Rd. For more information contact Rusk County Forestry Department (715-532-2113, ruskcounty.org/departments/forestry/camping-information).

Weyerhaeuser: See Southern Blue Hills Segment, p. 48. From CTH-F southern Trail access go east and south 6.6 mi. Also see Trail Access and Parking directions, above.

Rusk County

Southern Blue Hills Segment (Atlas Map 12f; Databook page 12)

SNAPSHOT

7.3 miles: Yuker Rd. at CTH-F to Old 14 Rd. (Bass Lake Rd)

  This remote and rugged segment continues through the Blue Hills, traversing ridges, kettles and ravines.

- From North Lake, Moose Ear Creek and other small intermittent streams/creeks and wetlands.
- Primitive camping on county forest land and at a walk-in campsite on the south shore of North Lake.
- The portion of the segment south of the Rusk County Forest boundary to Old 14 Rd. (Bass Lake Rd.) is closed during gun deer season.
- Dogs should be leashed (8-ft max) and under control at all times.
- Portions overlap logging/forest roads and dirt access road.

TRAIL ACCESS AND WALK-IN

Yuker Rd. at CTH-F: From Weyerhaeuser on USH-8 take CTH-F north 5.4 mi to Yuker Rd., an unsigned primitive road heading west. Roadside parking on Yuker Rd.

Old 14 Rd. (Bass Lake Rd.): From Weyerhaeuser on USH-8, take CTH-F (2nd St.) north 0.1 mi. At the first street north of the railroad tracks, unsigned Railway Ave., turn left and go west 1.0 mi. Railway Ave. becomes Old 14 Rd. (Bass Lake Rd). Angle left across the railroad tracks and continue west 1.9 mi to the Trail access. Roadside parking along the north side of the road.

THE HIKE

This segment starts at the intersection of CTH-F and Yuker Road, an unsigned primitive road used by fishermen and hunters for access to Rusk County Forest land. Hikers should head west on Yuker Road for 0.7 miles to a point (**RU9**) where the Trail leaves Yuker Road and heads south on a logging/forest road. Shortly, the segment splits off to the right on a narrow tread. Within the first few miles, the Trail twice crosses scenic Moose Ear Creek on primitive wooden and log bridges (second crossing: **RU4**). As the route makes its way to North Lake it follows or parallels forested ridges with views of trailside kettles and down glacial-formed ravines on a mix of two-track footpath and logging roads. Low-lying areas can be very wet and muddy, especially during rainy periods. Hilly, forested terrain characterizes this portion of the segment, most of which is on Rusk County Forest land. During growing season dense vegetation hugs the Trail; pay close attention to Trail signage.

The segment eventually emerges into a clearing and soon after intersects and briefly follows a dirt access road to the east. The segment curves around to the west and south of North Lake, a local fishing hole, then reaches the south shore of the lake and a walk-in campsite (**RU2**). The south shore offers scenic views of the lake and is a perfect place to view the many birds, including loons, who use the lake.

South of North Lake, the Trail soon comes to a gate and fence stile and enters private land. The segment crosses the outlet/small stream (**RU1**) from a small, unnamed lake then weaves in and out of woods, skirts daisy pastures and crosses the small stream two more times on a combination of forest roads, farm roads and narrower tread. Eventually the Trail climbs a ridge overlooking a lake through the forest, crosses another fence stile and comes to a gravel farm road (**RU13**) with excellent views of agricultural fields through an opening in the trees.

From here on its way to its terminus on Old 14 Road (Bass Lake Road), the segment includes a trek through a forested, more hummocky area, the crossing of a set of railroad tracks, the skirting of another wetland/lake and a pine, oak and birch forest with an undergrowth of ferns.

Mobile Skills Crew project site, 2013, 2014, 2016, 2017

AREA SERVICES

Audie Flowage-Perch Lake Recreation Area: See Northern Blue Hills Segment, p. 46. From Yuker Rd. at CTH-F go north and east ~9 mi.

Murphy Flowage Recreation Area: See Hemlock Creek Segment, p. 42. From Yuker Rd. at CTH-F go north ~10.5 mi.

Birchwood: See Tuscobia Segment, p. 38. From Yuker Rd. at CTH-F Trail access go north ~20 mi.

Weyerhaeuser: Restaurant, grocery store, convenience store, lodging. From Old 14 Rd. (Bass Lake Rd) Trail access go east 3.0 mi. Lodging at Country View Motel (715-353-2780).

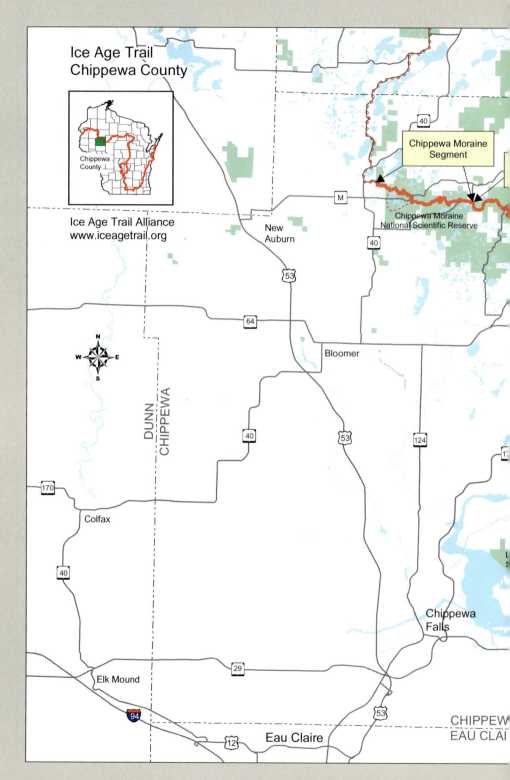

Chippewa County

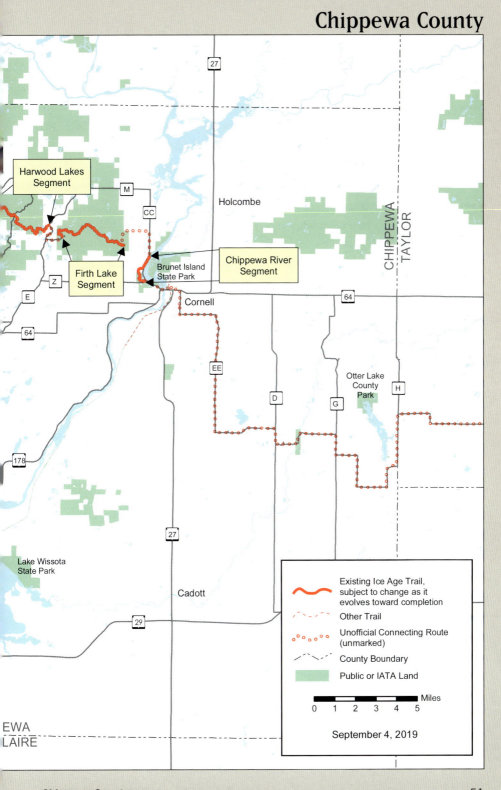

Chippewa County

Atlas Maps 14f–19f; Databook pages 14–18
Total miles: 58.3 (Trail 20.8; Connecting Route 37.5)

The Chippewa Lobe formed Chippewa County's prominent glacial features, including the Chippewa Moraine. The terminal moraine stands above the surrounding cultivated plains, with lakes and ponds set in a forested jumble of hills. Unlike the higher hills of the interlobate Kettle Moraine in southeastern Wisconsin, the features of the Chippewa Moraine are characterized by gentler hills of "dead ice" moraine. As the ice ceased to move, fissures crisscrossed the glacier. Surface debris, transported by sliding ice and flowing meltwater, filled many cracks and formed a variety of sharp ridges after the ice melted. When debris-covered blocks of ice melted, kettles formed, producing the area's knob-and-swale or hummocky landscape. Ice-walled lake plains, flatter-topped areas formed by glacial lakebeds, are abundant in this area.

The Chippewa Moraine National Scientific Reserve's David R. Obey Ice Age Interpretive Center is perched high atop an ice-walled lake plain and offers views of the lake-dotted countryside. It has a 4.5-mile Circle Trail with interpretive signs and shorter nature trails that explore the area. Inside, modern in-depth displays and hands-on exhibits describe the Wisconsin Glaciation and its legacy in the area. Both the reserve and nearby Brunet Island State Park are waypoints on the Great Wisconsin Birding and Nature Trail.

Primitive camping is permitted on Chippewa County Forest land. Please camp at least 200 feet from waterways and trails. There are also two developed walk-in campsites on the Chippewa Moraine National Scientific Reserve property; some portions of the reserve are open to primitive camping but others are not. A walk-in campsite and a Dispersed Camping Area (DCA) are found in the Harwood Lakes Segment. Refer to the maps for details on camping locations and county forest boundaries.

CHAPTER INFORMATION

The Chippewa Moraine Chapter officially formed in 1988 and sponsors hikes, work outings and presentations on glacial geology. The chapter maintains a close relationship with the Chippewa Moraine National Scientific Reserve's David R. Obey Ice Age Interpretive Center, where many events take place, such as the chapter's annual Parade of Colors hike in autumn. In addition to its chapter pages at **iceagetrail.org**, the chapter maintains its own external website, **iatchippewa.org**. The site features a wealth of information, including news items, detailed parking information, an archive of the chapter's *Trail Dispatch* newsletters and information for member volunteers and hikers. There is also information about the trail-related merchandise that the chapter offers for sale at the interpretive center. The chapter periodically broadcasts announcements on trail conditions and events via email and Twitter (**twitter.com/iatachippewa**).

COUNTY INFORMATION

Chippewa County Tourism: 866-723-0331, chippewacounty.com

Chippewa County Facilities and Parks Division: 715-726-7882

Chippewa County Land Conservation and Forest Management Division: 715-726-7920

A tuft of blue flag iris brightens a pond along the Firth Lake Segment.

Chippewa Moraine Segment

(Atlas Map 15f; Databook pages 15–16)

SNAPSHOT

7.6 miles: 267th Ave. (Oak Ln.) to 167th St. (Plummer Lake Rd.)

This very scenic segment passes near more than 20 kettle lakes and highlights several significant ice-walled lake plains, including the one the Obey Ice Age Interpretive Center is built on.

 At the Obey Interpretive Center.

 From numerous lakes.

 Primitive camping on portions of the Chippewa Moraine Reserve. Two walk-in campsites near the Interpretive Center.

 A small private campground and a county park campground are located north of the western endpoint (see Area Services).

 Restrooms are available at the Obey Interpretive Center and at the two walk-in campsites (privy) just off the Trail. Please respect those who have reserved the sites.

 Two ColdCache sites on segment.

 Dogs should be leashed (8-ft max) and under control at all times.

 Small portion overlaps 260th Ave. (Rattlesnake Hill Rd.).

 Chippewa Moraine National Scientific Reserve trail network. Spur trails (**CH25**, **CH26**) to walk-in campsites.

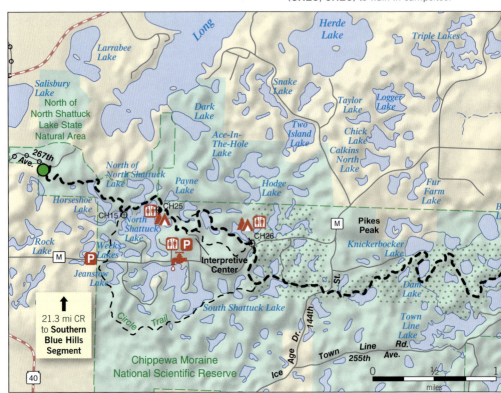

TRAIL ACCESS AND PARKING

267th Ave. (Oak Ln.): From USH-53 take the CTH-M/New Auburn exit (Exit 118). Take CTH-M east for 7.0 mi. At STH-40 turn left and go north 0.7 mi. At 267th Ave. (Oak Ln.) turn right and go east 0.7 mi to the Trail access on the south side of the road. Roadside parking just west of the Trail access. No overnight parking.

167th St. (Plummer Lake Rd.): From USH-53 take the CTH-M/New Auburn exit (Exit 118). Go east 12.6 mi on CTH-M. At 167th St. (Plummer Lake Rd.) turn right and go south 1.0 mi to the parking area on the west side of the road near the boat landing area. No overnight parking. The segment begins 0.2 mi north on Plummer Lake Rd. just south of the intersection with 260th Ave. (Rattlesnake Hill Rd.).

Additional Parking: (i) Circle Hiking Trail parking area on CTH-M near western boundary of Chippewa Moraine National Scientific Reserve. (No parking at CTH-M Trail access farther east.) (ii) Chippewa Moraine National Scientific Reserve's David R. Obey Ice Age Interpretive Center off CTH-M. (iii) 260th Ave. (Rattlesnake Hill Rd.) parking area 0.2 mi west of where the Trail heads off on the north side of the road. Parking area in the corner of a field. Overnight parking permitted.

THE HIKE

This segment traverses dramatic high-relief hummocky terrain with numerous scenic kettle lakes. The first portion of the segment travels through the North of North Shattuck Lake State Natural Area, a southern dry mesic forest. This area is heavily used by birds during spring migration, including red-headed woodpeckers, hairy woodpeckers, scarlet tanagers, American redstarts, yellow-throated vireos and eastern wood-pewees.

From its starting point on 267th Avenue (Oak Lane) the segment heads east and soon reaches the northern tip of the first of two lakes named "Horseshoe" that hikers will pass while hiking the segment. On the way toward the southeastern corner of the lake the segment climbs a hill; during leaf-off seasons hikers can see five bays from this point. Coming down from the hill the segment soon intersects the western junction (**CH15**) of the Chippewa Moraine Reserve's Circle Trail. To stay on the Ice Age Trail, hikers should turn left at this junction and continue east. This is the first junction with the reserve's other trails; signage is excellent throughout the trail network making it easy for hikers to navigate.

After the segment passes between North Shattuck Lake and the aptly named North of North Shattuck Lake, the route bends south and soon intersects (**CH25**) a spur trail that leads 750 feet to a walk-in campsite. This is one of two walk-in campsites on the reserve, each with a privy and fire ring. Hikers wanting to spend a night at either site should first check in at the interpretive center; there is a small fee.

A short distance south of the campsite spur the segment intersects the reserve's Dry Lake Trail and Mammoth Nature Trail, which branch off the Ice Age Trail route to the east. From this junction the Ice Age Trail continues southeast toward the interpretive center.

Harwood Lakes Segment

From the interpretive center, the segment heads north and wraps around the northern tip of a small lake, then continues southeast toward CTH-M. A short distance before the CTH-M crossing the segment intersects (**CH26**) a 300-foot spur trail leading north to the reserve's second walk-in campsite.

East of CTH-M the segment reaches the eastern junction with the Circle Trail and passes another scenic cluster of lakes before crossing 144th Street (Ice Age Drive). As the segment makes its way east, it crosses an earthen bridge on the south end of Dam Lake, skirts the north shore of the segment's second Horseshoe Lake and crosses 160th Street (Town Line Road).

The Trail shortly arrives at a bench overlooking Dumke Lake (**CH12**). The view here can give a hiker a visual appreciation of how ice-walled lake plains formed.

During the Wisconsin Glaciation period, small lakes filled depressions in the ice surface and became walled off by enormous ice blocks. Lakes often formed on debris-covered parts of the glacier, and over time, fine sediment accumulated on the lake's floor. When the ice surrounding the lake melted, the sediment that accumulated in the lake remained. This formed a high, flat-topped area on the landscape. Often dish-shaped, these plateau-like areas have rich soil for farming. The coarse material deposited near the ice block wall and glacial lake's shoreline forms a higher rim-like ridge around the lake plain. After the glacial lake drained, parts of the ice wall continued to melt and water flowed across the now dry lakebed, carving a channel that the segment crosses just east of the bench. The channel actually flowed away from Dumke Lake, demonstrating that the ice wall continued to melt long after the original glacial lake was dry. The ice block disappeared last, leaving Dumke Lake well below.

From Dumke Lake the segment continues east across the ice-walled lake plain, intersects and briefly follows 260th Avenue (Rattlesnake Hill Road) and passes one final lake (Plummer) before reaching the segment's terminus at 167th Street (Plummer Lake Road).

Mobile Skills Crew project site, 2004

POINTS OF INTEREST

Chippewa Moraine National Scientific Reserve and the David R. Obey Ice Age Interpretive Center: On Trail. (13394 CTH-M, New Auburn, 715-967-2800, dnr.wi.gov/topic/parks/name/chipmoraine/naturecenter.html).

The Ice Age Interpretive Center has many hands-on and interactive activities, including activity books, short films and various displays about geologic, cultural and natural history. The Center is generally open year-round Tuesday to Sunday from 8:30 am to 4:00 pm (closed Monday) and has maps, restrooms, drinking water and helpful staff. Three loop trails start here and share parts of the Ice Age Trail: Circle Trail (4.5 mi), Dry Lake Trail (1.8 mi) and Mammoth Nature Trail (0.7 mi). These trails feature numerous interpretive signs described in *Hiking Field Trip Guide for Glacial Landforms*, available at the Center..

AREA SERVICES

Bloomer: Restaurant, grocery store, convenience store, lodging, library, medical services. From the 267th Ave. (Oak Ln.) Trail access, go west on 267th Ave. (Oak Ln.) 0.7 mi. At STH-40, turn left and go south 11.3 mi. Lodging at Bloomer Inn and Suites (715-568-3234, bloomerinn.com).

Chippewa Moraine National Scientific Reserve and the David R. Obey Ice Age Interpretive Center: On Trail. (13394 CTH-M, New Auburn, 715-967-2800, dnr.wi.gov/topic/parks/name/chipmoraine

/naturecenter.html). Camping at the two walk-in campsites. Campers using the campsites need to register at the Interpretive Center before heading out.

New Auburn: Restaurant, convenience store, camping. Convenience store at the intersection of STH-40 and CTH-M, 2.0 mi west of the Obey Interpretive Center. Camping at Salisbury Campground (715-967-2782) and Morris Erickson County Park (715-726-7882, reservations.co.chippewa.wi.us/parks/camping/). Village of New Auburn, 6 mi west on CTH-M, has a restaurant and convenience store.

Cornell: See Firth Lake Segment and Chippewa River Segment, p. 60. From the Obey Interpretive Center on CTH-M go east ~19 mi.

> *Living in the UK and growing up in Germany, meeting animals like porcupines and bears just isn't something that happens as you're strolling through the woods. So certainly, it was an experience and memory to treasure for a lifetime.*
>
> JILL RAGER (AKA "GRITSCONSIN"), ICE AGE TRAIL THOUSAND-MILER

Harwood Lakes Segment (Atlas Maps 15f, 16f; Databook page 16)

SNAPSHOT

6.1 miles: 167th St. (Plummer Lake Rd.) to CTH-E

4 3 *This beautiful segment features large beaver dams, a massive glacial erratic and several scenic pristine lakes and wetland areas.*

 From numerous lakes, streams/creeks and wetland areas.

 A walk-in campsite between the two Harwood Lakes, a Dispersed Camping Area near the west shore of Picnic Lake and primitive camping on county forest lands.

 One ColdCache site on segment.

 A portion of the segment crossing private land between the eastern boundary of the Chippewa County Forest and CTH-E is closed during gun deer season.

 Dogs should be leashed (8-ft max) and under control at all times.

Portions overlap Plummer Lake Rd., the Nawakwa equestrian trail, and logging and forest roads.

Spur trail to walk-in campsite at Harwood Lakes, blue-blazed loop trail (**CH22**) to the DCA and Girl Scout Camp Nawakwa trail network.

TRAIL ACCESS AND PARKING

167th St. (Plummer Lake Rd.): From USH-53 take the CTH-M/New Auburn exit (Exit 118). Take CTH-M east for 12.6 mi. At 167th St. (Plummer Lake Rd.) turn right and go south 1.0 mi to the parking area on the west side of the road near the boat landing area. No overnight parking. The segment begins 0.2 mi north on Plummer Lake Rd. just south of the intersection with 260th Ave. (Rattlesnake Hill Rd.).

CTH-E: From Cornell take STH-64 west across the Chippewa River. At CTH-CC turn right and go north 1.0 mi. At CTH-Z turn left and go west 5.0 mi. At CTH-E turn right and go north 3.0 mi. Roadside parking.

Additional Parking: Deer Fly Trail. From CTH-M and Deer Fly Trail (gravel road), go south 2.6 mi on Deer Fly Trail to the parking area on west side of road.

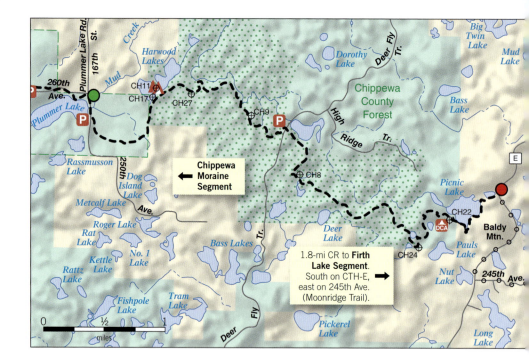

THE HIKE

From the segment's starting point on 167th Street (Plummer Lake Road) just south of the road's intersection with 260th Avenue (Rattlesnake Hill Road) hikers should head south along the road for 0.2 miles across a narrow causeway between Plummer Lake and a wetland. Across from the Trail access parking area the segment then departs from the road and heads east through the easternmost portion of the Chippewa Moraine Reserve property, which is relatively flat compared with the dramatic high-relief hummocky topography of the remainder of the segment. The wide path enters a second-growth forest with a high canopy and diverse understory of ferns and woodland plants. *Note: Camping is not permitted on Reserve property from Plummer Lake Road to the campsite (*CH11*) between the two Harwood Lakes.*

The segment leaves the Reserve and enters Chippewa County Forest lands just before arriving at a bench (CH17) that provides lovely views of the Harwood Lakes. About 200 feet east of the bench, a spur trail leads north steeply downhill to a small but picturesque walk-in campsite (CH11) (no privy) on the narrows between the two Harwood Lakes.

East of the Harwood Lakes in rolling topography, the segment crosses Mud Brook on a serpentine boardwalk/bridge (CH27) built by Mobile Skills Crew volunteers. The boardwalk and bridge includes a bench where hikers can relax and look out at Mud Brook Valley. The Trail briefly follows along the edge of the wetland and soon climbs steeply to the top of a well-defined hummocky ridge then drops down to follow alongside a swamp. Along the north side of the Trail, hikers may detect ruts from when loggers cut trenches in the ground and filled them with water to create iced tracks to run their logging sleds on.

The segment crosses a boardwalk/bridge (**CH9**) over a low wet area and passes a bench offering a quiet respite as it sits near the boardwalk surrounded by several old white pine trees.

The Trail climbs up out of the swamp and crosses a distinctive county ATV trail. It then crosses a bridge over a small stream, outlines the edge of another swamp/wetland area with toppled trees exposing their roots and soon arrives at Deer Fly Trail (a gravel road).

East of Deer Fly Trail, the segment passes a massive glacial erratic just 40 feet off trail and shortly crosses a footbridge at the base of a beaver dam. The dam creates a flowage to the south with several heron nests. The segment then continues to another bridge (**CH8**) spanning a small gulch. The bridge is named "Kim's Crossing" in memory of Kim Heidtke. Kim's family funded the bridge project to commemorate her love of the Ice Age Trail. This spot was home to an earthen beaver dam until backed up water overtook the dam and carved the gulch in its place. A wetland pond remains as habitat for waterfowl and other wetland creatures.

Moving along, the Trail quickly intersects and briefly overlaps an equestrian trail and soon skirts along the edge of a logged area. Leaving the logged area, the Trail meanders through the woods and soon comes to a Leopold bench (**CH24**) with a panoramic view of a tamarack bog. The Trail drops to a small intermittent stream with a rock crossing and immediately rises again, affording views of a small, isolated pond. Shortly after, the segment intersects (**CH22**) the western end of a marked loop trail that leads to a Dispersed Camping Area (DCA) for long-distance, multiday hikers. The site has a fire pit and log benches and is located on Girl Scout Camp Nawakwa property.

Continuing on the Trail, the segment passes the eastern end of the loop trail that leads to the DCA and quickly reaches a bridge on private property spanning an intermittent stream draining into Picnic Lake. Crossing the bridge, the Trail is back on Girl Scout property as it wraps around the eastern edge of Picnic Lake with many views of the pristine lake. In times of high water, portions of the Trail along Picnic Lake can become wet and flooded, requiring hikers to take brief detours. Just before reaching its terminus on CTH-E, the Trail skirts above a scenic hemlock-rimmed pond.

Mobile Skills Crew project site, 2013, 2014, 2018

AREA SERVICES

New Auburn: See Chippewa Moraine Segment, p. 54. From the 167th St. (Plummer Lake Rd.) Trail access go north and west ~13 mi. Also see Trail Access and Parking directions, above.

Cornell: See Firth Lake Segment and Chippewa River Segment, p. 60. From the CTH-E Trail access go south and east 9.0 mi. Also see Trail Access and Parking directions, above.

Firth Lake Segment and Chippewa River Segment (Atlas Map 16f; Databook pages 16–17)

SNAPSHOT

Firth Lake Segment—8.4 miles (5.2 IAT, 3.2 CR): 245th Ave. (Moonridge Trail) to CTH-CC
Chippewa River Segment—1.9 miles (1.8 IAT, 0.1 CR): CTH-CC to CTH-Z

 The **Firth Lake Segment**, an interesting and scenic hike, crosses an ice-walled lake plain and beaver dams in a generally forested setting and highlights beautiful Firth Lake.

- From Firth Lake and a few intermittent streams/creeks.
- Primitive camping on county forest lands.
- Two ColdCache sites on segment.
- Dogs should be leashed (8-ft max) and under control at all times.

 Portions overlap logging/forest roads and a blue-blazed connector trail.

 A short blue-blazed spur trail to a parking area next to Firth Lake and a blue-blazed spur trail to 250th Ave. connecting route.

 The short **Chippewa River Segment** highlights Perch Lake and features dramatic views of the Chippewa River.

- From the Chippewa River and Perch Lake.
- At nearby Brunet Island State Park (see Area Services).
- At nearby Millyard Park, Brunet Island State Park and the Cornell Visitor Center. Picnic area and playground also available at Brunet Falls Park.
- Dogs should be leashed (8-ft max) and under control at all times.
- Small portion overlaps CTH-CC.

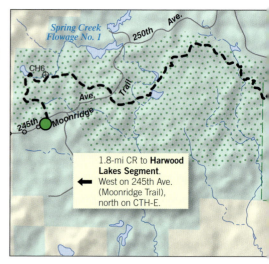

1.8-mi CR to **Harwood Lakes Segment**. West on 245th Ave. (Moonridge Trail), north on CTH-E.

TRAIL ACCESS AND PARKING

245th Ave. (Moonridge Trail): From Cornell take STH-64 west across the Chippewa River. At CTH-CC turn right and go north 0.9 mi. At CTH-Z turn left and go west 5.0 mi. At CTH-E turn right and go north 2.0 mi. At 245th Ave. turn right and go 0.9 mi. Roadside parking. *Note: Use caution as this is a narrow, curvy road.*

CTH-Z: From Cornell take STH-64 west across the Chippewa River. At CTH-CC turn right and go north 0.9 mi. At CTH-Z turn left and go west 0.1 mi to the Trail access on the north side of the road. Roadside parking on the south side of CTH-Z.

Additional Parking: (i) 250th Ave. parking area and boat launch, located south down a gravel drive. Best accessed from the east (CTH-CC). From the parking area, walk around a gate and follow the access trail 0.2 mi to the Ice Age Trail. (ii) CTH-CC parking area on east side of road, 1.2 mi north of CTH-Z intersection. (iii) Perch Lake parking area on the west side of CTH-CC, 0.3 mi north of CTH-Z intersection. *Note: No direct access to the IAT.*

THE HIKE

The **Firth Lake Segment** traverses a second-growth northern mesic forest of birch, red maple, ash and balsam, with an understory of fern, clintonia, blue bead lily, bloodroot, Indian pipe and red baneberry. There are board bridges throughout this segment as it can be very wet in spring due to beaver activity in the many lakes and ponds.

From its starting point on 245th Avenue (Moonridge Trail) to Firth Lake, the segment traverses rolling high-relief hummocky topography. Heading north and then east, the segment reaches a bridge (**CH6**) near a small stream; just beyond the bridge hikers can look north to a view of trailing arbutus on the north slope of the moraine.

After crossing 245th Avenue (Moonridge Trail), the segment quickly intersects and follows logging roads for 0.4 miles. The Trail then turns sharply left on single-track tread and passes a scenic pond with a bench where hikers can relax. The Trail soon climbs a rise overlooking a beaver dam and flowage.

Continuing, the segment meanders through hardwood forest and areas of aspen, briefly overlapping old forest roads. The Trail rock-hops across a small stream, climbs out of the ravine and travels alongside the babbling stream. The segment quickly comes to a bench (**CH29**) overlooking the stream where hikers can rest and enjoy the sounds of the stream and the forest.

Continuing on, the seg-

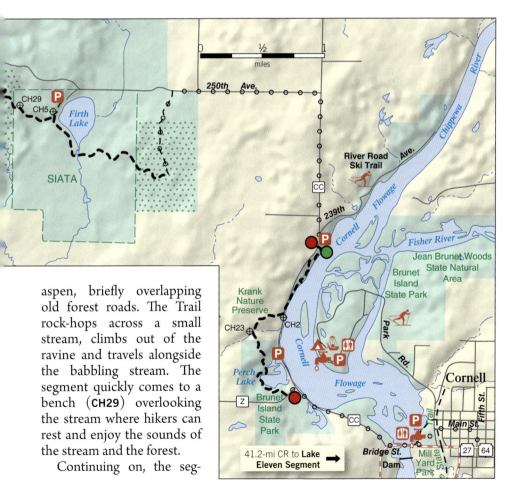

Chippewa County

ment makes its way toward Firth Lake, crossing an ATV trail (follow the ATV trail 50 feet to the right) and passes through a grooved-top ridge, a glacial feature characterized by two parallel ridges separated by a trench-like linear depression. Shortly, the segment intersects (**CH5**) a blue-blazed spur trail heading north to the 250th Avenue parking area and boat launch. From the spur trail junction, the segment turns sharply to the south and climbs a hill with a bench overlooking Firth Lake.

Leaving behind the high-relief hummocky topography, the segment skirts the southwest side of Firth Lake, a shallow kettle lake situated in an outwash plain. Located within the Firth Lake State Ice Age Trail Area, the 52-acre lake is surrounded by a northern sedge meadow and is home to water lilies, cattails, swamp milkweed, beaver lodges and loons.

The segment crosses a 500-foot boardwalk, over an old beaver dam that hikers should traverse cautiously and continues east into low-relief hummocky topography, crossing two bridges over small streams along the way. After reentering the Chippewa County Forest, the Trail turns left on a blue-blazed connector trail that leads north to 250th Avenue. The hike joins the connector trail north for 0.7 miles transitioning from a single-track trail to a forest road on its way to 250th Avenue. The segment continues as a connecting roadwalk east on 250th Avenue for 1.2 miles. At CTH-CC turn right and go south 1.2 miles to the large CTH-CC Ice Age Trail parking area on the east side of the road.

Mobile Skills Crew project site, 2017

The **Chippewa River Segment** starts out from the large CTH-CC parking area and heads south through a forest featuring stunning Chippewa River views from the edge of rolling bluffs, with braided, steep topography and vertical gains up to 70 feet. Several deep ravines transect the segment west to east and water drains seasonally to the river. The forest cover includes various species of ash, oak and maple, with an undergrowth of several varieties of seasonal woodland flowers.

After passing through the thin strip of land between the road and river, the segment reemerges onto CTH-CC, where hikers will follow the road south for 350 feet.

The segment resumes an off-road course (**CH2**) by heading west from CTH-CC into the Krank Nature Preserve. The Trail climbs a hill, shortly turns to the south and makes its way to a deep ravine and the crossing (**CH23**) of a picturesque stream. The segment continues to head south through the woods, crosses a power line right-of-way and soon reaches Perch Lake. It bends around the western shore of Perch Lake, then steers southeast away from the lake to the segment's endpoint on CTH-Z.

Mobile Skills Crew project site, 2006, 2014

AREA SERVICES

Cornell: Restaurant, grocery store, convenience store, lodging, camping, library, medical service. From the CTH-Z Trail access, go east 0.2 mi. At CTH-CC turn right and go south 1.0 mi. At STH-64 turn left and go east 0.6 mi. Most services are on Bridge St. (STH-64/27) or 1 block north on Main St. Camping at Brunet Island State Park (715-239-6888, dnr.wi.gov/topic/parks/name/brunetisland; reservations: 888-947-2757, wisconsin.goingtocamp.com).

A serpentine boardwalk/bridge along the Harwood Lakes Segment.

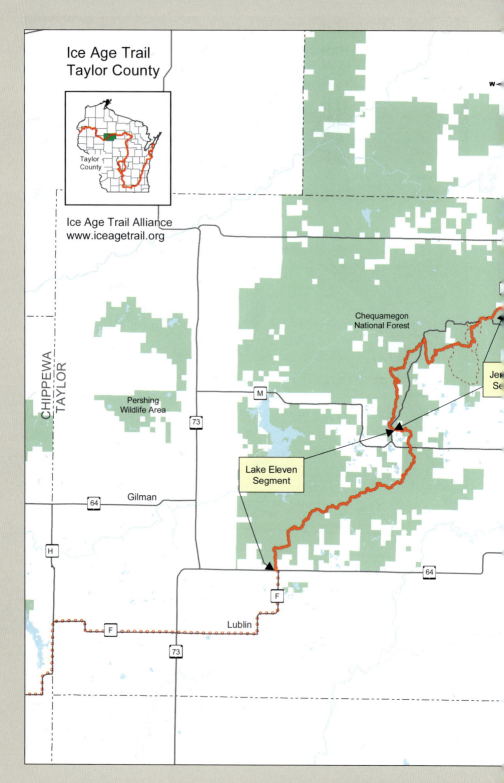

Taylor County

Taylor County

Atlas maps 19f–26f; Databook pages 19–24
Total miles: 87.2 (Trail 65.8; Connecting Route 21.3)

The Chippewa Lobe had the greatest influence on the present-day topography of Taylor County, sculpting all but the eastern edge of the county (shaped by the Wisconsin Valley Lobe, as seen in the Wood Lake moraine) and the southern part of the county (shaped by earlier glaciations). Glaciers left behind a hilly terrain with kettle lakes, erratics, ice-walled lake plains and eskers. Most of Taylor County lies within the end moraine zone near the recent glacier's southernmost extent.

The Menominee, Ho-Chunk, Chippewa and Sioux nations, French trappers, early missionaries and loggers once inhabited the area. Area forests thrive with hemlock, sugar maple, yellow birch and red and white pine trees. The Ice Age Trail goes through the Chequamegon National Forest and highlights the Mondeaux Dam Recreation Area, with the historic Mondeaux Lodge and Dam. The national forest is more than 850,000 acres and is rich in geologic and human history. Approximately 2,100 known archeological sites, containing more than half of the archeological sites recorded in northern Wisconsin's 15 counties, are present in the forest. Sites range from 10,000-year old prehistoric native American campsites to 20th-century homesteads. The North Country National Scenic Trail also passes through the Chequamegon National Forest about 100 miles north of the Ice Age Trail.

Primitive camping is allowed on Taylor County Forest lands and in the national forest. Please camp at least 200 feet from trails and waterways. The Rib Lake Segment includes a Dispersed Camping Area (DCA).

CHAPTER INFORMATION

The High Point Chapter was officially organized in 1986. The chapter is working with Taylor County officials, Wisconsin Department of Natural Resources and the National Park Service to identify the Ice Age Trail corridor for western Taylor County. The proposed corridor will line up with eastern Chippewa County's proposed corridor.

COUNTY INFORMATION

Taylor County Tourism Office & Medford Area Chamber of Commerce:
715-748-4729, taylorcountytourism.com

Chequamegon National Forest Medford—Park Falls District Ranger:
715-748-4875, fs.usda.gov/cnnf

Taylor County Forestry & Recreation Department: 715-748-1486, co.taylor.wi.us

A young hiker points the way forward on the Jerry Lake Segment.

Lake Eleven Segment (Atlas Maps 20f, 21f, 22f; Databook page 20)

SNAPSHOT

15.6 miles: STH-64 to Sailor Creek Rd. (FR-571)

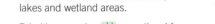 *This varied segment in the Chequamegon National Forest, with a distinct Northwoods feel, highlights the clear, deep kettle Lake Eleven and many other glacial features associated with the Perkinstown End Moraine.*

 From South Fork of the Yellow River, Lake Eleven, Beaver Creek and other small intermittent streams/creeks, lakes and wetland areas.

 Primitive camping on national forest lands. Several walk-in campsites are located at Lake Eleven.

At Chippewa Campground ~9 mi west of CTH-M Trail access (see Area Services).

 Two ColdCache sites on segment.

 Dogs should be leashed (8-ft max) and under control at all times.

 Small portions overlap horseback and snowmobile trails and logging/forest roads.

 Short side trails lead to campsites around Lake Eleven.

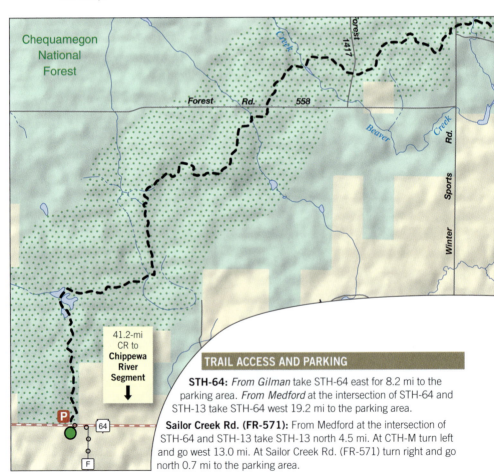

TRAIL ACCESS AND PARKING

STH-64: *From Gilman* take STH-64 east for 8.2 mi to the parking area. *From Medford* at the intersection of STH-64 and STH-13 take STH-64 west 19.2 mi to the parking area.

Sailor Creek Rd. (FR-571): From Medford at the intersection of STH-64 and STH-13 take STH-13 north 4.5 mi. At CTH-M turn left and go west 13.0 mi. At Sailor Creek Rd. (FR-571) turn right and go north 0.7 mi to the parking area.

THE HIKE

From its starting point on STH-64 the segment heads north and east and after 2.8 miles skirts around a beaver dam; hikers should watch for signage and avoid crossing the actual dam. A significant portion of the forest between STH-64 and FR-558, covering approximately the first 3.5 miles of the segment, was flattened by a tornado in 2002. The area's once towering hardwoods and pines have been replaced with underbrush, rapidly growing raspberry bushes and poplars. Due to lack of trees in some places, yellow-blazed Carsonite posts mark the Trail route. The area is beginning to return to its original state but caution is still recommended. This challenging portion of the segment can potentially be difficult to navigate and footing is rough in areas. Hikers should move slowly and pay close attention to signage. *Note: Throughout the segment, depending on the season, creek crossings*

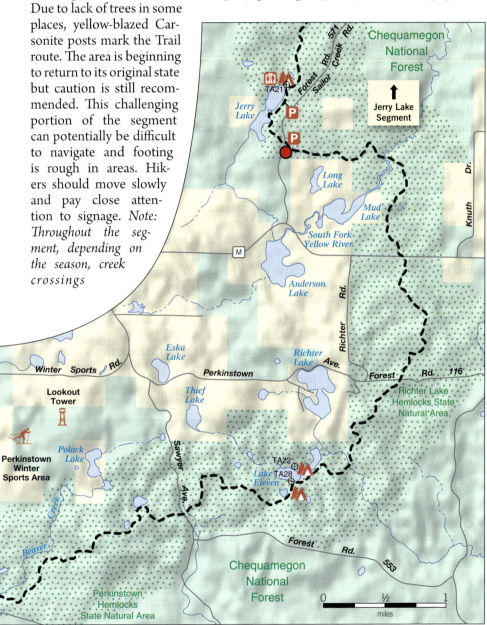

Taylor County

Meadow Road (FR-572) the Trail passes through an area of wetlands over several boardwalks and then crosses the South Fork of the Yellow River on an impressive 67-foot-long bridge built by volunteers. From the bridge, the segment bends northwest and runs alongside the river arriving at a walk-in campsite (**TA20**) situated on a ridge overlooking the river.

As the segment makes its way north from the river it soon makes the first of two crossings of FR-576. The first crossing is near the westernmost end of the road and is clearly designated as the "West" crossing. The second crossing is about 0.7 mi to the east and is clearly designated as the "East" crossing.

After the eastern crossing of FR-576 the segment continues northeast to Sailor Creek. Hikers will find a walk-in campsite (**TA26**) on the west side of the segment and north side of the creek about 150 feet northeast from the creek crossing. The campsite is marked by a large blue-gray boulder and is situated in a grove of hemlocks. It features a stone fire ring and nice flat area with space for several tents.

After the northern crossing of Sailor Creek Road (FR-571) the segment enters the Lost Lake

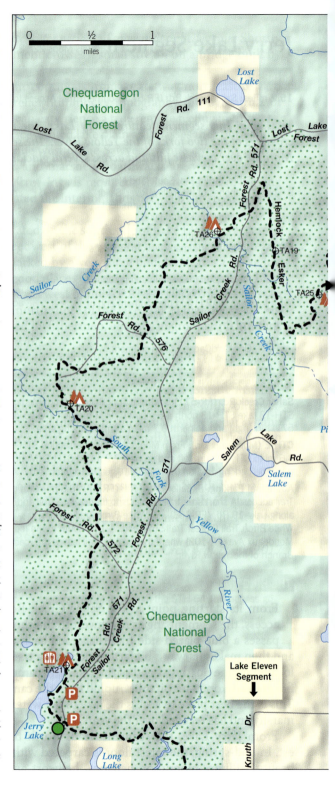

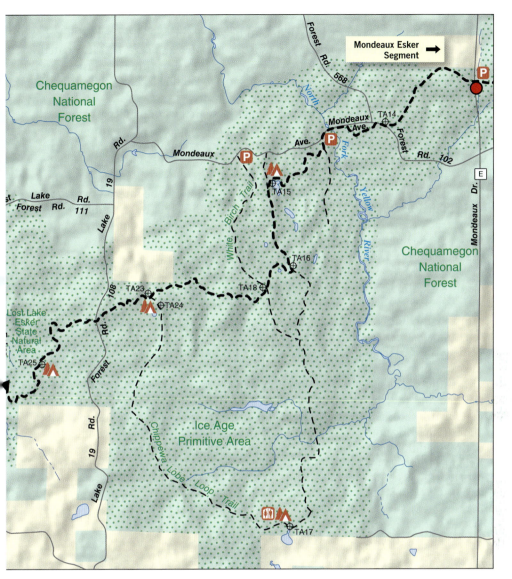

Esker State Natural Area, established in 2007 to protect the complex forest and wetland communities associated with the esker and the glacial till surrounding it. The Trail soon makes a sharp bend to the south and traverses the Hemlock Esker (**TA19**) for almost a mile, rising 80 feet above the forest floor. After descending from the Hemlock Esker the segment bends northeast and winds through hemlock-hardwood forest over hummocky terrain. After about 0.5 miles, it crosses an unnamed creek on a short boardwalk. A walk-in campsite (**TA25**) is located immediately atop the rise after the creek crossing, tucked under a hemlock canopy. The area is flat with space for several tents.

After crossing Lake 19 Road (FR-108) the segment follows the edge of a large bog before reaching the western intersection (**TA23**) of the Chippewa Lobe Interpretive Loop (see detailed description below) clearly marked by a wooden sign;

the Loop trail is marked by blue diamond blazes. From this intersection hikers can head south 0.1 miles on the Loop trail to a walk-in campsite (**TA24**). Situated on high, dry ground, the campsite has benches and a stone fire ring. Just across the Trail from the campsite, a log path leads to a small bog lake which is not visible from the Trail.

The segment continues east from the junction with the Loop trail past marshes, bogs and wetland areas. Portions of the trail along here may be swampy during wet weather. After about a mile the segment reaches a junction (**TA18**) with the White Birch Trail (Forest Trail 567). A walk north on White Birch Trail will take hikers to a parking area on Mondeaux Avenue (FR-102). A walk southeast on the White Birch Trail offers another access to the Chippewa Lobe Interpretive Loop.

Less than half a mile east of its junction with the White Birch Trail, the segment reaches the eastern junction (**TA16**) with the Chippewa Lobe Interpretive Loop. The segment turns left at the junction and heads due north. After 0.7 miles the segment reaches a junction with Forest Trail 350, which leads directly north to Mondeaux Avenue (FR 102). The segment turns right at this junction and heads east, almost immediately reaching a walk-in campsite (**TA15**) located on the west shore of a small unnamed lake which is not visible from the Trail. The campsite includes space for several tents around a stone fire ring. After passing the campsite, the segment winds downhill and skirts the lake for several hundred yards. Access to the water is easier here than from the steep, shrubby slope below the campsite.

Less than a mile east of the walk-in campsite, the segment intersects a forest trail and turns north to reach Mondeaux Avenue (FR-102). It joins the road to the east for 100 yards and crosses the North Fork of the Yellow River. A bench on the pedestrian bridge offers a spot to rest, listen to the water and view wildlife. East of the river, the segment soon dips back into the forest, then crosses Mondeaux Avenue (FR-102) (**TA14**) and meanders northeast to the segment's endpoint on CTH-E. This last section, through birch forest with an undergrowth of ferns, is mostly flat and tends to get swampy after heavy rain and during the spring thaw.

Mobile Skills Crew project site, 2003, 2012, 2014, 2015, 2016

SIDE TRAIL—CHIPPEWA LOBE INTERPRETIVE LOOP

6.1 miles: Includes 4.6 miles of Loop trail plus 1.5 miles of Ice Age Trail to close the loop

Access by foot only: (i) From the west, hike the Ice Age Trail 0.5 mi east from Lake 19 Rd. (FR-108) to a kiosk at the start of the Loop (**TA23**). (ii) From the north, hike the White Birch Trail (Forest Trail 567) south 1.1 mi, cross the Ice Age Trail (**TA18**) and continue south another 0.5 mi to its intersection with the Chippewa Lobe Interpretive Loop. This is less scenic than the Ice Age Trail access. (iii) From the east, hike the Ice Age Trail 1.6 mi west of where the Ice Age Trail leaves FR-102 after crossing the North Fork of the Yellow River. A steel sign marks the trail junction (**TA16**).

The Chippewa Lobe Interpretive Loop, also called the "Blue Diamond Trail" due to its blazes, is a rugged route that circles a remote roadless area called the Ice Age Primitive Area. Six posts mark the miles oriented counterclockwise, starting from the Ice Age Trail's western access to it at the kiosk. During wet weather, the loop may not be passable, as the Yellow River tributaries flow west to east through the entire section, with little structure at critical wet crossings. A walk-in campsite (**TA24**) is located on the loop 0.1 mi south of its western intersection with the Ice Age Trail. A second secluded walk-in campsite (**TA17**) is located at the southern end of the loop, 2.7 mi south of the Ice Age Trail's western intersection and 1.9 mi south of the Ice Age Trail's eastern intersection. Situated with pleasant views of the pond and beaver dam, this exceptional site has a log bench, fire pit and small cast iron table made from an old fire grate. A pit toilet is hidden a few yards to the southeast.

AREA SERVICES

Gilman: See Lake Eleven Segment, p. 68. From the Sailor Creek Rd. (FR-571) Trail access go west ~18 mi.

Mondeaux Dam Recreation Area: See Mondeaux Esker Segment, p. 76. From the CTH-E Trail access go north and east ~4 mi.

Medford: See Pine Line Segment and East Lake Segment, p. 80. From the CTH-E Trail access go east and south ~22 mi. Also see Trail Access and Parking directions, above.

Sunset solitude along the Jerry Lake Segment.

of the Mondeaux Flowage and turns north, paralleling the west side of the flowage. The segment climbs atop and follows the crest of the obvious Mondeaux Esker (**TA13**).

As the segment continues north toward the Spearhead Point campground hikers may want to consider jumping off the Ice Age Trail for two interesting side trips. A year-round glacial spring with cold, clear water can be found by following Park Road west a short distance from its intersection with Campers Road. The Leopold Nature Trail heads northwest from Park Road less than half a mile north of the Park Road and Campers Road intersection.

Back on the Trail, hikers should pay close attention to signage at the somewhat confusing crossing of the campground road near Spearhead Point. Toward the northern end of the flowage the segment passes the facilities of the Mondeaux Dam Recreation Area (MDRA). In addition to several developed campgrounds around the Mondeaux Flowage, the MDRA has picnic shelters, a swimming beach, boat rentals and a fishing pier. The segment passes a historic lodge built by the Civilian Conservation Corps.

The next portion of the segment, from the Mondeaux Dam to the Shady Drive and Fawn Avenue intersection, can be exceptionally challenging even for experienced hikers. All who pass through here should be prepared for a tough trek. There are plenty of slippery roots, rocks and wet sections. The Trail follows troads in some sections and parallels wetland areas and crosses unnamed creeks with no bridges or on beaver dams. Some areas may require a wet ford due to beaver activity or seasonally changing water levels. Signage can be sparse, undergrowth can be thick and cell phones may not work.

The segment crosses the Mondeaux Dam into the Lakeview Picnic Area (restrooms available) before heading south between the Eastwood Campground and the flowage. As the segment continues south along the east side of the flowage it passes through areas of new young forest where undergrowth can make the Trail very difficult to follow; pay close attention to signage.

The segment turns east, crosses Mondeaux Drive (FR-104) and continues east into more damp/wet forest. After about 0.3 miles the Trail takes a sharp right turn (**TA45**) and heads up a hill to an island of mature maples that tower overhead with a clear understory. Upon descending the backside of the hill, the Trail drops into an extended wet section. The segment soon crosses a wetland on an old beaver dam (**TA46**); the tread can be uneven and appropriate caution should be taken when crossing. Overgrown vegetation can cover yellow blazes and make the Trail difficult to follow in places. The segment continues to make its way east through wetlands and forests to its terminus at the Shady Drive and Fawn Avenue intersection.

Mobile Skills Crew project site, 2005

AREA SERVICES

Medford: See Pine Line Segment and East Lake Segment, p. 80. From the CTH-E Trail access go south and east ~18 mi. Also see Trail Access and Parking directions, above.

Chequamegon National Forest Medford—Park Falls District: Information (715-748-4875, www.fs.usda.gov/cnnf).

Mondeaux Dam Recreation Area (MDRA): Lodging, camping. On Trail. Cabin rental (seasonal) at Mondeaux Dam Lodge (W7969 Park Rd., Westboro, fs.usda.gov/detail/cnnf/recreation/?cid=fseprd529776). *Note: Lodge is closed for renovations but expected to reopen sometime in 2020. Seasonal concession stand is open.* Camping at Chequamegon National Forest Campgrounds: Eastwood, Spearhead Point, Picnic Point (group), West Point (first come, first served) and nearby North Twin Lake (877-444-6777, recreation.gov).

Westboro: See Pine Line Segment and East Lake Segment, p. 80. From the MDRA go east ~8.5 mi. Also see Trail Access and Parking directions, above.

A view down the Mondeaux Esker on the Mondeaux Esker Segment.

Pine Line Segment and East Lake Segment (Atlas Maps 24f, 25f; Databook pages 22–23)

SNAPSHOT

Pine Line Segment—0.9 miles: Fisher Creek Rd. at Fawn Ave. to STH-13

0.6-mile Connecting Route

East Lake Segment—6.4 miles: STH-13 Wayside to CTH-D

 *The very short **Pine Line Segment** retains a remote, deep-woods feeling.*

At Chelsea Lake County Park.

A walk-in campsite.

Segment is closed during gun deer season.

Dogs should be leashed (8-ft max) and under control at all times.

Crosses Pine-Line multiuse rail-trail at western end of segment.

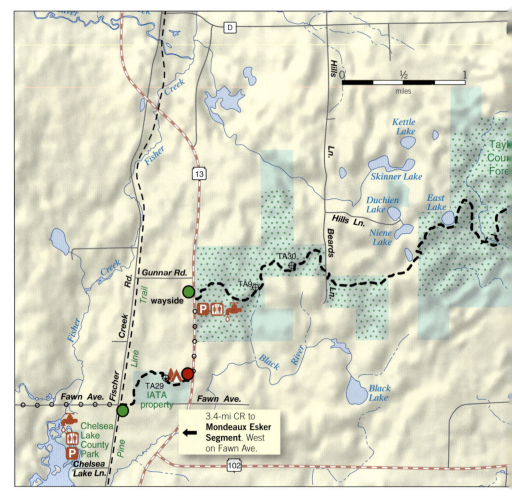

▲4 🐾 *The remote, hilly and scenic* **East Lake Segment** *highlights the headwaters of the Black River, historic logging sites and Moose Mountain and features signs along the route identifying points of interest.*

 At the STH-13 wayside.

 From East Lake and a few other small lakes and intermittent streams/creeks.

 Primitive camping ⋯ on county forest lands.

 Portion of the segment crossing private land east of Beards Ln. is closed during gun deer season.

 Dogs should be leashed (8-ft max) and under control at all times.

 Portions overlap cross-country ski/bike trails and with logging/forest roads.

 Rib Lake Nordic Ski Trails network.

TRAIL ACCESS AND PARKING

Fischer Creek Rd. at Fawn Ave.: From Medford, at the intersection of STH-64 and STH-13 take STH-13 north 13.0 mi. At Gunnar Rd. turn left and go west 0.5 mi. At Fischer Creek Rd. turn left and go south 1.0 mi. The Ice Age Trail is on the east side of the road at the Fawn Ave. intersection. No parking. Instead, park at nearby Chelsea Lake County Park (see Area Services, below).

CTH-D: From Rib Lake at the intersection of STH-102 and CTH-D, take CTH-D north for 2.0 mi to the Rib Lake School Forest/Ice Age Trail parking area on the right side of the road. From the parking area the Trail access is 300 ft west along CTH-D.

Additional Parking: STH-13 wayside.

THE HIKE

From its starting point at the Fischer Creek Road and Fawn Avenue intersection, the 0.9-mile **Pine Line Segment** crosses the Pine Line multiuse trail and then makes its way east along the edge of a farm field. The segment turns north and soon enters a wooded property owned by the Ice Age Trail Alliance. A small walk-in campsite (**TA29**), built by local Boy Scouts, is located in a wooded clearing west of the segment's endpoint on STH-13.

Upon reaching STH-13, hikers should head north on the shoulder of the highway for 0.6 miles to a wayside on the east side of the road. The wayside has water and restrooms available from late May to mid-September.

From the STH-13 wayside the **East Lake Segment** heads east through hilly terrain and mixed hardwood forest. Look for signs noting points of interest or identifying trees, including a faded sign at the beginning of the segment detailing the Wisconsin Conservation Corps' help in building the Ice Age Trail in Taylor County. The segment soon reaches the headwaters of the Black River (**TA9**) in a scenic hemlock grove. Farther on, the Trail enters (**TA30**) a Taylor County aspen regeneration project area. The segment follows a swath cut through the trees and crosses Beards Lane.

From here the segment continues northeast through a mix of Taylor County Forest and private lands, soon passing the shore of East Lake, a classic kettle lake, in a landscape of dramatic high-relief hummocky topography. After passing East Lake, the segment soon skirts a wetland area and crosses a bridge over an unnamed creek. From here the segment heads in a northeast direction through forested but slightly less hilly terrain and eventually climbs Moose Mountain (**TA31**). Here, hikers may glimpse a view of the surrounding area through the trees, especially when leaves are off. Hikers will notice erratics of various sizes, shapes and colors scattered across Moose Mountain and in some of the surrounding areas. The Trail descends and near its endpoint on CTH-D connects and overlaps the Rib Lake Nordic Ski Trail network.

Mobile Skills Crew project site, 2002

AREA SERVICES

Chelsea Lake County Park: From the Fawn Ave. and Fischer Creek Rd. intersection go south on Fisher Creek Rd. 0.5 mi. At the park's gravel road, turn right and go west 0.3 mi to the county park.

Westboro: Restaurant, library. At the STH-13 wayside go north 2.5 mi on STH-13. Library has limited hours.

Ogema: Restaurant, lodging. At the STH-13 wayside go north 9.0 mi on STH-13. Lodging at Ogema House Hotel (715-767-5620, ogemahousehotel.com).

Medford: Restaurant, grocery store, convenience store, general shopping, lodging, camping, library, medical service. At the STH-13 wayside go south 12.6 mi on STH-13. For area info, contact the Medford Area Chamber of Commerce (715-748-4729).

Rib Lake: See Rib Lake Segment, p. 84. From the CTH-D Trail access go south 2.0 mi.

A highlight was seeing mama bear and baby crossing a newly-mown hay field on the Pine Lake Segment. My companion and I were safely out of view so we could watch them unobserved. Baby bear was enthralled with the hay rolls and entertained himself by climbing up one side and sliding down the other. Mama lumbered on along beside him. Eventually, they entered the woods far from where we were headed. That was the day I lost my irrational fear of bears.

JANET WOOD, ICE AGE TRAIL THOUSAND-MILER

An early season snowfall doesn't deter intrepid backpackers on the Lake Eleven Segment.

Taylor County

Rib Lake Segment (Atlas Map 25f; Databook page 23)

SNAPSHOT

5.5 miles (2.7 IAT, 2.8 CR): CTH-D to STH-102

This segment's lengthy roadwalk is balanced by the wooded, off-road section highlighting a steep-sided esker and several picturesque streams and lakes.

 At Rusch Preserve (**TA5**).

 From Copper Creek, Sheep Ranch Creek and several lakes along the connecting route.

 Primitive camping in areas in the IATA's Marimor Preserve. Three walk-in campsites and Heilige Nacht Dispersed Camping Area in the Rusch Preserve.

 At nearby private campground 4.0 mi south of the Trail (see Area Services).

 At South Harper Lake public beach (no facilities) on the west end of the lake.

 Portion of the segment crossing private land between CTH-C and STH-102 is closed during gun deer season.

 Dogs should be leashed (8-ft max) and under control at all times.

 A significant portion is connecting route roadwalk. Off-road sections overlap a short portion of the Timm's Hill National Trail, cross-country ski trails and logging/forest roads.

The connecting route portion passes an access point for the Timm's Hill National Trail where it heads north from Rustic Road 1; off-road portion intersects (**TA41**) a blue-blazed spur trail to a DCA and ski trails of the Rib Lake Nordic Ski Trails system.

 Portions of this segment in the Rusch Preserve may be suitable for those using wheelchairs or similar devices.

TRAIL ACCESS AND PARKING

CTH-D: From Rib Lake at the intersection of STH-102 and CTH-D, take CTH-D north for 2.0 mi to the Rib Lake School Forest/Ice Age Trail parking area on the right side of the road. From the parking area the Trail access is 300 feet west along CTH-D.

STH-102: From Rib Lake at the intersection of STH-102 and CTH-D, take STH-102 east then north 5.5 mi to the parking area on the west side of the road.

Additional Parking: CTH-C Rib Lake Nordic Ski Trails accessible parking area in front of the Nordic Ski Trails kiosk. A second parking area is located at the large Rusch Preserve parking area slightly north of the kiosk area.

THE HIKE

The segment begins by following Rib Lake ski and snowmobile trails and cuts through the Rib Lake School Forest. From CTH-D, the segment follows a route parallel to the highway, ducks into the woods, then bears right and passes a flowing stream. The Trail climbs atop a steep-sided esker (**TA47**) then sharply descends the esker and follows and crosses Sheep Ranch Creek on a bridge. The segment winds its way through the forest to Harper Drive to begin a 2.8-mile connecting route road walk.

The segment heads north on Harper Drive for 1 mile. At Rustic Road 1 it heads east 1.8 miles past a swimming beach on South Harper Lake and an access point where the Timm's Hill National Trail (**timmshilltrail.com**) heads north to Timm's Hill (Wisconsin's highest point at 1951.5 feet). It continues to the point (**TA43**) where the Ice Age Trail and Timm's Hill National Trail both head off-road to the south into the Rusch Preserve.

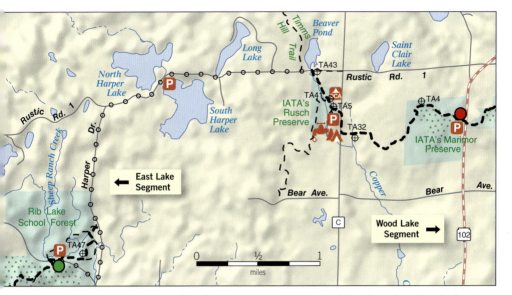

Departing Rustic Road 1, the segment passes a Trail kiosk with a detailed map of the 50-acre Rusch Preserve, historical information and a Trail register. The Trail continues through wooded, low-relief terrain and soon comes to a junction (**TA41**) with a spur trail that leads to the Heilige Nacht Dispersed Camping Area (DCA) for long-distance, multiday hikers. The site has two benches, a small "table" and a fire ring. The segment continues to the Rusch Preserve parking area, jogs right then left and quickly reaches CTH-C. Hikers may wish to explore other parts of the IATA-owned Rusch Preserve, which features three additional campsites (Stille Nacht campsites) with a well-water handpump (**TA5**). While visiting, hikers should watch carefully for private property markers and must stay within the preserve's boundaries. Upon reaching CTH-C hikers should turn right and head south to where the segment departs the road and continues east toward STH-102.

Between CTH-C and its endpoint on STH-102, the segment passes over private lands featuring areas of open fields and mature hardwoods. The segment briefly cuts through an area of pine trees and a field before entering the woods and crossing St. Claire Creek on a curving boardwalk (**TA32**). The segment climbs a hill and continues through alternating areas of woods and fields, intersects several logging roads on its way to its terminus at STH-102. Two of these open areas were once part of gravel pits, but little evidence of gravel pit activity remains today. In the second gravel pit area, however, hikers will pass a small cinder block cairn (**TA4**), which stands in contrast with the more natural surroundings.

Mobile Skills Crew project site, 2008, 2011, 2015, 2016

AREA SERVICES

Rib Lake: Restaurant, grocery store, convenience store, lodging, camping, library, medical service. From the CTH-D Trail access go 2.0 mi south on CTH-D. Lodging at Gasthaus B&B (715-427-5058) and Toad Hollow (715-427-5676; airbnb.com/rooms/12104978). Camping at Lakeview Park (715-427-5404). For area info, contact Village of Rib Lake (715-427-5404, riblakewisconsin.com).

Medford: See Pine Line Segment and East Lake Segment, p. 80. From CTH-D Trail access go south ~18 mi.

Wood Lake Segment (Atlas Maps 25f, 26f; Databook pages 23–24)

SNAPSHOT

13.4 miles: STH-102 to Tower Rd.

 This wild, remote segment highlights scenic Gus Johnson Creek, Wood Lake, wetlands and historic logging camp sites.

At Wood Lake County Park.

 From Gus Johnson Creek (**TA1**), Wood Lake and other small streams/creeks, small lakes and wetland areas.

 Primitive camping on county forest lands and on portions of the IATA's Marimor Preserve.

 A portion of the segment crossing private land east of STH-102 is closed during gun deer season.

 Dogs should be leashed (8-ft max) and under control at all times.

 Portions overlap logging/forest roads.

 A white-blazed loop north of Wood Lake.

TRAIL ACCESS AND PARKING

STH-102: From Rib Lake at the intersection of STH-102 and CTH-D, take STH-102 east then north 5.5 mi to the parking area on the west side of the road.

Tower Rd.: *From Rib Lake* at the intersection of STH-102 and CTH-D, take STH-102 east for 2.0 mi. At CTH-C turn right and go south 7.0 mi. At CTH-M turn left and go east 8.0 mi. At Tower Rd. turn left and go north 9.0 mi to the parking area on the west side of the road. *From Merrill* at the intersection of I-39/USH-51 and STH-64, take STH-64 west for 3.0 mi to the junction with STH-107. Continue west on STH-64/107 6.6 mi. At CTH-M continue west for 10.9 mi. At Tower Rd. turn right and go north 9.0 mi to the parking area on the west side of the road.

Additional Parking: (i) Second Bear Ave. Trail access (**TA33**) parking area. (ii) Wood Lake County Park (see Area Services, below). (iii) North Loop Rd. Trail access parking area.

THE HIKE

This segment is in a very remote area that provides welcoming habitat for deer, black bear, wolf, grouse and coyote. Wetlands and lakes are home to eagles, sandhill cranes, loons and beaver. The area has recovered

from extensive logging since the early 1900s, when logging camps (remains of which are found along the segment) dotted the forest landscape and were symbolic of the Northwoods way of life during the early part of the past century. Wayfinding can present a challenge in some areas and hikers can expect to cross unbridged creeks and seasonally flooded wetlands that occasionally swamp portions of the segment.

From its starting point on STH-102, the segment enters the IATA's Marimor Preserve and heads through an area that embraces the western end moraines left by the Wisconsin Valley lobe. The segment climbs one end moraine, drops to cross an intermittent stream at Six Stone Crossing, then courses along the outer side of another end moraine.

The segment continues east through a mix of Taylor County Forest land and the IATA's Moraine Preserve and private lands, and crosses Bear Avenue for the first time ("western crossing"). South of Bear Avenue, the segment follows an old railroad right-of-way constructed in 1902, which ran between Rib Lake and Tomahawk. The Trail soon reaches the site of Rib Lake Lumber Company Logging Camp 7; a sign and historic photo mark the spot. Camp 7 operated 1912–13 and the outline of its buildings can be seen in the clearing on top of the hill southwest of the sign. One hundred twenty-five lumberjacks worked at Camp 7 for two years cutting hemlock and other hardwood trees.

Departing the Camp 7 site, the segment leaves the old railroad grade and winds through the forest on its way to the second ("central") crossing of Bear

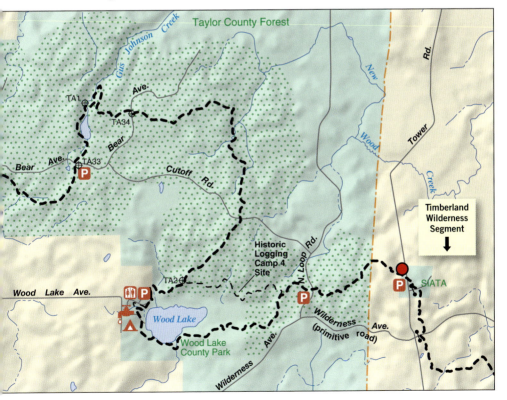

Avenue (**TA33**). From here the segment traverses the scenic and steep-sided valley of Gus Johnson Creek, set between two ice-walled-lake plains and formed by water gushing from under the ice at the outer edge of the Wood Lake Moraine. The segment has an especially intimate wilderness character to it, especially in the area where it crosses (**TA1**) Gus Johnson Creek. East of the creek near the third crossing of Bear Avenue (**TA34**), hikers may notice how the forest dramatically changes from hemlock, birch and maple to maple, oak and poplar.

The segment turns south, crosses Cutoff Road, travels through an area of spectacular high-relief hummocky topography and then reaches the western junction (**TA2**) with a 3.5-mile loop trail circling Wood Lake. The 67-acre lake is spring-fed with clear, blue waters. The Ice Age Trail uses the western and southern portions of the loop trail, a total of 2.5 miles, passing through Wood Lake County Park's swimming, picnic and camping areas, where water and restrooms are available seasonally. The white-blazed northern portion of the loop, known as Camp 4 Trail, highlights the historic Logging Camp 4 site, which was in operation from 1906 to 1910. As a joint 2019–20 project, the Taylor County Forestry Department, Rib Lake Historical Society, Ice Age Trail Alliance and local High Point Ice Age Trail Chapter are erecting twenty signs identifying historic and geological sites on the Wood Lake loop trail. They will have maps and photos focusing on the early logging history of the area.

From the eastern junction with the Wood Lake loop trail the segment crosses North Loop Road and continues eastward through high-relief hummocky topography toward the segment's endpoint on Tower Road, crossing from Taylor County into Lincoln County along the way.

Mobile Skills Crew project site, 2008, 2009, 2011, 2016

AREA SERVICES

Rib Lake: See Rib Lake Segment, p. 84. From the STH-102 Trail access go south 5.5 mi. Also see Trail Access and Parking directions, above.

Medford: See Pine Line Segment and East Lake Segment, p. 80. From the STH-102 Trail access go south ~22 mi.

Wood Lake County Park: Camping. On Trail. For information contact Taylor County Forestry & Recreation Department (715-748-1486). Camping is free Labor Day to Memorial Day. From Rib Lake at the intersection of STH-102 and CTH-D take STH-102 east and north 4.0 mi. At Wood Lake Ave. turn right and go east 3.3 mi.

Merrill: See Turtle Rock Segment and Grandfather Falls Segment, p. 101. From Tower Rd. Trail access go south and east ~30 mi. Also see Trail Access and Parking directions, above.

> *I loved the whole experience of planning, driving, navigating to the trail heads, organizing food and gear… and of course the hiking and the companionship! For me, this is the epitome of wellness and self-care. It's a perfect sort of mind-body effort shared with a beautiful friend. Connecting with nature; being part of a community of like-minded folks… guided by a simple yellow blaze.*
>
> PATRICE NICOLET, ICE AGE TRAIL THOUSAND-MILER

With the exception of the relatively small unglaciated portion, the entire surface of Wisconsin, the location of its rivers and lakes, its farmlands and marshes, its surface deposits of gravel, sand and till, is due principally to the Wisconsin Glacier. Nowhere else in the United States has glaciation left greater and more permanent marks on the face of the earth.

RAYMOND T. ZILLMER, FOUNDER,
ICE AGE TRAIL ALLIANCE

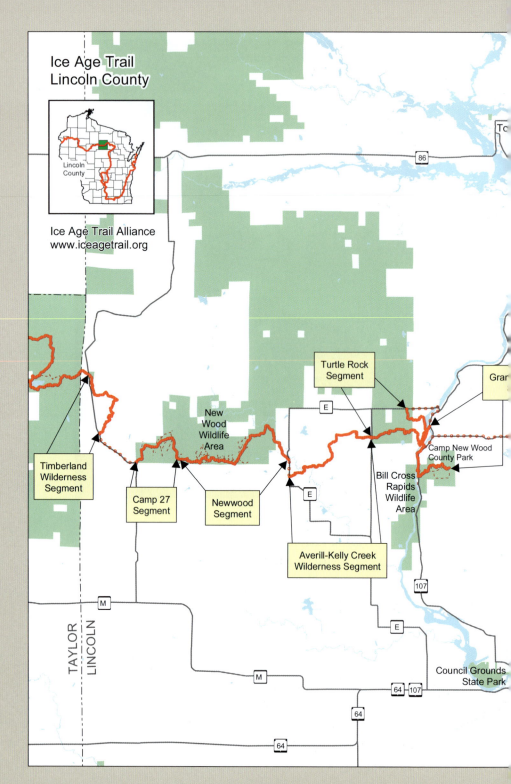

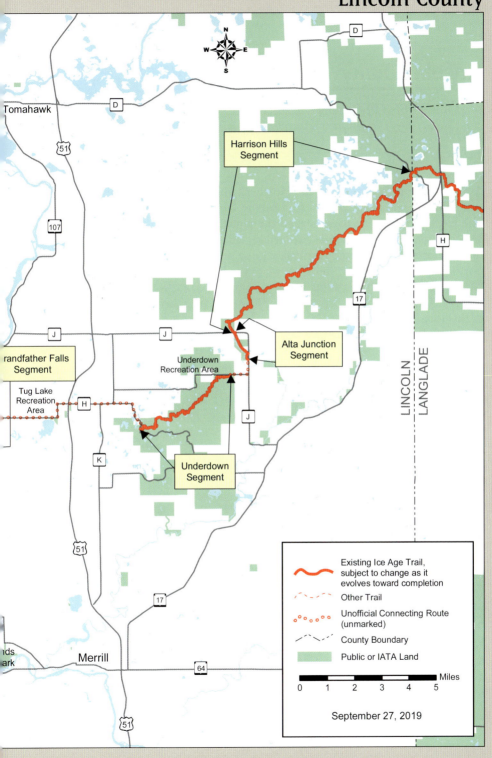

Lincoln County

Atlas Maps 26f–31f; Databook pages 25–30
Total miles: 65.8 (Trail 49.7; Connecting Route 16.1)

Lincoln County lies within the Northern Highlands. This was once a mountainous region that eroded to a rolling landscape long before the Ice Age. The Ice Age glaciers further scoured the higher bedrock hills and filled the valleys with glacial till and debris. The striking geographical features of this area are the landforms of the Wisconsin Valley Lobe, which covered most of central and northern Lincoln County. Aerial views of the land reveal parallel moraine ridge "waves" formed by the receding glacier 15,000 to 18,000 years ago. A spectacular band of high-relief hummocky topography marks the maximum southern extent of this lobe. The Ice Age Trail is bookended by the Wood Lake Moraine on the west and the Harrison Moraine on the east side of the advancing lobe. Within the Harrison Moraine are the Harrison Hills and Underdown segments, where the elevation often varies by more than 200 feet. This top-notch topography is marked by deep kettles, fragmented ridges, irregular hummocks and ice-walled lake plains. The Wisconsin River at Grandfather Falls provides an opportunity to see 1.8-billion-year-old exposed bedrock and large boulders smoothed by thousands of years of water flow.

The Ice Age Trail segments in Lincoln County provide some of the most isolated experiences on the Trail. The forest uplands include hemlock, maple, yellow and white birch, white cedar, balsam fir, poplar, black ash, white pine and tamarack. Black bear are common and timber wolves are present in the large tracts of public land in the area.

Dogs should be kept on a leash as they have been known to chase bears and deer and could be attacked should they wander near a den of cubs or wolf pups. Bringing dogs to these areas during hunting season may endanger the use of these lands.

For overnight parking contact the chapter coordinator for best locations and notify the county sheriff department. Primitive camping is permitted on county forest land. Please camp at least 200 feet away from waterways and trails.

Note: Throughout the county there are yellow paint markings found in areas about to be or recently logged. These markers are not Ice Age Trail navigational aids and differ from the traditional Ice Age Trail yellow blazes by their irregular shape and randomness.

CHAPTER INFORMATION

The Northwoods Chapter is one of the oldest IATA chapters. The chapter has a Trail segment "adoption" program that divides Trail segments into manageable distances for volunteers to maintain. It also has a rich history of working with youth groups, the Wisconsin Conservation Corps, Mobile Skills Crew program and volunteers from throughout the state to build new Trail segments and maintain existing ones in the county.

COUNTY INFORMATION

Lincoln County: co.lincoln.wi.us

Lincoln County Forestry, Lands & Parks Department: 715-539-1034

Lincoln County Sheriff's Office: 715-536-6272; contact for overnight parking permission.

A hiker carefully negotiates a creek crossing on the Turtle Rock Segment.

Lincoln County

Timberland Wilderness Segment

(Atlas Map 26f; Databook page 26)

SNAPSHOT

3.9 miles: Tower Rd. Northern Trail Access to Tower Rd. Southern Trail Access

  This remote segment through hardwood forests features ice-walled lake plains, ravines and several small streams.

- From several small intermittent streams/creeks.
- Portions overlap logging/forest roads.
- Dogs should be leashed (8-ft max) and under control at all times.

TRAIL ACCESS AND PARKING

Tower Rd. Northern Trail Access: *From Merrill* at the intersection of I-39/USH-51 and STH-64, take STH-64 west for 3.0 mi to the junction with STH-107. Continue west on STH-64/107 6.6 mi. At CTH-M continue west for 10.9 mi. At Tower Rd. turn right and go north 9.0 mi to the parking area on the west side of the road. *From Rib Lake* at the intersection of STH-102 and CTH-D, take STH-102 east for 2.0 mi. At CTH-C turn right and go south 7.0 mi. At CTH-M turn left and go east 8.0 mi. At Tower Rd. turn left and go north 9.0 mi to the parking area on the west side of the road.

Tower Rd. Southern Trail Access: *From Merrill* at the intersection of I-39/USH-51 and STH-64, take STH-64 west for 3.0 mi to the junction with STH-107. Continue west on STH-64/107 6.6 mi. At CTH-M continue west for 10.9 mi. At Tower Rd. turn right and go north 7.0 mi to the Trail access on the east side of the road. Roadside parking. No overnight parking. *From Rib Lake* at the intersection of STH-102 and CTH-D, take STH-102 east for 2.0 mi. At CTH-C turn right and go south 7.0 mi. At CTH-M turn left and go east 8.0 mi. At Tower Rd. turn left and go north 7.0 mi to the Trail access on the east side of the road.

THE HIKE

This segment passes through a 35,000-acre privately owned property that is a large undeveloped tract. Timber production and harvest have not hindered the eastern timber wolf, black bear, bobcat, deer, red fox or fisher populations. The signs of wildlife and the isolation of the region make for a true wilderness feeling. The state purchased a linear easement on this property to permanently protect the Ice Age Trail in 1999 and in 2002 the state purchased a Forest Legacy Easement over the entire 35,000 acres that prevents the land from being developed or subdivided.

The segment starts off from a point on Tower Road directly across from the Wood Lake Segment Trail access and crosses an overgrown forest road after a quarter mile. This is the first of four crossings of logging roads used as part of a 21st-century logging operation. Prior to that, the area was last logged in 1938. Beavers have embedded themselves in the area doing their own form of logging. As a result, new wetlands have formed changing the landscape and impacting the Trail in some locations.

After the second logging road crossing, the segment passes through an area with several trailside erratics and reaches a large beaver dam (**LI51**) with an expansive pond. The Trail crosses in front of and below the dam on a boardwalk and continues through the forest, traversing the top of a crescent-shaped ridge before reaching an old railroad grade.

As the segment makes its way southeast, it follows the edge of an ice-walled lake plain (**LI35**). Hikers can peer through the forest to see creek-filled ravines and forested lowlands of mature hemlock, balsam fir, white cedar and yellow birch. Pass a Leopold bench dedicated to Herb Schotz, volunteer and former coordinator of the Ice Age Trail Alliance's Northwoods Chapter, as the segment turns to the southwest.

The segment crosses a two-plank native material bridge (**LI36**) made on-site that spans a gully. Here steam engines moved timber via the old railroad grade to the main line south and east.

After crossing the third logging road (also an old railroad grade) the segment follows rolling ridges of two more ice-walled lake plains before crossing the final logging road and reaching its terminus at Tower Road.

Mobile Skills Crew project site, 2004, 2007

AREA SERVICES

Rib Lake: See Rib Lake Segment, p. 84. From the Tower Rd. southern Trail access go south and west ~9 mi. Also see Trail Access and Parking directions, above.

Medford: See Pine Line Segment and East Lake Segment, p. 80. From the Tower Rd. southern Trail access go south and west ~30 mi.

Merrill: See Turtle Rock Segment and Grandfather Falls Segment, p. 101. From the Tower Rd. southern Trail access go south and east ~27.5 mi. Also see Trail Access and Parking directions, above.

> *I started talking to the chipmunks, squirrels, and deer I encountered. When I admitted this online, a fellow hiker responded, "It is only polite to say hello when you are walking through someone else's home."*
>
> LOU ANN NOVAK, ICE AGE TRAIL THOUSAND-MILER

Camp 27 Segment and Newwood Segment (Atlas Maps 26f, 27f; Databook pages 26–27)

SNAPSHOT

Camp 27 Segment—2.9 miles: Tower Rd. to unnamed logging road
Newwood Segment—6.9 miles: Unnamed logging road to CTH-E

 The **Camp 27 Segment** traverses one of the most remote areas in the state—the New Wood State Wildlife Area—and includes the crossing of a large beaver dam and a river ford.

- From the North Fork of the Copper River (**LI31**), a wetland area (**LI32**) and other small streams/creeks.
- Dogs should be leashed (8-ft max) and under control at all times. By law, dogs **must** be leashed April 15 to July 31 in the State Wildlife Area.
- Portions overlap logging/forest roads.
- Short spur trail (gravel road) to the site of historic Camp 27 lumber camp.

 The remote **Newwood Segment** traverses a wide variety of terrain and highlights the beautiful New Wood River and three towering riverbank pines.

- From the New Wood River, Camp Twentysix Creek and other small streams/creeks and wetland areas.
- Primitive camping on a narrow band of county forest.
- Portion of segment crossing private land between the eastern boundary of the Lincoln County Forest and CTH-E is closed during gun deer season.
- Dogs should be leashed (8-ft max) and under control at all times. By law, dogs **must** be leashed April 15 to July 31 in the State Wildlife Area.
- Portions overlap logging/forest roads.
- A number of hunter access footpaths on old forest roads.

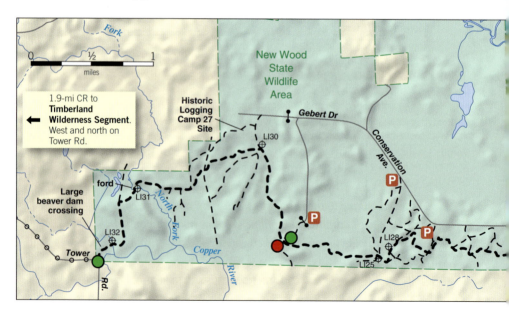

TRAIL ACCESS AND PARKING

Tower Rd.: *From Merrill* at the intersection of I-39/USH-51 and STH-64, take STH-64 west for 3.0 mi to the junction with STH-107. Continue west on STH-64/107 6.6 mi. At CTH-M continue west for 10.9 mi. At Tower Rd. turn right and go north 5.1 mi to the Trail access on the east side of the road. Roadside parking. *From Rib Lake* at the intersection of STH-102 and CTH-D, take STH-102 east for 2.0 mi. At CH-C turn right and go south 7.0 mi. At CTH-M turn left and go east 8.0mi. At Tower Rd. turn right and go north 5.1 mi to the Trail access on the east side of the road

CTH-E: From Merrill at the intersection of I-39/USH-51 and STH-64, take STH-64 west for 3.0 mi. At STH-107 turn right and go north 12.8 mi past Grandfather Falls and Dam. At CTH-E turn left across the Wisconsin River and go west then south for 7.5 mi to the parking area on the west side of the road.

Additional Parking: (i) Conservation Ave.: From the CTH-E access go south 0.2 mi on CTH-E. At Conservation Ave. turn right and go west 2.1 mi to the parking area. (ii) Additional parking areas farther west along Conservation Ave. near hunter access footpaths on old forest roads (see map). These are maintained mostly during hunting season and provide access to the Ice Age Trail.

THE HIKE

Both the Camp 27 and Newwood segments traverse the New Wood State Wildlife Area. The area dates back to 1945 when 960 acres of cutover and burned land were purchased by the state for wildlife and waterfowl management and public hunting purposes. Additional state purchases increased the Wildlife Area to today's 4,635 acres. The New Wood State Wildlife Area is one of the most remote areas in the state. Since the early 1980s timber wolf packs have returned and reestablished themselves in the area. The upland forest offers habitat for deer, ruffed grouse, snowshoe hare, timber wolves, hawks, bald eagles and a variety of thrushes and warblers.

From its starting point on Tower Road, the **Camp 27 Segment** quickly reaches a beaver dam more than 100 feet long that is used to cross a large wetland (**LI32**). Hikers will follow atop the narrow earthen embankments of the dam, which are marked on each end with metal Trail markers.

Farther along, the segment crosses (**LI31**) the North Fork of the Copper River on a rocky creek bed about 20 feet wide. Depending on the amount of snow melt or rain, this may be a relatively dry crossing or require a shallow ford. From here the segment switches back and forth between narrow, tree-lined corridors and wide, grassy logging trails.

About a mile and a quarter past the North Fork of the Copper River crossing, the segment intersects (**LI30**) a grass-covered logging road that leads 100 yards north to the site of the historic Camp 27 logging camp. Camp 27 was established in 1940 or 1941 by the Rib Lake Lumber Company of Delaware. Logs were transported by rail to the Company's sawmill in Rib Lake. At the time, hemlocks had grown so large two people could barely reach around the trunks. Loggers felled the trees by hand using crosscut saws and axes. They worked in winter, icing the roads to transport the logs by sled. Some winters there were as many as 150 men in Camp 27. The camp was self-sufficient as they even had their own cattle and pigs. By 1945 the area had been cut over and cleared. Little trace of Camp 27 remains at the site, except a small mound on the northern edge of the camp, probably a garbage dump site.

From the intersection (**LI30**) with the grass-covered logging road to Camp 27, the segment continues south, crosses a small stream on a footbridge and an ice-walled-lake plain just shy of its terminus at an unnamed logging road.

The **Newwood Segment** heads east from the unnamed logging road through a few boggy areas and marshland. Within a mile the segment intersects (**LI25**) the first of several old forest roads that are primarily used by hunters.

As the segment continues eastward, it traverses a classic esker (**LI28**) and highlights trailside erratics. Portions of the segment follow narrow and lightly treaded footpath sections that enhance the natural, semi-primitive experience. As the segment nears the Conservation Avenue Trail access and parking area, it transitions (**LI26**) from a narrow footpath to wide, grassy troads along the edge of an assortment of open meadows.

The eastern half of the Newwood Segment courses through rough terrain on state, county and private lands. This area along the entire Wisconsin River valley was logged for large pines from the 1850s through the 1890s. Rivers were used to transport the logs to the mills. By 1906, once the old growth pines were gone, the logging of hardwoods and hemlock began. The Stange & Kinzel Lumber Company of Merrill built a network of standard guage railroad spurs and used them until the area was completely logged off from the 1900s to 1920s. The spurs tied in with a line of the Milwaukee Road that went from the Newwood area into Merrill to the company's lumber mill. In 1925, the Rib Lake Lumber Company bought the land and held logging operations on it for the next 20 years.

North of Conservation Avenue the segment makes its way across the State Wildlife Area boundary into a mile-wide band of Lincoln County Forest, where primitive camping is permitted. Shortly after crossing into the Lincoln County Forest, hikers will find a Leopold bench (**LI27**) beneath a large pine and a hemlock. After the segment curves around to the south it reaches a point along the New Wood River where hikers will discover three giant white pines (**LI24**). These probably escaped the saw during the logging heyday due to their small size at the time. They have since thrived and offer a scenic, peaceful resting spot under their canopy. There is a bench and access to the New Wood River here.

Farther along, the segment reaches an overlook of the river featuring another Leopold bench in a small grove of hemlocks where hikers can relax and enjoy the memorable view. Hikers must not camp here as this spot and the remainder of the segment are on private land. The segment continues through hummocky glacial terrain to a crossing of Camp Twentysix Creek (**LI23**) before following the flat, grassy rail bed of a historic logging railway that rises above the surrounding wetlands and brings the segment to its terminus on CTH-E. Wolf scat is commonly seen on the old rail bed.

Mobile Skills Crew project site, 2003, 2004, 2005, 2006

AREA SERVICES

Rib Lake: See Rib Lake Segment, p. 84. From the Tower Rd. Trail access go west ~10 mi. Also see Trail Access and Parking directions, above.

Medford: See Pine Line Segment and East Lake Segment, p. 80. From the Tower Rd. Trail access go south and west ~27 mi.

Merrill: See Turtle Rock Segment and Grandfather Falls Segment, p. 101. From the CTH-E Trail access go east then south ~23 mi. Also see Trail Access and Parking directions, above.

Averill-Kelly Creek Wilderness Segment (Atlas Maps 27f, 28f; Databook pages 27–28)

SNAPSHOT

4.9 miles: CTH-E to Burma Rd.

 *This segment, entirely on private lands, features three water crossings in a forested, remote setting.*

 From the New Wood River (**LI21**), Averill Creek (**LI19**), Kelly Creek and a few smaller intermittent streams.

 Dogs must be leashed at all times.

Portions overlap logging/forest roads.

 The eastern portion of the segment is closed for all of October, November and December. A reroute is posted during this time. The entire segment is closed for the traditional 9-day gun deer season in November.

TRAIL ACCESS AND PARKING

CTH-E: From Merrill at I-39 and USH-51/STH- 64, take STH-64 west for 3.0 mi. At STH-107 turn right and go north 12.8 mi past Grandfather Falls and Dam. At CTH-E turn left, go across the Wisconsin River and go west then south for 8.1 mi. Roadside parking on the east side of the road.

Burma Rd.: From Merrill at the intersection of I-39/USH-51 and STH-64, take STH-64 west for 3.0 mi. At STH-107 turn right and go north 12.8 mi past Grandfather Falls and Dam. At CTH-E turn left across the Wisconsin River and go west 2.6 mi. At Burma Rd. turn left and go south 1.1 mi. NO PARKING. Instead, park roadside next to the Turtle Rock Segment Burma Rd. southern Trail access sign (**LI41**), 0.1 mi farther south on the east side of the road. *Note: DO NOT park in front of the private road with access gate on the west side of the road.*

THE HIKE

This segment offers hikers many opportunities for wildlife viewing. Watch for signs of bear activity, wolf scat and frogs at the water crossings. *Note: After periods of heavy rain the New Wood River and Averill-Kelly Creek swell and currents increase making these water crossings treacherous.* Check with the Ice Age Trail

Alliance (**800-227-0046, iceagetrail.org**) *for conditions. It is possible to bypass the segment at times of high water and during hunting season when the segment is closed. The alternative road walk is north and east on CTH-E, then south on Burma Road.*

From its starting point on CTH-E the segment passes through an open canopy of aspen and birch trees regenerating after a timber harvest from the beginning of this millennium. In the first half mile, the area has been intermittently logged off and hikers should pay close attention to signage. Continuing on, the segment soon reaches and then parallels the peaceful New Wood River before reaching a point where hikers will ford the river (**LI21**). The river is wide but generally only ankle- to knee-deep. However, water levels can reach hip-deep or higher. When water levels are high, extreme caution should be used when fording this waterway. It is recommended hikers take the alternate route.

On the other side of this ford, the segment reaches an open grassy area at an unsigned trail junction (**LI20**) and continues east 300 feet to a spot where hikers will rock-hop across Averill Creek (**LI19**). Following the creek crossing the segment passes through a large clear-cut timber harvest area regenerating with pioneer plants such as birch, aspen and cherry, along with blueberry and raspberry bushes, grasses and shrubs. The segment uses portions of an old railroad grade as it makes its way first to Kelly Creek—a trout stream—and then to its endpoint on Burma Road. The area around the Kelly Creek crossing can be very wet and swampy.

AREA SERVICES

Tomahawk: See Turtle Rock and Grandfather Falls Segment, p. 101. From Burma Rd. go north, east then north ~17 mi.

Merrill: See Turtle Rock Segment and Grandfather Falls Segment, p. 101. From Burma Rd. go north, east then south ~18 mi. Also see Trail Access and Parking directions, above.

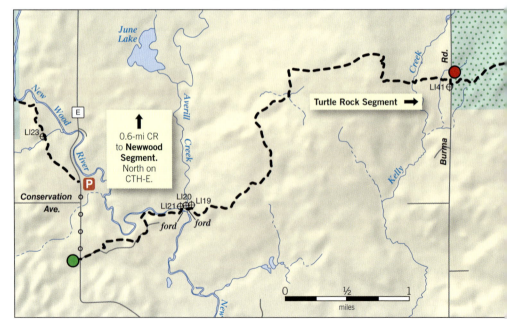

Turtle Rock Segment and Grandfather Falls Segment

(Atlas Map 28f; Databook pages 28–29)

SNAPSHOT

Turtle Rock Segment—5.1 miles: Burma Rd. Northern Trail Access to CTH-E

   2.1-mile Connecting Route

Grandfather Falls Segment—4.0 miles: STH-107 Grandfather Falls Hydro Northern Parking Area to Eastern Terminus of out-and-back section through the Merrill School Forest

The **Turtle Rock Segment** *includes a beautiful—and very challenging—trek along and near the banks of the Wisconsin River, where the ceremonial Turtle Rock is found.*

 From the Wisconsin River and other small streams/creeks.

 Primitive camping on county forest lands.

Eastern portion of the segment crossing private land along and near the Wisconsin River is closed during gun deer season.

 Dogs should be leashed (8-ft max) and under control at all times.

 Segment includes brief roadwalk on Burma Rd. Portions overlap logging/forest roads and multiuse trails open to snowmobiling and cross-country skiing.

The scenic **Grandfather Falls Segment** *highlights Ripley Creek, the Wisconsin River, Grandfather Falls and a unique hydroelectric plant.*

 From the Wisconsin River and Ripley Creek.

 Campground at Camp New Wood County Park.

 At Camp New Wood County Park. Also, portable toilet at STH-107 Grandfather Falls Hydro northern parking area.

 Dogs should be leashed (8-ft max) and under control at all times.

 Portions overlap logging/forest roads and gravel access roads.

 Unmarked spur trails off the northern portion along the Wisconsin River, the Merrill School Forest trail network and a spur trail crossing the Wisconsin Conservation Corps bridge over Ripley Creek.

TRAIL ACCESS AND PARKING

Burma Rd. Northern Trail Access: From Merrill at the intersection of I-39/USH-51 and STH-64, take STH-64 west for 3.0 mi. At STH-107 turn right and go north 12.8 mi past Grandfather Falls and Dam. At CTH-E turn left across the Wisconsin River and go west 2.6 mi. At Burma Rd. turn left and go south 1.1 mi. NO PARKING. Instead, park roadside next to the Turtle Rock Segment Burma Rd. southern Trail access sign (**LI41**), 0.1 mi farther south on the east side of the road. *Note: DO NOT park in front of the private road with access gate on the west side of the road.*

Eastern Terminus of out-and-back section through the Merrill School Forest: No parking. Instead, park at the Camp New Wood County Park day use parking area on the west side of STH-107 or Merrill School Forest parking area on the north side of the forest entrance road.

Additional Parking: (i) CTH-E parking area on the north side of the road across from the Trail access. (ii) Grandfather Falls Hydro northern parking area on west side of STH-107. (iii) Grandfather Falls Hydro southern parking areas on west side of STH-107. (iv) Wisconsin River canoe and tubing/float

Lincoln County

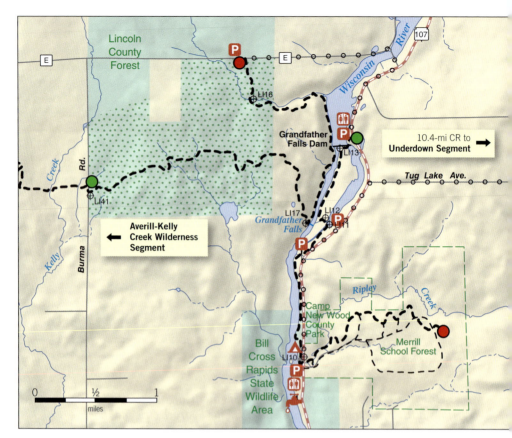

craft entry point parking area on west side of STH-107, a short distance south of Grandfather Falls Hydro southern parking area.

THE HIKE

The **Turtle Rock Segment** was named for a ceremonial rock used by Native Americans. The segment is diverse and rugged, traversing thickets and isolated forest, along a rocky river shoreline and around a marsh, and may require a few hours to hike going one way. The segment is lightly used and it is important that hikers watch for blazes and directional arrows to stay on course—bears in the area are famous for knocking down directional sign posts. This is a prime area for bird watching and wildlife viewing as the DNR maintains several wildlife and game clearings in the area. Expect the sudden rise of grouse, curious forest hawks swooping overhead and the sudden noisy commotion of deer crashing through the undergrowth.

From the endpoint of the Averill-Kelly Creek Wilderness Segment on Burma Road, hikers should head south 0.1 miles to a point where the segment leaves Burma Road (**LI41**) and heads east. Within half a mile, the segment reaches a 4-acre DNR wildlife clearing that hikers consider a good place for primitive camping. The first few miles of the the segment follow wide forest roads through county forest land before transitioning to a narrower, winding path on private land. The Trail in this area at times shares a snowmobile route.

The segment makes a sharp left turn off the wider multiuse trail and heads steeply down into the valley of the Wisconsin River (**LI17**). As the forest becomes dense near the river, the tread can become slippery with forest debris and can be uneven. Use special caution when climbing over rocks and crossing wet wooden planks. For more than a mile, the segment parallels the river through a scenic, rocky playground. This side of the river offers the best view of Grandfather Falls and one can climb out on rocks to watch cascading river water. Eventually, the segment passes the west end of Grandfather Falls Dam (**LI52**). Across the river, a bench overlook is near the start of the next segment. Careful hikers will spot Turtle Rock, a huge erratic with a "turtle head" protuberance jutting skyward amongst the forest's rock gardens.

The segment curves west and parallels an unnamed creek emptying into the Wisconsin River. Climbing out of the lush Wisconsin River valley, hikers will find a wooden bench that sits 20 feet above the creek on a scenic bank. The segment intersects a forest road where hikers can enjoy a birch-tree-lined trail corridor.

Farther along, the segment cuts sharply to the right and quickly crosses the creek (log and rock hop) (**LI16**) in front of a beaver dam, then comes to an open area overlooking the beaver pond and wetland area. The creek crossing can be tricky in times of high water. Shortly after passing through this area, the segment follows a wide multiuse path to its endpoint on CTH-E.

To reach the Grandfather Falls Segment, hikers should head east on a connecting route along lightly travelled CTH-E. After 1.3 miles hikers will reach a bridge and head east across the Wisconsin River to STH-107, then turn right and hike south 0.8 miles along STH-107.

The **Grandfather Falls Segment** starts at the Grandfather Falls Hydro northern parking area on STH-107. From the parking area, the segment heads south past a red gate and crosses a bridge over the inlet of a reservoir that is located east of the Wisconsin River. Once across the bridge, the segment heads west on a gravel drive to the base of Grandfather Falls Dam and the original red brick hydroelectric plant. From here the segment enters woods (**LI13**) and travels south along the river.

Below the dam, hikers can view the unique boulders and sculptured rock formations caused by thousands of years of cascading water. The sound is thunderous; this is the largest waterfall on the Wisconsin River, with a total drop of 89 feet. The rapids continue for about one mile. Hikers travel through an enormous pre-Cambrian rock outcrop, geologic evidence of a former mountain range exposed by weathering and the more recent scraping of the glaciers.

Native Americans and fur traders portaged here to bypass Grandfather Falls. Later, untold numbers of logs made their way down this stretch of the river. In 1846, history records 24 lumber mills on the Wisconsin River providing 20 million board feet of lumber per year. By 1857, there were 107 mills producing over 100 million board feet per year. The dam itself represents a living history of the taming of the river for hydroelectric power in the early 20th century.

The segment continues south and then turns east to cross a grassy swath and the reservoir's floodgate outlet on a bridge (**LI12**). The bridge is engineered to withstand floodwater and is a replacement for several others that were repeatedly washed out over the years. Be mindful of the floodgate warning sirens as the gates are opened once a week.

The segment then proceeds over a short section north of a set of huge tubes called penstocks and south of the reservoir. Once past the penstocks, the segment turns sharply south (**LI11**) paralleling the penstocks. The penstocks carry water hundreds of yards downriver from the reservoir. Up until recent years, the penstocks were made of wood, but high maintenance costs replaced the wood with steel. Hikers can view and walk through a section of wooden penstock displayed alongside the Trail.

Toward the downstream end of the penstocks, the segment continues around the east side of the current hydroelectric plant before reaching a Wisconsin River canoe and tubing/float craft entry point and parking area. It continues south through the camping area of Camp New Wood County Park, the historic site of a 1935 Civilian Conservation Corps (CCC) camp named Camp McCord. The segment then reaches a junction with a spur trail that heads south over the Wisconsin Conservation Corps bridge crossing Ripley Creek to the Camp New Wood County Park day use area entrance drive. From this junction hikers should turn left and briefly head east along Ripley Creek to the STH-107 crossing (**LI10**). Hikers should cross STH-107 to begin the 1.7-mile (one way) out-and-back portion of the segment. This is necessary to cover the segment's entire Ice Age Trail route.

The out-and-back portion of the segment starts by descending and intermittently following along a beautiful stretch of Ripley Creek on Merrill School Forest private property. This property came to be the school forest in 1944 when William T. Evjue, an 1898 graduate of Merrill High School, purchased 598 acres from Lincoln County and donated it to the school. The property became a memorial to William's father, Nels P. Evjue, a pioneer Merrill woodsman. Initially, students planted 2000 conifer trees and after purchase of an additional 80 acres of land, 60,000 more trees were planted on the property.

The out-and-back portion climbs steeply to a meadow above the creek. Trail conditions and markings may vary when the meadow is overgrown. The out-and-back portion intersects various roads and trails that are part of the Merrill School Forest trail network, passes an education center and continues until reaching the segment endpoint near the eastern boundary of the Merrill School Forest property. At the segment endpoint, hikers should turn around and return to the Trail's crossing of STH-107 (**LI10**).

Mobile Skills Crew project site, 2011, 2017

AREA SERVICES

Camp New Wood County Park: Camping. On Trail. Camping for a fee on a first come, first served basis. For info contact the Lincoln County Forestry, Lands & Parks Department (715-539-1034).

Council Grounds State Park: Camping. From Camp New Wood County Park on STH-107 go south 8.4 mi on STH-107 to the park entrance drive (715-536-8773, dnr.wi.gov/topic/parks/name/councilgrounds/; reservations: 888-947-2757, wisconsin.goingtocamp.com).

Merrill: Restaurant, grocery store, convenience store, general shopping, lodging, camping, library, medical service. From Camp New Wood County Park go south 10.2 mi on STH-107. For area info contact the Merrill Area Chamber of Commerce (715-536-9474, merrillchamber.org).

Tomahawk: Restaurant, grocery store, convenience store, lodging, camping, library, medical service. From Camp New Wood County Park go north ~17 mi on STH-107. For area info contact the Tomahawk Area Chamber of Commerce (715-453-5334, gototomahawk.com).

Underdown Segment and Alta Junction Segment (Atlas Maps 29f, 30f; Databook pages 29–30)

SNAPSHOT

Underdown Segment—6.3 miles: Horn Lake Rd. to Copper Lake Ave.

1.2-mile Connecting Route

Alta Junction Segment—1.2 miles: CTH-J Southern Trail Access to CTH-J Northern Trail Access

 *The very hilly and forested* **Underdown Segment** *passes through the popular Underdown Recreation Area and cuts through the primeval "Enchanted Forest," a beautiful hemlock grove next to a wetland area.*

At the Underdown Recreation Area main parking area 1.1 mi west of the eastern end of the segment.

From Dog Lake and Mist Lake.

Primitive camping on county forest lands. Walk-in campsites in the Mist Lake and Dog Lake area. The Dog Lake site has a shelter.

Campground at the Underdown Recreation Area main parking area. Primitive campground on south end of Horn Lake.

Dogs should be leashed (8-ft max) and under control at all times.

Much of the segment overlaps bike trails, horse trails, cross-country ski trails, snowshoe trails and logging/forest roads.

Underdown Recreation Area trail network.

The short **Alta Junction Segment** *follows a historic railroad grade for much of its route.*

From the North Branch of the Prairie River and a small intermittent creek.

Dogs should be leashed (8-ft max) and under control at all times.

TRAIL ACCESS AND PARKING

Horn Lake Rd.: From Merrill at the intersection of I-39/USH-51 and CTH-K, take CTH-K north 7.3 mi. At CTH-H turn right and go east 0.5 mi to gravel Horseshoe Lake Dr. As CTH-H turns north, continue east on Horseshoe Lake Dr. for 0.8 mi. At Horn Lake Rd. turn right and go south 1.2 mi. No parking. Instead, park at the Horn Lake primitive camping area (see additional parking below).

CTH-J Northern Trail Access: From Merrill at the intersection of I-39/USH-51 and STH-64, take USH-51 north 13.0 mi to Irma. At CTH-J turn right and go east 5.1 mi. Roadside parking.

Additional Parking: (i) Horn Lake camping area: From Horn Lake Rd. Trail access take Horn Lake Rd. south and then west at the T intersection 0.4 mi to the walk-in campsites on the south end of Horn Lake. (ii) Copper Lake Ave.: From Merrill at the intersection of I-39/USH-51 and CTH-K, take CTH-K north 7.3 mi. At CTH-H turn right and go east then north 1.0 mi to Copper Lake Ave. At Copper Lake Ave. turn right and go east 3.7 mi. Pass the Underdown Recreation Area main parking area and continue an additional 1.1 mi east to reach the Trail access. Roadside parking. (iii) CTH-J southern Trail access: From Merrill at the intersection of I-39/USH-51 and STH-64, take USH-51 north 13.0 mi to Irma. At CTH-J turn right and go east then south 6.6 mi to a DNR parking area on the west side of CTH-J. There is also an additional DNR parking area 0.25-mi north on CTH-J. (iv) Alta Springs Rd. parking area, about 0.1 mi north of CTH-J on Alta Springs Rd. A blue-blazed spur trail leads to the Ice Age Trail.

THE HIKE

The topography traversed by the **Underdown Segment** is part of the Harrison Moraine of the Wisconsin Valley lobe. Glacial debris remnants in the form of hummocks separate deep kettles. Some kettles remain lakes, but most are filled with sphagnum peat. Thick forests including frequent hemlock groves, white pine, mature maples and white birch hide the high-relief hummocky terrain that a hiker may not always see but will certainly feel with the climbs and descents. *Note: Single-track mountain bike trails and horse trails intertwine with the Ice Age Trail along this segment. Pay close attention at intersections.*

From its starting point on Horn Lake Road the segment heads east then north and after about a mile winds through a thick hemlock grove called the "Enchanted Forest." Sphagnum moss bogs lie amid the hemlocks and towering white pines. Steep climbs up and down hummocks greet the hiker as the segment closes in on Mist Lake and reaches a high point and a Leopold bench (**LI40**) high above the lake. Farther east along the segment another very steep ascent leads to a campsite (**LI39**) halfway between Mist Lake and Dog Lake. The site is very primitive and high above the surrounding forest. After descending through a mature hardwood forest hikers will encounter another hemlock grove that wraps around the northwest side of Dog Lake. On a small rise facing the lake is the Dog Lake backpack shelter (**LI5**). There is a fire ring and room for a few small tents near the shelter.

After leaving Dog Lake the segment crosses several small bridges and intermittently shares single-track trail. After crossing Loop Road (open to all vehicles including ATVs) the segment enters an open mature white birch forest home to nesting cooper's hawks. The segment continues past a Leopold bench through open forest and a previously logged area ascending to the high point of the seg-

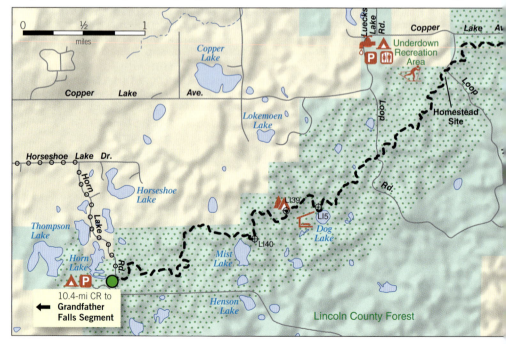

ment. Volunteers have worked hard to make this section easy to traverse with hand-built bench cuts carved into the hillside.

Just prior to crossing Loop Road a second time, hikers will reach the site of the original homestead of Bill Underdown. Remains of the cabin foundation can be found on the left side of the Trail. A sign marks the location. The segment crosses Loop Road and steeply climbs an esker. This very narrow ridge has steep sides falling off on both sides from the narrow ribbon of Trail. Another bench here lets the hiker rest and take in the surrounding deep woods. The segment descends and crosses an intermittent creek and climbs back up and through a recent timber harvest area before reaching its endpoint on Copper Lake Avenue.

To reach the Alta Junction Segment, hikers should head east for 0.7 miles on a connecting route along Copper Lake Avenue, then turn left and head north for 0.5 miles on CTH-J.

The **Alta Junction Segment** is named after the historic railroad junction of two rail lines at the village of Dunfield (now a ghost town). The segment follows the east side of the North Branch of the Prairie River. This area is known for the natural springs that bubble up from underground water tables. The Alta Springs Bottling Company (late 1800s) and Pay Brothers Alta Springs Bottling Company (1930s) bottled and sold the spring water for medicinal purposes.

From the southern Trail access on CTH-J the segment initially crosses a hummocky area, cuts through a parking area and then follows a rail grade built in 1908 that was part of the Milwaukee Road network that mainly serviced the logging industry in the area. Old railroad ties can still be seen in some places. The rail lines served the land Sigmund Heinemann owned and were used to transport timber to the mill town of Heinemann until it burned down in 1910. Traversing the hilly glacial terrain, trains also hauled freight along these lines to the lumber mills in Merrill and Tomahawk until 1931. The segment ends when it again intersects CTH-J near Alta Springs Road.

AREA SERVICES

Underdown Recreation Area: Camping. From the Copper Lake Ave. Trail access go west 1.1 mi. For info contact the Lincoln County Forestry, Lands & Parks Department (715-539-1034).

Merrill: See Turtle Rock Segment and Grandfather Falls Segment, p. 101. From Copper Lake Ave. Trail access go west then south ~17 mi. Also see Trail Access and Parking directions, above.

Gleason: See Harrison Hills Segment, p. 108. From the CTH-J southern Trail access go south then east ~6 mi.

Tomahawk: See Turtle Rock Segment and Grandfather Falls Segment, p. 101. From the CTH-J northern Trail access go west then north 15.5 mi.

Harrison Hills Segment (Atlas Maps 30f, 31f; Databook page 30)

SNAPSHOT

14.5 miles: CTH-J to First Lake Rd.

This beautiful, remote segment features roller-coaster topography, plentiful primitive camping options and long views from the top of Lookout Mountain.

 From the numerous trailside lakes, a trailside spring near the North Branch of the Prairie River and other small streams/creeks.

 Primitive camping on county forest lands. Two walk-in campsites on Chain Lake.

 At a walk-in campsite on Bus Lake accessible from Turtle Lake Rd. Large enough for groups.

 At an ATV shelter at the CTH-B Trail access.

 Dogs should be leashed (8-ft max) and under control at all times.

 Portions overlap logging/forest roads and two gravel roads.

 Blue-blazed spur trail to Alta Springs Rd. parking area and a spur trail to walk-in campsite on Bus Lake.

TRAIL ACCESS AND PARKING

CTH-J: From Merrill at the intersection of USH-51 and STH-64, take USH-51 north 13.0 mi to Irma. At CTH-J turn right and go east 5.1 mi. Roadside parking.

First Lake Rd.: From Merrill at the intersection of USH-51 and STH-64, take STH-64 east 0.3 mi. At STH-17 turn left and go northeast for 21.9 mi. At First Lake Rd. turn left and go north then west 1.5 mi to parking area on the north side of First Lake Rd., just before the intersection of First Lake Rd., Parrish Rd. and Fish Lake Rd. Additional roadside parking is available on Parrish Rd. just north of this intersection.

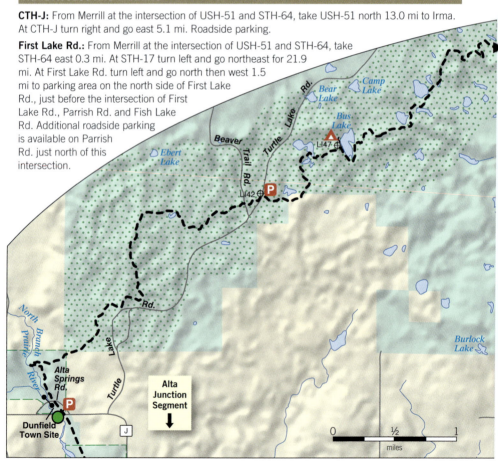

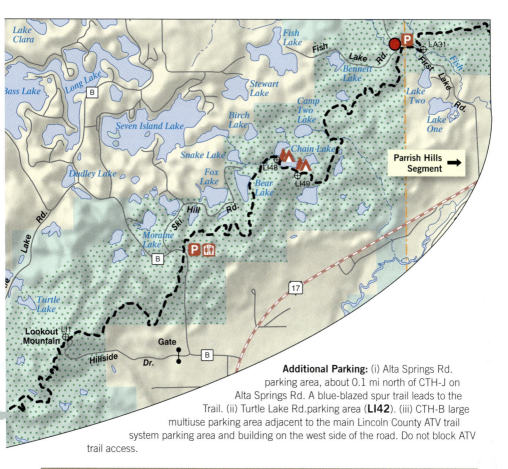

Additional Parking: (i) Alta Springs Rd. parking area, about 0.1 mi north of CTH-J on Alta Springs Rd. A blue-blazed spur trail leads to the Trail. (ii) Turtle Lake Rd. parking area (**LI42**). (iii) CTH-B large multiuse parking area adjacent to the main Lincoln County ATV trail system parking area and building on the west side of the road. Do not block ATV trail access.

THE HIKE

When the Wisconsin Valley lobe advanced, there was most likely a period where the lobe surged forward. Researchers have found that when today's glaciers rapidly advance they gather sediment on their surface, especially along the marginal edges. When the ice melts it leaves behind deep kettles and high-relief hummocks. The Harrison Moraine that this segment traverses is noted for this spectacular high-relief topography, including many glacially deposited ridges and hills such as Lookout Mountain, the highest point on the Ice Age Trail at 1,920 feet above sea level. Views are especially impressive when leaves are off.

Generally on public forest lands, this segment is remote (the Harrison Hills support a thriving wolf pack) and rugged. Ongoing timber harvest can make navigation challenging at times. The Trail corridor, while generally easy to follow, can be quite narrow in some areas. Watch carefully for Trail signage, especially at intersections and when on logging/forest roads.

This segment starts off at CTH-J and almost immediately intersects a blue-blazed spur trail leading to the Alta Springs Road parking area. It then quickly crosses primitive Alta Springs Road and soon brings hikers to a natural spring bubbling trailside and a bench with a view of the North Branch of the Prairie

River. The segment follows the river briefly before heading northeast to an area with a network of public ATV trails. ATVs are often seen or heard nearby; however, the segment does not overlap any of the ATV trails.

The segment crosses Beaver Trail Road and then Turtle Lake Road (**LI42**) before entering a region filled with small, beautiful, undeveloped lakes. It is common to see beavers swimming in some of the lakes at dusk. Portions of the segment in this area may be wet or flooded in early spring or during rainy periods. The trail wraps around the south end of Bus Lake. Near a bench overlooking the lake, the trail intersects (**LI47**) a spur trail leading north along the western edge of Bus Lake to a walk-in campsite (also accessible by car). A few open timber harvest areas on this portion of the segment are reestablishing with what is called a "gap" forest. Pioneer plants, such as grasses, shrubs and raspberry bushes, close in on the Trail and the new growth of aspen and birch trees offers little shade.

The segment reaches the top of Lookout Mountain (**LI1**), the second highest point in Wisconsin. There are several structures at the top, including two radio towers. The segment continues from Lookout Mountain. It travels through deciduous forest dominated by oak and maple trees on its way to CTH-B. It passes an ATV parking area with vault toilets. A popular fishing destination, the northeastern section of the segment passes many lakes. There are two angler campsites on Chain Lake: the first is along a spur trail (**LI48**) between the west and center lobes and is approximately 100 feet off the Trail; the second is also reached by a spur trail (**LI49**) between the center and east lobes and is approximately 400 feet off the Trail. The second campsite may be flooded when water levels are high.

From Chain Lake, the segment continues for about 2.0 miles to its terminus on First Lake Road, right on the Lincoln/Langlade county line.

AREA SERVICES

Tomahawk: See Turtle Rock Segment and Grandfather Falls Segment, p. 101. From the CTH-J Trail access go west then north 15.5 mi.

Gleason: Restaurant, convenience store. From the CTH-J Trail access, take CTH-J east, south and east 5.6 mi to STH-17. At STH-17, turn left (northeast) and go 1.9 mi. From the CTH-B parking area, take CTH-B east 1.2 mi to STH-17. At STH-17 turn right (southwest) and go 10.0 mi.

Harrison: Restaurant. From the CTH-B Trail access parking area go west and north ~7 mi.

Merrill: See Turtle Rock Segment and Grandfather Falls Segment, p. 101. From the First Lake Rd. Trail access go east then south ~24 mi. Also see Trail Access and Parking directions, above.

Rhinelander: See Parrish Hills Segment, p. 116. From the First Lake Rd. Trail access go east and north ~18 mi.

> *A highlight for us was learning that winter hiking was great. Frozen fog is beautiful. Snowshoeing at Harrison Hills was unforgettable. You see how alive the Trail is in winter by the tracks. We hiked, in two to four feet of snow, with snowshoes, and saw tracks from mice, squirrels, otter, deer, coyotes, and turkey but no humans. We didn't see bears but saw lots of poop and tracks on the Trail.*
>
> GEORGE (AKA "MOSS BACK GEORGE") AND VIOLET (AKA "DANCING TURTLE") BANE, ICE AGE TRAIL THOUSAND-MILERS

Autumn drenched in gold along the Harrison Hills Segment.

Lincoln County

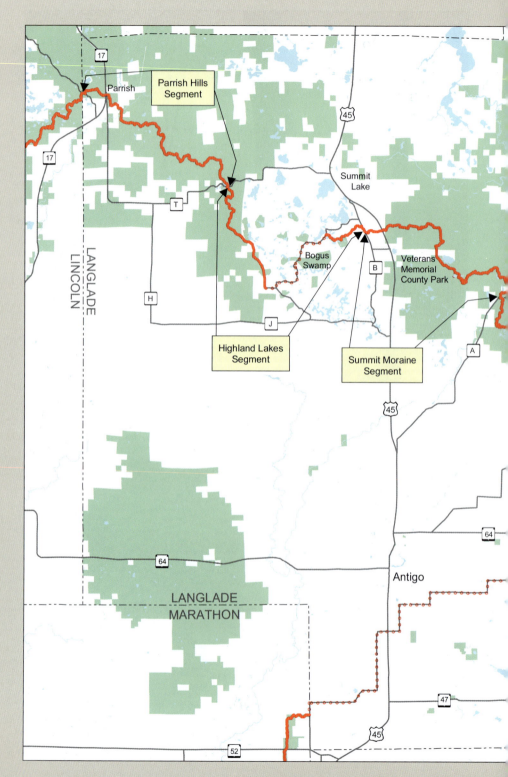

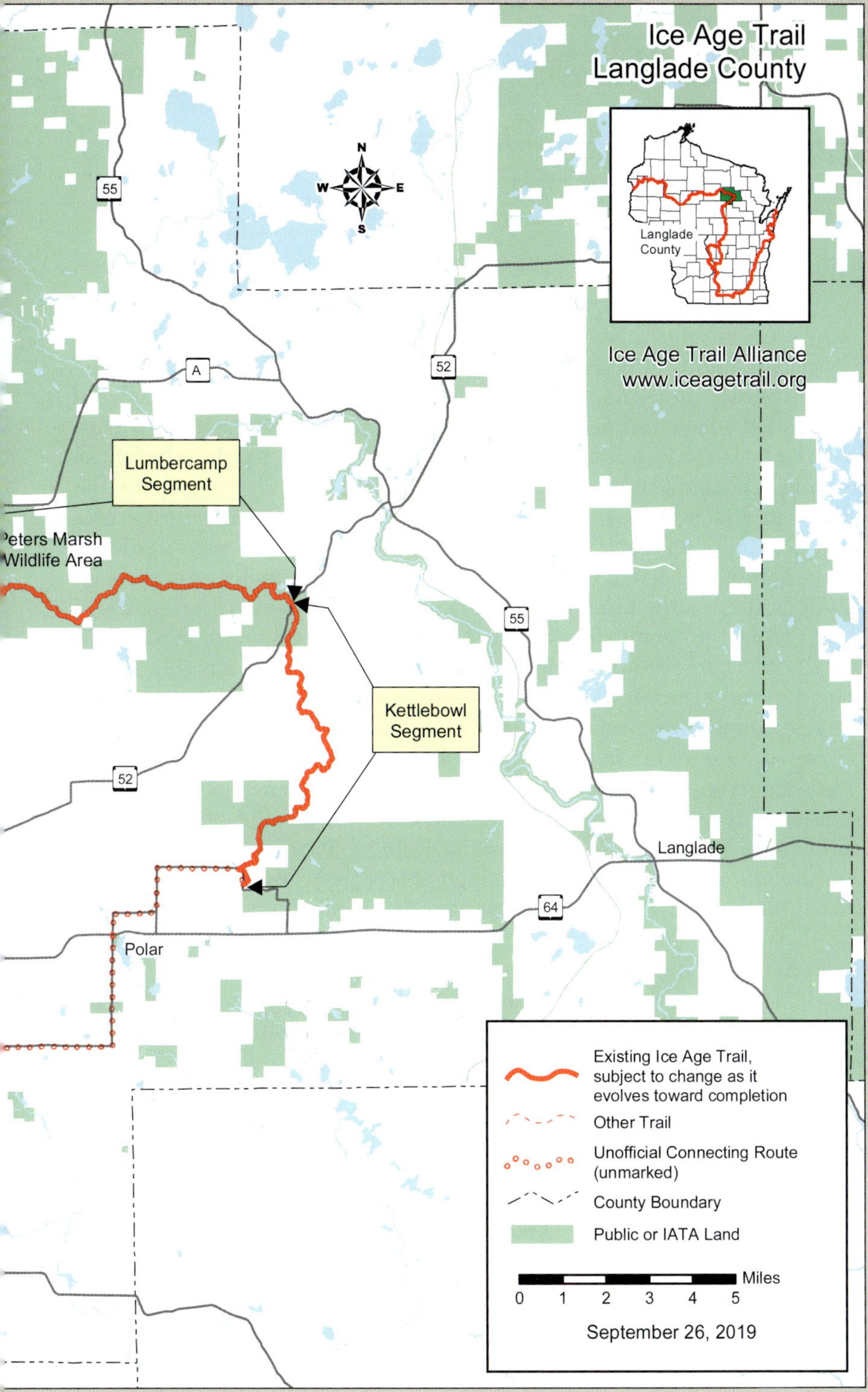

Langlade County

**Ice Age Trail
Langlade County**

Ice Age Trail Alliance
www.iceagetrail.org

- Lumbercamp Segment
- Peters Marsh Wildlife Area
- Kettlebowl Segment
- Langlade
- Polar

Legend:
- Existing Ice Age Trail, subject to change as it evolves toward completion
- Other Trail
- Unofficial Connecting Route (unmarked)
- County Boundary
- Public or IATA Land

Miles: 0 1 2 3 4 5

September 26, 2019

Langlade County 113

Langlade County

Atlas Maps 31f–39f; Databook pages 31–36
Total miles: 83.0 (Trail 54.3; Connecting Route 28.6)

The Wisconsin Valley, Langlade and Green Bay lobes shaped the landscape of Langlade County. In places, one can imagine the violent movement of the glacial lobes as they carved and crafted the county's landscape. These three glacial lobes deposited a large terminal moraine, 250 feet high in places, when the ice stopped and began to retreat 13,000 to 25,000 years ago. South and west of the end moraine is the broad outwash plain known as the Antigo Flats, named for the city of Antigo, which sits near its center. Langlade County is named for Charles de Langlade, son of a French man and an Ottawa woman, who was a leader in the region during the second half of the 1700s. The Ice Age Trail passes through hummocky end moraine terrain on county and private industrial forest lands. The county forest program started in 1928 (the first of its kind in Wisconsin) after local voters approved the establishment of a unit on a large acreage of a tax-delinquent, cutover land. Today, the county manages almost 130,000 acres, a fifth of its land area, and the state and federal governments own another 80,000 acres.

Logging is a way of life in this area and has a constant influence on the Ice Age Trail. Therefore, hikers are urged to contact the coordinator of the IATA's Langlade County Chapter before hiking in the area to get updates on logging activities and other issues affecting Trail navigability and wayfinding. Trail users here should carry a compass and topographic map. Yellow metal posts with and without Ice Age Trail signage are often used to signify the route through the county. They are used instead of the traditional wooden posts because wooden posts are often vandalized (by both humans and bears) in the area.

Because of all the county forest land, primitive camping opportunities are widespread. As with all parts of the Ice Age Trail open to primitive camping, hikers should set up their campsites at least 200 feet from trails and waterways. The Summit Moraine Segment now contains a Dispersed Camping Area (DCA). For overnight parking hikers should contact the coordinator of the IATA's Langlade County Chapter for best locations and also notify the county sheriff department. Water sources are scarce on the Kettlebowl and Lumbercamp segments.

CHAPTER INFORMATION

The Langlade County Chapter was formed in 1974 and within its first year mapped and marked five Ice Age Trail segments. Chapter volunteers maintain the Trail with help of area organizations. The chapter promotes the Ice Age Trail with outings, local news articles, a newsletter called the *Langlade Erratic*, service club presentations and exhibits at community events.

COUNTY INFORMATION

Langlade County Visitor Information: 715-623-2085, langladecounty.org

Langlade County Forestry Department: 715-627-6300, co.langlade.wi.us

Langlade County Sheriff Department: 715-627-6411; contact for overnight parking permission, co.langlade.wi.us

A summer view of Upper Ventor Lake on the Summit Moraine Segment.

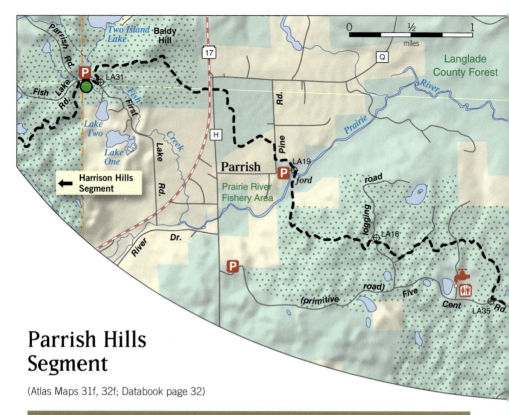

Parrish Hills Segment

(Atlas Maps 31f, 32f; Databook page 32)

SNAPSHOT

12.0 miles: First Lake Rd. western Trail access to CTH-T

This remote and rugged segment features the shoulder of Baldy Hill, a ford of the Prairie River, a scenic ridge with long views, several wetland areas and scenic Townline Lake.

Note: *A reroute is planned between Five Cent Rd. and Parrish Game Trail Fire Lane. Check with the Ice Age Trail Alliance (800-227-0046, iceagetrail.org) for details.*

 At a former ATV shelter north of Five Cent Rd. (see map icons).

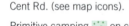 Primitive camping on county forest lands. Camping is not allowed in the immediate vicinity of the former ATV shelter north of Five Cent Rd.

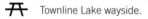 Townline Lake wayside.

 At a former ATV shelter north of Five Cent Rd. (see map icons) and the Townline Lake wayside.

 Dogs should be leashed (8-ft max) and under control at all times.

 Portions overlap roads, ATV and snowmobile trails and gravel or dirt logging roads.

TRAIL ACCESS AND PARKING

First Lake Rd. Western Trail Access: From Merrill at the intersection of I-39/USH-51 and STH-64, take STH-64 east 0.3 mi. At STH-17 turn left and go northeast for 21.9 mi. At First Lake Rd. turn left and go north then west 1.5 mi to the parking area on the north side of First Lake Rd. just before the intersection of First Lake Rd., Parrish Rd. and Fish Lake Rd.

CTH-T: From Antigo, at the intersection of USH-45/STH-47 and STH-64, take USH-45/47 north 16.6 mi to Summit Lake. At CTH-T turn left and go west 5.2 mi to the easternmost Townline Lake wayside parking area.

Additional Parking: Pine Rd. (Prairie River SFA) 0.1-mile south of where IAT departs Pine Rd.

THE HIKE

This segment is the oldest in the county. It was named after the town of Parrish, in the northwestern corner of Langlade County, and the Parrish End Moraine, a belt of moraine hills of boulders, sand and gravel deposited by a massive ice sheet over 10,000 years ago. The segment traverses the Parrish End Moraine, winding its way southeast through the typical hilly, hummocky terrain. The wetlands are so extensive that the Trail layout winds through the landscape to take advantage of beaver dams and narrow, high ridges. The segment is notable for the extent of evergreen forest (spruce, pine, fir, balsam, etc.) traversed by the route.

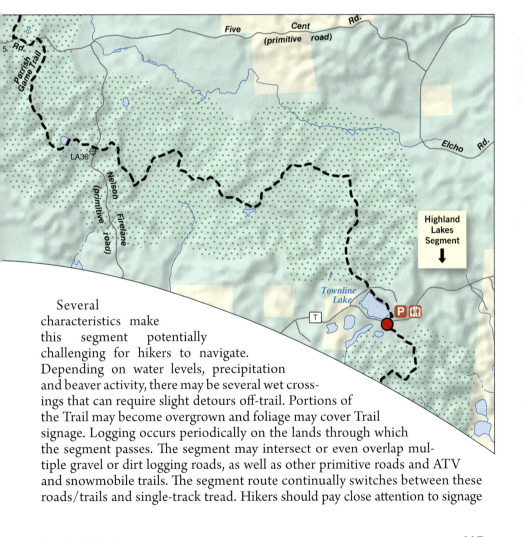

Several characteristics make this segment potentially challenging for hikers to navigate. Depending on water levels, precipitation and beaver activity, there may be several wet crossings that can require slight detours off-trail. Portions of the Trail may become overgrown and foliage may cover Trail signage. Logging occurs periodically on the lands through which the segment passes. The segment may intersect or even overlap multiple gravel or dirt logging roads, as well as other primitive roads and ATV and snowmobile trails. The segment route continually switches between these roads/trails and single-track tread. Hikers should pay close attention to signage

Langlade County

and navigate carefully through intersections. *Note: The logging roads between Pine Road and Townline Lake are ATV roads and are not maintained for general vehicular traffic. Hikers are strongly advised not to drive motor vehicles on these roads.*

From its starting point at the Lincoln/Langlade county line on First Lake Road, hikers should head east just under 0.2 miles to a point where the segment leaves the road (**LA31**) on a single-track tread. It briefly heads north then east through forested terrain, passing 1831-foot Baldy Hill and then meanders to where hikers will need to exercise caution when crossing STH-17 and then CTH-H, in short order, as the roads parallel one another at this location. The segment continues southeast over lands that are part of a glacial outwash fan from the Harrison Moraine. *Note: Portions of the segment here cross private and state lands where primitive camping is not permitted.*

After skirting south and eastward along a pine plantation, the segment emerges onto Pine Road, follows the road south for a short distance and then continues southeast to a crossing (river ford) of the Prairie River (**LA19**), which has a fairly firm bottom with water levels typically below the knees. With rocks and vegetation on the river bed, hikers may wish to use footwear appropriate for the crossing. There is an old building foundation near the river ford where hikers can sit to rest or change footwear.

A little more than a mile east of the river the segment reaches a small wooden shelter (**LA18**) in a grassy opening along a logging road. Much of the next portion of the segment traverses high-relief hummocky topography. The segment continues east and then bends south to its intersection (**LA35**) with primitive Five Cent Road. About 0.9 miles from the small wooden shelter, the Trail intersects a logging road. Hikers can follow this road south for 0.3 miles to reach a former ATV shelter with drinking water and pit toilets. The segment continues east and then bends south to its intersection with primitive Five Cent Road. Hikers can also head west from here 0.3 miles along Five Cent Road, then north on a logging road 0.2 miles to reach the ATV shelter.

Upon reaching Five Cent Road hikers should turn left and follow the road east for a short distance, less than 0.2 miles, before departing from the road to head south for less than a mile down the primitive Parrish Game Trail Fire Lane. The segment then departs from the Parrish Game Trail Fire Lane and heads east, soon reaching a nice grove of hemlocks along a small lake.

The segment crosses (**LA36**) Nelson Firelane and eventually joins the Parrish snowmobile and ATV trail for a short distance. Hikers here should be alert to motorized traffic. The segment continues east, passing large wetlands and through logged clear-cut areas. At one time, the segment traversed at least two active beaver dams. Reroutes were constructed over the years because the beavers' persistence in dam building caused flooding of the segment. The footbridge that hikers cross a mile north of the segment's terminus on CTH-T replaced one beaver dam.

The segment follows the northeast edge of scenic Townline Lake along the base of a hill through a stand of large hemlock. Townline Lake is one of two trout lakes in the county and loons can be seen here in season. Remains of a stone bench, fire pit and stairs built by the Civilian Conservation Corps in the 1930s are located along the Trail just before the picnic area. They are heavily overgrown and easily missed. The segment ends at the easternmost Townline Lake day-use picnic area on CTH-T, which features several picnic tables, grills, a fire ring and a privy about 50 yards up the Trail into the woods. Swimming is available nearby at the boat landing.

AREA SERVICES

Parrish: Restaurant (tavern). From the STH-17 Trail access go north 0.1 mi.

Rhinelander: Restaurant, grocery store, convenience store, general shopping, lodging, camping, library, medical service. From the STH-17 Trail access go north 15.5 mi. Area info available from the Rhinelander Chamber of Commerce (715-365-7464, explorerhinelander.com).

Gleason: See Harrison Hills Segment, p. 108. From the STH-17 Trail access go south 10.5 mi.

Merrill: See Turtle Rock Segment and Grandfather Falls Segment, p. 101. From STH-17 Trail access go south ~25 mi. Also see Trail Access and Parking directions, above.

Antigo: See Highland Lakes Segment, p. 120. From the CTH-T Trail access go east then south 21.7 mi. Also see Trail Access and Parking directions, above.

Winter solitude along the Highland Lakes Segment.

Highland Lakes Segment (Atlas Maps 32f, 33f; Databook pages 32–33)

SNAPSHOT

12.8 miles (8.3 IAT, 4.6 CR): CTH-T to CTH-B at snowmobile trail (old railroad grade).

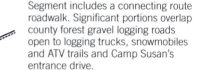 This segment is named for the abundance of lakes located in the area that serve as the headwaters for the Hunting, Eau Claire and Prairie rivers and features the Parrish Terminal Moraine.

 From the West Branch of the Eau Claire River (**LA16**), Deep Wood, Alga, Susan and Alta lakes.

 At Townline Lake wayside and Summit Lake Park on USH-45 (see Area Services).

 Primitive camping on county forest lands.

 Portion of segment crossing private land between CTH-B and USH-45/STH-47 is closed during gun deer season.

 Dogs should be leashed (8-ft max) and under control at all times.

Segment includes a connecting route roadwalk. Significant portions overlap county forest gravel logging roads open to logging trucks, snowmobiles and ATV trails and Camp Susan's entrance drive.

 Camp Susan's nature trail.

 Portions of this segment along Camp Susan's entrance drive may be suitable for those using wheelchairs or similar devices.

TRAIL ACCESS AND PARKING

CTH-T: From Antigo, at the intersection of USH-45/STH-47 and STH-64, take USH-45/47 north 16.6 mi to Summit Lake. At CTH-T turn left and go west 5.2 mi to the Townline Lake wayside and parking area.

CTH-B: From the north side of Antigo, at the intersection of USH-45/STH-47 with STH-64, take USH-45/STH-47 north 12.1 mi. At Koepenick Rd. turn left (CTH-J turns to the right) and go west 0.8 mi. At CTH-B turn right and go north 1.0 mi to a snowmobile crossing and the Trail access. No parking. Instead, park roadside along CTH-B at Camp Susan's gated entrance drive, 0.1 mi north on CTH-B. Parking permitted on the side of the access road. Do not block the gate!

Additional Parking: (i) Kleever Rd. (Sucker Rd.). Roadside parking. No overnight parking. (ii) Deep Woods Lake wayside located on the west side of Forest Rd. 0.2 mi north of the Trail access. No overnight parking. *Note: The wayside is unsigned and may be difficult to locate driveway entrance.*

THE HIKE

The first portion of the segment, the Trail between CTH-T and the crossing of the West Branch of the Eau Claire River, traverses the Parrish Terminal Moraine's high-relief hummocky topography. East of the river, the segment follows the base of a ridge that is the highest outer moraine ridge anywhere on the entire Ice Age Trail.

As the segment heads south from its starting point on CTH-T hikers will climb a ridge and during leaf-off seasons enjoy a view to the southwest of a large wetland that is a former glacial lake formed behind the Parrish Terminal Moraine. Over thousands of years, the shallow basin filled with soil and organic materials from the surrounding landscape to create the swamp viewed today. Over thousands of years, all lakes eventually become wetlands similar to the swamp seen here. There are a number of intersecting logging roads on this portion of the segment and hikers should watch carefully for blazes and directional arrows.

After 2.6 miles the segment crosses the West Branch of the Eau Claire River (**LA16**). The crossing can be tricky in high water, but rocks in the river can be used as steppingstones when water is low. A dry crossing of the river can be found by heading upriver ~300 yards, crossing over the river on a culvert and returning to the Trail by heading southwest on a logging road. The trek upstream to the dry crossing may be difficult requiring hikers to bushwhack through thick underbrush.

Just beyond the river crossing, the segment reaches a former rail line junction where five fire lanes or logging roads meet, known as "Five Points" (**LA15**). Eastbound hikers should follow the distinct logging road headed southeast. This is the second lane/road to the left or clockwise. Westbound hikers should follow the logging road headed northwest. Be careful not to follow ATV trail signs. A short side trip on the logging road headed northeast off the main route offers a view of the West Branch of the Eau Claire River dissecting the Parrish Terminal Moraine. Massive volumes of glacial meltwater now represented by the tame West Branch made the cut through the moraine.

From Five Points, the segment continues southeast through a mix of county forest and private land along an unimproved forest lane. Just past a second gate, a logging road intersects from the right; bear left to stay on the Trail. The segment soon reaches the west end of Kleever Road.

To reach the next portion of Trail on the segment, hikers should follow a 4.6-mile connecting route: turn left on Kleever Road and head east for 0.5 miles; turn left and go north and east on Forest Road 4.1 miles to the Trail access (**LA30**) on the right. Along the way, hikers will pass Bogus Swamp, a unique 870-acre wetlands complex that includes a variety of northern wetland types, none of which are swamp. Bogus Swamp, a large kettle filled with peat, is a State Natural Area and home to several rare plants, birds and butterflies.

Departing Forest Road, the segment heads east 250 feet on a wide logging road and makes a sharp right turn at an intersection (**LA11**) with another logging road. After another 100 feet, the segment makes a sharp left turn onto a wide track forest road and generally heads southeast through the woods. Hikers will soon see Alga Lake to the south.

Shortly after, the segment makes another sharp left turn onto a single-track tread to connect with Camp Susan's nature trails network with its many informational/educational signs. On this scenic part of the segment, hikers follow a rolling ridge that divides the area's lakes and wetlands and highlights elevated views of Lake Susan through white birch and pine forests. The ridge was formed from rocky material that sloughed off the ice masses that formed the area kettle lakes.

The segment leaves the footpath (**LA10**) and drops down to connect with Camp Susan's entrance drive and continues east on the drive for 1.8 miles through high-relief hummocky topography with erratics and some large conifers as it makes its way to CTH-B. There is a fine view of Alta Lake as the Trail skirts the north edge of a peat bog along the way. At CTH-B hikers should proceed south along the west side of CTH-B ~300 yards to the segment's terminus where a snowmobile trail crosses the road.

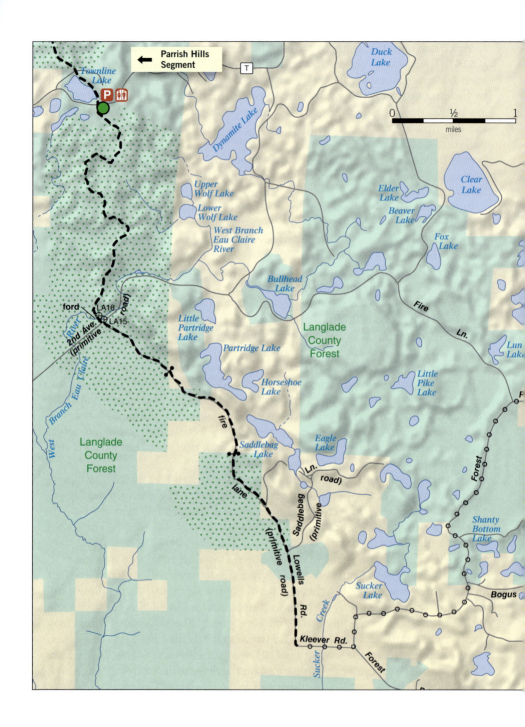

AREA SERVICES

Local Area: Restaurant, lodging. Lodging at Koeppel's Cottages on Deep Wood Lake near Forest Rd. Trail access (715-350-2570). Overnight lodging available to hikers if there are vacant cottages.

Summit Lake: Restaurant, convenience store. From the Camp Susan entrance road and CTH-B, take CTH-B north for 2.5 mi. Summit Lake Park (antigochamber.com) on the west side of USH-45 has swimming beach, picnic and playground area and pit toilets.

Elcho: Restaurant, grocery store, convenience store, medical service. From the Camp Susan entrance road and CTH-B, take CTH-B and USH-45/STH-47 north for 6.5 mi.

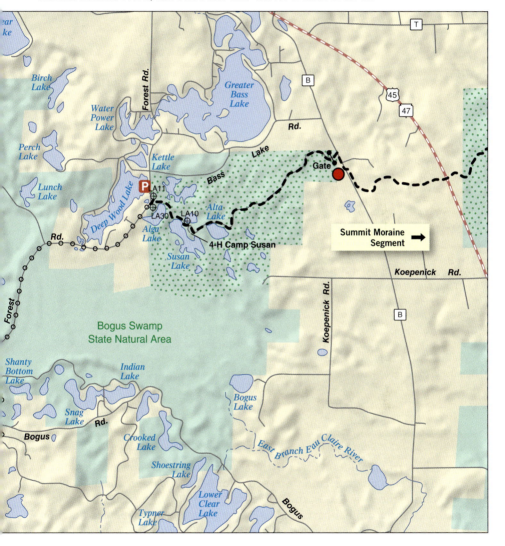

Veterans Memorial Park: Camping. See Summit Moraine Segment, p. 124. From CTH-B Trail access, go south 1.0 mi. At Koepenick Rd. (becomes CTH-J), go east 3.3 mi. At Park Rd. go south 0.2 mi to park entrance.

Antigo: See Summit Moraine Segment, p. 124. From CTH-B Trail access, go south, east and south ~ 15 mi.

Langlade County

Summit Moraine Segment (Atlas Maps 33f, 34f; Databook pages 33–34)

SNAPSHOT

12.2 miles: CTH-B at snowmobile trail (old railroad grade) to CTH-A

 Traveling near the outer edge of the Summit Moraine, this varied segment highlights the Jack Lake Ski Trails, Veterans Memorial Park and several scenic and remote lakes.

At Veterans Memorial Park. Portable toilet also available near the Jack Lake Ski Trails shelter.

From Game Lake, Upper Ventor Lake and several other lakes and ponds in the area.

 Primitive camping on county forest lakes , walk-in site on Game Lake and a Dispersed Camping Area on Upper Ventor Lake.

 Portion of segment crossing private land between CTH-B and USH-45/STH-47 is closed during gun deer season.

 Dogs should be leashed (8-ft max) and under control at all times.

 Portions overlap roads, Veterans Park campground road, logging/forest roads, snowmobile and ski trails.

 Segment intersects Jack Lake Ski Trails and the Veterans Memorial Park trail network including Game Lake Nature Trail.

TRAIL ACCESS AND PARKING

CTH-B: From the north side of Antigo, at the intersection of USH-45/STH-47 and STH-64, take USH-45/STH-47 north 12.1 mi. At Koepenick Rd. turn left (CTH-J turns to the right) and go west 0.8 mi. At CTH-B turn right and go north 1.0 mi to a snowmobile crossing and the Trail access. No parking. Instead, park roadside along CTH-B at Camp Susan's gated entrance drive, 0.1 mi north on CTH-B. Parking permitted on the side of the access road. Do not block the gate!

CTH-A: From the north side of Antigo, at the intersection of USH-45/STH-47 with STH-64, take USH-45/STH-47 north 3.5 mi. At CTH-A turn right and go northeast 8.6 mi to the Trail access. NO PARKING. Instead, park at the Peters Marsh Wildlife Area parking areas on the east side of CTH-A.

Additional Parking: (i) Jack Lake Cross-Country Ski Area. From the north side of Antigo at the intersection of USH-45/STH-47 with STH-64, take USH-45/STH-47 north 12.1 mi. At CTH-J turn right and go east 2.1 mi. (ii) Veterans Memorial Park (see Area Services, below). (iii) Pence Lake Rd. at the Trail crossing.

THE HIKE

From its starting point on CTH-B, the segment follows a snowmobile trail up on an old railroad grade and turns south for 0.2 miles. Railroads built in the area during the early 1900s, and active until the 1940s, were used to haul logs from the extensive timber harvest areas to the main line at Koepenick Junction during the county's logging period. These trains also carried men and supplies to the lumber camps. Hikers will pass through areas of yellow birch, tamarack and balsam in lowland bogs/wetlands and paper birch, maple and aspen in second growth hardwood forests which grew after the great white pines were logged. The Trail turns off the railroad grade to the east and travels through forested, relatively flat terrain. This portion of the segment is prone to flooding during wet periods, and water may extend across the segment for several feet. A metal gate and sign mark the segment's approach to busy USH-45/STH-47. Hikers should cross the highway with caution.

Continuing on, the segment heads east through mixed forest, crosses a powerline right-of-way, and then passes through a section of a towering old red pine plantation. Enter the Jack Lake Ski Trails area, where the Trail joins wide ski trails and is relatively flat to rolling. Even with the numerous ski trail intersections, the segment is very well marked and easy to follow. Eventually the segment reaches a cross-country ski trail warming shelter (LA41) with table, chairs and a fireplace. A portable toilet sits next to the shelter. The Trail continues to follow mostly ski trails as it makes its way to the Spychalla Lodge (day use only), a wonderful quaint wood shelter also with table, chairs and a fireplace. The Spychalla Lodge is the trailhead for the Jack Lake Ski Trails. The parking area serves the Ice Age Trail, the ski trails and an ATV/snowmobile trail that crosses the segment here. Beyond the parking area, the Trail continues south on CTH-J (Park Road) for 0.5 miles to the entrance of Veterans Memorial Park.

The segment meanders through Veterans Memorial Park, which includes a main campground, walk-in campsites, beach, showers, water and three cabins along with mountain bike, snowshoe and nature trails. Yellow blazes and signposts easily guide hikers through the campground road onto shared trails and then north and east out of the campground. Just outside of the campground, the segment enters the Langlade County Arboretum, which offers interpretive information on native trees and shrubs. A visit to the arboretum is worth it for those interested in seeing a collection of native plants suitable for landscaping. A marker recognizes Ray Webber, who designed and laid out the arboretum. A former Department of Natural Resources forester, Webber had a personal desire to foster a greater aesthetic appreciation for the natural landscape.

Leaving the arboretum, the trail runs alongside a small bog lake and hemlock grove as it nears Game Lake and soon intersects with the Game Lake Nature Trail. Bearing left, the Trail becomes more glaciated, twisty and hilly. A sharp esker leads the segment up along the north side of Game Lake dividing it from a massive bog marsh. The segment intersects (LA42) a short spur trail that leads to a walk-in campsite. The site has a fire ring, privy, two picnic tables and room for four tents.

There are several lakes in the area but Game Lake is one of four lakes (along with High, Low and Jack) reported to be named by card-playing loggers. Look for sign of beaver feeding, lodges and a floating bog that migrates over the surface of the lake depending on prevailing wind direction. A "bog-walk" structure (LA37) crosses at the east end of the lake and can be submerged at times of high water. Watch for birds, bog laurel, leatherleaf, Labrador tea, pitcher plants and other unique wetland flora and fauna. Should high water prevent crossing the bog-walk, hikers can take the Game Lake Nature Trail, which circles Game Lake on the south side and rejoins the Ice Age Trail just past the bog-walk.

At the junction point with the Game Lake Nature Trail, on the southeast end of Game Lake, the segment turns left and climbs a steep hill in a southeasterly direction. The segment turns, twists and climbs up and down before reaching a Leopold bench (LA7) at the south end of Narrow Neck Pond. From here the segment follows a mix of

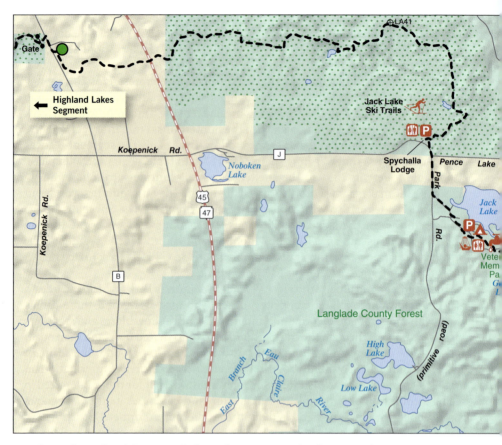

wide-track tread and forest roads through mature stands of aspen and younger age managed forest before reaching Pence Lake Road.

East of Pence Lake Road, the segment winds through hummocky topography across skillfully constructed tread. Mobile Skills Crew volunteers completed several projects along this portion of trail including two boardwalks, sustainable tread and stone steps. There is a variety of narrow footpaths and wide forest roads as the segment makes its way through multi-aged mixed forest. Look for exposed multicolored glacial drift stones and erratics, along with grouse and wild turkey coveys, woodcock, deer, bear and wolves. There are several wildlife openings along the trail maintained by the Wisconsin Department of Natural Resources as a wildlife management measure. Swallowtail and mourning cloak butterflies frequent these sunny areas filled with milkweed, blue beebalm, butterfly weed and blue aster.

Shortly after leaving Pence Lake Road, the segment reaches a scenic unnamed lake with a bench overlooking it. The Trail continues mostly on forest roads in rolling terrain and eventually follows a narrow footpath up a hill on a series of wonderfully crafted stone steps. Here the segment travels near the outer edge of the Summit Moraine. Continuing on, the segment reaches Upper Ventor Lake and soon passes a Dispersed Camping Area (DCA) (**LA38**) for long-distance, multiday hikers in a beautiful hemlock stand. A bench sits near the shore of Upper Ventor Lake. The segment continues south passing a large white pine (**LA39**) and then skirts the edge of private property along Ventor Lake before reaching CTH-A. The Trail parallels CTH-A southwest, crosses a private driveway, ducks north toward Ventor Lake, then back out to the segment's endpoint and gate at CTH-A.

Mobile Skills Crew project site, 2018

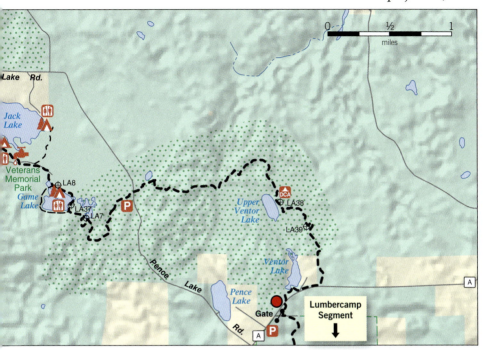

Summit Lake: See Highland Lakes Segment, p. 120. From the USH-45/STH-47 Trail access go north 2.5 mi.

Elcho: See Highland Lakes Segment, p. 120. From the USH-45/STH-47 Trail access go north ~7 mi. Also see Trail Access and Parking directions, above.

Antigo: Restaurant, grocery store, convenience store, general shopping, lodging, camping, library, medical service. From the USH-45/STH-47 Trail crossing go south 13.0 mi on USH-45/STH-47. Most services on USH-45/STH-47 and STH-64. INN Style lodging at Spychalla Family Farm House (715-623-5773, airbnb.com/rooms/38451928). Camping at Antigo Lake RV Park and Campground (715-623-3633, antigochamber.com). Area info available from the Antigo Chamber of Commerce (888-526-4523, antigochamber.com).

Veterans Memorial Park (Jack Lake Campground): Camping. On Trail. (N8375 Park Rd., Deerbrook, 715-623-6214, jacklakecampground.com). The County Park has a campground, walk-in campsites, three rental cabins, showers, beach, hiking, mountain biking and snowshoe trails. From the north side of Antigo at the intersection of USH-45/STH-47 with STH-64, take USH-45/STH-47 north 12.1 mi to CTH-J. At CTH-J turn right and continue east then south 2.6 mi as CTH-J becomes Park Rd. to the park's entrance.

Lumbercamp Segment (Atlas Maps 34f, 35f; Databook pages 34–35)

SNAPSHOT

12.0 miles: CTH-A to STH-52

  This segment highlights the historic Norem Lumber Camp and the dramatic Baker Lake basin.

- No reliable sources of water.
- Primitive camping on county forest lands and "Hillbilly Hilton" shelter at the Norem Lumber Camp site.
- Dogs should be leashed (8-ft max) and under control at all times. By law, dogs **must** be leashed April 15 to July 31 in the State Wildlife Area.
-   A significant portion of the segment overlaps snowmobile trails and logging/forest roads.
- Trails in the Peters Marsh State Wildlife Area.

TRAIL ACCESS AND PARKING

CTH-A: From the north side of Antigo, at the intersection of USH-45/STH-47 with STH-64, take USH-45/STH-47 north 3.5 mi. At CTH-A turn right and go northeast 8.6 mi to the Trail access. NO PARKING. Instead, park at the Peters Marsh Wildlife Area parking area 0.1 mi south on the east side of CTH-A.

STH-52: From the north side of Antigo, at the intersection of USH45/STH-47 with STH-64, take STH-64 east 1.6 mi. At STH-52 turn left and go northeast 15.0 mi. At the Kettlebowl Ski Area turn right and park along the road between the gate for Kettlebowl Ski Area and STH-52. Please park vehicles on the side of the access road to allow authorized traffic beyond the gate.

Additional Parking: (i) Hill Rd. Peters Marsh Wildlife Area parking area. A logging road leads 0.3 mi to the Trail. (ii) CTH-S parking area.

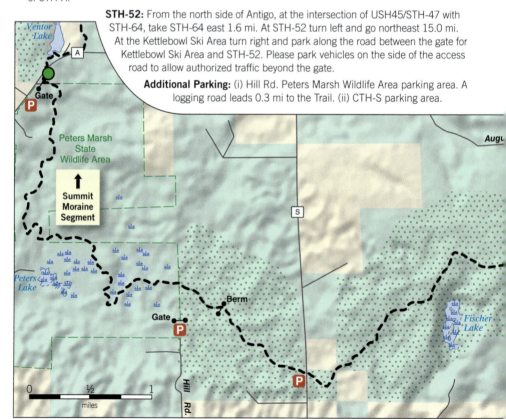

THE HIKE

Heading east from the CTH-A Trail access, the western end of the segment passes through a portion of the 1,687-acre Peters Marsh State Wildlife Area. The wildlife area has a network of other hiking trails and is made up of a variety of habitats home to numerous wildlife species. Spring wildflowers include spring beauty, Dutchman's breeches, yellow trout lily, trillium, hepatica and bloodroot. All lakes shown on the map, except Baker Lake, are subject to seasonal groundwater fluctuations and hikers should not regard them as a dependable water source as they are known to go dry. Baker Lake has significant amounts of sediment in the water.

East of CTH-S the segment transitions from the more open landscape of the Peters Marsh State Wildlife Area to more forested land cover. For most of the remainder of the segment the route travels across the relatively flat surface of a pitted outwash plain deposited by streams flowing away from the Summit Lake Moraine. Logging can occur along this portion of the segment and there are several intersecting logging roads; hikers should pay close attention to signage in this area as some of the intersections can be confusing.

Just west of primitive Otto Mauk Firelane/Norem Camp Road, in a trailside clearing, are the remains of Norem Lumber Camp (**LA5**). From the 1920s until 1938, the camp contained several log structures, including a bunkhouse, hayshed, stable, community kitchen and mess hall. All that remain are the root cellar and several log foundations. The root cellar has been renovated and is affectionately called the "Hillbilly Hilton." Inside are sleeping platforms, a small table and shelving to welcome hikers out of the elements. Hikers who use the shelter should practice responsible stewardship by leaving the "Hilton" in as good condition or better than they found it. *Note: This structure is not sponsored or maintained by the Langlade County Chapter.*

Langlade County

The segment continues east from the primitive road and, a short distance west of Baker Lake, enters the high-relief hummocky topography representing the front of the Summit Lake Moraine. This portion of the segment is well marked but is rocky and can be a challenging hike. As the Trail reaches the far western end of Baker Lake, hikers will notice a wooden boat slide used for getting small boats and canoes down to the water. As hikers make their way through the Baker Lake basin toward the segment's endpoint on STH-52 they will see a dramatic exposure of massive boulders deposited by the ice on the north slope of the Summit Lake Moraine.

AREA SERVICES

Veterans Memorial Park: See Summit Moraine Segment, p. 124. From the CTH-A Trail access go north and west ~7 mi.

Antigo: See Highland Lakes Segment, p. 120. From the STH-52 Trail access go south and west ~17 mi. Also see Trail Access and Parking directions, above.

The "Hillbilly Hilton," a former logging camp root cellar on the Lumbercamp Segment

Kettlebowl Segment (Atlas Maps 35f, 36f; Databook page 35)

SNAPSHOT

9.9 miles: STH-52 to Oak Rd./Sherry Rd.

This rugged and isolated segment winds through hilly terrain dotted with huge granite erratics and kettles and has the most topographical relief of all segments in Langlade County.

 No reliable sources of water.

 Primitive camping on county forest lands.

 At the Kettlebowl Ski Area.

 Dogs should be leashed (8-ft max) and under control at all times.

 Portions overlap cross-country ski trails. A significant portion overlaps logging/forest roads; some of these are frequently used by ATVs and snowmobiles.

 Spur trails to the Big Stone Hole, Kent Hill and Oak Rd./Sherry Rd. parking area.

TRAIL ACCESS AND PARKING

STH-52: From the north side of Antigo, at the intersection of USH45/STH-47 with STH-64, take STH-64 east 1.6 mi. At STH-52 turn left and go northeast 15.0 mi. At the Kettlebowl Ski Area turn right and park along the road between the gate for Kettlebowl Ski Area and STH-52. Please park vehicles on the side of the access road to allow authorized traffic beyond the gate.

Oak Rd./Sherry Rd.: From the north side of Antigo, at the intersection of USH-45/STH-47 with STH-64, take STH-64 east 9.0 mi. At Price-Polar Rd. turn left and go north 1.6 mi. At Oak Rd. turn right and go east 1.5 mi to where Sherry Rd. and Oak Rd. join. Continue on Oak Rd./Sherry Rd. east and south for 0.9 mi to the Trail access on the east side of the road. No parking. Instead, park at the parking area near Evergreen Cemetery 0.1 mi north of the Sherry Rd. Trail access. (Park respectfully.) Do not park vehicles on the lanes within the cemetery. Overnight parking permitted.

Additional Parking: ATV parking area located on Sherry Road 0.9 mi southeast of the Sherry Rd. Trail access.

THE HIKE

The Kettlebowl Segment generally follows a variety of logging and forest roads in various conditions that are used by and signed for multiple users, including Ice Age Trail hikers, snowmobilers, skiers and ATV users. There are numerous intersections with logging and forest roads. Segment signage can be obscured during growing seasons and can be sparse in some areas. Hikers should pay careful attention to Ice Age Trail signage, which can consist of yellow blazes, black block arrows on yellow signs and yellow and black signs with the Ice Age Trail logo. Hikers should carry maps and a compass and/or a GPS unit.

From its starting point on STH-52 the segment follows the Kettlebowl Ski Area access road southeast, passing a minimally maintained pit toilet, to the base of the ski slopes. Kettlebowl Ski Area is not actually located in a kettle; the ski runs are located on the north slope of the recessional Summit Lake Moraine. The segment departs from the ski area at a yellow marker near the bottom of the southernmost ski run (**LA25**).

The segment highlights deep "frost pockets," a local expression for depressions with steep sloping sides. In some cases, they may represent "kettles," "kettle holes" or "kettlebowls" formed by remnants of huge blocks of ice that broke from the ice sheet. The timber or tree line observed in the frost pockets is "inverted" or the reverse of the same phenomenon seen on many mountaintops. Because heavier, cooler air prevails at the lower elevations in the pocket, the lower levels are usually devoid of woody vegetation. These areas were more pronounced in years past. However, with warmer year-round temperatures, woody species have started to populate the once distinctive grassy bottoms. One such frost pocket (**LA21**) is found shortly after crossing a primitive private road just off the Trail.

The area south of this private road is lined with large rocks, often Wolf River granite, on both sides of the Trail. About one mile south of the frost pocket the segment reaches a short, unmaintained spur trail that leads to "Big Stone Hole" (**LA3**), a large kettle loaded with granite erratics; use caution. Less than a mile south of the intersection with the spur trail to the Big Stone Hole, the segment reaches an intersection (**LA22**) with a logging lane marked by a yellow metal post without a sign that leads 0.8 miles east to Kent Hill, the highest point in Langlade County at 1,903

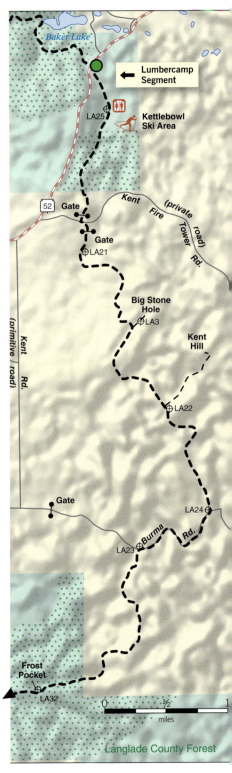

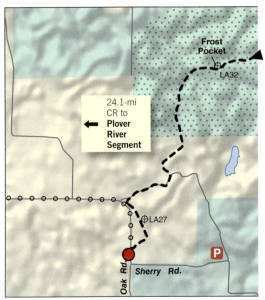

feet above sea level. It is just 50 feet below Timm's Hill, the state's highest point, and 45 feet lower than the peak at Rib Mountain. The vista from Kent Hill is tremendous during leaf-off. Views to the southwest include distant Rib Mountain. Visible to the northeast, across the Wolf River valley, are McCaslin and Thunder mountains in Oconto and Marinette counties.

As the segment continues south and west it makes its way through the high-relief hummocky topography of the terminal Parrish Moraine, which in this area runs roughly parallel with the recessional Summit Lake Moraine. The segment reaches primitive Burma Road (**LA24**) in an active logging and ATV area. The segment bends west and follows Burma Road for approximately one mile before departing from the road (**LA23**) and continuing south.

Portions of the segment south of Burma Road are rough and can be overgrown due to a recent clear-cut. An early successional forest of young aspen, birch and cherry trees, as well as grasses, shrubs and other vegetation have started to recolonize the area, taking advantage of the lack of forest canopy. Deer, bear, grouse, turkey and porcupines inhabit the area. The segment skirts another frost pocket (**LA32**) shortly before it turns south and begins to make its way to Oak Road/Sherry Road. As the segment approaches Oak Road/Sherry Road, it sharply turns south to follow a former railroad grade on the east side of Oak Road/Sherry Road. Hikers may notice some railroad ties underfoot. Besides the timber and lumber camp supplies this railroad grade carried, stock cars of sheep were also hauled over it in the 1920s and early 1930s. On the east side of the railroad grade in a clearing, about 0.2 miles south of where the Trail turned south, is the foundation of a huge barn (**LA27**), formerly part of a large sheep ranch owned by Endre Norem, one of the area's early settlers. As the segment approaches Oak Road/Sherry Road, it turns sharply south to follow a former railroad grade on the east side of Oak Road/Sherry Road.

AREA SERVICES

Antigo: See Highland Lakes Segment, p. 120. From the STH-52 Trail access go south and west ~17 mi or from the Oak Rd./Sherry Rd. Trail access go west and south ~12 mi. Also see Trail Access and Parking directions, above.

Kettlebowl Ski Area: On Trail.

Polar: Restaurant. From the Oak Rd./Sherry Rd. Trail access go east and south 4.5 mi. Mueller Lake Town Park at Polar Rd. and STH-64 has swimming beach and picnic area.

> *It's a dark 3:30 a.m. We are heading toward an Ice Age Trail segment, one of 37 such trips. For four-plus hours, filling our senses with staticky radio noise, speeding traffic and rushing sights and sounds. Later, ten minutes into the woods, we encounter another world entirely, one of blissful natural marvels, soft hums and twitters, and being on nature's relaxed timeline.*
>
> JANE AND DAVID LECOUNT, ICE AGE TRAIL THOUSAND-MILERS

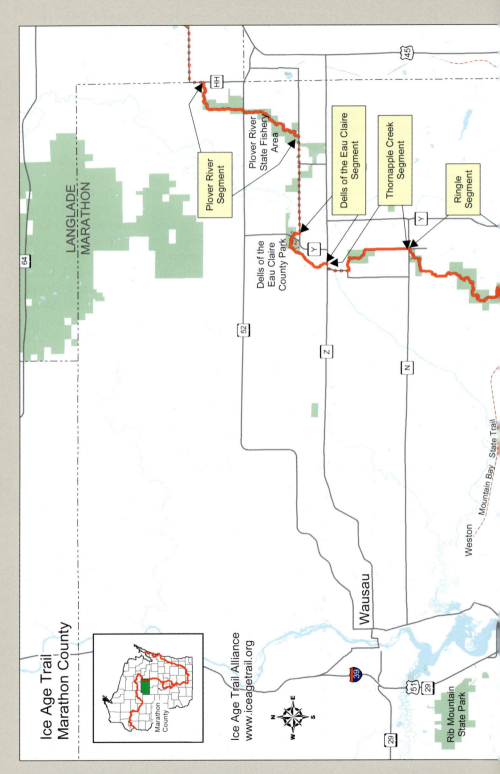

Marathon County

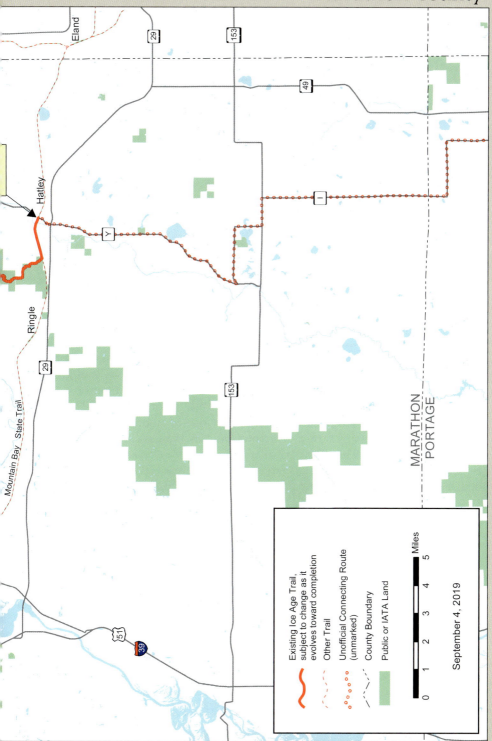

Marathon County

Atlas Maps 39f–44f; Databook pages 37–40
Total miles: 42.7 (Trail 20.0; Connecting Route 22.8)

The glacial deposits in Marathon County vary in age and time periods. The eastern part of the county was the only portion covered by the Green Bay Lobe, where it abutted the Langlade Lobe. Glacial deposits in central and western Marathon County are from an earlier glaciation. The Ice Age Trail follows the Hancock Moraine, an end moraine of the Green Bay Lobe, for several miles north of the town of Ringle, before dipping into the previously glaciated landscape.

The main feature of the Trail west of the moraine is its walk along the Eau Claire River (French for "clear water") and the Dells of the Eau Claire. The Dells of the Eau Claire are metamorphic rock bluffs carved when ice from the Green Bay and Langlade lobes thawed and the rush of a tremendous amount of meltwater found a fault in the bedrock. The mylonite bedrock is dated at about 1.8 billion years old and is similar in strength to granite, although it looks more like sandstone. This oldest type of exposed bedrock along the Ice Age Trail is also found along the Wisconsin River's Grandfather Falls in Lincoln County.

Today, the Dells of the Eau Claire County Park features the 65-foot-deep gorge with water cascading into a series of pools formed among the rock ledges. The county park contains several structures built by the Civilian Conservation Corps (CCC) in the 1930s. The park offers a number of individual camping sites as well as a group camping site. Dispersed Camping Areas (DCAs) have been established on the Ringle Segment and at the Rice Lake Preserve, south of Hatley.

CHAPTER INFORMATION

The Central Moraines Chapter formed in the early 1970s. Chapter volunteers built the first six miles of Ice Age Trail in the county, now known as the Ringle Segment, in 1973. Three years later, volunteers built six more miles of what are now the Thornapple Creek and Dells of the Eau Claire segments. The momentum of these projects led to numerous Mobile Skills Crew (MSC) events dedicated to building the Plover River Segment. Following on the heels of these successes, the chapter has been instrumental in the reroute of the Ringle Segment, away from multiuse trails and onto land dedicated to the Ice Age Trail. MSC volunteers have committed many hours and significant trailbuilding efforts to bring this "Landscape Crossroads" to fruition. The chapter promotes use of the Trail for recreation and education. It hosts several trail improvement days and hikes throughout the year, including a snowshoe hike, a spring wildflower hike, and a fall color hike.

COUNTY INFORMATION
Wausau/Central Wisconsin Convention & Visitors Bureau: 888-948-4748 or 715-355-8788, visitwausau.com

A line of boulders awaits the next adventerous rock hopper on the Plover River Segment.

Plover River Segment (Atlas Map 39f; Databook page 38)

SNAPSHOT

5.9 miles: CTH-HH to Sportsman Dr.

 This beautiful segment highlights a dramatic traverse of the terminal moraine and the peaceful Plover River.

From the Plover River.

One ColdCache site on segment.

 Dogs should be leashed (8-ft max) and under control at all times.

 A spur trail to a parking area on CTH-HH and a blue-blazed spur trail to a parking area on Hatchery Rd.

TRAIL ACCESS AND PARKING

CTH-HH: *From Wausau* on US-51 exit onto STH-52 and go east ~26 mi. At CTH-HH turn left and go north 1.5 mi to the Trail access on the west side of the road. Park at the Ice Age Trail parking area 0.1 mi south on CTH-HH on the west side of the road. A blue-blazed spur trail leads to the Ice Age Trail. *From Antigo* at the intersection of USH-45/STH-47 and STH-52/STH-64, take USH-45/STH-47/STH-52 south 11.0 mi. Continue on STH-52 west for 1.3 mi. At CTH-HH turn right and go 1.5 mi to the Trail access on the west side of the road. Park at the Ice Age Trail parking area 0.1 mi south on CTH-HH on the west side of the road. A blue-blazed spur trail leads to the Ice Age Trail.

Sportsman Dr.: From Wausau take STH-29 east to Exit 185 for Hatley/CTH-Y. Take CTH-Y north 7.5 mi. At CTH-Z turn right and go east 2.0 mi. At North Pole Rd. turn left and go north 1.0 mi. At Sportsman Dr. turn right and go east 1.0 mi to the parking area on the north side of the road.

Additional Parking: (i) STH-52: From Wausau on US-51 exit onto STH-52 and go east ~25 mi to the parking area on north side of highway at the STH-52 and Hatchery Rd. intersection. (ii) Hatchery Rd.: From the STH-52 and Hatchery Rd. intersection, go south on Hatchery Rd. 0.7 mi to the DNR parking area at the junction with Village Rd. A blue-blazed spur trail leads 0.1 mi to the Ice Age Trail (**MR12**).

THE HIKE

The Plover River State Fishery Area includes hardwood and cedar forests, lowlands and spring ponds along the Plover River, a Class I, high-quality trout stream that has a naturally sustaining trout population.

From the CTH-HH Trail access head west across rolling, forested hills lined by mossy boulders and bright green ferns. Watch for wetlands, a variety of wildflowers, deep kettles, a stone hole and a boulder train as you cross the terminal moraine. Over 1,000 feet of volunteer-built boardwalk will keep boots high and dry through wetlands just north of STH-52. On the north section of boardwalk there is a welcoming observation deck with comfortable benches (**MR14**).

There is a good line of vision at the STH-52 crossing, but it still requires caution. Just south of STH-52, hikers will reach a stretch of puncheon and native timber bridge before continuing southward through a pine forest on the west side of the Plover River. Near the river, the trail is rock strewn and swampy. Footing can be treacherous with rocks and roots in the path. After about one-third of a mile, hikers will reach a crossing of the river and can choose to either have their feet cooled by the river's waters or step across on boulders rising above the surface. Listen for the symphony of a "babbling brook" while seated on a nearby bench as the peaceful Plover River tumbles through the rocks at this crossing.

Now on the east side of the river, the segment continues southward through

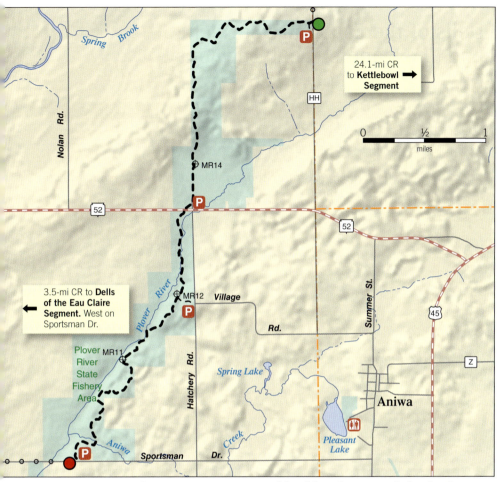

a riparian zone. The segment intersects a blue-blazed spur trail that leads east 0.1 miles to the Hatchery Road Trail parking area (**MR12**).

As the segment continues southward, it travels along a ridge through thick stands of balsam fir, northern white cedar and hemlock before returning alongside the rippling waters of the river. The segment traverses an interesting stone-lined glacial wash (**MR11**) and again travels a ridgetop before it transitions to rolling, open grassland. It crosses Aniwa Creek and reaches its endpoint at the Sportsman Drive parking area and informational kiosk.

Mobile Skills Crew project site, 2010, 2011, 2012, 2013

AREA SERVICES

Antigo: See Highland Lakes Segment, p. 120. From the STH-52 Trail access go east then north ~13 mi. Also see Trail Access and Parking directions, above.

Wausau: See Ringle Segment, p. 143. From the STH-52 Trail access go west ~25 mi. Also see Trail Access and Parking directions, above.

Rural Aniwa: Restaurant east of USH-45 and STH-52 intersection.

Birnamwood: Restaurant, lodging. Take Hatchery Rd. south until it becomes CTH-D. Continue south to CTH-N, then turn left (southeast on CTH-N).

Dells of the Eau Claire Segment and Thornapple Creek Segment

(Atlas Maps 40f, 41f; Databook pages 38–39)

SNAPSHOT

Dells of the Eau Claire Segment—2.6 miles: Sportsman Dr. to CTH-Z

Thornapple Creek Segment—4.0 miles (3.0 IAT, 0.9 CR): CTH-Z to CTH-N

 The **Dells of the Eau Claire Segment** shows off one of the most dramatic sites on the entire Ice Age Trail.

One ColdCache site on segment.

At Dells of the Eau Claire County Park.

The portion of the segment between Dells of the Eau Claire County Park and CTH-Z is closed during gun deer season.

Dogs should be leashed (8-ft max) and under control at all times.

From the Eau Claire River.

Dells of the Eau Claire County Park trail network.

 The **Thornapple Creek Segment** crosses a small creek in a quiet, primitive area.

From Thornapple Creek.

Dogs should be leashed (8-ft max) and under control at all times.

Portions of the segment crossing private land between Thornapple Creek Rd. and Gold Dust Rd. are closed for hunting Sept. 1 to Dec. 31.

Segment includes a connecting route roadwalk. Portions overlap gravel Helf Rd. and a snowmobile trail.

TRAIL ACCESS AND PARKING

Sportsman Dr.: From Wausau, take STH-29 east to Exit 185 for Hatley/CTH-Y. Take CTH-Y north 9.5 mi. At Sportsman Dr. (gravel road) turn right and travel east 0.3 mi to the Trail access on the north side of the road. Roadside parking.

CTH-N: From Wausau, take STH-29 east to Exit 185 for Hatley/CTH-Y. Take CTH-Y north 4.5 mi. At CTH-N turn left and go west 1.0 mi. At Helf Rd. turn south for roadside parking. Parking is also available 0.4 mi west in a parking area (**MR8**) on the south side of CTH-N.

Additional Parking: (i) Parking areas in Dells of the Eau Claire County Park. (ii) CTH-Z parking area. (iii) Gold Dust Rd. Roadside parking.

THE HIKE

From the Trail access on Sportsman Drive the **Dells of the Eau Claire Segment** heads north along a mowed path for a quarter mile then bends west near a trail junction where a Dells of the Eau Claire County Park trail continues straight ahead to CTH-Y. Hikers should turn right and cross the Eau Claire River on a walkway above a dam that makes a small lake for the park's campground. Above the dam are the safe swimming and beach area, ample parking, rest rooms and a picnic ground.

After crossing the dam the segment heads west, past the Park Manager's office, on the park's North River Trail. Hikers will find several places to step out on ancient volcanic rock palisades for a closer view and feel of the river's roaring rapids before reaching CTH-Y. Shortly after crossing the road hikers will pass near the county park's main picnic shelter (constructed by the Civilian Conservation Corps [CCC]) and picnic tables scattered beneath large shade trees.

The segment continues westward along the north bank on the bluff high above the river. There are multiple scenic overlooks with stone walls at the edge. The area is quite spectacular in spring and after rainy periods when water levels are up. The cascading river winds through a series of ledges and pools in the mylonite bedrock gorge formed thousands of years ago from the glacial meltwater of the Green Bay Lobe. In addition, potholes up to five feet in diameter are found along the river.

The segment crosses 30 feet above the river on the Dells High Bridge that was built by the CCC in the 1930s and spans 120 feet. South of the bridge hikers will encounter a trail junction; the Ice Age Trail heads southwest along the river while county park trails head south into Dells of the Eau Claire River State Natural Area.

The segment continues southwest along the quiet and peaceful east bank of the river past two benches near the trail that were an Eagle Scout service project and eventually encounters large Sandberg Island, the southern foot of which marks the boundary of the county park. Just south of the park boundary, after a roped area, steps lead down to the river. This is the point at which the Ice Age Trail crosses the 45th parallel (**MR4**) and is considered the halfway point between the North Pole and Equator.

Continuing south, the pine forest along the river gives way to deciduous woods as the segment makes its way to its terminus at CTH-Z.

Mobile Skills Crew project site, 2005

The **Thornapple Creek Segment** starts with a 0.9-mile connecting route west along CTH-Z and then south on Thornapple Creek Road. The segment leaves the road (**MR9**) along a farm field and continues east and south toward the Gold Dust Road and Helf Road intersection. *Note: This rough and rugged stretch is often wet and may be difficult to pass. Hikers may bypass this area—and must bypass it from September 1 to December 31 for hunting seasons—by continuing south on Thornapple Creek Road and then heading east on Gold Dust Road to Helf Road intersection.*

After departing from Thornapple Creek Road and then crossing Thornapple Creek, the segment emerges from a wooded area onto a powerline right-of-way for a short stretch before winding through the wooded area to the west. After crossing the powerline right-of-way again, the Trail reenters the woods to the east on a snowmobile trail and eventually intersects a wide, grassy two-track logging road where the segment turns to the south. When the logging road goes around a gate and intersects Gold Dust Road, it becomes Helf Road and gradually transitions from grassy two-track and the edge of a cultivated field to gravel as it makes its way south. Moderate-size erratics are strewn off the edge of the path among spring-blooming trilliums. When the road reaches a stretch of open farmland, hikers may note a fire tower perched atop a hill just east of the road in the distance. The Trail reaches the segment's endpoint at the intersection of CTH-N and Helf Road.

AREA SERVICES

Dells of the Eau Claire County Park: Camping. On Trail. For information contact Marathon County Park and Recreation Department (715-261-1550; reservations: 715-261-1566).

Wausau: See Ringle Segment, p. 143. From the CTH-N. Trail access go west ~13 mi. Also see Trail Access and Parking directions, above.

Ringle Segment (Atlas Map 41f; Databook page 39)

SNAPSHOT

8.5 miles: CTH-N to Curtis Ave. (CTH-Y)

 This segment traverses the terminal moraine of the Green Bay Lobe and prominently features kames, kettles and erratics.

Note: A reroute is planned between Helf Rd. and Poplar Ln. Check with the Ice Age Trail Alliance (800-227-0046, iceagetrail.org) for details.

At the Hatley Library.

From small streams and ponds and the Plover River.

 At a Dispersed Camping Area north of Poplar Ln. Camping also available at a Dispersed Camping Area on the Rice Lake Preserve (see Area Services).

 Two ColdCache sites on segment.

 Portions of the segment crossing private lands north of Mole Brook Rd. are closed during gun deer season. Hikers will need to use alternative road walks to pass through the area during gun deer season.

Dogs should be leashed (8-ft max) and under control at all times.

 Portions overlap Phoenix St., snowmobile trails, a cross-country ski trail and the multiuse MBST.

 The MBST continues west and east.

 Portions of this segment may be suitable for those using wheelchairs or similar devices.

TRAIL ACCESS AND PARKING

CTH-N: From Wausau, take STH-29 east to Exit 185 for Hatley/CTH-Y. Take CTH-Y north 4.5 mi. At CTH-N turn left and go west 1.0 mi. At Helf Rd. turn south for roadside parking. Parking is also available 0.4 mi west in a parking area (**MR8**) on the south side of CTH-N.

Curtis Ave. (CTH-Y): From Wausau, take STH-29 east to Exit 185 for Hatley/CTH-Y. Take Curtis Ave. (CTH-Y) go north 0.5 mi to the intersection with the Mountain-Bay State Trail (MBST) and Ice Age Trail access. Parking area at the Hatley Branch Library just north of the Trail.

Additional Parking: Poplar Ln. parking area on the north side (just east of Trail crossing) and south side of road.

THE HIKE

From the intersection of CTH-N and Helf Road the segment heads south for approximately 30 yards along Helf Road and then departs the road heading southwest. The Trail passes through beautiful, heavily wooded country with maples, oaks and pines. After 0.5 miles the segment intersects (**MR7**) a blue-blazed spur trail that leads north 0.2 miles to the CTH-N parking area (**MR8**). From this intersection the segment continues south on a mix of single- and wide-track tread and forest roads and eventually reaches a private drive. The segment turns right and follows the drive for 300 feet to the intersection of Mole Brook Road and Phoenix Street.

Upon reaching this intersection, hikers will continue south for 0.3 miles on Phoenix Street, then onto a private driveway for 450 feet. The Trail leaves the driveway to the left at a sign and snakes through the woods, crossing a series of

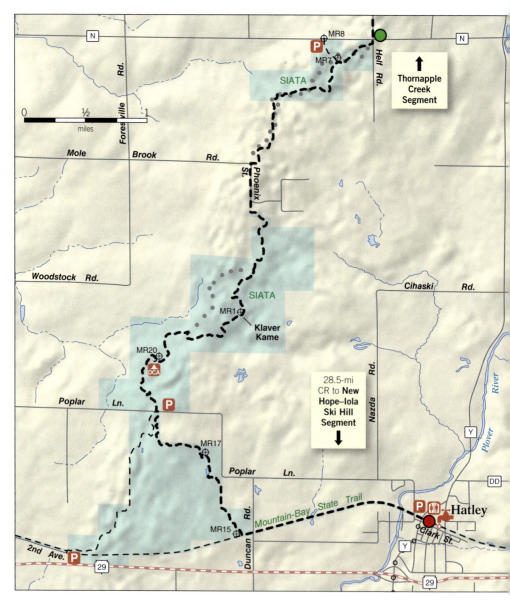

boardwalks and bridges over wet areas and small streams. After 0.8 miles the segment intersects a forest road. For the next 1.0 mile the segment mostly follows forest roads, snowmobile/ski trails and wide-track tread. Be sure to watch for blazes and pointers for the Ice Age Trail at intersections and stay alert for markers where the trail departs from the larger forest roads/snowmobile trails. Soon after intersecting the forest road, the segment passes a large open meadow that is covered in wildflowers and black raspberries in summer and then climbs over Klaver Kame, which features a bench (**MR1**) at the top. Continuing on, the Trail eventually leaves the forest roads/snowmobile trails, turning left onto single-track tread and meandering through the forest. The segment crosses another series of four boardwalks. After crossing the third boardwalk, the Trail quickly intersects (**MR20**) a short blue-blazed spur trail that leads to a Dispersed Camping Area (DCA) for long-distance, multiday hikers. The segment courses up and down through the woods and passes numerous erratics of various sizes on its way to Poplar Lane.

The segment crosses Poplar Lane, jogging slightly to the left, and continues southward through slightly more open forest. The Trail turns toward the east and soon arrives at an impressively large glacial erratic called the Stone Lion (**MR17**). Soon thereafter, hikers will reach a bench overlooking a small, peaceful pond.

After leaving the pond, the Trail emerges from the woods into a clearing and skirts along the edge of the Marathon County landfill, where hikers can see and may hear landfill operations, a stark contrast to the previous woodland tranquility. The segment turns away from the landfill, reenters the woods and makes it way to its intersection with (**MR15**) the 83.4-mile-long Mountain-Bay State Trail (MBST), which occupies the former Chicago and Northwestern Railroad right-of-way between Wausau and Green Bay. Hikers will turn left and head east toward Hatley on the MBST's crushed limestone surface. The segment ends in Hatley at Curtis Avenue (CTH-Y) at the site of an Ice Age Trail/MBST kiosk.

Mobile Skills Crew project site, 2017, 2018, 2019

AREA SERVICES

Mountain-Bay State Trail (MBST): On Trail (715-261-1550, dnr.wi.gov/topic/parks/name/mountainbay).

Ringle: Restaurant. From the Poplar Ln. parking area, go west on Poplar Ln. 1.3 mi, then southwest on CTH-Q 1.2 mi. From the MBST trail intersection go west 3.0 mi.

Hatley: Restaurant, convenience store, library. On Curtis Ave. (CTH-Y) and on State Rd. (STH-29 frontage road).

Dispersed Camping Area (DCA) at IATA's Rice Lake Preserve: Camping for long-distance, multiday hikers. From the intersection of the Mountain-Bay State Trail and Curtis Ave. (CTH-Y), go south on CTH-Y for 4.0 mi.

Pike Lake: Restaurant, lodging. From the intersection of the Mountain-Bay State Trail and Curtis Ave. (CTH-Y), go south on CTH-Y for 5.0 mi, at intersection of CTH-Y and N. South Shore Dr.

Wausau Area: Restaurant, grocery store, convenience store, general shopping, lodging, camping, library, medical service. From the Curtis Ave. (CTH-Y) Trail access, go south 0.5 mi, then take STH-29 west 14.5 mi. Also see Trail Access and Parking directions, above. For area info, contact Wausau/Central Wisconsin Convention & Visitors Bureau (888-948-4748, visitwausau .com).

> *Being novice hikers, hiking the Ice Age Trail was a real learning experience. We learned about proper trail footwear, clothing, equipment, and nutrition. We learned how to navigate to trailheads and about the geology of glacial formations. But most of all, we learned about the incredible people and places of our wonderful state.*
>
> DAVE AND LINDA VOELZ, ICE AGE TRAIL THOUSAND-MILERS

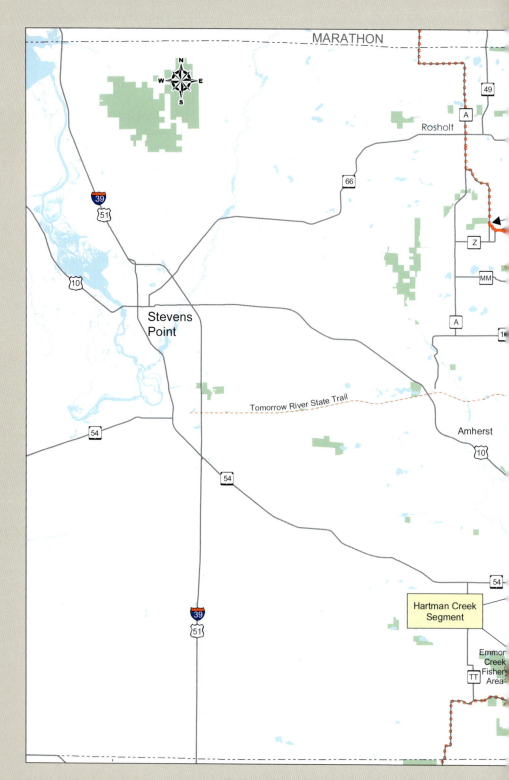

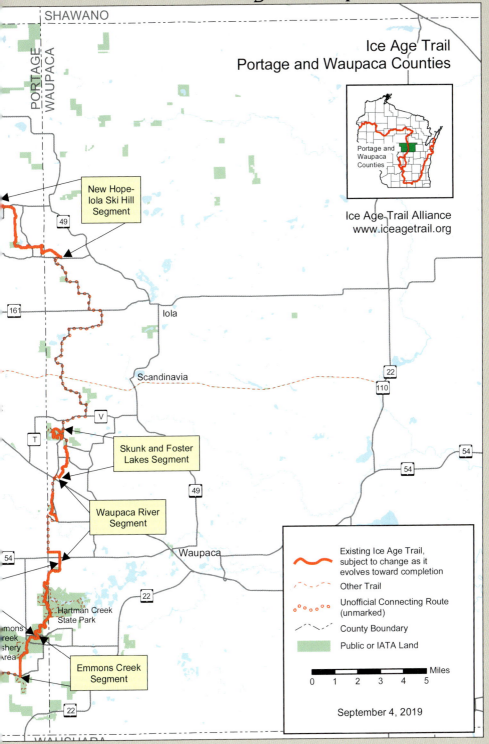

Portage & Waupaca Counties

Atlas Maps 44f–49f; Databook pages 41–45
Total miles: 51.8 (Trail 19.6; Connecting Route 32.2)

Several glacial advances formed the landscape of eastern Portage County and all of Waupaca County. The Green Bay Lobe moved from the east, with its farthest advance extending a few miles east of Stevens Point. Successive glacial advances often stopped short of previous ones, each leaving their own set of moraines. The Ice Age Trail along the county border passes over several Elderon Moraines, deposited approximately 13,000 years ago. These moraines, like several others to the west, are narrow and noncontiguous, broken by channels cut by westward torrents of glacial meltwater and pitted outwash. The meltwater drainageways flushed glacial debris of sand and gravel onto stagnant glacier ice. After the buried ice melted, the deposited glacial debris collapsed onto the underlying ground forming the undulating and irregular landscape of ridged hills and knobs interspersed with steep-sided depressions that later filled and became kettle lakes. The geological area known as the Farmington Drumlins is the largest swarm of drumlins along the entire Ice Age Trail. Miles from the terminal moraine the drumlins were formed beneath a continental glacier through the sculpting of sand, pebbles and other glacial debris. Found in clusters called swarms, drumlins have a distinctive shape that has been described as a teardrop, oval or cigar-shaped.

"Waupaca," a Menominee word for both the county and its river, has been translated as either "pale water" or "tomorrow." These two counties have many plant communities, including oak barrens, prairie and northern hardwood forests. The Ice Age Trail passes through several state fishery areas, state natural areas and Hartman Creek State Park. In addition to camping at Hartman Creek State Park, the Portage County Parks Department offers camping near the Ice Age Trail at Collins and Lake Emily county parks.

CHAPTER INFORMATION

The Portage County Chapter and the Waupaca County Chapter formed in 1986 and 1987, respectively. The Ice Age Trail crosses back and forth between these two counties and the two chapters have shared in its care. Members from the chapters came together and initiated a merger. The Portage/Waupaca County Chapter of the Ice Age Trail Alliance will be official by mid-2020. Chapter volunteers promote the Trail segments in their counties by staffing numerous outreach events, planning seasonal hikes, and hosting an annual fund-raising event, the Fall Hike-a-Thon, in October. The chapter works closely with Hartman Creek

State Park and local landowners on Trail stewardship issues and maintenance of Trail privileges.

COUNTY INFORMATION

Portage County Information: co.portage.wi.us

Portage County Parks Department: 715-346-1433, https://www.co.portage.wi.us/department/parks

Stevens Point Area Convention and Visitors Bureau: 715-344-2556, stevenspointarea.com

Waupaca County Visitor and Promotional Council: visitwaupacacounty.com

A grassy path on the Hartman Creek Segment.

New Hope-Iola Ski Hill Segment

(Atlas Map 45f; Databook page 42)

SNAPSHOT

5.6 miles (5.6 IAT, 0.1 CR): Sunset Lake Rd. to CTH-MM at Iola Winter Sports Club

This segment traverses areas of high-relief hummocky topography and has a strong Northwoodsy character.

Note: Reroutes are planned west of CTH-T and between Stoltenberg Rd. and CTH-MM. Check with the Ice Age Trail Alliance (800-227-0046, iceagetrail.org) for details.

 At Iola Winter Sports Club lodge (winter only).

 From Severson Lake.

 Walk-in shelter just off the segment on Iola Winter Sports Club property.

 At Iola Pines Campground ~6 mi east and Collins County Park ~9 mi west (see Area Services).

 At Sunset Lake County Park.

 One ColdCache site on segment.

 Segment is closed during gun deer season.

 Dogs should be leashed (8-ft max) and under control at all times.

 Portions overlap a farm road, Stoltenberg Road and the Iola Winter Sports Club ski trails (hike well off to the side when groomed).

 A farm road, forest roads and the network of Iola Winter Sports Club ski trails, including access (**PW26**) to a shelter.

TRAIL ACCESS AND PARKING

Sunset Lake Rd.: *From Stevens Point* at the intersection of I-39 and USH-10, take USH-10 east 8.0 mi. At STH-161 turn left and go east 3.8 mi. At CTH-A turn left and go north 4.0 mi. At CTH-Z turn right and go east 1.5 mi. At Sunset Lake Rd. turn left and go north 0.9 mi to the Trail access on the east side of the road. No parking. Instead, park at the roadside parking area 200 ft north on the east side of Sunset Lake Rd. *From Waupaca* at the intersection of STH-49, USH-10 and STH-54, take STH-49 north 20.5 mi. At CTH-Z turn left and go west 2.8 mi. At Sunset Lake Rd. turn right and go north 0.9 mi to the Trail access on the east side of the road. No parking. Instead, park at the roadside parking area 200 ft north on the east side of Sunset Lake Rd.

CTH-MM at Iola Winter Sports Club: *From Stevens Point* at the intersection of I-39 and USH-10, take USH-10 east 8.0 mi. At STH-161 turn left and go east 3.8 mi. At CTH-A turn left and go north 2.3 mi. At CTH-MM turn right and go east 4.0 mi to the Iola Winter Sports Club parking area. *From Waupaca* at the intersection of STH-49, USH-10 and STH-54, take STH-49 north 17.5 mi. At CTH-MM turn left and go west 1.6 mi to the Iola Winter Sports Club parking area.

Additional Parking: (i) New Hope Pines State Natural Area parking area on the west side of Sunset Lake Rd. 0.1 mi north of the Trail access. (ii) CTH-Z parking area (**PW15**).

THE HIKE

Before starting off on this segment, hikers looking for an extra adventure should walk 0.1 miles north from the segment's starting point on Sunset Lake Road to pay a visit to New Hope Pines State Natural Area. It features one of the largest and least disturbed northern dry-mesic forests remaining in central Wisconsin and is reminiscent of the vast "pineries" found in this region prior to European settlement. A primitive yet easily navigable path winds through the

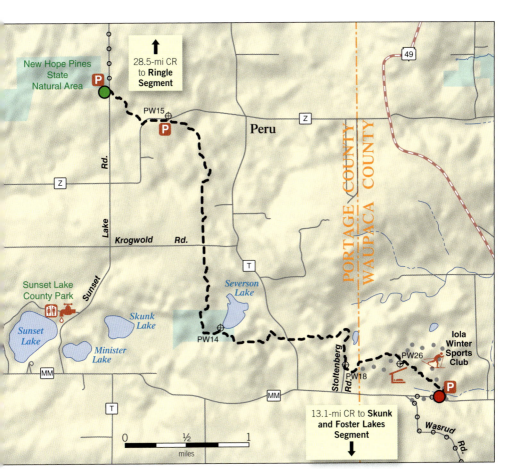

SNA, which is likely to one day host a segment of the Ice Age Trail.

From Sunset Lake Road the segment heads southeast through dense forest, dropping down into a low area and then climbing out as the route approaches CTH-Z. Upon arriving at CTH-Z hikers should cross to the opposite side of the road, turn left and follow the road around to the east for 0.2 miles to the CTH-Z parking area (**PW15**). From here, the segment then reenters the woods and continues south then southeast.

Between CTH-Z and CTH-T the segment moves through dramatic high-relief hummocky topography. The area's high water table and clay-laden soil produce marshes in the small depressions that harbor nesting ducks. A few larger kettles contain lakes, including Severson (Budsberg) Lake (**PW14**). This portion of the segment traverses open meadows and climbs in and out of three steep wooded ravines. Short bridges cross wet marshy areas and may be partially submerged during rainy periods. Northwoods red and white pine and birches mix with Hill's oak; several of the oaks and pines are assumed to be well over 100 years old.

The Trail crosses CTH-T and briefly follows a farm road before reentering the woods to the right. After climbing uphill, the Trail passes several trailside benches offering hikers a place to rest and moments of solitude in the woods. The segment continues meandering up and down through the forest, passing

Portage & Waupaca Counties

several deep kettles on its way toward Stoltenberg Road. Shortly before reaching the road, hikers will pass a unique "snake sculpture" made of plastic tubing with carved wooden head and tail, hanging from a tree, along with other similar sculptures visible through the trees. The Trail reaches a gravel driveway, jogs left onto Stoltenberg Road and follows the road 0.1 miles before the segment turns left and heads east, departing the road (**PW18**).

From Stoltenberg Road, the segment soon enters the grounds of the Iola Winter Sports Club, a full service winter sports area, and follows wide grassy ski trails. There are a number of intersecting trails so hikers should pay close attention and look carefully for yellow blazes and directional arrows. The Sports Club also offers a shelter for overnight use by Ice Age Trail hikers; the trail (**PW26**) to the shelter is located between Sports Club numbered intersections 44 and 43. The club's ski jump is located on the top of Norseman Hill and uses the relief and steep slopes of a deep kettle. The total relief is approximately 100 feet suggesting the ice block buried here was at least 100 feet thick.

AREA SERVICES

Alban: Restaurant, grocery store. From the Sunset Lake Rd. access, go north to CTH-T. Continue north on CTH-T then CTH-A to STH-66. Small grocery store at CTH-A and STH-66. Restaurant (seasonal) is 0.7 mi east on STH-66.

Rosholt: Restaurant, grocery store, camping, library. From the Sunset Lake Rd. access go north to CTH-T. Continue north on CTH-T then CTH-A to STH-66. Go west 1.0 mi on STH-66. Camping at Collins County Park (715-346-1433, co.portage.wi.us/department/parks/collins-park), 3.5 mi south and west of town. The library has limited hours.

Iola Winter Sports Club: Seasonal facilities (winter) (715-445-3411, iolawintersportsclub.org/). A full-service winter sports area with 20 km of groomed cross-country trails and ski jump, rentals, lessons and chalet. Primitive shelter available for camping for long-distance, multiday hikers.

Iola: Restaurant, grocery store, lodging, camping, library, medical service. From the CTH-MM access go east on CTH-MM to STH-49. Turn right and follow STH-49 for 3.5 mi. Camping at Iola Pines Campground (715-445-3489, iolapines.com).

Stevens Point: See Skunk and Foster Lakes Segment and Waupaca River Segment, p. 154. From the CTH-MM Trail access go west then south ~18 mi. Also see Trail Access and Parking directions, above.

Waupaca: See Skunk and Foster Lakes Segment and Waupaca River Segment, p. 154. From the CTH-MM Trail access go east then south ~21 mi. Also see Trail Access and Parking directions, above.

> *Go hike Wisconsin, go explore your own state, go donate a day to trail maintenance, go motivate someone else to hike. Be one with a fall forest, trip over snow covered roots in your snowshoes, soak your feet in a cold lake after a long summer hike, pee your pants when startled by your first grouse. Yell at the rain.*
>
> DAVID CLOUSTON (AKA "WALKA WALKA"), ICE AGE TRAIL THOUSAND-MILER

Late autumn solitude on the Emmons Creek Segment.

Skunk and Foster Lakes Segment and Waupaca River Segment (Atlas Map 47f; Databook pages 43–44)

SNAPSHOT

Skunk and Foster Lakes Segment—4.4 miles (3.6 miles IAT, 0.8 miles CR): N. Foley Dr. Northern Trail Access to USH-10

Waupaca River Segment—4.9 miles (2.2 miles IAT, 2.7 miles CR): USH-10 to STH-54

*The **Skunk and Foster Lakes Segment** passes through a beautiful State Natural Area, highlights a drumlin swarm and features clear, undeveloped kettle lakes, hilly topography and huge trailside erratics.*

 From trailside lakes and streams.

 Segment includes two connecting route roadwalks.

 A white-blazed loop on northwest end, a blue-blazed spur to a parking area and several DNR access trails.

 Portion of the segment crossing private land between Indian Valley Rd. and Rieben Rd. is closed during gun deer season.

 Dogs should be leashed (8-ft max) and under control at all times.

*The varied **Waupaca River Segment** highlights a steep ridge with a trailside ridgetop cabin and the scenic Waupaca River.*

 From the Waupaca River.

 The WCC trailside cabin (first come, first served) just west of Foley Dr.

 Portions of the segment crossing private lands both north and south of the Waupaca River State Fishery Area are closed during gun deer season.

 Dogs should be leashed (8-ft max) and under control at all times.

 Segment includes two connecting route roadwalks.

 A blue-blazed loop trail west of the segment near the Waupaca River and a blue-blazed spur trail to the Foley Dr. parking area.

TRAIL ACCESS AND PARKING

N. Foley Dr. Northern Trail Access: *From Waupaca* at the intersection of highways STH-49 and USH-10, take USH-10 west 6.0 mi. At Foley Dr. turn right and go north 2.1 mi. *Note: Foley Dr. becomes N. Foley Dr. at Floistad Rd.* No parking. Instead park at the Skunk and Foster Lakes SNA parking area 0.1 mi south of the N. Foley Dr. northern Trail access on the west side of the road. A blue-blazed spur trail leads to the Trail. *From Stevens Point* at the intersection of I-39 and USH-10, take USH-10 east 18.0 mi. At Foley Dr. turn left and go north 2.1 mi. *Note: Foley Dr. becomes N. Foley Dr. at Floistad Rd.* No parking. Instead park at the Skunk and Foster Lakes SNA parking area 0.1 mi south of the N. Foley Dr. northern Trail access on the west side of the road. A blue-blazed spur trail leads to the Trail.

STH-54: *From Waupaca* at the intersection of STH-49, USH-10 and STH-54, take STH-54 west 5.0 mi to the parking area on the north side of the road. *From Stevens Point* at the intersection of I-39 and USH-10, take I-39 south 6.5 mi. Exit STH-54 and go east 17.0 mi to the parking area on the north side of the road to the parking area on the north side of the road.

Additional Parking: (i) Indian Valley Rd. Roadside parking. (ii) Grenlie Rd. Roadside parking. (iii) Foley Dr. Waupaca River State Fishery Area parking area, 1.4 mi south of USH-10. A blue-blazed spur trail leads to the Trail.

THE HIKE

The first half of the **Skunk and Foster Lakes Segment** is a horseshoe-shaped route in the Skunk and Foster Lakes State Natural Area (SNA) with several undeveloped kettle lakes and loop and side trail options. From its starting point at the North Foley Drive northern Trail access the segment heads west and parallels Sannes Creek, which flows through the ancient meltwater channel that surrounds the SNA. As the segment bends south through white and red pines, it approaches the north shore of 11-acre spring-fed Skunk Lake and arrives at an intersection (**PW12**) with a white-blazed loop trail and a DNR access forest road. Hikers looking for additional adventures can head west on the 0.8-mile loop trail, which explores a scenic, mature maple forest set in more rolling topography.

From the junction with the loop trail, the segment continues southeast, crossing another access path that leads to the shore of Skunk Lake, which is surrounded by a wetland dominated by cattails and bulrush. The Trail continues into hummocky terrain east of Skunk Lake. Numerous impressive-sized Wolf River granite boulders are scattered throughout the area. The route descends through second growth forest for a brief view of 7-acre shallow, hard water Foster Lake, then circles east toward Grenlie Lake, a clear lake fed by seepage and springs.

On the southwest corner of Grenlie Lake, the segment passes a hillside filled with large ferns then follows along the north shore of the lake. The blue-blazed spur trail that

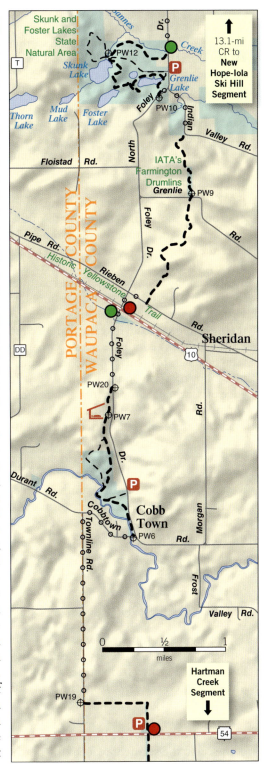

Portage & Waupaca Counties

leads to the parking area on North Foley Drive intersects the segment near the east end of the lake. From here the segment heads south across the lake's outlet on a bridge. The Trail then follows the shoreline with views of waterfowl habitat and soon ascends through a glacial erratic field, fern garden and pine forest on the way to the North Foley Drive southern Trail access (**PW10**).

From here, hikers follow a 0.5-mile connecting route roadwalk: northeast on North Foley Drive and then southeast and south on Indian Valley Road to the spot where Indian Valley Road turns sharply east.

The segment goes off road and continues south under the cover of woods on an uneven forest road. Erratics of various sizes populate the Trail between here and the end of the segment. The route climbs steadily up the side of a drumlin on the western edge of the Farmington Drumlins swarm, the most significant swarm of drumlins along the entire length of the Ice Age Trail. Drumlins are elevated tear-shaped land formations that indicate the flow of the glaciers. The steep end faces the flow of the ice and the tail end tapers to the ground like a ramp. Drumlins are always found in groups called a drumlin field or swarm.

The canopy opens up to a fenced pasture with a large cell/transmission tower in the middle. The Trail hugs the tree line along the field, then enters the Farmington Drumlins Preserve and descends through woods and open prairie. As the segment reaches Grenlie Road, hikers will notice huge erratics lined up alongside it.

The segment continues across Grenlie Road (**PW9**) and follows the edge of a farm field before diving left into the woods where the Trail weaves under a beautiful canopy of hardwoods and intersects several forest roads. It reemerges along the edge of a farm field for a short distance before again entering the woods through a stand of red pine. Continuing along the western edge of the drumlin swarm, the Trail climbs steeply before descending ~100 feet down a steep dirt path. Footing can be treacherous, especially when the tread is wet. The segment jogs right then left and emerges along a farm field that takes the hiker to Rieben Road.

From Rieben Road hikers should follow a 0.3-mile connecting route roadwalk west on Rieben Road, then south on Foley Drive across the Canadian National Railroad tracks to the segment's terminus on the north side of USH-10.

Mobile Skills Crew project site, 2005, 2009, 2012

The **Waupaca River Segment** begins with a 0.6-mile connecting route roadwalk south on Foley Drive. Hikers should head south and cross four-lane USH-10 with extreme caution. USH-10 is on the route of the historic Yellowstone Trail, the first transcontinental highway in the northern tier of the United States. Hikers should follow Foley Drive south to where the off-road portion of the segment heads west (**PW20**) from the road.

The segment's topography is mainly pitted outwash made up of glacial debris left behind when the glaciers retreated. The steep slope just east of the first part of the segment resulted from buried ice melting and the outwash surface collapsing. The Trail ascends steeply from the road and hikers may hear equipment operating from a sand and gravel pit just west of the Trail. After 0.2 miles the segment arrives at a small, simple trailside cabin (**PW7**) built on private land by the Wisconsin Conservation Corps in 1986 that is open to the public for overnight stays. South of the cabin the segment reaches the northern junction with a scenic blue-blazed loop trail that splits off to the west. The Trail continues through rolling terrain with steep slopes on the sides of the Trail in mixed oak woodland and pine forest. South of the southern junction with the loop trail, the segment flattens out to follow the placid Waupaca River. Native Americans living in this area named the river "Waupaca," which translates to "tomorrow" because it took them 24 hours to paddle the river's length. Portions of the Trail along the river can become wet or flooded. The segment leaves the river bank briefly, intersects a blue-blazed spur trail leading to the parking area on Foley Drive, then returns to the river before emerging at the Cobbtown Road and Foley Drive intersection (**PW6**).

From this point hikers follow a 2.0-mile connecting route roadwalk. Hikers should cross the river on the bridge and head west following Cobbtown Road, then turn left and follow Townline Road south until the segment heads east (**PW19**) from the road. Here the segment crosses a pitted outwash landscape along a field edge, then heads south to the segment terminus at STH-54. A prominent field of drumlins sits about half a mile east of the parking area.

Mobile Skills Crew project site, 2009, 2012

POINTS OF INTEREST

Lake Emily County Park: 8 mi west of the Ice Age Trail. From the Skunk and Foster Lakes SNA parking area on N. Foley Dr., take N. Foley Dr. north to CTH-V, turn left and go 7.6 mi, turning left on CTH-A and turning right on CTH-KK. Take Lake Dr. to Park Dr. (3968 Park Dr., Amherst Junction).

Lake Emily County Park has 15 conical, oval and linear Indian mounds in various groups out of a previous 22 or more. Look for an information board citing locations in the park.

AREA SERVICES

Waupaca: Restaurant, grocery store, convenience store, general shopping, lodging, camping, library, medical service. From the USH-10 Trail access, go ~6 mi east on USH-10. Most services in the area of USH-10 and STH-54/49. INN Style program lodging at the Apple Tree Lane B&B (715-258-3107, appletreelanebb.com), Green Fountain Inn (715-258-5171, green-fountain-inn.com) and Crystal River Inn (715-258-5333, crystalriver-inn.com). Area info available from the Waupaca Area Chamber of Commerce (715-258-7343, waupacaareachamber.com).

Amherst: Restaurant, grocery store, lodging, camping, library, medical service. From the USH-10 Trail access go ~5 mi northwest on USH-10. INN Style program lodging at Artha Sustainable Living Center B&B (715-824-3463, arthaonline.com). Additional lodging at The Amherst Inn B&B (888-211-3555, amherstinn.com). The library has limited hours.

Manawa: INN Style lodging at Lindsay House B&B (920-407-1416, lindsayhouse.com).

Amherst Junction: Convenience store, lodging, camping. From the USH-10 Trail access go ~7 mi northwest on USH-10. Camping at Lake Emily County Park (3968 Park Dr., 715-346-1433, co.portage.wi.us/department/parks/lake-emily-park).

Stevens Point: Restaurant, grocery store, convenience store, general shopping, lodging, library, medical service. From the USH-10 Trail access go ~18 mi northwest on USH-10. INN Style program lodging at A Victorian Swan on Water (715-345-0595, victorianswan.com) and Dreams of Yesteryear B&B (715-341-4525, dreamsofyesteryear.com). Area info available from the Stevens Point Area Convention and Visitor Bureau (715-344-2556, stevenspointarea.com).

Turner's Fresh Market: See Hartman Creek Segment, p. 158. From the STH-54 Trail access go west 0.2 mi.

Hartman Creek State Park: See Hartman Creek Segment, p. 158. From the STH-54 Trail access go east and then south on Hartman Creek Rd. 2.5 mi.

Hartman Creek Segment (Atlas Map 48f; Databook page 44)

SNAPSHOT

5.6 miles: STH-54 to Emmons Creek Rd.

 This segment features the forested, hilly terrain of Hartman Creek State Park (HCSP) and one of the largest erratics on the entire Ice Age Trail.

 At various locations throughout HCSP.

 From Allen Creek and Allen Lake.

One ColdCache site on segment.

 Portion of segment crossing private land between STH-54 and HCSP is closed during gun deer season.

 Dogs should be leashed (8-ft max) and under control at all times.

 Portions overlap HCSP trails. Hike well off to the side when ski trails are groomed.

 Several unsigned side trails and the extensive HCSP trail network.

TRAIL ACCESS AND PARKING

STH-54: *From Waupaca* at USH-10 and STH-54, take STH-54 west 5.0 mi to the parking area on the north side of the road. *From Stevens Point* at the intersection of I-39 and USH-10, take I-39 south 6.5 mi. Exit STH-54 and go east 17.0 mi to the parking area on the north side of the road.

Emmons Creek Rd.: *From Stevens Point* at the intersection of I-39 and USH-10, take I-39 south. Exit STH-54 and go east 15.0 mi. At CTH-D turn right and go south 2.5 mi. Continue south on Stratton Lake Rd. 0.8 mi. At Emmons Creek Rd. turn left and go east 0.5 mi to the Trail access. Watch carefully for Trail signage on the north side of the road. No parking. Instead, continue 0.2 mi east of the Ice Age Trail to a DNR parking area on the north side of the road. *From Waupaca*, at USH-10 and STH-54, take STH-54 west 6.6 mi to CTH-D. Follow the directions described above from CTH-D to the Trail access.

Additional Parking: (i) Edminster Ln. parking area at Trail access. (ii) Hartman Creek State Park (HCSP) parking areas on Windfeldt Ln.

THE HIKE

From its starting point on STH-54 the segment heads south between farm fields, enters a hilly wooded area, crosses Allen Creek and then passes through a pine plantation before emerging onto Edminster Road. The Allen Creek crossing can be very muddy and wet in times of heavy rain or high water. In this initial portion the segment intersects several unsigned side trails.

South of Edminster Road the segment enters Hartman Creek State Park (HCSP), which has a long history. The Wisconsin Conservation Department, the precursor to the Wisconsin Department of Natural Resources (DNR), bought 309 acres from the Allen and Hartman family estates in 1939 for $8,500. The Conservation Department dammed a creek and created Allen Lake, in honor of George W. Allen, and named the property "Hartman Creek State Fish Hatchery" in honor of the Hartman family. Today, the park consists of approximately 1,400 acres.

The park is located on terrain formed as the Wisconsin glacier retreated down a regional slope. The eastern part of the park lies on gently rolling ground moraine and pitted outwash where flowing rivers from the melting glacier deposited layers of gravel and sand. The resulting topography is pitted outwash to the west; as the glacier melted back from this position it left a substantially lower land surface to the east.

The segment makes its way south through the park, intersecting and sharing portions of the park's extensive trail network. At a huge erratic (**PW25**) next to a Leopold bench, hikers can depart from the segment and access the HCSP's campground and facilities by heading east 0.2 miles then south 0.1 miles on park hiking and biking trails. In the summer look for a large tepee, a part of the campground, which can be reserved for camping.

Nearly the entire portion of the segment through the northern part of the park (north of Winfeldt Lane) is on rolling, forested terrain. A kiosk explaining the geological landscape of the Elderon Moraine and the outwash plain is a short distance east of the segment's route at a parking area on Windfeldt Lane.

South of Windfeldt Lane the segment courses through the forest and cuts across areas of open prairie near the edge of an old orchard where bluebirds and other songbirds thrive. The segment then intersects several mountain bike paths. As the segment enters Emmons Creek Barrens State Natural Area, the most hilly portion of the segment, the forest clears away and hikers can see a large clearing. The segment narrows and descends into the clearing as it approaches its endpoint on Emmons Creek Road.

Mobile Skills Crew project site, 2012, 2015

AREA SERVICES

Turner's Fresh Market: From STH-54 parking area go 0.2 mi west on STH-54. Seasonal farmer's market with fresh fruits, vegetables and drinks (715-258-3355, turnersfreshmarket.com).

Waupaca: See Skunk and Foster Lakes Segment and Waupaca River Segment, p. 154. From the STH-54 Trail access go east ~5 mi. Also see Trail Access and Parking directions, above.

Stevens Point: See Skunk and Foster Lakes Segment and Waupaca River Segment, p. 154. From the STH-54 Trail access go west ~23.5 mi. Also see Trail Access and Parking directions, above.

Hartman Creek State Park (HCSP): Camping, summer concession stand and recreational rentals. On Trail. (715-258-2372, dnr.wi.gov/topic/parks/name/hartman; reservations: 888-947-2757, wisconsin.goingtocamp.com).

Emmons Creek Segment (Atlas Map 48f; Databook pages 44–45)

SNAPSHOT

2.6 miles: Emmons Creek Rd. to 2nd Ave.

  This segment and its accompanying Faraway Valley Loop highlight charming Emmons Creek and oak woodland and savanna areas.

- From Emmons Creek.
- Dogs should be leashed (8-ft max) and under control at all times.
- Green-blazed Faraway Valley loop and white-blazed loop south of 2nd Ave.

TRAIL ACCESS AND PARKING

Emmons Creek Rd.: *From Stevens Point* at the intersection of I-39 and USH-10, take I-39 south. Exit STH-54 and go east 15.0 mi. At CTH-D turn right and go south 2.5 mi. Continue south on Stratton Lake Rd. 0.8 mi. At Emmons Creek Rd. turn left and go east 0.5 mi to the Trail access. Watch carefully for Trail signage on the north side of the road. No parking. Instead, continue 0.2 mi east of the Ice Age Trail to a DNR parking area on the north side of the road. *From Waupaca*, at USH-10 and STH-54, take STH-54 west 6.6 mi to CTH-D. Follow the directions described above from CTH-D to the Trail access.

2nd Ave.: *From Stevens Point* at the intersection of I-39 and USH-10, take I-39 south. Exit STH-54 and go east 12.0 mi. At CTH-TT turn right and go south 2.5 mi. Join CTH-D south for another 0.5 mi. Where CTH-D turns west, continue south on 16th Rd. for another 2.2 mi. At 2nd Ave. turn left and go east 1.5 mi to the Trail access on the north side of the road. No parking. Instead, continue east on 2nd Ave. for 50 yards to the parking area for the Murry Creek loop trail. *From Waupaca*, at USH-10 and STH-54, take STH-54 west 8.2 mi. At CTH-TT turn left. Follow the directions described above from CTH-TT to the Trail access.

Additional Parking: Stratton Lake Rd. parking area with informational kiosk.

THE HIKE

From its starting point on Emmons Creek Road, the segment heads south through the Emmons Creek State Fishery Area, climbing a dramatic ridge through oak woodlands. The river valley below is revealed when leaves are off trees. Leopold benches along the Trail provide convenient resting places. The segment descends from the ridge through a pine plantation to Stratton Lake Road and the segment's main parking area. The green-blazed Faraway Valley Loop leaves the segment from the parking area and heads west through a meadow, crosses Emmons Creek on the 3rd Avenue road bridge, returns to the woods and heads south to rejoin the segment south of Emmons Creek.

Back on the Trail, south of Stratton Lake Road, the segment passes through a large meadow before crossing Emmons Creek on a scenic footbridge (**PW2**). Boardwalks take the segment through a seasonally wet area noted for skunk cabbage and marsh marigolds. The segment overlooks the Emmons Creek valley, reaches the southern junction with the Faraway Valley Loop and heads south on a straight line toward its endpoint on 2nd Avenue.

Upon arriving at 2nd Avenue, hikers may explore a white-blazed lollipop loop (with a total distance of 2.7 miles) that heads south from 2nd Avenue, crosses narrow Murry Creek and then winds through pine plantations. Small meadows here sometimes yield sightings of the rare and endangered Karner blue butterfly.

Mobile Skills Crew project site, 2012, 2015

AREA SERVICES

Almond: Restaurant, library. From the 2nd Ave. Trail access go west ~9 mi. The library has limited hours.

Hartman Creek State Park: See Hartman Creek Segment, p. 158. From the 2nd Ave. Trail access go east then north ~7 mi.

Waupaca: See Skunk and Foster Lakes Segment and Waupaca River Segment, p. 154. From the 2nd Ave. Trail access go east then north ~12 mi. Also see Trail Access and Parking directions, above.

Stevens Point: See Skunk and Foster Lakes Segment and Waupaca River Segment, p. 154. From the 2nd Ave. Trail access go west then north ~28 mi. Also see Trail Access and Parking directions, above.

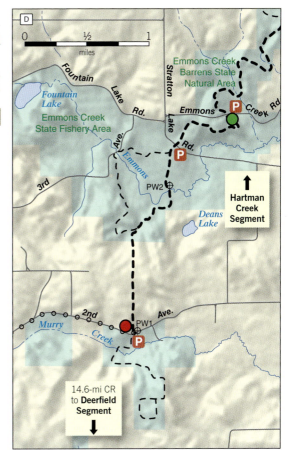

If there is one thing the Ice Age Trail does well, it is to create an environment for exploration. That exploration may be with the outdoors itself, but more importantly it is with what I will refer to as the indoors. In this case, indoors may be that part of yourself where you explore your thoughts, feelings, relationships, good and bad memories and develop into who you are... Ultimately this creates understandings and then passions which may have been provoked while walking alone, gathering deep thoughts.

JEFF DOHLBY, ICE AGE TRAIL THOUSAND-MILER

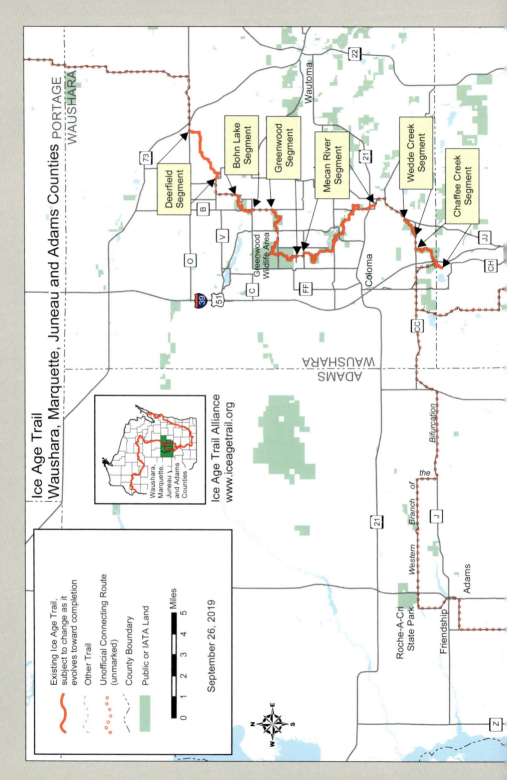

Waushara & Marquette Counties

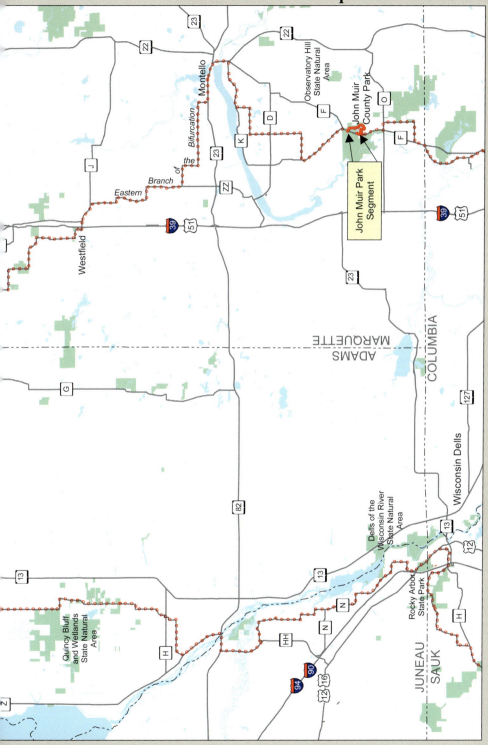

Waushara County

Atlas Maps 49f–53f-E and 53f-W;
Databook pages 47–50
Total miles: 41.1 (Trail 20.7; Connecting Route 20.4)

Within the Central Sand Hills region, the Ice Age Trail corridor in Waushara County courses through a complex terminal moraine zone of the westward-flowing Green Bay Lobe. The moraines along the Trail were deposited during the late Wisconsin Glaciation. Most of these moraines were deposited after the Green Bay Lobe reached its maximum extent about 18,000 years ago. As the ice sheet retreated and advanced, it deposited a series of moraines. When the westward torrents of glacial meltwater flowed through the region, the moraines became pitted and meltwater channels sliced through them. The moraines were also partially buried by the glacial outwash debris.

A mixture of farmland, woodlots, wetlands, small kettle lakes, cold-water streams and rural communities characterizes the county. The Ice Age Trail passes through land managed by the Wisconsin Department of Natural Resources (DNR), including Bohn Lake State Ice Age Trail Area/State Natural Area, Greenwood State Wildlife Area and Mecan River System State Fishery Areas, which include Wedde Creek and Chaffee Creek. These public lands protect a wide range of plant communities, including wetlands, restored prairie and rare oak and pine barrens. Private landowners host Trail segments through handshake agreements or easements providing permanent Trail protection.

In southern Waushara County the eastern and western routes of the Ice Age National Scenic Trail "bifurcation" split (or rejoin, depending on hike direction). Currently, several Ice Age Trail segments have been completed along the eastern branch and only one along the western route, in the city of Baraboo in Sauk County. In addition to the Whistler Mounds Group on the eastern branch, the western connecting route passes near such significant historical sites as the rock art of Roche-a-Cri State Park in Adams County and Indian Mounds Park and Cranberry Creek Mound Group State Natural Area in Juneau County. Contact the Ice Age Trail Alliance for more information on the bifurcation. Camping is available at a Dispersed Camping Area (DCA) in the Mecan River Segment and at private campgrounds near Hancock and Coloma.

Note: Hikers should be aware that many of the roads in Waushara County share the same name and differ only in the road "suffix" paired with the road name (e.g., Beechnut Dr., Beechnut Rd.; 7th Ave., 7th Ln., 7th Dr.).

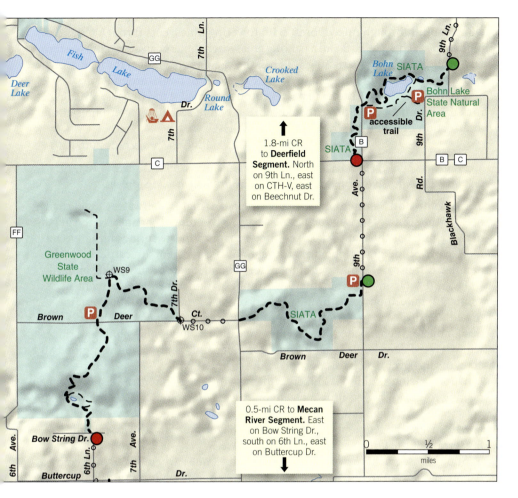

Lake, were created from buried blocks of ice left behind when the tunnel collapsed. The northwest part of the property contains a portion of an end moraine.

From its starting point on 9th Lane, the segment travels through an oak forest mixed with pine and makes its way downhill to Bohn Lake and the intersection with the eastern end of the white-blazed Lake Loop trail. The Lake Loop trail goes around the south side of the lake, intersecting with a blue-blazed spur trail leading to the 9th Drive parking area. The Lake Loop continues past a handsomely crafted log bench and interpretive panel explaining the creation of kettle lakes. This overlook section of the Lake Loop, coupled with the blue-blazed spur trail, make up the Bohn Lake Accessible Hiking Trail, an "all access" 0.2-mile route built by local volunteers offering a compacted surface with minimal grade.

From the eastern junction of the Lake Loop, the Ice Age Trail crosses a boardwalk between Bohn Lake and a small pond. Fluctuating lake levels have joined the two water bodies, necessitating the boardwalk to keep the Trail open. Continuing on from the boardwalk, the Trail courses along the north and west shores of the lake. Evidence of the fluctuating lake levels can be seen through tipped over trees and mature pines and oaks surrounded by water. Departing the lake, the segment climbs uphill through mixed forest with towering pines, cuts through a stand of pines and reaches CTH-B and a parking area, where hikers can access the western end of the Lake Loop. Crossing CTH-B, the segment meanders through scotch and white pines before the canopy opens as the Trail hooks around a dry kettle and fallow farm fields. The Trail passes through a small stand of oaks, revealing a rock garden and a good place to take a break before reaching its terminus at the intersection of CTH-B (9th Avenue) and CTH-C.

Mobile Skills Crew project site 2007, 2019

From the CTH-B (9th Avenue) at CTH-C Trail access, hikers should cross CTH-C and hike 1.0 miles south on 9th Avenue to reach the Greenwood Segment.

The **Greenwood Segment** is located between two major meltwater tunnel channels. To the south of the segment is the Mecan River tunnel channel. To the north of the segment is the Hancock Lakes tunnel channel. In late spring and early summer, many of the grassy openings throughout the segment are carpeted in blue lupine creating a welcome environment for the endangered Karner blue butterfly.

From its starting point at the 9th Avenue parking area, the segment heads south 0.1 mile then west through pitted outwash of the Almond Moraine. A mixed forest of stately oaks and various other woodland species keeps this portion of the segment shaded. The segment meanders along rolling hills and ridges with views of deep kettles. George and Lois Siler and family generously gifted 80 acres of land over which this portion of the segment passes.

Upon reaching CTH-GG hikers will cross the road and head west on a connecting route, following Brown Deer Court west for 0.5 miles. At 7th Drive hikers should turn right and head north for a few yards to reconnect with the Trail (**WS10**). Here the segment leaves the road and continues northwest into the rolling terrain of the Greenwood State Wildlife Area.

Soon the segment arrives at Pine Tree Point (**WS9**) where hikers can enjoy a panoramic view of an open prairie edged by oak savanna while putting up their feet on the beautifully crafted (and very comfortable) log couch and ottoman tucked under the shady pines. The restored prairie is one square mile (the largest in Waushara County) and features bottle gentian, blazing star, leadplant and prairie willow.

From Pine Tree Point, the Kettle Trail, a blue-blazed spur trail, heads west then north through the prairie for 0.7 miles (one-way) to an impressive, open view of an entire 78-foot-wide dry glacial kettle.

The segment continues southwest from Pine Tree Point along the edge of the Almond Moraine. South of Brown Deer Court the segment heads southeast, taking hikers a short distance back from the moraine's outer edge. The segment continues southwest and then west before dropping down toward a 200-foot-deep glacial kettle that was likely part of a tunnel channel running out to the Hancock Moraine several miles west. The narrow banana-shaped kettle is almost a mile long and has four separate ponds in the bottom. A white-blazed loop trail weaves along the north and east ridge overlooking the ponds at the bottom of the kettle and rejoins the segment on the south side of the kettle. From the junction with the white-blazed loop trail, the segment heads south to its endpoint on Bow String Drive.

Mobile Skills Crew project site, 2010, 2011, 2013, 2019

POINTS OF INTEREST

Whistler Mounds Group & Enclosure: Located in Whistler Mounds Park on Fish Lake just east of Hancock. From Hancock, take CTH-FF east 1.0 mi, then continue straight on Beechnut Dr. 0.3 mi to 6th Ave. (N4140 6th Ave., Hancock).

The Whistler Mounds Group & Enclosure, listed on the National Register of Historic Places, consists of two rows of conical mounds (13 mounds) and a low earthen double enclosure, one of only a few enclosures surviving development in Wisconsin. Archaeologists think the double enclosure was a sacred space where special ceremonies were held. The mounds and enclosure are believed to have been constructed by Woodland Indians during the period 650 to 1200 AD. A short trail travels past the mounds and enclosure area.

AREA SERVICES

Hancock: Restaurant, convenience store, lodging, camping, library. From the CTH-B (9th Ave.) Trail crossing, go north on CTH-B for 1.1 mi. At CTH-V turn left and go west 3.9 mi. Camping at Hancock Village Campground (715-249-5521) and Tomorrow Wood Campground (715-249-5954, tomorrowwood.com). Library has limited hours.

Coloma: See Mecan River Segment, p. 172. From the Bow String Dr. Trail access go south then west 5.6 mi. Also see Trail Access and Parking directions, above.

Wautoma: See Mecan River Segment, p. 172. From the Bow String Dr. Trail access go south then east ~14 mi.

Mobile Skills Crew volunteers built this boardwalk (see page 165) on the Bohn Lake Segment.

Mecan River Segment (Atlas Map 52f; Databook pages 48–49)

SNAPSHOT

7.5 miles (7.1 IAT, 0.4 CR): Buttercup Dr. to Cumberland Ave.

  This segment traverses a variety of natural communities from wetland to grassland to forest and includes outstanding views of the Mecan Springs and Mecan River.

Note: *A reroute is planned for the eastern portion of the segment. Check with the Ice Age Trail Alliance (800-227-0046, iceagetrail.org) for details.*

- From the Mecan River.

 A Dispersed Camping Area south of Buttercup Dr.

 At a nearby private campground (see Area Services).

- One ColdCache site on segment.

- Portion of the segment crossing private land between CTH-GG and 9th Ave. is closed during gun deer season.

 Dogs should be leashed (8-ft max) and under control at all times.

 Road walk along 9th Ave.

 A blue-blazed spur trail (**WS14**) to the DCA, a blue-blazed spur trail to the CTH-GG parking area and a blue-blazed spur trail (**WS6**) to the Mecan River vista.

TRAIL ACCESS AND PARKING

Buttercup Dr.: From I-39 take Exit 124 (Coloma) and follow STH-21 east 1.4 mi. At 6th Ave. turn left and go north 2.6 mi. At Buttercup Dr. turn right and go east 0.8 mi to the parking area on the south side of the road.

Cumberland Ave.: From I-39 take Exit 134 (Coloma) and follow STH-21 east 3.9 mi. At 9th Ave. turn right and go south 0.2 mi, merging with Cumberland Ave. Curve east and continue on Cumberland Ave. 0.1 mi to the Trail access on north side of the road. No parking. Instead, park at the STH-21 parking area between 9th Ave. and the Mecan River.

Additional Parking: (i) 6th Ln. parking area. (ii) CTH-GG parking area. A blue-blazed spur trail leads 0.1 mi to the Trail. (iii) 9th Ave. DNR parking areas located 0.6 and 0.8 mi north of STH-21.

THE HIKE

From its starting point at the parking area on Buttercup Drive, the segment heads south on a grass-and-dirt access road. The segment then heads west through a pine plantation, where one of the Waushara County Chapter's signature log benches offers a shady respite. The segment intersects a signed spur trail (**WS14**) leading to a nearby Dispersed Camping Area (DCA) for long-distance, multiday hikers. The segment continues through a State Ice Age Trail Area property that contains rolling hills with steep slopes and scenic panoramas of the rural farm countryside. The property is a mix of pine plantations, upland woods and grasslands. As the segment makes its way south toward Chicago Road, it passes through a large, open field where whitetail deer are often spotted at dawn and dusk.

South of Chicago Road the segment heads into the Mecan River headwaters area and intersects an outstanding example of a tunnel channel. The channel extends west several miles through the Almond Moraine to the edge of the Han-

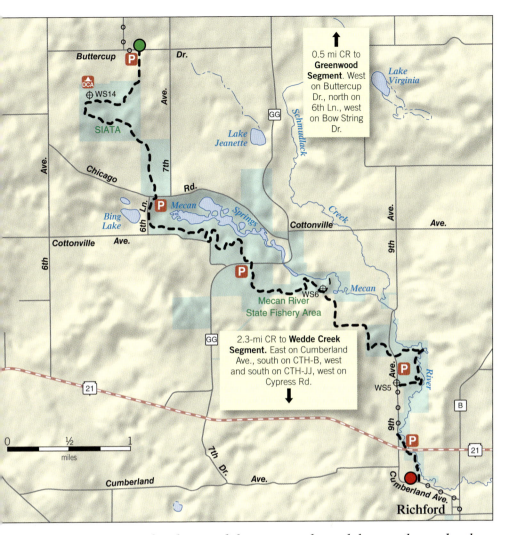

cock Moraine. As it bends around the western edge and then southern edge the segment offers outstanding views of the Mecan Springs more than a hundred feet below. Many migratory and wetland birds visit the area including sandhill cranes, northern bobwhite quail, red-shouldered hawks and bald eagles.

The segment bends south away from the springs, crosses CTH-GG and intersects a blue-blazed spur trail that leads 0.1 miles to the CTH-GG parking area. The Trail continues south and east for a short distance before arriving at a spot above the banks of the Mecan River, renowned as one of the finest trout streams in central Wisconsin. A little farther on, a rewarding side trip on the blue-blazed Mecan Vista Trail (**WS6**) offers views of the Mecan River.

The segment departs from the Mecan River State Fishery Area briefly and passes over the Wisconsin Operating Engineer training grounds. For safety's sake, hikers should stay on the Trail to avoid the heavy equipment operated on the grounds.

As it approaches 9th Avenue, the segment reenters the fishery area property.

Hikers will cross through a recent timber harvest area, part of an oak regeneration project. East of 9th Avenue the segment hits another recent pine timber harvest area. Pay close attention to Trail signage in these logged areas.

From 9th Avenue the segment continues past rock piles cleared from pioneer farmers' fields and through deciduous forest and openings of prairie and wetlands along the river. The segment bends back to the west and passes through a pine plantation before emerging back onto 9th Avenue (**WS5**). Here, hikers should turn left and walk south 0.4 miles along the road. The segment then leaves the road again, heading southeast along the river for a short distance before reaching STH-21. Hikers should cross STH-21 carefully and continue south as the Trail follows a beautiful section of the Mecan River. The Trail passes a log bench and crosses a 70-foot-long boardwalk and a 32-foot-long bridge built by volunteers as it makes its way to the segment terminus at the Cumberland Avenue parking area.

Mobile Skills Crew project site, 2003, 2010, 2014, 2019

AREA SERVICES

Hancock: See Bohn Lake Segment and Greenwood Segment, p. 168. From the Buttercup Dr. Trail access go west then north ~6 mi.

Coloma: Restaurant, convenience store, lodging, camping, library. From the STH-21 Trail access go west 4.0 mi on STH-21. INN Style lodging at the Coloma Hotel (715-228-2401, colomahotel.com) and Caribou Bay Retreat (920-716-5918, cariboubayretreat.com) and Whispering Pines of Pleasant Lake (715-347-7005, airbnb.com/rooms/14083416).

Wautoma: Restaurant, grocery store, convenience store, lodging, camping, library, medical service. From the STH-21 Trail access go east ~10 mi on STH-21. Lodging at Super 8 (920-787-4811, wyndhamhotels.com/Super-8), Boarders Inn and Suites (920-787-5050, staycobblestone.com/wi/Wautoma), Silvercryst Resort and Motel (920-787-3367, silvercryst.com; includes restaurant). Area info available from Waushara Area Chamber of Commerce (920-787-3488, wausharachamber.com).

Richford: Restaurant, lodging. From the Cumberland Ave. Trail access go east 0.5 mi. Lodging at Mecan River Inn (866-322-6466 or 715-228-2555, mecanriverinn.net).

> *I touched every large tree encircling Ennis Lake, as if to make a personal connection with John Muir. I wondered if he had carefully examined these same trees when they were mere saplings. Among countless ranks of swaying tan cattails, I observed a trio of Amish youth launch a wooden rowboat from a carriage pulled by a handsome black horse. Did the youthful, inquisitive Muir play on the same shoreline to usher in a similar summer morning?*
>
> JAMES KING (AKA "J.J."), ICE AGE TRAIL THOUSAND-MILER

Wedde Creek Segment and Chaffee Creek Segment (Atlas Maps 52f, 53f-E; Databook pages 49–50)

SNAPSHOT

Wedde Creek Segment—1.2 miles: Cypress Rd. to Czech Ave.

0.7-mile Connecting Route

Chaffee Creek Segment—2.5 miles: Czech Ave. to I-39 Southbound Wayside

  *The short **Wedde Creek Segment** passes through oak woodlands and highlights quiet Wedde Creek.*

From Wedde Creek.

Dogs should be leashed (8-ft max) and under control at all times.

 Portion of the segment overlaps a snowmobile trail.

 Short spur trail to parking area.

  *The **Chaffee Creek Segment** highlights savannas, meadows and a charming creek and the Chaffee Creek valley.*

At the Interstate 39 wayside.

From Chaffee Creek.

 At a nearby private campground (see Coloma Area Services, p. 174).

 Dogs should be leashed (8-ft max) and under control at all times.

 Short blue-blazed spur trail (**WS1**) to 6th Ave. parking area.

TRAIL ACCESS AND PARKING

Cypress Rd.: From I-39 take Exit 124 (Coloma) and follow STH-21 east 4.9 mi. At CTH-B turn right and go south 0.7 mi. At CTH-JJ turn right and go southwest 1.5 mi. At Cypress Rd. turn right and go west 0.1 mi. Roadside parking.

I-39 Southbound Wayside: From Coloma on I-39, go south 3.5 mi and exit at the highway wayside at Mile Marker 120. The Trail access is at the kiosk on the west end of the wayside.

Additional Parking: (i) Czech Ave. parking area 0.3 mi east of the Wedde Creek Segment Czech Ave. Trail access. A short spur trail leads north to the Ice Age Trail. (ii) 6th Ave. cul-de-sac. A blue-blazed spur trail leads 0.2 mi south to the Ice Age Trail.

THE HIKE

From its starting point on Cypress Road the **Wedde Creek Segment** heads south through hardwood forest and a prairie restoration area to a crossing on a wooden bridge of the South Branch of Wedde Creek. Shortly before crossing the creek, the segment intersects a snowmobile trail and shares this trail for about 0.4 miles. The segment follows a ridge above the south side of the creek for a short distance before heading south and then west along the crest of a small end moraine. As the segment continues, hikers should look for a large erratic in an oak opening south of the Trail. The segment intersects a spur trail that leads south to a parking area on Czech Avenue, then continues west through conifer forests and oak barrens to the segment's endpoint on Czech Avenue, a short distance west of the parking area.

To reach the next segment, hikers should head 0.7 miles west on a connecting route along Czech Avenue.

Waushara County

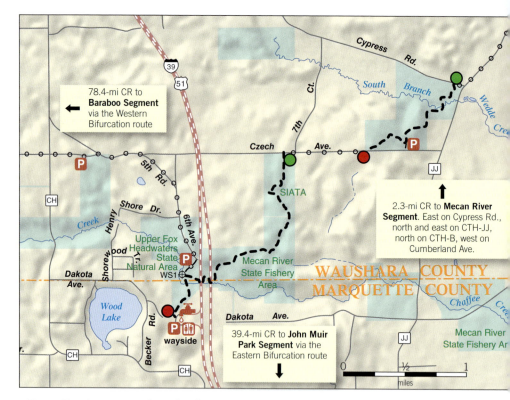

From Czech Avenue, the **Chaffee Creek Segment** heads south on a narrow strip between two agriculture fields. As it makes it way southwest toward the Chaffee Creek valley the segment passes several trailside kettles while traversing grassy meadows and savanna woodlands. After almost 1.5 miles, the segment crosses into the Upper Chaffee Creek Meadow, one of three units of the Upper Fox Headwaters State Natural Area, and continues on toward Chaffee Creek.

The Upper Chaffee Creek Meadow recognizes the unique flora that grow in the Chaffee Creek valley including wet-mesic prairie, wetland fen complex and sedge meadow. The area boasts over 100 native plants species. Prairie grasses include big and little bluestem, blue-joint grass and slender wheat grass.

The segment soon arrives at Chaffee Creek and continues west under I-39. A short distance west of the I-39 underpass the segment arrives at a T-intersection (WS1). A blue-blazed spur trail heads north from the intersection 0.2 miles to the 6th Avenue cul-de-sac.

Continuing south beyond the meadow the segment reaches its endpoint at an Ice Age Trail kiosk in the I-39 southbound wayside.

AREA SERVICES

Richford: See Mecan River Segment, p. 172. From the Cypress Rd. Trail access go east and north ~2 mi.

Coloma: See Mecan River Segment, p. 172. From the Cypress Rd. Trail access go northwest ~7 mi. Also see Trail Access and Parking directions, above.

Wautoma: See Mecan River Segment, p. 172. From the Cypress Rd. Trail access go east and north ~12 mi.

The Trail wends its way through a rock garden along the Bohn Lake Segment.

Marquette County

Atlas Map 53f-E–56f-E; Databook pages 51–52
Total miles: 41.9 (Trail 1.8; Connecting Route 40.1)

Marquette County was entirely covered by the Green Bay Lobe. The region is part of the central sands of Wisconsin. The county is mostly undeveloped, with pine and oak forests and extensive grass marshes. The mucky-peat soils of these marshes owe their origin to two major geologic events. The glacier ice, advancing across east central Wisconsin, gouged out the original basins. Then water from the melting glaciers transformed them into lake basins. The lake basins were sandy along the beach areas, but the deep-water areas had fine water-sorted deposits. As the climate warmed, vegetation started to encroach upon the water areas. Over the last 13,000 years, sedges and marsh grasses slowly replaced the water areas. The wet environment of the marsh inhibits the decomposition of these plant remains, so it accumulates. The organic soils we see today are simply decayed plant residue accumulated over thousands of years. Each winter, another layer of dead plants is added. Research on bogs in Wisconsin shows that these organic soils form at a rate of about one inch every 40 years. Some marshes in the area have an organic layer more than ten feet thick.

John Muir, known as the father of America's National Parks, grew up on a farm near Fountain Lake, now called Ennis Lake, in an area that had been home to the Winnebagos. It now is the site of a national historic landmark, state natural area and county park. The Trail segment mostly surrounds the lake and highlights the landscape where Muir developed a profound love for nature. Although the county has few off-road Ice Age Trail miles, it has plenty of other places of interest to explore, such as Page Creek Marsh State Natural Area and Observatory Hill State Natural Area, a site often visited by Muir.

The National Park Service, Wisconsin Department of Natural Resources and Marquette County have started the planning process for determining the future Ice Age Trail corridor through the county. It will be several years before the Ice Age Trail corridor will be determined.

CHAPTER INFORMATION

The Marquette County Chapter focuses on (i) supporting IATA activities, Trail maintenance and advocacy for the Ice Age Trail corridor planning process; (ii) building outdoor family traditions by planning a variety of Trail-related events and (iii) developing relationships with community organizations with interests in health, conservation and preservation. The chapter has created the *John Muir*

Park Ice Age Trail Guide that enhances a hiker's experience in the park. It is available from the Marquette County Chapter's home page on the IATA website.

COUNTY INFORMATION

Marquette County Convention and Visitors Bureau:
travelmarquettecounty.com

Marquette County Information: co.marquette.wi.us

Sunset over Ennis Lake on the John Muir Park Segment.

John Muir Park Segment (Atlas Map 56f-E; Databook page 52)

SNAPSHOT

1.8 miles: CTH-F to John Muir Memorial County Park entrance drive

 This segment highlights the boyhood playground of John Muir, "Father of the National Parks."

Note: *New Ice Age Trail is planned south of John Muir Memorial County Park. Check with the Ice Age Trail Alliance (800-227-0046, iceagetrail.org) for details.*

	From Ennis Lake.		Dogs should be leashed (8-ft max) and under control at all times.
	In John Muir Memorial County Park.		A blue-blazed trail leading to the John Muir Memorial County Park parking area and a few side trails leading to Ennis Lake.
	One ColdCache site on segment.		

TRAIL ACCESS AND PARKING

CTH-F: From Portage, take STH-33 north. At CTH-F turn left and continue north 10.4 mi. The parking area is on the west side of the road (N1595 CTH-F).

John Muir Memorial County Park Entrance Drive: From Portage, take STH-33 north. At CTH-F turn left and continue north 10.0 mi. The park is on the east side of the road and has a large parking area.

THE HIKE

On this segment hikers will explore and experience the land that was the boyhood home of John Muir and that made such a positive and lifelong impression on the eminent naturalist and founder of the Sierra Club. Portions of the segment pass across land that was homesteaded in 1849 by the Ennis and Muir families; the Muirs lived on the northeast side of Ennis Lake, known as Fountain Lake at the time, from 1849 to 1856. Although John Muir traveled all over the world, he never forget his family homestead and tried several times to buy and preserve it. He said, "Even if I should never see it again, the beauty of its lilies and orchids is so pressed into my mind, I shall always enjoy looking back at them in imagination, even across the seas and continents and perhaps after I am dead."

The segment passes through prairie and meadows that fill with wildflowers in the summer, features views of picturesque Ennis Lake and passes through and by open oak forests, sedge meadows and fens bordered by tamarack and bog birch. It begins at CTH-F near the parking area, which is a site on the Marquette County John Muir Nature and History Route and includes interpretive signage regarding the Eggleston Family, farming and John Muir's boyhood home. The segment crosses CTH-F into the IATA's Muir Preserve and travels east through a field that is being converted into a prairie. The segment then turns south and follows a tree line between another field and sedge meadow before reaching Gillette Drive.

Crossing Gillette Drive, the segment enters Muir Park State Natural Area (SNA) and climbs to the top of a rise with outstanding panoramic views of Ennis Lake, a spring-fed 30-acre kettle lake occupying a marshy pocket in a ground moraine. The segment follows along the edge of a mesic prairie and shortly inter-

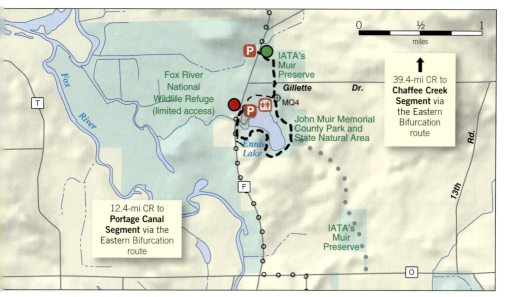

sects (**MQ4**) a blue-blazed trail that heads around the north side of Ennis Lake to the John Muir Memorial County Park parking area.

From here the segment begins to circle around the eastern and southern shores of Ennis Lake. Trailside benches offer hikers the chance to enjoy the natural surroundings and contemplate the rich history of the area. Many unusual and rare plants can be found in Muir Park SNA, and a guide is available on the Marquette County Chapter's home page on the IATA website (**iceagetrail.org/volunteer/chapters/marquette-county**).

The segment crosses the rich fen that surrounds the lake's eastern inlet on a boardwalk bridge. The calcareous fen and surrounding prairies contain a diversity of unusual and rare species. The segment then curves around the southern end of the lake. The bog near the lake's southeast corner offers the right environs for the northern wet forest dominated by tamarack, poison sumac and bog birch, with numerous pitcher plants beneath. Continuing on, the Trail eventually crosses the fen surrounding the western outlet of the lake on another boardwalk bridge and enters John Muir Memorial County Park, quickly reaching the segment's endpoint at the park entrance.

Several memorials to John Muir exist in the park: a granite monument, a wooden sign and an extensive informational display near the parking area. There is also an exhibit on his life at the Montello Museum (55 West Montello Street). But the parks and preserve are likely the best memorial to the man; hikers can literally walk in Muir's footsteps and see a landscape that has changed little since he lived here.

AREA SERVICES

Montello: Restaurant, grocery store, convenience store, lodging, camping, library, medical service. From John Muir Memorial County Park, go north on CTH-F 7.8 mi. At STH-22 (Main St.) turn left and continue north for 0.8 mi. Area info available from the Montello Area Chamber of Commerce (608-297-7420, montellowi.com).

Portage: See Portage Canal Segment, p. 186. From John Muir Memorial County Park go south ~10 mi. Also see Trail Access and Parking directions, above.

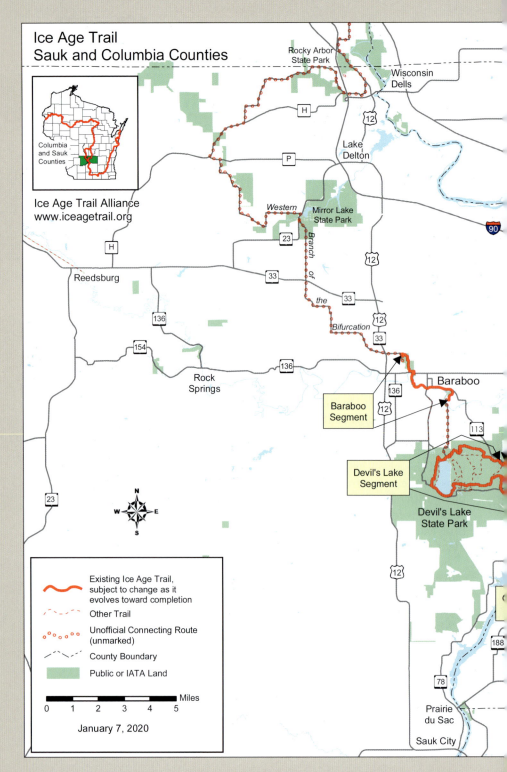

Sauk & Columbia Counties

Northern Columbia County

Atlas Maps 56f-E–58f-E; Databook pages 53–54
Total miles: 17.6 (Trail 3.0; Connecting Route 14.5)

The Green Bay Lobe covered nearly all of Columbia County during the Wisconsin Glaciation. When the ice sheet receded, the Green Bay Lobe left behind the Fox River, one of the few major rivers in Wisconsin that flows northward. The Fox River empties into Lake Winnebago and then flows northward to Green Bay. From there the waters eventually flow through the Great Lakes and out the St. Lawrence River to the north Atlantic. North of the Wisconsin River, the Ice Age Trail traverses low, rolling topography with large, open wetlands, grasslands and forested woodlots. Portage lies on a large outwash plain deposited by the Wisconsin River when it carried meltwater from the retreating glacier. The Ice Age Trail winds its way through the city of Portage, highlighting the history of the area and the Portage Canal. The Portage Canal Segment is dotted with historical sites including the Portage Canal and locks and the Historic Indian Agency House, setting of scenes in Juliette M. Kinzie's *Wau-Bun: The "Early Day" in the Northwest* that recorded transactions with Winnebago (Ho-Chunk) populations.

The Ice Age Trail route in the northern part of Columbia County is yet to be determined. Currently the connecting route (see map on p. 183) highlights the Fox River and French Creek State Wildlife Area. The western connecting route near Wisconsin Dells passes not far from the Kingsley Bend Mound Group, both a historical and a religious Ho-Chunk location.

CHAPTER INFORMATION

The Baraboo Hills/Heritage Chapter cares for the Ice Age Trail as it winds through Northern Columbia County and through Sauk County. The chapter works with the City of Portage and local conservation agencies to build and maintain the Trail. The Trail's route through the city helps highlight important Native American history alongside early European settlement in the area. The chapter also works to develop, maintain and protect the Ice Age Trail in Sauk County where the Trail passes through popular Devil's Lake State Park and heads into Southern Columbia County.

COUNTY INFORMATION

Columbia County Visitor Bureau: 608-742-6161, travelcolumbiacounty.net

A pedestrian bridge spans the Wisconsin River along the Portage Canal Segment.

Sauk County

Atlas Maps 58f-E–59f-E, 58f-W–60f-W and 61f–62f
Databook pages 53–57
Total miles: 35.0 (Trail 18.5; Connecting Route 16.5)

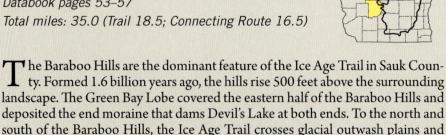

The Baraboo Hills are the dominant feature of the Ice Age Trail in Sauk County. Formed 1.6 billion years ago, the hills rise 500 feet above the surrounding landscape. The Green Bay Lobe covered the eastern half of the Baraboo Hills and deposited the end moraine that dams Devil's Lake at both ends. To the north and south of the Baraboo Hills, the Ice Age Trail crosses glacial outwash plains and small moraines.

Devil's Lake State Park is one of the Ice Age National Scientific Reserve units and the Ice Age Trail winds through the park and around the lake. A combination of interesting geology, diverse fauna, prehistoric effigy mounds, historic Civilian Conservation Corps (CCC) buildings and spectacular scenery make Devil's Lake a popular destination. Parfrey's Glen State Natural Area anchors the current Ice Age Trail route in the county to the east of Devil's Lake State Park. The state recognizes several other designated State Natural Areas within in the park, including East Bluff State Natural Area, Devil's Lake Oak Forest State Natural Area and South Bluff/Devil's Nose State Natural Area. The name "Devil's Lake" is a mistranslation from several different Native American names for the lake, which was believed to be the abode of good and evil spirits. In addition to the Bird Effigy Mound and other mounds in Devil's Lake State Park, Man Mound Park, a National Historic Landmark near Baraboo, contains the only human-shaped effigy in North America.

In Devil's Lake State Park the two branches of Ice Age Trail's bifurcation, which had split in Waushara County, reunite (or split depending on hike direction). The western branch arrives after passing through the lakebed of Glacial Lake Wisconsin, the Wisconsin Dells, Mirror Lake and Baraboo. The eastern branch, with more established segments of the Ice Age Trail at this time, arrives after passing through Marquette County, the city of Portage and Pine Island State Wildlife Area. Contact the Ice Age Trail Alliance for more information on the bifurcation. Camping is available at Devil's Lake State Park and at private campgrounds near Baraboo and is mentioned in the area services for the Devil's Lake and Merrimac Segments.

CHAPTER INFORMATION

The Baraboo Hills/Heritage Chapter works to develop, maintain and protect the Ice Age Trail in Sauk County. The Baraboo Hills/Heritage and Lodi Valley chapters of the Ice Age Trail Alliance have partnered to create the "Glacial Drifters" hiking award program. Participants in the program earn a patch for hiking the entire Ice Age Trail as it winds its way through Sauk County and southern Columbia County, for a total of about 50 miles. Registered participants will receive maps and information on the various segments, along with a hiking log.

COUNTY INFORMATION

Sauk County Tourism Information: co.sauk.wi.us

A young family soaks up the view from the quartzite bluffs on the Devil's Lake Segment.

Baraboo Segment (Atlas Map 60f-W; Databook page 112)

SNAPSHOT

4.0 miles: UW-Baraboo/Sauk County to Effinger Rd. at Manchester St.

 This segment shows off the Baraboo River along a network of city parks and includes a stop at Circus World Museum.

On the UW-Baraboo/Sauk County Campus, Ochsner Park and Zoo, Attridge Park, Mary Rountree Park, Statz Park and Maxwell-Potter Conservancy Area.

From the Baraboo River.

At several of the city parks. Restroom also available at UW-Baraboo/Sauk County Campus.

 Segment is entirely in the city of Baraboo.

 By law, dogs must be leashed in city parks.

 Portions follow sidewalks or roads and the Baraboo Riverwalk. The Riverwalk is also open to bikes.

 Other trails in some city parks.

 Portions of this segment may be suitable for those using wheelchairs or similar devices.

TRAIL ACCESS AND PARKING

UW-Baraboo/Sauk County: From I-90/94 take Exit 92 and follow USH-12E south for 7.0 mi. Take Exit 218 for STH-33 East and STH-136 and follow STH-33 (Linn St.) east for 0.6 mi. At Connie Rd. turn left and go north 0.5 mi. Trail access is at the north end of the parking area to the west of the disc golf kiosk.

Effinger Rd. at Manchester St.: From I-90/94 Exit 106 for STH-33 Baraboo/Portage. Take STH-33 west 11.9 mi. At Washington St. turn left and go south 0.6 mi. At Water St. (STH-113) turn left and go east less than 0.1 mi. At Effinger Rd. turn right and go south 0.4 mi to its intersection with Manchester St. The Trail access is on the northwest corner of the intersection. No parking. Instead, park on Water St. along the Trail route.

Additional Parking: (i) Ochsner Park and Zoo. (ii) Attridge Park. (iii) Lower Ochsner Park. (iv) Mary Rountree Park. (v) Statz Park. (vi) Maxwell-Potter Conservancy Area on Mill Race Dr. at Hill St.

THE HIKE

From its starting point at the UW-Baraboo/Sauk County parking area the segment follows a ridge with fine views toward the Baraboo Range and passes through campus property featuring mixed hardwoods, remnant prairie and oak savanna. Near the beginning of the segment, hikers will pass a small, scenic, glacial kettle with cattails and a rock ledge. The segment passes through the campus's disc golf course and then bends south, skirting athletic fields for area schools, passing through Baraboo High School's parking area and then intersecting Berkeley Boulevard.

The segment heads east then south a short distance on Berkeley Boulevard, then continues east on 9th Avenue for 0.2 miles. At Draper Street the segment turns south, crosses 8th Avenue (Ringling Boulevard/STH-33) and continues through a wooded area in Ochsner Park and Zoo, then down steep stone stairs to an intersection with the Baraboo Riverwalk. The Riverwalk parallels the Baraboo River for most of its route as it goes through or connects to several city parks.

Once on the Riverwalk route, the segment heads south through Lower

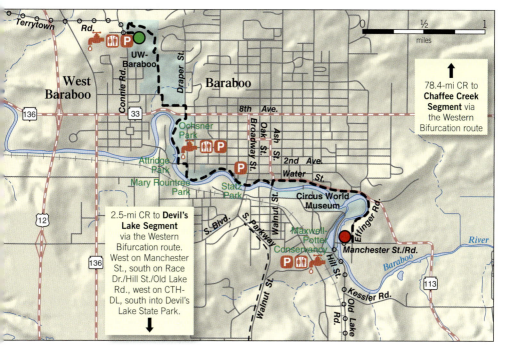

Ochsner Park, passing an old bridge crossing the Baraboo River to Attridge Park. The Trail bends east on 2nd Avenue a short distance to skirt private property along the river, then heads south into Mary Rountree Park and back toward the river before resuming an eastward course into Statz Park. The segment crosses underneath Broadway Street and continues to follow the Baraboo Riverwalk to Water Street (STH-113).

On Water Street (STH-113) the segment passes the Circus World Museum. This National and State Historic Landmark was the site of Ringlingville, the Ringling Bros. Circus winter quarters from 1884 to 1918. It is home to 200 preserved circus wagons and has extensive historical circus exhibits on display.

The segment departs from Water Street at Effinger Road and heads south for 0.4 miles to its terminus at Manchester Street.

Mobile Skills Crew project site, 2008

POINTS OF INTEREST

Man Mound Park: 4.7 mi from the Ice Age Trail. From Water St. (STH-113), head east and turn left on Washington Ave., then right on 8th St. (STH-33), then left on CTH-T, then right onto Man Mound Rd. to the park (E13085 Man Mound Rd., Baraboo).

Man Mound is the only surviving anthropomorphic (human-shaped) effigy in North America, a National Historic Landmark, measuring 214 ft by 48 ft, its legs damaged by road construction.

AREA SERVICES

Baraboo and West Baraboo: Restaurant, grocery store, convenience store, general shopping, lodging, camping, library, medical service. On Trail. INN Style lodging at Pinehaven (608-356-3489, pinehavenbnb.com) and Inn at Wawanissee Point (608-305-2241, innatwawanisseepoint.com). Baraboo area info available from the Baraboo Chamber of Commerce (800-227-2266, baraboo.com).

Devil's Lake State Park: See Devil's Lake Segment, p. 197. From the UW-Baraboo/Sauk County campus go south ~5 mi.

Sauk Point Segment (Atlas Map 61f; Databook page 55)

SNAPSHOT

3.9 miles (3.9 IAT, 0.1 CR): CTH-DL to STH-113

 This segment covers a very quiet corner of Devil's Lake State Park (DLSP) and offers access to spectacular Parfrey's Glen.

	Parfrey's Glen Creek is ~ 0.1 mi from the Trail on the Parfrey's Glen Trail.	Dogs are not allowed in Parfrey's Glen State Natural Area (SNA) except on the IAT. By law, dogs **must** be leashed when hiking on the Trail in Parfrey's Glen SNA and Devil's Lake State Park.
	At Parfey's Glen parking area.	
	Two ColdCache sites on segment.	Trail into Parfrey's Glen State Natural Area and blue-blazed spur trail (**SA7**) to Solumn Ln. parking area.

TRAIL ACCESS AND PARKING

CTH-DL: From the Baraboo area on USH-12, take exit 218 for STH-33 East and STH-136. Take STH-33 (Linn St. becomes 8th Ave.) east for 2.9mi. At Washington Ave. turn right and go south 0.6 mi. At STH-113 turn left and continue south 5.4 mi. At CTH-DL turn left and go east 2.0 mi to the parking area for Parfrey's Glen State Natural Area on the north side of the road. Overflow roadside parking available.

STH-113: From the Baraboo area on USH-12, take exit 218 for STH-33 East and STH-136. Take STH-33 (Linn St. becomes 8th Ave.) east for 2.9 mi. At Washington Ave. turn right and go south 0.6 mi. At STH-113 turn left and continue south 3.8 mi to the parking area on the west side of the road.

Additional Parking: Solum Ln. parking area. A blue-blazed spur trail leads to the Ice Age Trail (**SA7**).

THE HIKE

The segment starts at the information kiosk and parking area for Parfrey's Glen State Natural Area, Wisconsin's first State Natural Area. Native wildflowers are abundant along portions of the segment during the spring and summer. From the parking area, the segment climbs gently but consistently uphill on a narrow, single-track trail through a mixed hardwood forest including pockets of red cedar and groves of aspen. Occasional large "wolf trees," surrounded by mostly younger trees, indicate this area was probably used as farmland or open pasture before being allowed to transition back to forest a few decades ago. After a mile, the segment passes into Devil's Lake State Park (DLSP) and a more mature forest including red oak, white oak, sugar maple, red elm, shagbark hickory, jack-in-the-pulpit and trillium. Hikers may note oak trees with double trunks, indicating harvested trees from 60 to 80 years ago that have regenerated multiple trunks.

As the segment passes through a number of openings in the forest, a hiker may catch a glimpse of a nearby cell tower that marks Sauk Point, the highest point in Sauk County. The segment heads west and soon reaches a junction (**SA7**) with a blue-blazed spur trail that leads 0.3 miles south to a parking area on Solum Lane.

West of the spur trail, the segment reaches its highest elevation at the "Blue Mounds Vista" (**SA8**), with a bench in a grassy area (may be overgrown in the summer) offering spectacular views of the lower Wisconsin River valley and (about 30 miles away) Blue Mounds. On a clear day when leaves are down, hik-

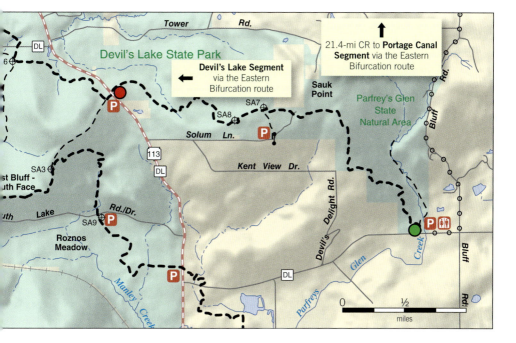

ers can look southeast and see the state capitol's dome in Madison.

From here the Trail moves slowly downhill amongst hummocky ridges, rocky downhill stretches and a few dry stream crossings. Hikers reach a farm and briefly cross a farm field before following a rolling ridge to the segment's endpoint on STH-113.

Mobile Skills Crew project site, 2009, 2019

POINTS OF INTEREST

Parfrey's Glen State Natural Area: On Trail. (1377 CTH-DL, Merrimac, dnr.wi.gov/topic/Lands/naturalareas/index.asp?SNA=1 or devilslakewisconsin.com/parfreys-glen).

Designated in 1952 as Wisconsin's first State Natural Area (SNA), Parfrey's Glen offers a 0.7-mi nature trail that passes through a spectacular deep gorge carved into the sandstone conglomerate of embedded quartzite pebbles and boulders on the south flank of the Baraboo Hills. The uppermost part of the Glen, with its jumble of huge fallen rocks, is nearly 100 feet deep. Hikers will pass moss-covered walls moist from seepage before the trail ends at a small waterfall. The Glen's unique microclimate grows northern flora, including white pine, yellow birch, mountain maple and rare cliff plants. An unusual aquatic ecosystem flourishes in the fast, cold, hardwater stream that flows through the gorge and the Glen harbors a diverse insect fauna with a few rare and threatened species. Pets are not allowed in Parfrey's Glen SNA except along the Ice Age Trail. The Area is open from 6 am to 8 pm.

Durward's Glen Retreat & Conference Center: From the CTH-DL Trail Access, head east on CTH-DL, turn left (north) on STH-78 N, then turn left (north) onto Durwards Glen Rd, turn left (west) onto McLeisch Rd. to the entrance of the grounds (W11876 McLeisch Rd., Baraboo, 608-356-8113, durwardsglen.org). INN Style lodging option.

Durward's Glen is located in the beautiful Baraboo Hills National Natural Landmark. The pristine 40-acre property offers scenic hiking trails, picturesque picnic areas, a pond, a rambling brook and a white oak tree over 350 years old. Durward's Glen is recognized as a place for reflection, peace and inspiration. Grounds are open to the public daily from dawn until dusk.

AREA SERVICES

INN Style lodging: Durward's Glen Retreat & Conference Center (608-356-8113, durwardsglen.org). See Points of Interest p. 195.

Devil's Lake State Park (DLSP): See Devil's Lake Segment, p. 197. From the STH-113 Trail access go west ~3 mi.

Baraboo and West Baraboo: See Baraboo Segment, p. 193. From the STH-113 Trail access go north ~5 mi. Also see Trail Access and Parking directions, above.

A path through summer woods on the Sauk Point Segment.

Devil's Lake Segment (Atlas Map 61f; Databook pages 55–56)

SNAPSHOT

10.9 miles: STH-113 Northern Trail Access to STH-113 Southern Trail Access

This is arguably the most dramatic Ice Age Trail segment of all, exploring Wisconsin's largest and most-visited state park and offering magnificent views from 500-foot quartzite bluffs overlooking a 360-acre lake.

At various locations throughout Devil's Lake State Park (DLSP).

From Devil's Lake.

At DLSP campgrounds and several nearby private campgrounds (see Area Services).

Six ColdCache sites on segment.

By law, dogs must be leashed in DLSP.

Portions overlap DLSP roads, bike and ski trails. Hike well off to the side when ski trails are groomed.

Extensive DLSP trail network.

TRAIL ACCESS AND PARKING

STH-113 Northern Trail Access: From the Baraboo area on USH-12, take exit 218 for STH-33 East and STH-136. Take STH-33 (Linn St. becomes 8th Ave.) east for 2.6 mi. At Washington Ave. turn right and go south 0.6 mi. At STH-113 turn left and continue south 3.8 mi to the parking area on the west side of the road.

STH-113 Southern Trail Access: *From Baraboo area* on USH-12, take exit 218 for STH-33 East and STH-136. Take STH-33 (Linn St. becomes 8th Ave.) east for 2.6 mi. At Washington Ave. turn right and go south 0.6 mi. At STH-113 turn left and continue south 5.3 mi to the parking area on the west side of the road. *From Merrimac* at the intersection of Baraboo St. and STH-113/78, take STH-113/78 west for 2.5 mi. Continue on STH-113 north for 2.3 mi to the DLSP Roznos Meadow parking area on the west side of the road.

Additional Parking: Parking areas throughout DLSP.

THE HIKE

Devil's Lake State Park (DLSP) is a place of striking contrasts. The purple rock, called Baraboo quartzite, in the walls of Devil's Lake gorge is more than 1.6 billion years old. The glacially deposited ridges or moraines that block both ends of the gorge are only about 16,000 years old. A three-dimensional topographical map of the park, found at the park's Nature Center, shows that the moraines wrap around high points in the landscape. Ice filled the lowlands in the eastern part of the park and flowed into both ends of the gorge but did not advance onto the higher western parts of the landscape. The ice left behind two prominent moraines that plugged both ends of the ancient gorge, now occupied by Devil's Lake.

These two moraine "plugs" and the way they create the lake are unique in the entire world. Breathtaking views of the western part of the park, part of the unglaciated Driftless Area, can be had from the many rock ledges the Ice Age Trail passes along the rim of the East Bluff. Cold airflow from the bluffs provides habitat for unusual northern plant species. Areas of dry prairie, red oak and maple forest are found atop the bluffs.

From the northern Trail access parking area on STH-113, a short blue-blazed spur trail leads to the Trail. From here the segment heads southwest and quickly intersects DLSP's Upland Trail Loop. Hikers should turn right and hike northwest (following the loop counter-clockwise) for about a mile to a junction (**SA6**) with the park's Johnson Moraine Loop. At the junction, hikers should turn right and head north across CTH-DL.

The segment makes its way west through a mix of meadows and woodlands, then drops down to the park's Ice Age campground and intersects (**SA5**) the campground road between sites 419 and 420. The segment follows the campground road south and then west, then follows a park road out of the campground and under CTH-DL. The segment continues southwest along the park road, skirting the Northern Lights campground, turns sharply left past the park's amphitheater, cuts through woods, eventually joins the Ice Age and Northern Lights campgrounds' exit road and shortly reaches the park's main exit road. Upon reaching the intersection (**SA10**) with the DLSP main exit road, hikers have arrived at the spot where the two branches of the Ice Age Trail bifurcation reunite. The connecting route from the western branch arrives from the Baraboo Segment down the park's exit road.

From the bifurcation intersection, the segment crosses a set of railroad tracks and passes through the North Shore Picnic Area with a seasonal concession stand and continues west paralleling the north shore of Devil's Lake on an asphalt path. The segment then makes its way northward from the lakeshore to connect with the park's West Bluff Trail.

The portion following the West Bluff Trail climbs steeply to the top of the West Bluff, 500 feet above lake level. Along the top of the bluff there are lookout points where hikers will have excellent views of Devil's Lake and the surrounding hills and moraines. Because it is in the Driftless Area, there are no erratics on the West Bluff. This is a popular rock climbing area that is said to have more than 2,000 possible climbing routes. The segment here passes through mixed woodlands with hardwoods and pine and features many woodland wildflowers such as jack-in-the-pulpit, Solomon's seal, wild geranium, tinkers weed, tick trefoil and woodland milkweed.

The segment descends gradually down the West Bluff to the South Lake Road (South Lake Drive)(**SA4**). Hikers should head east along the left side of the road and the south shore of Devil's Lake. At the point where the road leaves the lake, the segment turns left along a boardwalk and passes through the South Shore Picnic Area, with a seasonal concession stand, water and restrooms. Here the segment passes Bird Effigy Mound, the largest and most impressive of a number of Native American mounds in the park.

The segment crosses railroad tracks, turns left and follows the park's Balanced Rock Trail up steep stone steps, past Balanced Rock (slightly off-trail) to an intersection with the park's East Bluff Trail. This short section of Ice Age Trail can be a strenuous and challenging climb. Use caution when climbing on the rocks (especially when wet) and pay close attention to Trail signage. At the intersection with the East Bluff Trail, hikers should turn right and head east along the East Bluff Trail, which offers spectacular views of the South Bluff, Baraboo Hills and the

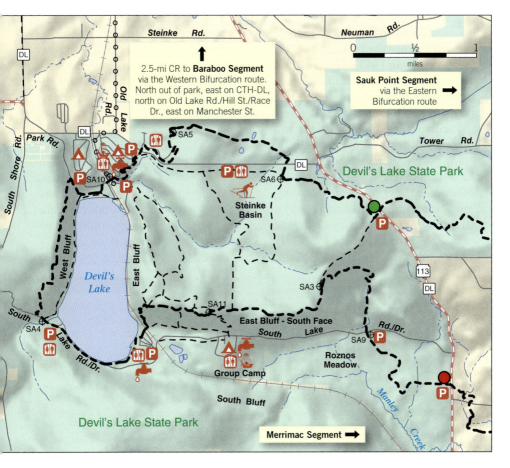

terminal moraine below. This portion of the segment is shaded in places by small oaks and gnarled red cedars. There are remnants of dry prairie here with flora including blazing star, leadplant, yellow false foxglove, shooting star, sunflower, goldenrod, aster and big bluestem grass. From the many rock ledges along the south face of the East Bluff, hikers can watch for turkey vultures and raptors soaring, sometimes at eye level. Signage points to a short loop trail to Devil's Doorway, the iconic rock formation of the park.

Moving along, the Trail quickly reaches a junction with the Potholes Trail. Hikers looking for an interesting but strenuous side trip can create a "loop trail" by hiking down the bluff on the Potholes Trail, turning east at the bottom of the bluff on the Grotto Trail and climbing back up the bluff on the CCC Trail to reconnect with the Ice Age Trail near the Moldy Buttress Cliffside rock formation. The Potholes Trail passes ancient potholes or depressions, not far below the top of the bluff, that were carved in the rock from fast moving water. The CCC Trail helps commemorate the CCC workers who built many of the trails in the park in the 1930s during the Great Depression. They were not allowed to use dynamite, so rocks were placed by hand labor.

Continuing east the segment departs (SA11) from the park's East Bluff Trail by the Moldy Buttress cliffside rock formation via a connector trail heading north then east about 0.25 miles to reconnect with the park's Upland Trail Loop. The segment follows the Upland Trail Loop east through woodlands and at another trail intersection (**SA3**) departs from the Upland Trail Loop and continues east, dropping down the south face of the East Bluff. Hikers may catch views of the largest unbroken sandstone escarpment in the park, a rare hanging sedge meadow and many rock outcrops. The segment passes a babbling brook in a diverse woodland with several species of fern and wildflowers such as mayapple, milkweed, goldenrod, aster and tick trefoil.

The segment crosses South Lake Road (South Lake Drive) and enters Roznos Meadow. Here the segment traverses open prairie and grassland, giving 360-degree views of the surrounding Baraboo Hills towering above. A National Park Service interpretive sign (**SA9**) explains the moraine dam, an important glacial feature that had a major influence on the creation of the surrounding landscape. The segment ends at the STH-113 southern Trail access parking area.

Mobile Skills Crew project site, 2002, 2003, 2004, 2008, 2009, 2012, 2017, 2018

POINTS OF INTEREST

Aldo Leopold Legacy Center: From the Baraboo area on USH-12, take exit 218 for STH-33 East and STH-136. Take STH-33 (Linn St. becomes 8th Ave.) east for 2.9 mi. At CTH-T turn left and go north 7.0 mi. At Levee Rd. (Rustic Road 49) turn left and go east 2.4 mi to the entrance of the Legacy Center on the right (E13701 Levee Rd., Baraboo, 608-355-0279, aldoleopold.org).

The Aldo Leopold Foundation operates the Aldo Leopold Legacy Center, which is an educational and interpretive facility near the Leopold "Shack." Here Aldo Leopold converted a chicken coop on his farm and wrote part of his conservation classic masterpiece on land ethics, A Sand County Almanac. This is also the very same land where Aldo Leopold died in 1948 fighting a brush fire. The Legacy Center is an excellent place to learn more about this famous American naturalist and see how the Leopold Foundation is carrying out his message of land ethics today. The Center is open from mid-April to the end of October with more limited hours during winter. Various guided and self-guided tours are available. Visit the website or contact the Aldo Leopold Foundation and Legacy Center for more information.

International Crane Foundation (ICF): From the Baraboo area on USH-12, exit 214 for North Reedsburg Rd. Take N. Reedsburg Rd. east 0.4 mi. At CTH-BD turn left and go north 1.0 mi. At Shady Lane Rd. turn right and go 1.0 mi. (E11376 Shady Lane Rd., Baraboo, 608-356-9462, savingcranes.org).

The International Crane Foundation (ICF) works worldwide to conserve cranes and the ecosystems, watersheds and flyways on which they depend. ICF is dedicated to providing experience, knowledge and inspiration to involve people in resolving threats to these ecosystems.

At its Baraboo headquarters, visitors can see all 15 species of cranes. The site offers guided and self-guided tours, an interactive educational center, live crane exhibits and over 4.0 mi of hiking trails over 100 acres of restored prairie, oak savanna and wetlands. The Baraboo headquarters is open to visitors from April 15 to October 31. Tours are provided daily from Memorial Day to Labor Day and on weekends in April, May, September and October.

AREA SERVICES

Devil's Lake State Park (DLSP): Seasonal concession stand, camping. On Trail (608-356-8301, dnr.wi.gov/topic/parks/name/devilslake; reservations: 888-947-2757, wisconsin.goingtocamp.com).

Local Area: Restaurant, camping at Double K-D Ranch Campground (608-434-0346, doublekdranch.com); Wheeler's Campground (608-356-4877, wheelerscampground.com) and Green Valley Campground (608-355-0090).

Baraboo and West Baraboo: See Baraboo Segment, p. 192. From the STH-113 northern Trail access go north ~5 mi. Also see Trail Access and Parking directions, above.

A mother-daughter trio pauses for reflection on the bluffs along the Devil's Lake Segment.

Merrimac Segment (Atlas Map 61f; Databook pages 56–57)

SNAPSHOT

3.7 miles: STH-113 to Marsh Rd. Southern Trail Access

 This segment highlights the diverse landscape of Riverland Conservancy's Merrimac Preserve and offers a quiet break from the crowds at Devil's Lake.

Note: Riverland Conservancy requires all visitors to the Merrimac Preserve (this entire segment) to wear blaze orange during gun deer and muzzleloader hunting seasons.

 From creeks and wetland areas.

At nearby private campground (see Area Services) and Devil's Lake State Park.

 Dogs should be leashed (8-ft max) and under control at all times.

 Briefly overlaps snowmobile trails.

 Riverland Conservancy trail network.

TRAIL ACCESS AND PARKING

STH-113: *From Baraboo area* on USH-12, take exit 218 for STH-33 East and STH-136. Take STH-33 (Linn St. becomes 8th Ave.) east for 2.6 mi. At Washington Ave. turn right and go south 0.6 mi. At STH-113 turn left and continue south 5.3 mi to the parking area on the west side of the road. *From Merrimac* at the intersection of Baraboo St. and STH-113/78, take STH-113/78 west for 2.5 mi. Continue on STH-113 north for 2.3 mi to the DLSP Roznos Meadow parking area on the west side of the road.

Marsh Rd. Southern Trail Access: From STH-113/78 at Merrimac turn north on Baraboo St. and go 0.3 mi. At Cemetery Rd., which becomes Marsh Rd., turn left and go west then north 0.9 mi to parking area on the northeast side of the road.

THE HIKE

This segment passes through the Merrimac Preserve, which is owned and managed by the Riverland Conservancy, and encompasses more than 1,800 acres. The preserve provides an integral wildlife corridor between the Baraboo Bluffs and the Wisconsin River. Riverland Conservancy began in 1997 as Wisconsin Power and Light Stewardship Trust through the generous donation of lands and equipment by Wisconsin Power and Light Co.

The segment heads east from STH-113 and quickly enters a wooded area, passes a hidden stream in an intimate setting and enters a prairie opening that leads to CTH-DL. Across the road, the segment continues south through a diverse prairie before descending toward a wetland and boardwalk crossing. The segment climbs gently and enters a savanna area with informational signs about groundwater and invasive species. Through this savanna area, views to the west feature the bluffs of Devil's Lake State Park and the terminal moraine between them. The segment returns to the woods then crosses another wetland area on a long boardwalk protecting fragile soils underneath. The segment continues alongside a meadow and briefly joins a snowmobile trail before reaching the northern Trail access on Marsh Road.

East of Marsh Road the segment winds through a mix of wooded areas, recent timber harvest areas and restored oak savannas and prairies. At one point the segment skirts past an area that was a primitive mowed airstrip which is being allowed to return to prairie. Toward the end, the segment drops down and out of a wooded

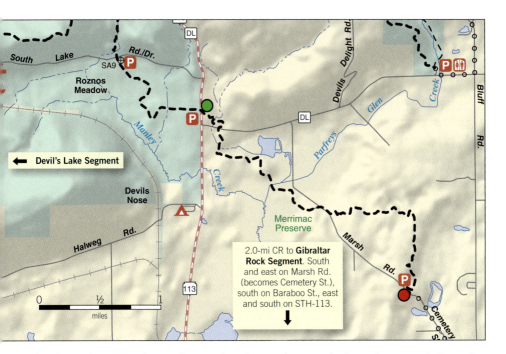

kettle. At this point the Trail turns sharply east then south through a recently logged area before gently curving through the woods to the segment's terminus at the southern Trail access on Marsh Road.

Mobile Skills Crew project site, 2012, 2016

POINTS OF INTEREST

Merrimac Ferry: On Trail. STH-113 across Lake Wisconsin (608-246-3872, wisconsindot.gov/Pages/travel/water/merrimac).

Listed in the National Register of Historic Places, the *Colsac III* ferry (commonly referred to as the Merrimac Ferry) is the lone survivor of about 500 ferries that used to operate in the 19th century across Wisconsin. The name "Colsac" is the phonetic rendering of the two counties the ferry connects, Columbia and Sauk. The ferry crosses the Wisconsin River at a wider part of the river known as Lake Wisconsin, which is a reservoir produced by a dam downstream. At that spot, it is both the Wisconsin River and Lake Wisconsin. The ferry takes seven minutes to cross approximately 0.45 mi. State operated, the service is free to all, including cars, bikes and pedestrians, and runs 24 hours, 7 days a week April 15 through November 30. The ferry is closed December 1 through April 14. There is a separate lane for pedestrians and bicycles, boarding from the sidewalk on the east (upriver) side of the ferry.

AREA SERVICES

Merry Mac's Campground: Camping. 0.7 mi south of Roznos Meadow lot on STH-113 (608-493-2367, merrymacscampground.com).

Devil's Lake State Park (DLSP): See Devil's Lake Segment, p. 197. From the STH-113 Trail access go north and west ~5 mi.

Baraboo and West Baraboo: See Baraboo Segment, p. 192. From the STH-113 Trail access go north ~6 mi. Also see Trail Access and Parking directions, above.

Merrimac: Restaurant, lodging and convenience store. From the Marsh Rd. southern Trail access go south and east 0.9 mi on Marsh Rd., which becomes Cemetery Rd. At Baraboo St. turn right and go south 0.3 mi. For area info, contact Merrimac Visitor Information (townofmerrimac.net).

Southern Columbia County

Atlas Maps 62f–63f; Databook pages 58–60
Total miles: 17.8 (Trail 12.4; Connecting Route 5.4)

Southern Columbia County is home to iconic Gibraltar Rock and the Lodi Marsh State Wildlife Area. The Ice Age Trail in this region passes through some unique geological features and diverse ecological habitats, giving hikers an excellent experience of glacially shaped valleys, bluffs and drumlins while passing through prairies, savannas and woodlands. The Trail also wanders through the historic city of Lodi, an official Ice Age Trail Community.

Following recent land acquisitions volunteers have built several more miles of the Ice Age Trail in the area over the past few years, giving hikers the opportunity to walk from the Merrimac Ferry on Lake Wisconsin, over several glacial bluffs, including Gibraltar Rock, and out to Lodi Marsh with much less road walking along the way. Conveniently, there is a Dispersed Camping Area (DCA) on the Gibraltar Rock Segment and one along the Eastern Lodi Marsh Segment, as well.

CHAPTER INFORMATION

Lodi Valley Chapter volunteers construct and maintain the Ice Age Trail, lead hikes and field trips, educate and assist in land stewardship. They are visible in their community, participating in and hosting local events. Notable activities include Art on the Trail, Mammoth Fun Run and Hike and a Fall Colors Run, along with Tyke Hikes and Full Moon hikes.

In partnership with the Baraboo Hills/Heritage Chapter, the Lodi Valley chapter's hiking program, the Glacial Drifters, offers participants the opportunity to earn a patch for hiking the entire Ice Age Trail as it winds its way through Sauk County and Southern Columbia County, for a total of about 50 miles. Registered participants will receive maps and information on the various segments, along with a hiking log. The care of the Eastern Lodi Marsh Segment, which spans the Dane/Columbia county border, is shared with the Dane County Chapter.

COUNTY INFORMATION

Columbia County Visitor Bureau: 608-742-6161, travelcolumbiacounty.net

Spectacular views are enjoyed from the Gibraltar Rock Segment.

Gibraltar Rock Segment (Atlas Map 62f; Databook page 58)

SNAPSHOT

4.8 miles (4.0 IAT, 0.8 CR): Merrimac ferry south landing wayside to CTH-V

This segment is a rolling ramble through mixed woodlands, prairies and fields. It features dramatic climbs and wide ranging views of Lake Wisconsin, a pastoral valley and the Baraboo Hills.

 At Merrimac ferry north landing and south landing wayside.

 At a Dispersed Camping Area .

Two ColdCache sites on segment.

 Dogs should be leashed (8-ft max) and under control at all times.

 Segment includes a connecting route roadwalk.

 A spur trail (**SC17**) to the DCA, three white-blazed loop trails (two north of Slack Rd. and one near the top of Gibraltar Rock) and Gibraltar Rock State Natural Area trails and road.

TRAIL ACCESS AND PARKING

Merrimac ferry south landing wayside: In Lodi, from the intersection of STH-113 and STH-60, take STH-113 north 6.0 mi to the parking area.

CTH-V: In Lodi, from the intersection of STH-113 and STH-60, take STH-113 north 4.0 mi. At CTH-V turn left and go west 1.7 mi to the parking area on the east side of the road.

Additional Parking: (i) Slack Rd. parking area. (ii) Gibraltar Rock Rd. parking area.

THE HIKE

The segment starts at the Merrimac ferry south landing wayside at the ferry ramp near a large six-panel kiosk providing information on the Ice Age Trail. Yellow-blazed posts guide hikers through the grassy wayside area. The Trail then passes through a woods of white oak, shagbark hickory and maple before crossing (**SC6**) busy STH-113 (cross with caution) near Northern Cross Arm Road.

The segment then ascends the north face of a 200-foot hill, taking in fine views of Lake Wisconsin through a screen of large oaks. The Trail continues southeast through red cedar and existing remnant prairie areas with big bluestem, Indian grass, little bluestem and other native grass species. More scenic views of Lake Wisconsin and the surrounding landscape are offered from different points along the route. This portion of the segment also includes a white-blazed trail that makes a short loop to the west of the main route.

Shortly after the white-blazed trail reconnects with the main route the segment intersects (**SC17**) a spur trail with signage pointing west to a Dispersed Camping Area (DCA) for long-distance, multiday hikers. Continuing on the main segment route, after a steady climb in open prairie for about a quarter mile, the Trail reaches a stunning panoramic vista (**SC8**) of the Wisconsin River and Baraboo Hills.

Continuing on, hikers will arrive at a junction with another white-blazed trail that makes a loop to the west of the main route. From the junction, the main seg-

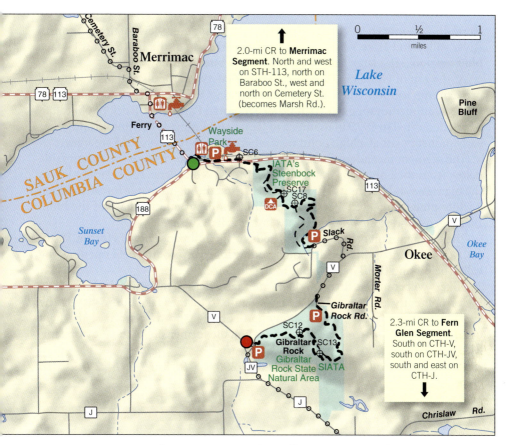

ment route soon reaches a viewpoint that offers great views during the leaf-off season of the surrounding hills and Wisconsin River Valley. From here, the segment drops almost 200 feet on a series of switchbacks through a woods of white pine and oaks, eventually reaching a boulder-studded dry ravine. The segment crosses the ravine and ascends to the Slack Road parking area and rejoins with the white-blazed loop.

From the parking area, hikers should follow a 0.9-mile connecting route. From the Slack Road parking area go east and south 0.4 miles. At CTH-V turn right and continue southwest 0.4 miles to Gibraltar Rock Road. Hikers should turn left on Gibraltar Rock Road and walk through the parking area for the Gibraltar Rock State Ice Age Trail Area to a kiosk and the start of the next portion of the segment.

The Trail enters the forest, quickly intersects a mixed gravel and crumbling blacktop DNR access road leading to the top of Gibraltar Rock, then continues to wind its way through a second-growth forest of white pine, hickory and oak. Hikers will climb a series of 50 steps constructed by volunteers that lead to the top of Gibraltar Rock. Just after the last steps, a marked loop trail stretching across the backside of Gibraltar Rock provides hikers with another option to pass across the top, thus avoiding proximity to sheer cliffs.

Rising 1,234 feet above sea level, Gibraltar Rock is a flat-topped butte, an outlier of the Magnesian escarpment, with a thin dolomite cap over St. Peter sandstone. Its 200-foot sheer cliffs offer spectacular panoramic views of the Wisconsin River valley and Lake Wisconsin. On the south side of the butte is a rock face bluff overlooking a large leather-leaf bog and a bucolic valley.

At the top of Gibraltar Rock there are no safety guardrails and hikers should use extreme caution when hiking near or along the bluff. A memorial plaque (**SC13**) commemorating the Richmond Memorial Park of the Rock of Gibraltar, a park dedicated in 1929 in memory of James and Emma F. Richmond and other early pioneers, sits at a high point near where the DNR access road emerges.

The segment meanders along the top offering several views of the countryside below from rock outcrops framed by weathered red cedars. The segment leaves the big views and begins its gradual descent, first through a maple forest and then a white-pine-dominated woods as the Trail winds around the base of the bluff. Black locust and stone retaining walls line much of the route.

The segment emerges from the woods to the full panoramic "Horton Vista" (**SC12**). This vantage point offers outstanding long views of the field opening, the valley below and the Baraboo Hills in the distance.

Hikers will continue through the former farm field to the mulberry tree growing prominently along the Trail and can pause to further take in the views. The segment returns to a wooded canopy and continues to descend past the field opening and soon reaches the parking area on the former site of the Horton family homestead.

Mobile Skills Crew project site 2005, 2009, 2010, 2013, 2014, 2015, 2016

POINTS OF INTEREST

Merrimac Ferry: See Merrimac Segment, p. 202.

AREA SERVICES

Merrimac: See Merrimac Segment, p. 202. From the ferry wayside Trail access take the ferry across to the north side of Lake Wisconsin. On STH-113 go north then east 1.0 mi.

Devil's Lake State Park: See Devil's Lake Segment, p. 197. From the ferry wayside Trail access take the ferry across to the north side of Lake Wisconsin. Take STH-113 north and west ~10 mi.

Baraboo and West Baraboo: See Baraboo Segment, p. 192. From the ferry wayside Trail access take the ferry across to the north side of Lake Wisconsin. Take STH-113 north ~12 mi.

Lodi: See Fern Glen Segment and City of Lodi Segment, p. 209. From the ferry wayside Trail access take STH-113 south 6.0 mi. Also see Trail Access and Parking directions, above.

Okee: Restaurant, lodging. From the CTH-V Trail access, go east on CTH-V for 2.0 mi.

Fern Glen Segment and City of Lodi Segment (Atlas Maps 62f, 63f; Databook pages 58–59)

SNAPSHOT

Fern Glen Segment—1.3 miles: CTH-J to Bilkey Rd.

2.4-mile Connecting Route

City of Lodi Segment—2.2 miles: Lodi School Complex to Corner St. (STH-113)

*The quiet, hilly **Fern Glen Segment** features dense woods, diverse vegetation and a steep climb.*

 No reliable sources of water.

 Dogs should be leashed (8-ft max) and under control at all times.

 Segment is closed during gun deer season.

A short spur trail to "Susie's Rock"

*The **City of Lodi Segment** saunters through a charming Ice Age Trail Community and highlights the impressive Rainbow Bridge.*

 At town public buildings. Restrooms also available at Goeres Park.

 Hikers will not have any interaction with hunting on this segment.

 From Spring Creek.

 Dogs should be leashed (8-ft max) and under control at all times.

 At private campground (see Area Services).

 Most of the segment follows city roads and sidewalks.

 At Strangeway Playlot and Veterans Memorial Park and at nearby Goeres Park and Pool (175 Fair St.).

 Portions of this segment may be suitable for those using wheelchairs or similar devices.

TRAIL ACCESS AND PARKING

CTH-J: In Lodi, from the intersection of STH-113 and STH-60, take STH-113 north. At CTH-J turn left and go west 2.0 mi to the parking area on the south side of the road just before the intersection with Lovering Rd.

Corner St. (STH-113): In Lodi, from the intersection of STH-113 and STH-60, take STH-113 south 0.7 mi to the parking area on the west side of STH-113.

Additional Parking: (i) Bilkey Rd. In Lodi from the intersection of STH-113 and STH-60, take STH-113 north. At CTH-J turn left and go west 1.0 mi. At Bilkey Rd. turn left and go south then west 0.5 mi. Roadside parking. (ii) At 1100 Sauk St. Park at the pool parking area on the northeast side of high school. Starting from the kiosk, walk southeast along a ravine and across a bridge, then continue along the Trail. (iii) City of Lodi public parking area. From the intersection of STH-113 and STH-60, take STH-113 south 0.1 mi, follow the right bend on STH-113 and immediately turn right into the public parking area.

THE HIKE

The **Fern Glen Segment** is in an area of rounded hills covered with a thin layer of glacial till supporting area fields and woods. The Ice Age Trail travels through a dense hardwood forest and climbs up and down a steep ravine. Several species of ferns and spring ephemerals highlight the segment, although be wary of poison ivy and wild parsnip.

The segment departs the CTH-J parking area and shortly begins its steady climb up a steep hill with a bench near a beautiful oak tree at its apex. The plaque

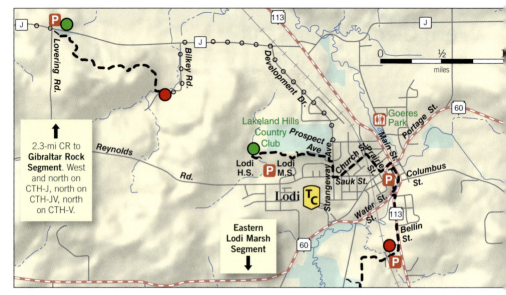

on the bench recognizes the Groves family's Fern Glen Farm and the conservation easement which protects 436 acres and several miles of Ice Age Trail. From here the segment begins a steep descent. It intersects a short (less than 0.1 mile) signed spur trail that leads to "Susie's Rock," a favorite spot of Susan Groves (1860–1906) and a place of remembrance for the Groves family. Just before the segment reaches its terminus at Bilkey Road, it crosses a low spot prone to flooding during rainy periods.

From the Bilkey Road Trail access, hikers can reach the next segment via the following 2.4-mile connecting route: hike northeast on Bilkey Road for 0.5 miles. Turn right and hike east on CTH-J for 0.8 miles. Turn right and hike south on Development Drive (which turns into Strangeway Avenue) for 1.1 miles to the intersection of Strangeway Avenue and Prospect Avenue.

From the intersection of Strangeway Avenue and Prospect Avenue, the first order of business for those wanting to explore the full **City of Lodi Segment** is to hike a short out-and-back stretch of Ice Age Trail to the west of Strangeway Avenue. Head west on Prospect Avenue and go 100 feet to Strangeway Playlot. The segment leaves the pavement here. Follow the posts with blazes through the playlot, across the street and into the woods paralleling Lodi Golf Club.

The segment passes prairie restoration efforts behind Lodi Middle School before crossing a 150-foot-long footbridge spanning a ravine between Lodi's middle and high schools. Based on the 16th-century Chinese Rainbow Bridge, the accessible structure was designed by U.S. Forest Products Lab forester and IATA Lodi Valley Chapter member Ron Wolfe. The twin arches, decking and railing are constructed of black locust and demonstrate the economical use of small-diameter invasive species. This bridge is a traditional centerpiece in Lodi High School's senior graduation ceremony.

From the western end of the bridge, the Trail continues another 200 feet to the end-of-segment sign. From here, backtrack 0.7 miles to Strangeway Avenue to resume hiking the remainder of the City of Lodi Segment.

Dane & Green Counties

Dane & Green Counties

Dane County

Atlas Maps 63f–68f; Databook pages 61–67
Total miles: 63.5 (Trail 35.3; Connecting Route 28.2)

Dane County straddles two distinct physical landscapes. Western Dane County is an unglaciated area of narrow, stream-cut valleys and angular ridges of exposed sandstone and dolomite, part of the Driftless Area. The eastern two-thirds of the county is covered with layers of sand, clay and gravel left by a series of glacial advances. The Green Bay Lobe covered most of this eastern portion 15,000 years ago. The Ice Age Trail weaves back and forth between the two landscapes. Prairie Moraine County Park, near Verona, is a great place to see the Johnstown End Moraine that marks the farthest advance of the Green Bay Lobe. A string of public lands protects portions of the Ice Age Trail in Dane County. These include, from north to south, Lodi Marsh State Wildlife Area; Indian Lake County Park; the Cross Plains National Scientific Reserve; Ice Age Junction Area, Badger Prairie and Prairie Moraine County Parks and Brooklyn State Wildlife Area. Increase Lapham wrote in 1846 that Dane County was "almost entirely oak openings or prairie." Seventeen mound sites of considerable variety still exist in the Valley View Segment and the Madison Segment of the Ice Age Trail. The trail also passes through two Ice Age Trail Communities, Cross Plains and Verona.

Five Dispersed Camping Areas (DCAs) are spread across Dane County, with campsites in the Eastern Lodi Marsh, Springfield Hill, Cross Plains, Verona and Montrose segments.

CHAPTER INFORMATION

One of the original IATA chapters, the Dane County Chapter sponsors many events each year such as trailbuilding and maintenance outings, hikes and interpretive walks and prairie and woodland restoration projects. The chapter promotes public awareness of the Ice Age Trail through displays at community functions, annual outdoor shows and restoration events. The chapter's newsletter, the *Ice Age Drift*, is available on the chapter's home page on the IATA website.

COUNTY INFORMATION

Greater Madison Convention and Visitors Bureau: 800-373-6376, visitmadison.com
Dane County Parks: 608-242-4576, parks-lwrd.countyofdane.com
Camping in Dane County Parks: 608- 224-3730, reservedane.com

Lodi Marsh Segment

This segment is located in Dane County just south of the Dane/Columbia county line. It is linked with the Eastern Lodi Marsh Segment and described in the Southern Columbia County chapter of this book (pp. 211–213).

Morning view on the Lodi Marsh Segment.

Springfield Hill Segment and Indian Lake Segment (Atlas Map 64f; Databook pages 62–63)

SNAPSHOT

Springfield Hill Segment—1.6 miles: Loop trail east of Ballweg Rd.

2.6-mile Connecting Route

Indian Lake Segment—2.9 miles: STH-19 Eastern Trail Access at Indian Lake County Park to STH-19 Western Trail Access at Indian Lake County Park

 The **Springfield Hill Segment** is a loop hike featuring impressive vistas, mature oak woodlands and remnant oak savanna and prairie.

No reliable sources of water.	Dogs should be leashed (8-ft max) and under control at all times.
At a Dispersed Camping Area.	A blue-blazed spur trail (**DA39**) to the DCA.

 The **Indian Lake Segment** highlights charming Indian Lake County Park and its wooded, hilly terrain.

> **Note:** New Ice Age Trail is planned north of Indian Lake County Park through Halfway Prairie Wildlife Area between Matz Rd. and STH-19. Check with the Ice Age Trail Alliance (800-227-0046, iceagetrail.org) for details.

By open-sided shelter.	Group camp area available for official youth groups (see Area Services) located near warming house (**DA24**). See the Dane Co. Park's website for more on camping (parks-lwrd.countyofdane.com/park/IndianLake).
From Indian Lake.	Dogs should be leashed (8-ft max) and under control at all times.
	Portions overlap ski trails. Hike off to the side when groomed.
	Park's trail network.

TRAIL ACCESS AND PARKING

Ballweg Rd.: From the intersection of USH-12 and USH-14 in Middleton, take USH-12 west 12.0 mi. At Ballweg Rd. turn right and go 0.2 mi to the parking area on the east side of the road.

STH-19 Western Trail Access at Indian Lake County Park: From the intersection of USH-12 and USH-14 in Middleton, take USH-12 west 10.0 mi. At STH-19 turn left and go west 2.8 mi to Indian Lake County Park's gravel parking area for the lake access and dog training/exercise area.

Additional Parking: (i) Indian Lake County Park's main parking area off of STH-19. The entrance road leading to the main parking area is 1.0 mi east of the dog training/exercise area parking. (ii) Halfway Prairie Wildlife Area parking area, 350 ft west of Indian Lake County Park's eastern entrance on STH-19.

THE HIKE

The **Springfield Hill Segment** is a short loop that can be hiked in either direction. Extensive restoration work has already been completed but continues on the segment. In 2009, the U.S. Fish and Wildlife Service constructed a grassy drainage way which has failed in recent years, resulting in a small but picturesque lake towards the center of the loop for hikers to enjoy.

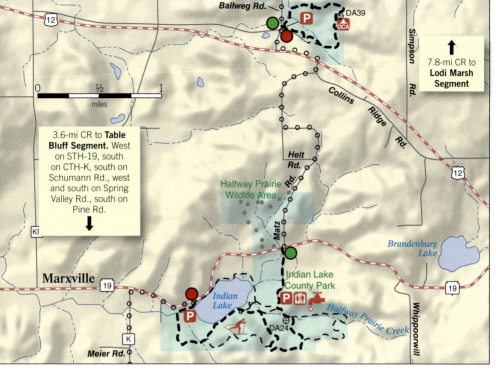

From the parking area, hikers taking the left branch of the loop will gradually ascend on a berry-lined path to the crest of a south-facing slope offering dramatic views to the west. A nearby bench offers hikers the chance to rest and enjoy the view and summer wildflowers including monarda, spiderwort and coreopsis. After descending off the ridge, the segment intersects (**DA39**) a short spur trail that climbs a short staircase and leads to a Dispersed Camping Area (DCA) for long-distance, multiday hikers. The segment descends through beautiful oak savanna and woodlands, then crosses a boardwalk before passing near the remains of Frederic Hahn's log outbuilding, dating to the late 19th century. Both the DCA staircase and boardwalk were Eagle Scout projects. The segment continues along a grassy goat-prairie hillside and passes an old cattle road underpass, the small central lake and an agricultural field before arriving back at the parking area.

Mobile Skills Crew project site, 2013, 2014

To reach the Indian Lake Segment, hikers should follow a 2.6-mile connecting route by heading south on Ballweg Road 0.2 miles. At USH-12 turn left and walk east on the gravel shoulder for 0.4 miles. Cross USH-12 at Collins Ridge Road and go south 0.1 miles. At Matz Road turn right and go west and south 0.6 miles to the first left. Turn left and continue to follow Matz Road 1.3 miles east and south to STH-19. Jog right and turn left into Indian Lake County Park.

Before starting the **Indian Lake Segment**, hikers may want to make an interesting side trip to the Halfway Prairie Wildlife Area, 0.1 mile west on STH-19. The wildlife area features hiking trails and the stone ruins of the Matz farmstead, built in 1907 and burned in 1948.

From its starting point on STH-19 at the Indian Lake County Park eastern entrance, the segment follows the park entrance road to the main parking area, with water, restrooms and a picnic shelter nearby. A trail from the parking area leads about 0.5 miles to historic St. Mary of the Oaks Chapel (look for signage behind and to the right of the pit toilets). Wildflowers near the parking area include monarda, Queen Anne's lace and coreopsis.

Indian Lake County Park has 8 miles of ski and hiking trails. The segment overlaps some of the park's ski trails, which have their own color-coded markings and directional designations, and at times may follow the ski trail in the "wrong" direction. The Trail is generally well blazed. Hikers should pay attention to the yellow-blazed route. Please respect the ski trails in winter. A number of benches for resting spots are scattered along the Trail.

From the parking area, the Trail heads south past the Indian Lake Trailhead sign, quickly turns left, then right at a brown gate onto a gravel path. The old stairs straight ahead provide hikers another way to access the historic chapel. When the segment leaves the gravel path for a large grassy area, hikers will find off to the right and up a slight hill the warming house (**DA24**), with a restroom nearby, that is open during ski season. Past the warming house the Trail alternates between grass and woods, then enters a woods where the segment climbs up and down steep hills. The segment exits the woods near a large erratic to the left of the Trail with a memorial marker to Gerald Klurfield Baer (1949–1976), a gentle lover of man and nature. From here, the segment follows along the south side of Indian Lake. After crossing a meadow and passing a marsh the segment skirts around a dog exercise area, crosses a bridge over Halfway Prairie Creek and reaches its terminus at Indian Lake County Park's dog exercise/lake access parking area on STH-19.

AREA SERVICES

Sauk City: Restaurant, grocery store, convenience store, lodging, library, medical service. From the Ballweg Rd. Trail access go south 0.2 mi. At USH-12 turn right and go northwest for 7.0 mi. For area info contact the Sauk Prairie Area Chamber of Commerce (608-643-4168, saukprairie.com).

Middleton: See Valley View Segment and Madison Segment, p. 227. From the Ballweg Rd. Trail access go south 0.2 mi. At USH-12 turn left and go east then south ~12 mi. Also see Trail Access and Parking directions, above.

Indian Lake County Park: Camping. For official youth groups and long-distance, multiday hikers with advanced permission only from the Dane County Parks Department (608-224-3730, parks-lwrd.countyofdane.com). The group camp area is located near the park's warming house (**DA24**).

Cross Plains: See Cross Plains Segment, p. 223. From the STH-19 western Trail access go west then south ~10 mi.

Table Bluff Segment (Atlas Map 64f, 65f; Databook page 63)

SNAPSHOT

Table Bluff Segment—4.8 miles (3.6 IAT, 1.2 CR): Pine Rd. to Scheele Rd.

  The segment offers a trek through a stunning prairie with long ridgetop views and showcases the results of some remarkable land stewardship efforts.

	No reliable sources of water.		Between Table Bluff Rd. and Scheele Rd., the southern two-thirds of the segment crossing private land are closed during gun deer season.
	At the top of the bluff 0.4 mi north of Scheele Rd.		Dogs must be leashed.
	One ColdCache site on segment.		Two white-blazed loop trails and additional informal trails.

TRAIL ACCESS AND PARKING

Pine Rd.: From the Ice Age Trail Alliance Headquarters in Cross Plains, take USH-14 west 1.2 mi. At CTH-KP turn right and go north 2.9 mi. At Pine Rd. turn right and go northeast 0.4 mi to the Trail access on the east side of the road. The main parking area is located 0.1 mi north on Pine Rd. A blue-blazed spur trail leads to the Trail.

Scheele Rd.: From the Ice Age Trail Alliance Headquarters in Cross Plains, take USH-14 west 1.2 mi. At CTH-KP turn right and go north 0.3 mi. At Scheele Rd. turn left and go west 0.3 mi to a gated gravel road on the north side. Roadside parking in mowed area. Do not block the gate.

Additional Parking: Table Bluff Rd. parking area, 0.3 mi west of CTH-KP on the south side of Table Bluff Rd.

THE HIKE

The segment begins with a lollipop loop trail around the Liebetrau Prairie, a culmination of nearly 15 years of prairie restoration efforts. In spring, hikers will see shooting stars and other early prairie flowers; in summer, prairie flowers include an ever-changing explosion of compass plants, monarda, rudbeckia, coneflowers, coreopsis, milkweed, liatris and many more.

The segment leaves Pine Road and quickly comes to an intersection with a blue-blazed spur trail that leads 0.1 mile to the Pine Road parking area. A little farther on, the segment reaches the junction of the lollipop loop. Following the loop to the right, the Trail begins a gradual descent, leaves the prairie and enters an area of mixed hardwoods and then crosses a small partially stone-lined ravine and begins to gradually climb back up to the prairie. The Trail climbs gradually to its highest point. Hikers will enjoy sweeping views in multiple directions, including views of the Blue Mounds to the west, particularly impressive at sunset. The segment returns to the junction of the lollipop loop and makes its way back to Pine Road.

Here hikers should turn left and head south 0.4 miles on Pine Road. At CTH-KP they should turn left and continue south 0.5 miles. At Table Bluff Road, hikers should turn right and go west 0.3 miles to the Trail access and parking area.

This portion of the segment, located in the Driftless Area of southwestern Wisconsin, traverses restored prairie as well as steep rocky slopes. There is approximately 200 feet of total vertical relief, and several vistas from the heads of two valleys and two prominent goat prairies offer great views of the Driftless Area.

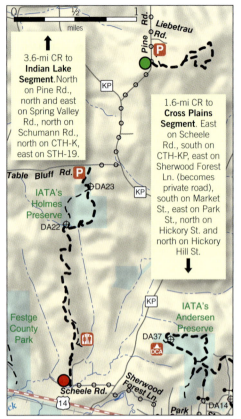

Meltwater from the Laurentide ice sheet poured through a preglacial valley depositing sand and gravel and partially filling the valley floors, which now hold wetlands and a tributary stream of Black Earth Creek, a Class I trout stream.

From the Trail access on Table Bluff Road, the segment heads south across the IATA's 73-acre Holmes Preserve. After passing through a prairie hikers will come to an intersection (**DA23**) with a white-blazed loop trail that offers a 0.5-mile "bubble" to the west. The loop trail traverses up a ridge through a mixed hardwood forest containing a grove of several large oaks.

Back on the main segment, from its initial encounter with the white-blazed loop trail, the Trail continues south across a large restored prairie with a thriving population of rare pale purple coneflower. This area is a wildflower treasure trove—shooting star, rattlesnake master, stiff gentian, hoary vervain, prairie smoke, cream gentian and cream baptisia have all been identified here. The segment then enters a wooded area and dips down onto a valley floor before making its second connection with the white-blazed loop trail (**DA22**).

The remainder of the segment traverses the privately owned Swamplovers property. From the valley floor, the segment climbs up a ridge and traverses nearly a mile of woodlands of oak and hickory before entering a prairie/oak savanna area that owners of the Swamplovers property are faithfully restoring to its native state. This area, including a second white-blazed loop, features dramatic rock outcroppings of Ordovician dolomite and views southwest to the Blue Mounds. At the top of the bluff area are a portable toilet and a shelter with picnic tables that is available to hikers when not already in use by the property owners. From the top of the bluff the segment drops precipitously on a series of switchbacks to the segment's endpoint on the Swamplovers property access road.

Mobile Skills Crew project site, 2006

AREA SERVICES

Cross Plains: See Cross Plains Segment, p. 223. From Scheele Rd. and CTH-KP, go south and then east on USH-14 ~1 mi. Also see Trail Access and Parking directions, above.

Middleton: See Valley View Segment and Madison Segment, p. 227. From Scheele Rd. and CTH-KP, go south and then east on USH-14 ~9 mi.

Madison: See Valley View Segment and Madison Segment, p. 227. From Scheele Rd. and CTH-KP, go south then east on USH-14 ~14 mi.

Cross Plains Segment (Atlas Map 65f; Databook page 64)

SNAPSHOT

9.0 miles (5.3 IAT, 3.6 CR): Hickory Hill St. to Timber Ln.

This diverse segment highlights a Trail Community, the Ice Age Trail Alliance headquarters and the surprisingly remote-feeling bluffs, prairies and woodlands north of town.

 At the public library, public pool (seasonal) and IATA headquarters (**DA34**).

 From Black Earth Creek.

 At a Dispersed Camping Area on the IATA's Andersen Preserve.

 At Legion Park, 1 block west of the Trail on American Legion Dr. and at municipal pool on Caesar St.

 One ColdCache site on segment.

 Dogs should be leashed (8-ft max) and under control at all times.

 Portions follow town streets and sidewalks.

A blue-blazed spur trail (**DA37**) to the DCA and informal trail in Hickory Hill Conservation Area and trails in the John I. Hillenbrand Glacial Valley Conservancy. At the Ice Age Complex Trail Access on the south side of Old Sauk Pass Road there is a white-blazed loop trail from the parking lot and a network of unsigned, mowed trails on the north side of the road.

 Portions of this segment may be suitable for those using wheelchairs or similar devices.

TRAIL ACCESS AND PARKING

Hickory Hill St.: From the Ice Age Trail Alliance Headquarters in Cross Plains, take USH-14 west for 0.3 mi. At Hickory St. turn right and go north 0.2 mi until the road curves east. At Hickory Hill St. turn left and continue north to the Hickory Hill Conservation Park gate. Roadside parking.

Timber Ln.: From west of Madison on the Beltline Hwy.(USH-12/14), take Exit 254 for Mineral Point Rd. (CTH-S) and go west on Mineral Point Rd. for 4.0 mi. At Timber Ln. turn right and go north 0.4 mi. Roadside parking.

Additional Parking: (i) Roadside parking at Lewis St. Trail access. (ii) Parking area at Village of Cross Plains Municipal Park pool at 2106 Lewis St. (behind the library). (iii) Parking area on the west end of Mill Creek Parkway. Take footpath south across Black Earth Creek to Trail. (iv) Roadside parking at Bourbon Rd. Trail access. (v) Roadside parking at Old Sauk Pass Rd. Trail access. Do not block gate. (vi) Old Sauk Pass Rd. parking area, 0.2 mi east of the Old Sauk Pass Rd. Trail access. A portion of a white-blazed loop trail leads to the Trail. (vii) Goth Conservancy parking area, 0.3 mi east of Timber Ln. on W. Old Sauk Rd.

THE HIKE

The segment highlights the Cross Plains Unit of Ice Age National Scientific Reserve, one of nine such units, which represents a world-renowned example of the interface of glaciated and unglaciated terrain. It also shows off the village of Cross Plains, an Ice Age Trail Community, which is situated along Black Earth Creek in a valley between tall bluffs. It sits at the boundary of the most recent glaciation to the east and north and the Driftless Area to the west and south. Meltwater from the receding glacier eroded and carried the terminal moraine downstream from the site of the village. Cross Plains is named for the intersection of two early roads: the military road from Fort Crawford (Prairie du Chien) to Fort Howard (Green Bay) and the lowland road from Arena to Madison.

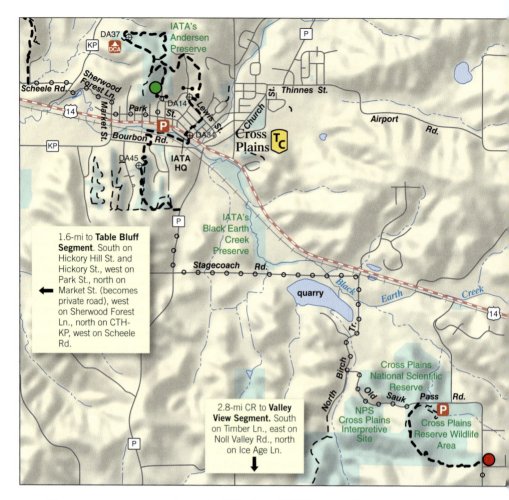

The segment starts at the end of Hickory Hill Street, where a gate crosses an access road that leads north uphill into the Hickory Hill Conservation Park. Departing from the access road, the segment enters a former agricultural field restored to native prairie. Shortly after entering the former agricultural field, hikers will encounter signage for a "cut-off" path that heads east. To continue with the full segment hikers should veer northwest at this junction, continue across the field, and enter the IATA's Andersen Preserve. The segment soon enters a woodland that features not only native flora such as jack-in-the-pulpit, shooting stars and wild ginger but also the glacial drainage network known as "Three Gorges." Shortly after entering the woodland the segment intersects (**DA37**) a blue-blazed spur trail that leads a few hundred yards to a Dispersed Camping Area (DCA) for long-distance, multiday hikers.

The segment exits the forest and once more crosses the former agricultural field. After passing the cut-off path, the segment continues southeast through an oak savanna enjoying restoration and gains elevation up the side of a dolomite ridge. At the head of the ridge hikers will find views to the south and east displaying what conservationist Increase Lapham described as the "Great Dividing Ridge." On the distant ridge to the south hikers may see a lone majestic white pine, marking the approximate location of the Cross Plains National Scientific Reserve. The Blue Mounds are also clearly visible to the west.

At this point the segment drops steeply 150 feet down a series of switchbacks to emerge at Lewis Street (**DA14**) between two houses. From here, the segment continues on sidewalks and roads through residential Cross Plains.

The segment heads east 0.2 miles on Lewis Street to its intersection with Caesar Street, where hikers should turn right and head southwest on the east side of Caesar Street, passing the Rosemary Garfoot Public Library and Village of Cross Plains Municipal Park and Pool.

At the intersection of Caesar Street and Julius Street signage directs hikers to continue southwest on Caesar Street but first to cross to the opposite (west) side of the street. The segment then reaches busy Main Street (USH-14), which hikers should cross cautiously and then turn left to head east down Main Street.

Hikers will soon encounter the Ice Age Trail Alliance's headquarters building (**DA34**) on the south side of the road at 2110 Main Street. Here the segment leaves Main Street and turns southwest to cross the IATA headquarters property, through the gardens in front of the building.

The headquarters building is open 8 a.m. to 5 p.m. weekdays except in the case of off-site special events. Though it's not a true "Visitor Center," hikers are encouraged to stop in—IATA staff love to chat with Trail users! Restrooms and drinking water are available for all, as are shower and laundry facilities for thru-hikers. Ice Age Trail merchandise can be purchased here as well. On site, the property features a rain garden, lawn with native prairie plants and boulders along the segment route bearing the names of the IATA's 19 volunteer chapters and the organization's key partners—the Wisconsin Department of Natural Resources and the National Park Service.

The segment exits the IATA headquarters property, crosses Mill Creek Parkway/Jovina Street and heads for the bridge spanning Black Earth Creek. After crossing the bridge, hikers will turn right and follow the paved path until the first time they can turn left on a boardwalk, which crosses the creek and railroad tracks. At the next intersection, hikers will turn left and make a quick right to stay on a sidewalk that parallels the Cross Plains fire station. The segment crosses Bourbon Road and heads south between buildings into the John I. Hillenbrand Glacial Valley Conservancy.

The Trail climbs sharply and meanders southward along the top of a wooded ridge, overlapping and crossing portions of the Conservancy Trail. Along the way hikers can rest on a bench (**DA45**) and enjoy views of neighborhoods below and the countryside in the distance. After passing behind a dairy farm, the segment exits the forest and begins its descent, down a steep hill to CTH-P.

To reach the next portion of Trail hikers should turn right on CTH-P and head south for 0.5 miles. At Stagecoach Road turn left and go east 1.5 miles. At North Birch Trail (a road), turn right and go south 0.8 miles. At Old Sauk Pass Road turn left and head east, south and east 0.8 miles to the Trail access at the Ice Age National Scenic Trail Interpretive Site kiosk.

The segment follows an asphalt driveway into the former Wilkie family homestead and quickly intersects a 0.4-mile white-blazed lollipop loop trail that highlights the view of a proglacial lakebed and accesses the Old Sauk Pass Road parking area.

The Trail then passes the house, garage and large red barn of the homestead and enters a prairie with wide mowed paths. At a high point are scenic long views to the east, north and west. The segment soon enters a woods and meanders gradually downhill through the forest. The segment passes a rock outcropping where hikers may also notice a sandstone outcropping in the distance to the east. From here the segment skirts a farm field, passes the sandstone rock outcropping and winds its way uphill to its terminus on Timber Lane near a cell tower and an electric substation.

Mobile Skills Crew project site, 2004, 2009, 2018, 2019

POINTS OF INTEREST

Cross Plains National Scientific Reserve and Future National Park Service Ice Age National Scenic Trail Interpretive Site: On Trail. (8075 Old Sauk Pass Rd., Cross Plains, nps.gov/iatr/planyourvisit/int_site.htm).

This area features a complex of lands owned by Dane County, the Wisconsin Department of Natural Resources (DNR) and the National Park Service (NPS) and includes the Cross Plains Unit of Ice Age National Scientific Reserve, one of nine such units. The area represents a world-renowned example of the interface of glaciated and unglaciated terrain. The relationship between moraine and glaciated landscapes on one side of the moraine and unglaciated bedrock landscapes on the other side is strikingly exhibited. Rugged ridges of the moraine formed during the Wisconsin Glaciation meet the eroded Driftless Area to the south and west.

Unsigned hiking trails penetrate land owned by the DNR north of Old Sauk Pass Rd. South of Old Sauk Pass Rd, land owned by NPS and Dane County hosts a portion of the Cross Plains Segment. Dogs are welcome on leash. There are no public restrooms or other visitor facilities at this time. View a General Management Plan for the site at home.nps.gov/iatr/learn/management/crossplainsgmp.htm.

AREA SERVICES

Cross Plains: Restaurants, grocery store, convenience store, library, medical service. On Trail. Most services on Main St. (USH-14). Restaurant. Crossroads Coffeehouse (2020 Main St., 608-798-2080, crossroadscoffeehouse.net). Area info available from the Cross Plains Chamber of Commerce (608-843-3166, crossplainschamber.net).

Ice Age Trail Alliance Headquarters (DA34): On Trail. (2110 Main St., 800-227-0046, iceagetrail.org). Headquarters hours: 8 am to 5 pm weekdays except during special events. Hikers welcome, though not a true "Visitor Center." Shower and laundry facilities for thru-hikers. Trail information and updates.

Mendota County Park: Camping. From the IATA headquarters go east ~10 mi. (5133 CTH-M, Middleton, 608-224-3730, reservedane.com).

Cedar Hills Campground: Camping. From the IATA headquarters go ~8 mi west on USH-14. At STH-78 go 3.0 mi north to the campground entrance (seasonal; 608-795-2606).

Middleton: See Valley View Segment and Madison Segment, p. 227. From the IATA headquarters onUSH-14 go east ~8 mi. Also see Trail Access and Parking directions, above.

Madison: See Valley View Segment and Madison Segment, p. 227. From the IATA headquarters on USH-14 go east ~13 mi.

Valley View Segment and Madison Segment (Atlas Map 66f; Databook pages 64–65)

SNAPSHOT

Valley View Segment—1.8 miles (1.5 IAT, 0.3 CR): Ice Age Ln. to Mid Town Rd. at Shady Oak Ln.

1.8-mile Connecting Route

Madison Segment—3.0 miles: Woods Rd. to CTH-PD (McKee Rd.).

  The **Valley View Segment** is a delightful suburban jaunt through a restored prairie with good interpretive signage and views west to the Blue Mounds.

Note: New Ice Age Trail is planned between Timber Ln. and Ice Age Ln. Check with the Ice Age Trail Alliance (800-227-0046, iceagetrail.org) for details.

- No reliable sources of water.
- Hikers will not have any interaction with hunting on this segment.

- Dogs must be leashed.
- An extensive, color-coded trail network through the prairie area.

  For being on the outskirts of town, the **Madison Segment** retains a surprisingly remote feel as it passes unobtrusively through a scenic golf course and residential neighborhoods.

- At the University Ridge Golf Course clubhouse (seasonal).
- Hikers will not have any interaction with hunting on this segment.

- Dogs are not allowed between Woods Rd. and CTH-M.
- Portions overlap golf course paths, city roads (including dangerous CTH-M), a driveway and sidewalks and a multi-use recreation path.

TRAIL ACCESS AND PARKING

Ice Age Ln.: From west of Madison on the Beltline Hwy. (USH-12/14), take Exit 254 for Mineral Point Rd. (CTH-S) and go west on Mineral Point Rd. (CTH-S) for 4.0 mi. At Timber Ln. turn left and go south 1.3 mi. At Noll Valley Rd. turn left and go east 0.3 mi. At Ice Age Ln. turn left and go north 0.1 mi. Roadside parking on the right side of the road by the gate.

CTH-PD (McKee Rd.): From Verona, at the intersection of Verona Ave. (Bus. Rt. USH-18/151) and CTH-M (Main St./Pleasant View Rd.), take CTH-M (Main St./Pleasant View Rd.) north 1.7 mi. At CTH-PD (McKee Rd.) turn right and go east east 0.8 mi (under the segment's pedestrian bridge) to S. High Point Rd. Turn right into the Ice Age Trail Junction Area parking area. A blue-blazed spur trail leads 0.1 mi to the Trail.

Additional Parking: (i) Parking area at Middleton Ice Age Trail Access park (**DA10**) on Moraine Ridge Rd. (ii) Roadside parking on Woods Rd. (iii) University Ridge Golf Course lower parking area, open seasonally during golf course hours. Accessed by car from the main golf course entrance along CTH-PD (McKee Rd.). Gate is sometimes locked. (iv) O.J. Noer Turfgrass Research and Education Center parking area on the west side of CTH-M (Pleasant View Rd.). Available only on weekends and after 4:00 p.m. on weekdays.

THE HIKE

The **Valley View Segment** starts at the Ice Age Lane Trail access along the brown fence to the right of the gate. After passing through a patch of woods, the segment crosses a residential driveway at a white lantern post. From there it enters the highlight of the segment, an open prairie with a series of looped side trails and trailside benches. Hikers should be very alert and watch for each Ice Age Trail post when hiking through the prairie. This portion of the segment is on the terminal moraine and is a

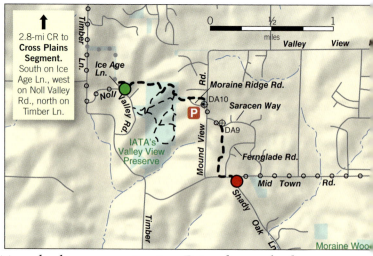

fine example of prairie and oak savanna restoration. Driven by area landowners, with a collaboration of various community volunteer groups, 14 acres spanning parts of three properties were returned to their native habitat.

On a clear day, hikers can see the Blue Mounds from the prairie. Increase Lapham wrote that the Blue Mounds "were very important landmarks to guide the traveler in his course through the boundless prairies." Their Indian name is Mucha-wa-ku-nin or "Smoky Mountains."

After exiting the prairie the segment passes through a residential area featuring prairie-style homes drawing their inspiration from Wisconsin-born architect Frank Lloyd Wright. Please respect private property by staying on the Trail. The segment then arrives at the Ice Age Trail Access parking area (**DA10**), a Town of Middleton park. From this spot hikers will continue on the following 0.3-mile connecting route to reach the next off-road portion of the segment: Head south out of the parking area and hike east on Moraine Ridge Road, turn right and hike south on Mound View Road, turn left and hike east approximately 0.1 mile on Saracen Way.

From the Saracen Way access (**DA9**) the segment works its way south through a wooded area. Emerging from the woods, hikers should continue walking south on the grassy path between the residential area and the farm fields. The segment then bends east and parallels Mid Town Road. Hikers will pass a residential sign for Glacier's End and cross Fernglade Road before reaching the segment terminus at a yellow-blazed Trail post on the northeast side of the intersection of Shady Oak Lane and Mid Town Road.

To reach the Madison Segment, hikers should follow a 1.8-mile connecting route by heading east on Mid Town Road for 1.3 miles and then turning right and heading south on Woods Road for 0.6 miles.

From the access point on Woods Road the **Madison Segment** makes its way eastward through woods located between two holes of University Ridge, the University of Wisconsin-Madison's golf course. Please respect the Trail host by walking quietly when passing those enjoying a round of golf.

The segment emerges briefly from the woods and crosses the cart path before

continuing southwest through another wooded area. The segment emerges again from the woods and intersects another paved path; hikers can turn left and access the golf course's clubhouse, which features water, restrooms and a restaurant. Ice Age Trail hikers are welcome to use the clubhouse. Shortly after crossing the road to the clubhouse hikers will come to another path, this one leading to the golf course's lower parking area.

The segment continues southeast through a grassland area located west of a fairway, bends east and passes between two tee boxes and then intersects and briefly follows a cart path. The segment leaves the cart path to the right, travels through a small wooded area and again crosses a cart path. The Trail makes its way up a moraine with expansive views to the east and south and continues north through grassland before bending east and cutting through woods adjacent to the golf course's practice area.

The segment exits the woods, runs past an agricultural field, goes between two small patches of woods and runs along the southern edge of a grassy area until it intersects a paved path that leads to the University's Noer Turfgrass Research Center. Hikers should turn left and follow the paved path northeast, briefly follow the Noer Center's driveway ~50 feet, then turn left onto a gravel path. From here the segment bears to the right on the gravel path, crosses a covered bridge and makes it way to a multiuse path. Join and follow this path underneath CTH-M (Pleasant View Road).

After leaving the underpass, the Trail follows the multiuse path for ~300 feet then leaves this path by turning sharply right and heading through a field of tall grasses and wildflowers and then a small wooded area. The segment crosses Raymond Road, passes along the west side of a large drainage basin and makes its way due south into a small aspen and oak grove that gives way to prairie. *Note: Along the north/south stretch between Raymond Road and CTH-PD, a multiuse paved path separate from the Ice Age Trail parallels the segment a short distance to the west.*

Passing through an area of native grasses and wildflowers that is part of a restoration project begun by Veridian Homes, the segment climbs to the top of a grassy moraine. It crosses a paved multiuse walkway and passes two interpretive signs about the presence of glaciers in the area. From here the Trail quickly intersects the paved multiuse path again and then turns sharply right onto a multiuse path to cross CTH-PD (McKee Road) on a pedestrian bridge.

AREA SERVICES

University Ridge Golf Course: Restaurant. On Trail. Open seasonally (9002 CTH-PD, Madison, 608-845-7700 or 800-897-4343, universityridge.com).

Middleton: Restaurant, grocery store, convenience store, general shopping, lodging, camping, library, medical service. From the CTH-M (Pleasant View Rd.) Trail access, go north on CTH-M 2.5 mi. At CTH-S (Mineral Point Rd.) turn right and go east 0.3 mi. At USH-12 go north 2.6 mi to the USH-14 Exit. Area info available from the Middleton Chamber of Commerce (608-827-5797, middletonchamber.com).

Madison: Restaurant, grocery store, convenience store, general shopping, lodging, camping, library, medical service. From CTH-PD (McKee Rd.) Trail access go east and north ~5 mi to West Towne Mall area. Outfitter/camping supplies at REI (608-833-6680, rei.com/stores/madison) behind West Towne Mall. Area info available from the Greater Madison Chamber of Commerce (608-256-8348, greatermadisonchamber.com).

Mendota County Park: See Cross Plains Segment, p. 223. From the CTH-PD (McKee Rd.) Trail access go west then north ~10 mi.

Verona: See Verona Segment, p. 231. For access to Verona's downtown, from the CTH-PD (McKee Rd.) Trail access go west then south ~3 mi. Also see Trail Access and Parking directions, above.

The Valley View Segment, in early spring, provides a spot for writing and reflection.

Verona Segment (Atlas Map 66f; Databook pages 65–66)

SNAPSHOT

6.4 miles: CTH-PD (McKee Rd.) to Prairie Moraine County Park at Wesner Rd.

 This suburban segment makes good use of three county parks and links up to a variety of additional hiking and biking trails.

 At Reddan Soccer Park parking area, Verona Public Library, Badger Prairie County Park main shelter and Ceniti Park Baseball Complex.

 At a Dispersed Camping Area in Badger Prairie County Park.

At Reddan Soccer Park and Badger Prairie County Park. Playground also available at Ceniti Park Baseball Complex.

 One ColdCache site on segment.

 Dogs should be leashed (8-ft max) and under control at all times.

Portions overlap multiuse paths, town sidewalks and roads and the Military Ridge State Trail (MRST).

 MRST continues east and west from the Trail; also numerous bike trails and spur trails.

TRAIL ACCESS AND PARKING

CTH-PD (McKee Rd.): From Verona, at the intersection of Verona Ave. (Bus. Rt. USH-18/151) and CTH-M (Main St./Pleasant View Rd.), take CTH-M (Main St./Pleasant View Rd.) north 1.7 mi. At CTH-PD (McKee Rd.) turn right and go east 0.8 mi (under the segment's pedestrian bridge) to S. High Point Rd. Turn right into the Ice Age Trail Junction Area parking area. A blue-blazed spur trail leads 0.1 mi to the Trail.

Prairie Moraine County Park at Wesner Rd.: From USH-18/151 south of Verona take Exit 79 onto CTH-PB and drive south 1.0 mi. At Wesner Rd. turn left to enter the Prairie Moraine County Park parking area.

Additional Parking: (i) Reddan Soccer Park parking area on Cross Country Rd. (No parking during tournaments.) (ii) Verona Public Library. (iii) Badger Prairie County Park (Exit 81 from USH 18/151). (iv) Military Ridge State Trail (MRST)/Ice Age Trail access on Old PB Rd. just south of Verona Ave. (Exit 81 from USH 18/151). (v) Ceniti Park Sports Complex on the south side of E. Verona Ave. (vi) Lincoln St. foot/bike bridge parking at end of street. (vii) IATA's Moraine Kettles Preserve on CTH-M.

THE HIKE

The segment travels through several park areas including the Ice Age Trail Junction Area, Badger Prairie County Park and Prairie Moraine County Park. Hikers will encounter a number of spur/side trails and bike trails in these parks and therefore should pay close attention to Trail signage as only some of these trails are noted below.

The segment starts from CTH-PD at the pedestrian bridge, turns right off the multiuse trail and begins to journey across a prairie and shortly intersects a blue-blazed spur trail leading 0.1 mi to the Ice Age Trail Junction Area parking area. The green space from CTH-PD south to Cross Country Road is the Ice Age Trail Junction Area, an open space managed by the Dane County Parks Department that visually and physically separates Verona from southwest Madison. It hosts the Ice Age Trail and a paved bike trail. About 200 acres is restored prairie.

As the segment makes its way south through the prairie, it begins a slight descent toward a wooded area. A look to the south offers a fine overview of features hikers

will encounter—the old water tower at Badger Prairie and the moraine on the horizon at the end of the segment, with CTH-PB cut through it.

The segment enters the wooded area and follows to the left at a fork. The segment travels south through another prairie before reaching a short spur trail (near a maintenance shed) that leads west to picnic tables and a kiosk display explaining the Dane County Parks Department's prairie restoration and seed collection program. Additional displays about the Upper Sugar River Valley and the Ice Age Trail are located on the kiosk or nearby. Just beyond the kiosk is the northeast corner of the Reddan Soccer Park parking area. There are several mowed paths that intersect the Trail near Reddan Soccer Park; continue to follow the Trail straight toward Cross Country Road.

The segment continues south and reaches Cross Country Road. The Trail runs west along a fence on the north side of Cross County Road to the entrance of the soccer park and crosses the road at a marked pedestrian crossing. Hikers can find several restaurants 0.3 miles west on Cross Country Road. After crossing the road the segment enters Badger Prairie County Park and continues southward. The Trail quickly intersects a mowed park path and briefly follows it west before turning south and ascending a ridge. Hikers can look to the southwest to see the prominent red-orange roof of the Verona Public Library, which is accessible via a spur trail that runs south to the park road or by a mowed bike path.

The segment crosses the top of the ridge and begins its descent first on a gravel road then on a mowed path. Just before reaching the park's main shelter, the segment passes a Dispersed Camping Area (DCA) (**DA21**) for long-distance, multi-day hikers, in the restored prairie that dominates the park.

After passing the DCA and the main park shelter and parking area, the segment continues south, hooking up with a bike trail as it makes its way to Verona

Avenue (CTH-MV). To access town services, hikers can head west on Verona Avenue 0.4 miles to a motel and another 0.5 miles to the town center.

The segment goes under Verona Avenue (CTH-MV) via a tunnel and continues southeast on the bike path to the Military Ridge State Trail (MRST) Park & Ride parking area off Old County Road PB. The multiuse MRST, connecting Madison to Dodgeville, is located on a railroad grade abandoned in the 1970s that once extended to Galena, IL.

The segment heads west on the MRST for approximately a quarter mile, then just past mile marker 3 it departs from the MRST and makes its way south along the west side of Badger Mill Creek, which flows through a meltwater gap in the moraine. The segment passes a spur trail with a bike/pedestrian bridge over the creek with trails heading east and south to a residential neighborhood.

Continuing southwest the segment passes through a wetland area, running on top of a berm for part of the route. After dropping off the berm, the Trail meanders through a wooded creek bottom and a pine grove, then turns left to cross a bridge to the east side of the creek. The segment turns right, shortly crosses a swampy area on a 275-foot boardwalk/puncheon span and eventually intersects a paved spur trail that connects two residential neighborhoods. To the west, the spur trail leads across the creek on the Lincoln Street footbridge and connects with the street's dead end. Lincoln Street provides access to Verona's city center less than a mile away. To reach several restaurants, a supermarket and a hardware store, hikers can walk northwest via Lincoln Street, left on Valley View Street and right on South Main Street.

The segment moves south through woods in the meltwater gap, makes a steep ascent from the creek and heads around the east side of a quarry passing a small shed before reaching CTH-M. The Trail continues southeast near or along CTH-M, crosses USH-18/151 on an overpass, crosses CTH-M and makes its way south through a restored prairie and quickly intersects a spur trail that leads to the CTH-M parking area. From here, the segment enters the woods and passes several kettle ponds in the IATA's Moraine Kettles Preserve. Leaving the woods, the Trail cuts through another prairie with tall grasses and wildflowers and reenters the woods on its way to CTH-PB. Shortly before reaching CTH-PB, the segment passes a sign noting a section of roadway from the County Farm—Paoli Road that was in use from 1882 to 1929. At the intersection with CTH-PB, hikers will need to briefly walk north to cautiously cross the road at the end of a median (**DA6**). *Note: Traffic along CTH-PB is very heavy; hikers should exercise caution at the Trail crossing described here and also along the subsequent connecting route to the Montrose Segment.*

Upon crossing CTH-PB the segment enters a wooded area of the 160-acre Prairie Moraine County Park, which features a 0.8-mile-long stretch of the terminal moraine on St. Peter sandstone bedrock. The segment briefly makes its way south before heading southeastward, gently ascending along the north-northeast side of the terminal moraine through restored prairie and savanna. At the top of the moraine, a spur trail heads east to a viewing platform that offers views of a ravine cut in the moraine by meltwater and of the upper Sugar River Valley in the Driftless Area to the south.

From a saddle on the moraine, the segment descends westward using several short switchbacks, then curls southward to reach the Trail access at a gate in the northwestern corner of the park's parking area near CTH-PB. The moraine and the Ice Age Trail are fenced off from a heavily used dog exercise area located in the southeastern area of Prairie Moraine County Park.

AREA SERVICES

Madison: See Valley View Segment and Madison Segment, p. 227. From the CTH-PD (McKee Rd.) Trail access go east and north ~5 mi to the West Towne Mall area.

Verona: Restaurant, grocery store, convenience store, general shopping, lodging, camping, library, medical service. From the E. Verona Ave. (CTH-MV) Trail crossing go west 0.9 mi on E. Verona Ave. Area information available from the Verona Chamber of Commerce (608-845-5777, veronawi.com).

Military Ridge State Trail (MRST): On Trail (608-437-7393, dnr.wi.gov/topic/parks/name/militaryridge).

A restored prarie in full bloom on the Table Bluff Segment.

Montrose Segment (Atlas Map 67f; Databook pages 66–67)

SNAPSHOT

7.5 miles: Purcell Rd. to CTH-D

This segment has two distinct experiences: a jaunt down a quiet multiuse rail trail and a beautiful off-road trek featuring dense forests, bedrock outcroppings, restored prairies and long views.

 No reliable sources of water.

 At a Dispersed Camping Area north of CTH-D.

 One ColdCache site on segment.

 Dogs should be leashed (8-ft max) and under control at all times.

 Portions overlap the multiuse Badger State Trail (BST) and Piller Rd.

BST continues north and south. Also, prairie spur trails and blue-blazed spur trail (**DA33**) to the DCA.

 Portions of this segment may be suitable for those using wheelchairs or similar devices.

TRAIL ACCESS AND PARKING

Purcell Rd.: From USH-18/151 south of Verona, take CTH-PB south 2.2 mi. At Purcell Rd. turn left and go east 1.7 mi. At Sayles Trail turn right and immediately turn right again into the Badger State Trail/Ice Age Trail parking area with kiosk.

CTH-D: From Madison, take Fish Hatchery Rd. (CTH-D) ~14 mi south. No parking. Instead, park at the CTH-DD parking area just west and south of the CTH-D endpoint. Access the segment via the Brooklyn Wildlife Segment.

Additional Parking: (i) CTH-A (**DA5**) roadside parking near the intersection where CTH-A heads west from STH-69. The Ice Age Trail/Badger State Trail is 100 ft to the east across STH-69. (ii) Frenchtown Rd./Piller Rd. parking area on the south side of the road.

THE HIKE

The segment starts out from Purcell Road by heading southwest along the Badger State Trail (BST), which extends north to Madison's Capital City Trail and south to the Illinois border. The BST is called a "well-connected trail," with links to the Capital City, Military Ridge and Sugar River state trails; Capital Springs and New Glarus Woods state parks; the Albany State Wildlife Area; numerous local parks and the Jane Addams State Trail in Illinois. Just south of the Purcell Road Trail access the segment crosses the Johnstown Moraine (**DA20**) through a cut in the moraine made by railroad construction crews before traversing several refurbished trestle bridges spanning intermittent creeks.

After 3.6 miles, the segment departs from the BST near the southern intersection of CTH-A and STH-69 at a point (**DA5**) where CTH-A heads west and the Ice Age Trail heads due east. The segment makes its way between two agricultural fields, crosses a 40-foot-long bridge over a ditch and meanders through a small wooded area before making its way to Piller Road, where the segment turns south and follows a field edge and then the road itself.

From the intersection of Piller Road and Frenchtown Road, site of a large parking area, the segment continues due south between two agricultural fields before entering a wooded area. Once in the wooded area the segment immedi-

ately winds uphill then bends west, south, then east as it climbs up to an agricultural field, passing along the way an impressive bedrock outcropping dotted with ferns. The segment heads southeast through the open fields to a high plateau from which hikers can enjoy long views, especially in leaf-off seasons.

The segment turns east when entering another wooded area and drops down a ridge, then continues south across a farm field and reenters the woods. From this point the segment climbs gradually up the west side of a sandstone ridge, eventually making its way to a fine goat prairie and trailside bench (**DA4**) where hikers will enjoy outstanding views across a glacial outwash plain to the Sugar River watershed and the city of Belleville.

The segment takes a turn northeast and crosses a high prairie plateau. On this high plateau volunteers are hard at work with prairie restoration activities. Right before the segment reenters the woods, hikers will reach a junction (**DA33**) with a blue-blazed spur trail and a sign indicating directions to a Dispersed Camping Area (DCA) for long-distance, multiday hikers. The spur trail leads 0.1 miles to the DCA. From the junction with the spur, the segment enters the woods and turns southeast to reach its terminus on CTH-D.

Mobile Skills Crew project site, 2009, 2011, 2012

AREA SERVICES

Verona: See Verona Segment, p. 231. From the Purcell Rd. Trail access go west then north ~4 mi. Also see Trail Access and Parking directions, above.

Paoli: Restaurant. From the Purcell Rd. Trail access go west 1.6 mi, then south 1.1 mi on CTH-PB, then west on Sun Valley Pkwy. *Note: There is no access to Sun Valley Parkway from the Ice Age Trail/Badger State Trail.*

Badger State Trail (BST): On Trail (608-523-4427, dnr.wi.gov/topic/parks/name/badger).

Basco: Restaurant, lodging. INN Style program lodging at the Cameo Rose Victorian County Inn, 0.7 mi east of the Trail crossing with Henry Rd. (866-424-6340, cameorose.com).

Belleville: See Brooklyn Wildlife Segment, p. 238. From the CTH-D Trail access go west then south ~3 mi.

Staff and volunteers celebrate a new bridge on the Cross Plains Segment.

Brooklyn Wildlife Segment (Atlas Map 68f; Databook page 67)

SNAPSHOT

3.3 miles: CTH-D to Hughes Rd.

 This segment follows a rolling course over glacial outwash and bedrock hills through the Brooklyn State Wildlife Area.

From a hand pump south of the southern CTH-DD parking area (**DA2**).

One ColdCache site on segment.

 Dogs should be leashed (8-ft max) and under control at all times. By law, dogs **must** be leashed April 15 to July 31 in the State Wildlife Area.

 Two blue-blazed spur trails to parking areas.

TRAIL ACCESS AND PARKING

CTH-D: From Madison, take Fish Hatchery Rd. (CTH- D) ~14 mi south. No parking. Instead, park at the CTH-DD parking area. See Additional Parking below.

Hughes Rd.: From Belleville at the intersection of STH-92 and STH-69, take STH-92 east then south 3.0 mi to Dayton. At Dayton take Green County's CTH-D north 1.0 mi. At Hughes Rd. turn right and go east 0.3 mi to a parking area on the north side of the road (N9362 Hughes Rd.).

Additional Parking: There are two parking area on CTH-DD that have blue-blazed spur trails to access the Ice Age Trail. (i) "North" CTH-DD parking area is just south of the intersection of Dane County's CTH-D and CTH-DD. (ii) "South" CTH-DD parking area is 1.2 mi north of the Green County CTH-D and Hughes Rd. intersection or 0.8 mi south of the "North" CTH-DD parking area.

> **Note:** A potential source of confusion in the area is the naming of county roads. In Dane County, the county's CTH-D crosses the Ice Age Trail as the road is making its way southwest toward Belleville. In Green County, the county's CTH-D runs north/south, passing through the town of Dayton on its way to the Green/Dane county line. Upon reaching the county line, Green County's CTH-D becomes CTH-DD, which in turn connects up a mile north with Dane County's CTH-D.

THE HIKE

The segment traverses an area featuring highly eroded glacial deposits from an earlier glacial advance more than 60,000 years ago. The segment highlights meadows, woodlands, oak savannas and colorful prairies. The variety of habitat in the area results in great bird-watching opportunities. Herons and cranes fish in the Story Creek wetlands and plenty of turkeys resting with their young can be stirred up on sandy portions of the segment. Volunteers from the Friends of Brooklyn Wildlife Area and the Ice Age Trail Alliance's Dane County Chapter have worked extensively on prairie restoration and removal of invasive species throughout the Brooklyn Wildlife Area. During periods of rain or snow melt, portions of the Trail can become wet and muddy.

From its starting point at the CTH-D Trail access the segment heads south. Several side trails make loops with the Ice Age Trail and give access to Story Creek. Two blue-blazed spur trails lead to the parking areas on CTH-DD. Hikers should pay attention to signage as intersections can be confusing. In addition to designated spur trails, there are numerous side trails to/on private property; please stay off these side trails. About 1.8 miles south of CTH-D hikers will encounter a particularly impressive overlook (**DA27**) and view from the Trail of the Story Creek wetlands and the Johnstown Moraine. Another 0.6 miles farther on hikers will find a trailside hand water pump (**DA2**). From the site of the hand water pump the segment continues its course to the Hughes Road Trail access.

AREA SERVICES

Belleville: Restaurant, grocery store, convenience store, library, medical service. From the Dane County CTH-D Trail access go west 2.6 mi on CTH-D and then south 0.3 mi on STH-69. John Frederick Memorial Park (Library Park), downtown on Main St., has a drinking fountain. Additional village parks with restrooms, picnic areas and playgrounds. Public swimming pool with showers at the Belleville Aquatic Center (seasonal).

New Glarus: See Monticello Segment, p. 242. From the CTH-D Trail access go west then south ~11 mi.

Cooksville: From the Hughes Rd. Trail access go south then east ~15 mi. INN Style program lodging at Cooksville Farmhouse Inn (608-335-8375, cooksvillefarmhouseinn.com).

I don't know when it first happened, but soon hiking the Ice Age Trail became a spiritual experience for me. I began to learn the history of the Trail and to understand the majestic forces that carved the landscape. Here on this erratic, or that esker, I saw eternity compressed into a single moment.

LOU ANN NOVAK, ICE AGE TRAIL THOUSAND-MILER

Green County

Atlas Maps 68f–71f; Databook pages 68–69
Total miles: 22.7 (Trail 15.9; Connecting Route 6.8)

Green County was largely untouched by the Green Bay Lobe of the late Wisconsin Glaciation. At its maximum extent, roughly 15,000 years ago, this lobe crept as far south as the village of Brooklyn. Much earlier glacial advances covered most of the county, except a portion to the northwest that is part of the Driftless Area. The county has a rich history of Native American occupation, including Sauk and Winnebago populations and European settlement. French explorers, traders and trappers were the first wave of Europeans in the region. Miners seeking lead ore came later.

Describing Green County in 1846, Increase Lapham wrote, "The mineral country extends nearly to the eastern part of this county, where the lead bearing rock crops out…There are already several very valuable discoveries of lead, and many flattering prospects of more. These mines are nearer Lake Michigan than any other in the mining country."

In the northern part of the county the Ice Age Trail follows the Badger State Trail (BST). A 2007 addition to the state's rail-trail system, the BST runs on the former Illinois Central Railroad corridor from Madison's Capital City Trail across the state line to Orangeville, IL, joining the Grand Illinois Trail system. Near the town of Exeter, the BST goes through the historic Stewart Tunnel, the 27th longest rail tunnel in the country. *Note: Old Ice Age Trail segment signs dot the countryside in the Exeter and Dayton area. These segments are no longer open for public use.*

In Monticello the Ice Age Trail switches over to the Sugar River State Trail (SRST). On the former Milwaukee Road ("Limburger Special"), the SRST was created in 1974 after the Wisconsin Department of Natural Resources purchased the abandoned rail bed. The crushed limestone rail-trail stretches 23.1 miles from New Glarus to Brodhead, and with its 1% grade, it is perhaps one of the few flat surfaces in the county. It follows the Sugar River and crosses it 14 times on various trestle bridges. The Ice Age Trail shares the SRST as it passes over rushing streams and through picturesque rolling hills, dairy farms, verdant meadows and state wildlife refuges. Wild edible plants can be found along this wildlife corridor during warmer months. The SRST is a popular weekend destination for bicyclists.

Hiking on these two rail-trails is free; bike use requires a pass and fee payable at trailheads. Snowmobiles use the SRST in winter. There is no camping allowed along either rail-trail. Camping is available at New Glarus Woods Park and at private campgrounds near Albany.

CHAPTER INFORMATION

The Green County Chapter is currently inactive. Contact the IATA for more information.

COUNTY INFORMATION

Green County Visitor Information: 888-222-9111, greencounty.org

Sugar River State Trail: 608-523-4427, dnr.wi.gov/topic/parks/name/sugarriver

Badger State Trail: 608-523-4427, dnr.wi.gov/topic/parks/name/badger

Inside the 1,260-foot-long Stewart Tunnel on the Monticello Segment.

Monticello Segment (Atlas Maps 68f, 69f; Databook page 68)

SNAPSHOT

6.5 miles: CTH-W to Monticello's Old Train Depot

This segment follows multiuse rail-trails and offers the unique experience of hiking through the long, dark Stewart Tunnel.

 At Monticello's Old Train Depot.

From the Little Sugar River.

 At nearby New Glarus Woods State Park ~3 mi west of the Trail (see Area Services).

 At a small pavilion south of Stewart Tunnel and at the Monticello Old Train Depot area.

 By law, dogs must be leashed on the Badger State Trail (BST) and Sugar River State Trail (SRST).

 The BST and SRST are open to bicycles and snowmobiles.

 The BST and SRST both continue north and south.

 Portions of this segment may be suitable for those using wheelchairs or similar devices.

TRAIL ACCESS AND PARKING

CTH-W: From Belleville take STH-92 south 3.0 mi. At CTH-W turn left and go west 1.3 mi. No parking on CTH-W or on CTH-CC north of CTH-W. Instead, park roadside at the CTH-CC Trail crossing located another 0.2 mi west on CTH-W and then south on CTH-CC 0.3 mi.

Monticello's Old Train Depot: From STH-69 at Monticello, turn east on Lake Ave. and go 1.0 mi. At Pratt Rd. turn right and go 1 block south to parking area at Old Trail Depot, just north of CTH-EE.

Additional Parking: Tunnel Rd. northern Trail access (**GR6**). Roadside parking.

THE HIKE

This segment starts off from CTH-W in a southwesterly direction on the wide, crushed-gravel-surfaced Badger State Trail (BST). After crossing CTH-CC and then Tunnel Road (**GR4**) the route reaches the northern end of the Stewart Tunnel (**GR3**). Completed in 1887, the 1,260-foot-long train tunnel is named after James Stewart of Pennsylvania, the contractor for the railroad construction. In 1886, he was killed nearby when he was thrown from his buggy while driving the proposed rail route. Blasted through limestone, the tunnel's opening is 14 by 22 feet. Hiking through the cool, dark, damp tunnel is quite an experience. It is lightless due to the curve midway through it. Hikers should have a flashlight ready! Springs above the tunnel trickle water down along the sides and onto the trail floor. Like a cave, it maintains a steady temperature. In summer it offers a cool retreat with temperatures staying between 50 and 60 degrees.

After exiting the tunnel at its south end, the segment passes a small timber frame pavilion (with a picnic table) highlighting the history of Stewart Tunnel. It crosses Tunnel Road a second time and then Exeter Crossing Road (**GR2**). Shortly after crossing the Little Sugar River on a long wooden bridge, the Ice Age Trail leaves the BST and switches to the Sugar River State Trail (SRST) at the signed crossover (**GR5**). The Ice Age Trail continues south on the SRST to Monticello. (*Heading north opposite the Ice Age Trail's route, the SRST takes users first to*

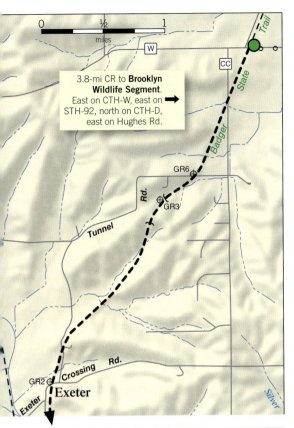

New Glarus Woods State Park and then to the Swiss-style village of New Glarus, known as "America's Little Switzerland.")

The segment ends at the historic Monticello train depot. The depot's history is explained at a small historical museum in a converted drugstore located in town.

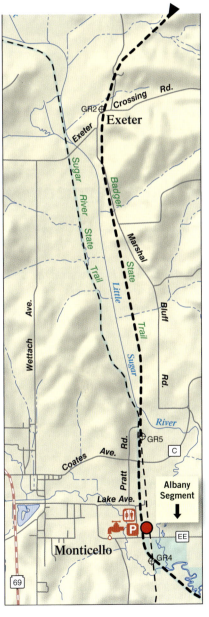

AREA SERVICES

Badger State Trail (BST): On Trail (608-523-4427, dnr.wi.gov/topic/parks/name/badger).

New Glarus Woods State Park: Camping. From Exeter Crossing Rd. Trail access go west 2.5 mi on Exeter Crossing Rd. then north on STH-69 2 mi. Or walk from the Exeter Crossing Rd. Trail access: Go west 0.4 mi. At the Sugar River Trail walk north and west 3.4 mi. (608-523-4427, dnr.wi.gov/topic/parks/name/ngwoods/; reservations: 888-947-2757, wisconsin.goingtocamp.com).

New Glarus: Restaurant, grocery store, convenience store, lodging, camping, library, medical service. From E. Lake Ave. in Monticello take the Sugar River State Trail north ~6 mi or drive north from Monticello on STH-69. Area info available from the New Glarus Chamber of Commerce and Tourist Information (608-527-2095, swisstown.com).

Sugar River State Trail (SRST): On Trail (608-523-4427, dnr.wi.gov/topic/parks/name/sugarriver).

Monticello: Restaurant, grocery store, convenience store, library. On Trail. From the Lake Ave. Trail access go west six blocks to most services.

Green County

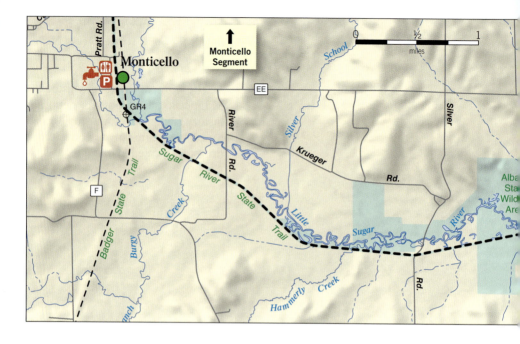

Albany Segment (Atlas Maps 69f, 70f; Databook pages 68–69)

SNAPSHOT

9.4 miles: Monticello's Old Train Depot to Bump Rd.

This very straight and flat segment highlights the quiet, twisty Little Sugar and Sugar rivers.

Note: New Ice Age Trail is planned in Evansville in northwestern Rock County, approximately 10 mi northeast of Albany. Check with the Ice Age Trail Alliance (800-227-0046, iceagetrail.org) for details.

 At Monticello's Old Train Depot and Sugar River State Trail (SRST) parking area in Albany.

 From the Little Sugar and Sugar rivers.

 Private campground south of Bump Rd. (see Area Services).

 One ColdCache site on segment.

 By law, dogs must be leashed on the SRST.

 The SRST is open to bicycles and snowmobiles.

 The SRST continues north and south. The Badger State Trail continues south.

 Portions of this segment may be suitable for those using wheelchairs or similar devices.

TRAIL ACCESS AND PARKING

Monticello's Old Train Depot: From STH-69 at Monticello, turn east on Lake Ave. and go 1.0 mi. At Pratt Rd. turn right and go 1 block south to parking area at Old Trail Depot, just north of CTH-EE.

Bump Rd.: From STH-59 in Albany, turn south on Cincinnati St. and go 0.8 mi. At Bump Rd. turn left and go 0.1 mi to the Trail access. No parking. Instead, park at the Sugar River State Trail parking area on 4th St. From STH-59 in Albany, turn south on Cincinnati St. and go 0.4 mi. At 4th St. turn left and go 0.1 mi; parking area on left.

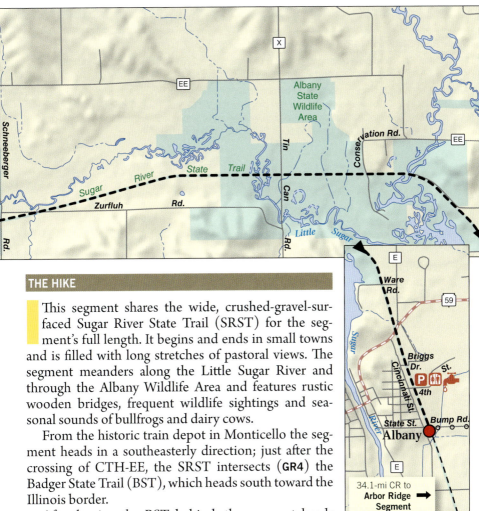

THE HIKE

This segment shares the wide, crushed-gravel-surfaced Sugar River State Trail (SRST) for the segment's full length. It begins and ends in small towns and is filled with long stretches of pastoral views. The segment meanders along the Little Sugar River and through the Albany Wildlife Area and features rustic wooden bridges, frequent wildlife sightings and seasonal sounds of bullfrogs and dairy cows.

From the historic train depot in Monticello the segment heads in a southeasterly direction; just after the crossing of CTH-EE, the SRST intersects (**GR4**) the Badger State Trail (BST), which heads south toward the Illinois border.

After leaving the BST behind, the segment heads east, paralleling the Little Sugar River. Watch for wild turkeys, pheasant, deer, sandhill cranes, snakes and turtles, who cross the path to lay their eggs.

As it nears the village of Albany, the segment crosses the Little Sugar River and then, on a long curving bridge with a picturesque view, the Sugar River. The latter crossing is just upstream from where the two rivers converge.

Upon reaching Albany, hikers can walk a few blocks off-Trail to the town's historical museum, which offers a nice slice of area history. It explains that the Ho-Chunk people called the river "Tonasookarah," meaning sugar, referring to the maple trees along the riverbank. They set up camps along the river in spring, cultivated gardens and fished in the Sugar River. As Europeans migrated west, the first settlers came to the area from New York State and New England and later Norway, Germany, Ireland, Wales and Switzerland. At the end of the 19th century, the Sugar River was called "River of Pearls," due to its abundance of oysters and clams, which are now protected.

Green County

AREA SERVICES

Sugar River State Trail (SRST): See Monticello Segment, p. 242.

Monticello: See Monticello Segment, p. 242. From the Monticello Old Train Depot go north then west 7 blocks. Also see Trail Access and Parking directions, above.

Albany: Restaurant, grocery store, convenience store, lodging, library, medical service. On Trail. From the Trail access, the business district is a few blocks west. INN Style program lodging at the Albany House B&B (608-862-3636, albanyhouse.com). Camping is available 2.4 mi south of Bump Rd. on CTH-E at Sweet Minihaha Campground (608-862-3769, sweetminihaha.com).

I appreciate my wife, family and friends who encouraged me along the way. At the start I said one of the reasons for doing this was that I wanted to be away from people. It became clear to me that you don't really do this alone. Every day I was reminded of people who were rooting me on and there for my success. Words of encouragement, donations to the cause and practical logistical support were available and ongoing. What I gained in self-reliance was outweighed by their ongoing generosity.

PAT ENRIGHT, ICE AGE TRAIL THOUSAND-MILER

I appreciated the small towns I walked through. I sometimes changed connecting roads to walk through a town. I loved the endless little hamlets, campgrounds and bars I stopped in to talk to locals about life, the weather, or my hike. Luck, Haugen, Cornell, Gilman, Antigo, Weyerhaeuser, Birchwood and countless others in the southern and eastern parts of the state. I hope the Trail stays close to or includes these little places. They are gems of Wisconsin, and to someone not of the state, a real taste of the culture that makes this wacky Trail special. You can get too much of woods and bogs sometimes.

DAVID CLOUSTON (AKA "WALKA WALKA"), ICE AGE TRAIL THOUSAND-MILER

A summer afternoon along the banks of the Sugar River flowing alongside the Albany Segment.

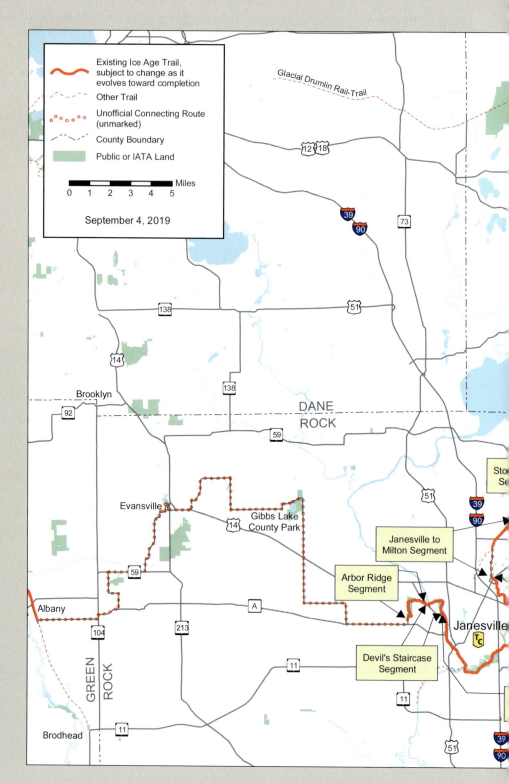

Rock, Walworth & Jefferson Counties

Rock County

Atlas Maps 71f–77f; Databook pages 70–75
Total miles: 64.0 (Trail 22.1; Connecting Route 41.9)

In Rock County, home to the southernmost segments of the Ice Age Trail, the Green Bay Lobe lost power and began to retreat about 20,000 years ago. The northern third of the county has hills, kettles and other landforms left behind when the ice sheet came to a stop. The Johnstown Moraine can be seen along the Ice Age Trail route between Janesville and Milton. This terminal moraine was formed when the Green Bay Lobe worked like a conveyor to drop glacial material near the ice edge. The Johnstown Moraine is named after a town in eastern Rock County and extends north to Waushara County. The remainder of Rock County was glaciated more than 100,000 years ago and is part of an area that stretches south beyond the Illinois border as prairie flatlands. The Ice Age Trail crosses the Rock River, which was a massive glacial meltwater channel during the last glacial advance and retreat. Today the river carries a smaller volume of water and can trace its origin north through Horicon Marsh and to the west edge of the Kettle Moraine near Allenton in Washington County.

The Sauk, Fox, Illinois, Potawatomi and Ho-Chunk nations all were in this area at one time. They named the Rock River after the rocks that caused the rapids at the mouth of the river where it empties into the Mississippi. Historical sites significant to Black Hawk War events are located throughout the county, including a few noted along the Ice Age Trail route. The Trail winds through two Ice Age Trail Communities, Janesville and Milton, highlighting their Ice Age and cultural history.

CHAPTER INFORMATION

The Rock County Chapter hosts trail improvement days and special events throughout the year. Chapter members work in collaboration with the Rock Trail Coalition in developing trails in the county for hiking and biking. The chapter's "Walk Across Rock County" program rewards hikers who have walked all Ice Age Trail segments in the chapter's territory. Trail users are urged to check out the chapter's page on the IATA website. Among other things, the page has information to connect hikers with volunteers interested in lending a hand with shuttling and other support.

COUNTY INFORMATION

Rock County Tourism Council: 866-376-8767, rockcounty.org
Rock County Parks Department: 608-757-5450

A gnarled tree captures the imagination on the Arbor Ridge Segment.

Arbor Ridge Segment and Devil's Staircase Segment (Atlas Maps 73f, 74f; Databook page 72)

SNAPSHOT

Arbor Ridge Segment—2.1 miles: Robert Cook Memorial Arboretum Upper Parking Area to N. Washington St. (CTH-E)

Devil's Staircase Segment—1.8 miles: N. Washington St. (CTH-E) to Riverside Park South Pavilion

The scenic **Arbor Ridge Segment** through the Robert Cook Memorial Arboretum is handy to Janesville but feels miles away.

 At the Arboretum Outdoor Educational Lab area.

 From Marsh Creek.

 In the Arboretum near the Marsh Creek area.

 Hikers will not have any interaction with hunting on this segment.

 By law, dogs not permitted in Janesville Parks May 15 to Sept. 15; must be leashed at other times.

 Small portion overlaps asphalt walkway in the arboretum.

 Robert Cook Memorial Arboretum trail network.

 Portions of this segment are suitable for those using wheelchair or similar device. In addition, there is a network of paved trails accessible from the Arboretum's upper parking area.

Like the Arbor Ridge Segment, the remarkable, remote-feeling **Devil's Staircase Segment** will make hikers forget they are in a city.

 At Riverside Park North and South pavilions.

 From the Rock River.

 Two ColdCache sites on segment.

 Hikers will not have any interaction with hunting on this segment.

 By law, dogs not permitted in Janesville Parks May 15 to Sept. 15; must be leashed at other times.

 Small portions overlap golf course paths.

TRAIL ACCESS AND PARKING

Robert Cook Memorial Arboretum Upper Parking Area: From Janesville at the intersection of Washington St. and Memorial Dr., take W. Memorial Dr. west 1.4 mi. Memorial Dr. becomes CTH-A. Continue west on CTH-A 0.4 mi to the paved entrance drive for the Arboretum on the right shortly after passing the Arbor Ridge subdivision entrance. The Ice Age Trail is accessed from the upper parking area. Additional parking in the lower parking area.

Riverside Park South Pavilion: From I-39/90 at Janesville, take Exit 171B onto USH-14 and go west 4.0 mi. At N. Washington St. (CTH-E) turn left and go south 2.5 mi. At Parkside Dr. turn left and go northeast for 0.4 mi to the pavilion. Roadside parking.

Additional Parking: (i) Roadside parking in Arbor Ridge subdivision. (ii) N. Washington St. (CTH-E) parking area on the east side of the road across from the entrance to the Arbor Ridge subdivision. (iii) Riverside Park parking areas on Parkside Dr. One is located along the road between the pavilions and another is located at the end of the road near the North Pavilion.

THE HIKE

The **Arbor Ridge Segment** traverses an area of bedrock hills covered with till from glacial advances much older than those explored by most of the Ice Age Trail. From its starting point at the upper parking area for the Robert Cook Memorial Arboretum–Janesville Schools Outdoor Laboratory, the segment heads under an archway and into the heart of the arboretum property. Trailside signage provides educational information on trees and local flora. The arboretum is a 160-acre City of Janesville park (managed by the Janesville school district) that is open to the public sunrise to sunset.

The segment route heads east from the parking area, then turns off the paved path at the log cabin and enters the woods. The Arboretum's Outdoor Educational Lab area and buildings are visible through the trees and can be accessed by several short spur trails. The segment descends a long bedrock ridge to the valley floor lined with intermittent tributaries of Marsh Creek. Upon reaching a junction where one of the larger tributaries flows into the creek, the segment turns east. Here there is a picnic table and access to other trails in the Arboretum's trail network. The segment then skirts a prairie with benches before exiting the Arboretum's property after passing under a power line.

The segment bends away from Marsh Creek within a 30-foot-wide wooded easement granted to the IATA for foot traffic only. Volunteers have worked hard to remove invasive species in the area and open the mixed hardwood forest to views of magnificent oaks. The segment parallels an active railway, then intersects an Arbor Ridge subdivision road, Northridge Drive. Here hikers should turn left and follow Trail signage east a short distance to the segment's endpoint at the Ice Age Trail parking area across North Washington Street (CTH-E).

Mobile Skills Crew project site, 2011

From its starting point at the parking area on the east side of North Washington Street (CTH-E), the **Devil's Staircase Segment** heads southeast a short distance parallel to the road, then emerges onto the City of Janesville's Riverside Golf Course property. As the segment continues, hikers will walk past a couple of the golf course's tee and green areas, crossing a set of railroad tracks in the process.

Hikers are asked to be respectful of golfers when passing through this area; keep voices low and yield to those in the process of teeing off, hitting approach shots or putting. Hikers should stay on the mulched pathway and off the grass.

The segment parallels a high-tension power line and then enters a wooded area. For the next half mile, hikers will traverse one of the more unique portions of the entire Ice Age Trail and may have a hard time remembering they are in the city of Janesville. The Public Works Department built this trail in the late 1920s as the City of Janesville was developing Riverside Park. During the intervening years, however, it deteriorated to the point where it became impassible. The Ice Age Trail Alliance, along with great cooperation from the city, golf course, environmental groups, local businesses and dozens of local and statewide volunteers, rebuilt the Trail with an emphasis on keeping the area as natural as possible. As a result, when hiking the segment hikers will not see the golf course but will enjoy outstanding views of the Rock River. Skillfully placed rock steps, blending into the landscape, take the hiker up and down steep hills. A portion of the route incorporates and preserves stonework attributed to the original crew of trailbuilders from the 1920s.

As hikers begin this unique section of the Ice Age Trail, the segment descends a steep switchback into the natural feature known as the Devil's Staircase (**R015**). This area features a huge gully (usually dry) descending from the golf course down across the Trail to the river. Lining the gully are large rocks that appear as though purposely placed as steps, thus leading to the name "Devil's Staircase."

The segment departs from the Devil's Staircase gully and continues along to the shore of the Rock River. The route then ascends from the river's shore up into the wooded area between the golf course and the river. On the uphill (south) side of the segment hikers will soon encounter carbonate calcareous rock faces, some of which rise up to 50 feet above the Trail. Numerous cliff-dwelling plants and woodland wildflowers highlight this portion of the segment.

Continuing east the segment arrives at a hand-crafted stone bench, where hikers will leave the wooded area by descending a steep set of manmade steps (**R010**) and arrive at Riverside Park's North Pavilion area. From here to its endpoint at the park's South Pavilion the segment hugs the shoreline, generally sticking to the thin strip of land between the Rock River and Parkside Drive.

Mobile Skills Crew project site, 2007, 2009

AREA SERVICES

Janesville: See Janesville Segment, p. 256. From the N. Washington St. (CTH-E) Trail access go south into the city. Also see Trail Access and Parking directions, above.

Evansville: Restaurant, grocery, convenience store, general shopping, lodging, library, medical service. From the N. Washington St. (CTH-E) Trail access go north 1.3 mi. At USH-14 go west 12.5 mi. Refer to Atlas maps 71f–73f. Lodging at Boarder Inn & Suites (608-882-0730, cobblestoneinns.com). Area parks with possible future Ice Age Trail are Magnolia Bluff County Park, Leonard-Leota Park in Evansville and Gibbs Lake County Park. Area information at City of Evansville (ci.evansville.wi.gov). The Wisconsin Historical Society identified Evansville as home to "the finest collection of 1840s to 1915 architecture of any small town in Wisconsin." The area is also known for its historic barn quilts.

Stone steps built in the 1920s along the Devil's Staircase Segment.

Janesville Segment (Atlas Map 74f; Databook pages 72–73)

SNAPSHOT

10.3 miles: Riverside Park South Pavilion to West Rotamer Ct.

This segment uses the City of Janesville's extensive paved trail system that links parks to create an urban greenbelt.

 At the Riverside Park South Pavilion, JTS Downtown Transfer Center and the many other parks along the segment's route.

 At the Riverside Park South Pavilion, downtown's Town Square and many other parks along the segment's route.

 From the Rock River.

 Hikers will not have any interaction with hunting on this segment.

 By law, dogs not permitted in Janesville Parks May 15 to Sept. 15; must be leashed at other times.

 Portions overlap multiuse recreational paths, sidewalks and roads.

 Side trails in city parks.

 Portions of this segment may be suitable for those using wheelchairs or similar devices.

TRAIL ACCESS AND PARKING

Riverside Park South Pavilion: From I-39/90 at Janesville, take Exit 171B onto USH-14 and go west 4.3 mi. At N. Washington St. (CTH-E) turn left and go south 2.5 mi. At Parkside Dr. turn left and go northeast for 0.4 mi to the pavilion. Roadside parking.

W. Rotamer Ct.: From I-39/I-90 take Exit 171A and go north on STH-26 (Milton Ave.). At Kettering St. turn left and go 0.1 mi. Turn right and go northeast on Whitney St. for 0.2 mi. Turn right at W. Rotamer Ct. Roadside parking.

Additional Parking: (i) Ashland Ave. at N. Washington St. parking area. A 0.2-mi spur leads to the Trail. (ii) N. River Rd. parking area (2 hour parking) just north of Mineral Point Ave. (iii) W. Milwaukee St. at the Rock River. (iv) S. River St. parking areas. (v) Dawson Ball Field. (vi) Rotary Botanical Gardens. (vii) Palmer Park. (viii) Blackhawk Meadows Park. (ix) N. Wright Rd. Roadside parking. (x) Amhurst Rd. Roadside parking. A short spur from the cul-de-sac leads to the Trail. (xi) Deerfield Dr. parking area between Home Depot and theaters. A short spur leads to the Trail.

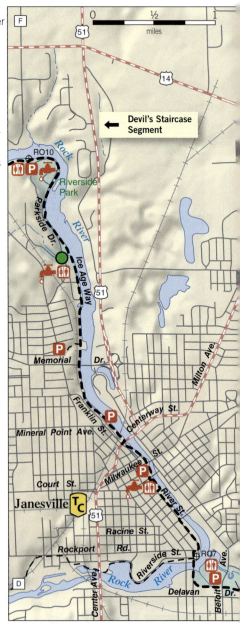

THE HIKE

From its starting point at Riverside Park's South Pavilion, the Janesville Segment exits the park and follows Ice Age Way for two blocks and then continues south along the Rock River on the Kiwanis Bike Trail. The segment passes a portion of the Rock River opposite Traxler Park, where in summer the Rock Aqua Jays water ski team performs free world-class shows on the river every Sunday and Wednesday evening. A bench allows viewing the shows across the river. This section of Trail can flood in spring or after periods of heavy rain.

The segment continues along a dirt trail built in the early 1990s by the Wisconsin Conservation Corps and goes by the ruins of the Croak Brewery (1904–1920), one of Janesville's many pre-prohibition breweries. It crosses Centerway Street and enters the City of Janesville's downtown area, which is undergoing revitalization as part of its Rock Renaissance Area redevelopment. The Town Square area, between East Milwaukee Street and West Court Street, consists of a Great Lawn gathering space, a bandstand, a pedestrian bridge across the Rock River, river edge seating, a canoe and kayak launch platform, an interactive water feature and a floating fountain. Continuing

Rock County

development on both banks of the Rock River is anticipated, including new lodging and restaurants. South of West Court Street, the segment passes on the river side of the JTS Downtown Transfer Center then continues on South River Street or along the river on a mix of sidewalk and bike trail.

At the end of River Street the segment heads west for a short distance on Rockport Road sidewalks, turns south on the City of Janesville's Spring Brook Bike Trail, passes the City of Janesville's trail hub (**R07**) and then crosses the Rock River on a pedestrian bridge on the site of an old railroad bridge. This bridge has a section where you can enjoy the river passing without being in the flow of traffic.

After heading a short distance south from the pedestrian bridge the segment bends east and follows an intermittent stream that was once a large glacial meltwater river. For portions of the Spring Brook Trail hikers may forget they are in a city as they walk through sections of forest and restored prairies. The segment passes a historical marker near Dawson Field that commemorates the site of the winter and eventual year-round grounds of the Burr Robins Circus. In the 1870s, the circus was the third largest in the world and had a significant economic impact on Janesville.

The segment then bends north to intersect Palmer Drive. Just a bit west down Palmer Drive hikers can explore the Rotary Botanical Gardens and Lions Beach (details below in Points of Interest section).

The segment continues northeast along Palmer Drive and passes the Blackhawk Golf Course; the Black Hawk War Grove historical marker that indicates where men, women and children of the Sac, Fox and Kickapoo Nations camped during the Black Hawk War; Palmer Park; and Black Hawk Meadows Park.

The segment continues northeast and crosses under I-39/90. Shortly before crossing North Wright Road the Trail intersects a paved spur trail near a kiosk. As an interesting side trip, hikers can take the spur trail 0.6 miles to walk through a recently restored prairie. At North Wright Road the segment bends north and eventually crosses under USH-14. From here the Trail turns northwest along USH-14, north along the backside of a big-box retail shopping area, west to skirt Briar Crest Park and north again, passing behind a Walmart and a Sam's Club on the way to the south side of East Rotamer Road. Cross East Rotamer Road at Tanglewood Drive and continue north and west on Tanglewood Drive 0.1 miles, picking up the multiuse path and crossing the STH-26 pedestrian bridge to the end of the segment at West Rotamer Court.

POINTS OF INTEREST

Lincoln-Tallman House: From the intersection of the Trail and N. River St. go north (right), N. River St. becomes Ravine St., turn right onto N. Jackson St. (440 N. Jackson St., Janesville, 608-756-4509, rchs. us/sites/lincoln-tallman-house).

The Lincoln-Tallman House is Rock County's most iconic historical structure. Constructed between 1855 and 1857, this six-floor mansion is an excellent example of Italianate-style architecture. From the basement to the cupola, each floor offers visitors a unique glimpse of daily life in 19th century Rock County. Over seventy percent of the furniture is original, making it one of the most complete historic houses in the Midwest. In October of 1859, Abraham Lincoln stayed at the house after a series of speeches in Beloit, forever cementing the reputation of the Lincoln-Tallman House as "where Lincoln slept."

Rotary Botanical Gardens and Lions Beach: Just west of the Trail's western intersection with Palmer Dr. (1455 Palmer Dr., Janesville, 608-752-3885, rotarybotanicalgardens.org).

The 20-acre Rotary Botanical Gardens, dedicated to international peace and friendship, showcase 18 different thematic gardens, many with an international theme, along with award winning roses, unusual plant combinations, special collections of annuals and more. There is an admission fee. Just west of the Gardens is Lions Pond and Beach, with its large swimming area and changing rooms.

AREA SERVICES

Janesville: Restaurant, grocery store, convenience store, general shopping, lodging, library, medical service. On Trail. Area info available from the Janesville Area Convention and Visitors Bureau (seasonal visitor center located on the Trail in Palmer Park; 800-487-2757, janesvillecvb.com), City of Janesville Parks Department (608-755-3025) and City of Janesville Recreation Department (608-755-3030, www.ci.janesville.wi.us/home). Access to services: (i) From the Trail at N. Washington St. (CTH-E) go east to Golf Course Rd. to access restaurants. (ii) From the Trail through the downtown area along the river find nearby restaurants, convenience store, lodging, library and medical service. (iii) From the Trail at Mt. Zion Ave. go west 0.3 mi for restaurants and convenience store. (iv) Near Briar Crest Park find access to restaurants, groceries, convenience store, general shopping, lodging and medical services in the vicinity of Deerfield Dr. and Humes Rd. (USH-14) and Milton Ave. (STH-26).

Janesville to Milton Segment

(Atlas Map 75f; Databook pages 73–74)

SNAPSHOT

3.2 miles (1.7 IAT, 1.5 CR): W. Rotamer Ct. to Manogue Rd. (High St.) at Vincent St.

This segment links two suburban areas via a portion of a pleasant, tree-lined converted railway path.

  No reliable sources of water.

  By law, dogs must be leashed on the multiuse path.

  Segment shares a multiuse recreational path and includes a portion of road walk.

  The multiuse path on the abandoned railroad bed extends southwest from the segment into Janesville.

  Portions of this segment may be suitable for those using wheelchairs or similar devices.

TRAIL ACCESS AND PARKING

W. Rotamer Ct.: From I-39/I-90 take Exit 171A and go north on STH-26 (Milton Ave.). At Kettering St. turn left and go 0.1 mi. Turn right and go northeast on Whitney St. for 0.2 mi. Turn right at W. Rotamer Ct. Roadside parking.

Manogue Rd. (High St.) at Vincent St.: From I-39/90 at Janesville, take Exit 171A and go north on STH-26 for 1.1 mi. At E. McCormick Dr. turn left and go west for 0.3 mi. At CTH-Y turn right go north for 2.2 mi to Vincent St. At Vincent St. turn left and go west and north for 0.4 mi to Manogue Rd. (High St.). The Trail access is on the southwest corner. Roadside parking along Vincent St.

Additional Parking: NW Rotamer Rd. parking area (**RO12**), just south of Townline Rd.

THE HIKE

From its starting point on West Rotamer Court the segment heads northwest 0.1 miles. At West Rotamer Road/Whitney Street hikers should turn right and continue north on West Rotamer Road. The road crosses railroad tracks

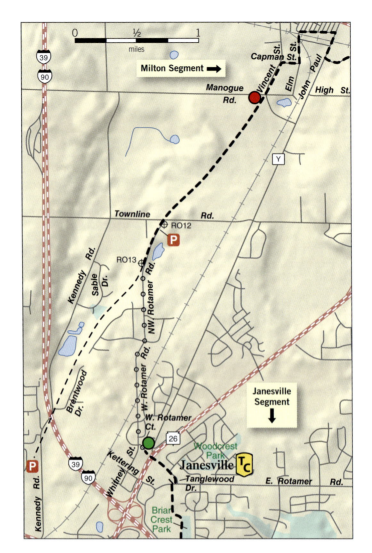

and becomes a narrow, paved country road with no shoulders. As the segment approaches Townline Road hikers will depart from the road and merge (**RO13**) onto an abandoned railroad bed that has been converted for public use as a multiuse recreational path. The segment continues northeast on the railroad bed, crossing Townline Road and then continuing through a tree-lined corridor in agricultural landscape to the segment's endpoint at the intersection of Vincent Street and Manogue Road (High Street).

AREA SERVICES

Janesville: See Janesville Segment, p. 256. From the West Rotamer Court Trail access go west then south 1.0 mi to a large commercial area. Also see Trail Access and Parking directions, above.

Milton: See Milton Segment and Storrs Lake Segment, p. 261. From Manogue Rd. Trail access go north and east into town. Also see Trail Access and Parking directions, above.

Milton Segment and
Storrs Lake Segment (Atlas Map 75f, 76f; Databook pages 74–75)

SNAPSHOT

Milton Segment—4.3 miles: Manogue Rd. (High St.) at Vincent St. to Storrs Lake Rd.

Storrs Lake Segment—1.8 miles: Storrs Lake Rd. to Bowers Lake Rd.

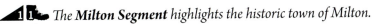 The **Milton Segment** highlights the historic town of Milton.

At Central Park, Veterans Park, South Goodrich Park and North Goodrich Park.

 Hikers will not have any interaction with hunting on this segment.

 By law, dogs must be leashed on the entire segment.

 Almost entirely on sidewalks and roads.

At South Goodrich Park.

At private campgrounds ▲ north of Milton (see Area Services).

 Portions of this segment may be suitable for those using wheelchairs or similar devices.

  The **Storrs Lake Segment** passes through woods where Abraham Lincoln camped and features wetlands and mixed forest teeming with songbirds and waterfowl.

From Storrs Lake and Bowers Lake.

Dogs should be leashed (8-ft max) and under control at all times. By law, dogs **must** be leashed April 15 to July 31 in the State Wildlife Area.

Portion of the segment crossing private land south of Bowers Lake Rd. is closed during gun deer season.

 Hunting/social trails in the State Wildlife Area.

TRAIL ACCESS AND PARKING

Manogue Rd. (High St.) at Vincent St.: From I-39/90 at Janesville, take Exit 171A and go north on STH-26 for 1.1 mi. At E. McCormick Dr. turn left and go west for 0.3 mi. At CTH-Y turn right go north for 2.2 mi to Vincent St. At Vincent St. turn left and go west and north for 0.4 mi to Manogue Rd. (High St.). The Trail access is on the northeast corner. Roadside parking along Vincent St.

Bowers Lake Rd.: From I-39/90 at Janesville, take Exit 171A and go north on STH-26 for 4.7 mi. Take Exit 8 and go west on STH-59 for 0.6 mi. At Janesville St. turn right and go north for 1.3 mi. At Bowers Lake Rd. turn right and go east 1.5 mi to the parking area on the north side of the road.

Additional Parking: (i) Storrs Lake State Wildlife Area Ice Age Trail parking area on Storrs Lake Rd. The Trail access is on the north side of the parking area. *Note: There is no access from STH-26 to Storrs Lake Rd. or Bowers Lke Rd. The closest exit ramp is at STH-59 (south of Storrs Lake Rd.).* (ii) Bowers Lake access DNR parking area, 0.8 mi west and south on Bowers Lake Rd. from the Bowers Lake Rd. Trail access. A blue-blazed spur trail leads 0.4 mi to the Trail (alternative route when Trail is flooded).

THE HIKE

From its starting point at the corner of Vincent Street and Manogue Road (High Street) the **Milton Segment** heads north on a grassy path along the east side of Vincent Street and enters a short section of a tree-lined Trail. The segment turns right onto Capman Street and heads east two blocks to Elm Street. This area, with an old railroad depot, used to be a separate community named

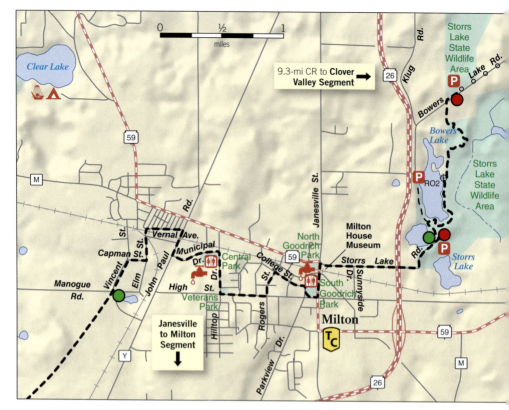

Milton Junction until a merger with Milton in 1967. It is considered Milton's second downtown area and hosts restaurants, bars, specialty shops and parks. Yellow blazes, on utility poles and street signs, guide hikers along Elm Street, Vernal Avenue, John Paul Road (CTH-Y) and Municipal Drive to reach Milton High School and the school's outdoor laboratory, which exhibits a restored prairie project.

The segment continues south along Hilltop Drive to High Street where it passes the Milton Area Veterans Memorial noted for a soaring bronze eagle atop an obelisk, flanked by the "Cost of Freedom" and "POW/MIA" memorials with benches to allow hikers to rest and reflect. Following the yellow blazes on High Street, Rogers Street and College Street, the segment travels past Milton College Historic District, which sits atop the terminal moraine of the Green Bay Lobe. Milton College closed in 1982 and is now home to a museum, office buildings, public library, guest house and park. The Milton College Preservation Society (**miltoncollege.org**) owns and operates the "Main Hall" as a museum of Milton College history. The buildings on this historic site were built in the mid-1800s.

At College Street turn right and go east three blocks through the Milton historic area. Upon reaching Parkview Drive cross the road and continue southeast through South Goodrich Park to High Street and on to Janesville Street. Turn left on Janesville Street and go north 0.3 miles past the historic Milton House Museum (see Points of Interest) to Storrs Lake Road.

The route heads east on Storrs Lake Road for 1.1 miles before reaching the segment's endpoint at the northeast corner of the large parking area for the Storrs

Lake State Wildlife Area.

The 950-acre Storrs Lake State Wildlife Area traversed by the **Storrs Lake Segment** is a rich brocade of old oak trees, tall prairie grasses, dry kettles, wildflowers and lakes teeming with northern pike, walleye and sunfish. It is home to sandhill cranes, deer, wood ducks, mallards, turkey, egrets, pheasants and barred and great horned owls. On July 1, 1832, young Abraham Lincoln camped beside Storrs Lake as one of 4,500 soldiers commanded by Brigadier General Henry Atkinson. They were in pursuit of Sauk Chief Black Hawk, who was fleeing north and west along the Rock River with 400 warriors and 1,200 women and children.

From its starting point on the north side of the parking area for the Storrs Lake State Wildlife Area the segment heads north and winds through tranquil forest of old bur and white oaks, glacial kettles and mixed hardwoods. The route offers delightful views of Bowers Lake along an upland terrace before emerging from the forest at a signed intersection (**RO2**) with a gravel service road. The quarter mile north of the intersection can experience periods of standing water. *Note: Check for current Trail conditions and alternate route options on the Ice Age Trail Alliance's website (**iceagetrail.org**) or call the Alliance (**800-227-0046**).*

The segment continues north, east and then north again, meandering between wetlands and forest to head onto the Milton Moraine. The segment exits the woods and continues north past an old apple orchard and along the edge of a cornfield before reaching Bowers Lake Road. Hikers should cross the road and follow the segment to the right to reach its endpoint at the parking area on Bowers Lake Road.

Mobile Skills Crew project site, 2004, 2015

POINTS OF INTEREST

Milton House Museum: On Trail. (18 S. Janesville St., Milton, 608-868-7772, miltonhouse.org).
The Milton House is one of twelve Underground Railroad National Historic Landmarks. This hexagonal stagecoach inn was built by Joseph Goodrich, Milton's founder, in 1844. The Underground Railroad was a secret network of people and places that helped individuals escape slavery. Freedom seekers would have traveled through Illinois and Wisconsin with the goal of reaching Lake Michigan and boarding a ship with a sympathetic captain to travel the Great Lakes and escape into Canada. Visitors walk through a secret passageway that ushered formerly enslaved people to shelter on the Underground Railroad. Seasonal hours; please call first.

AREA SERVICES

Milton: Restaurant, grocery store, convenience store, lodging, camping, library, medical service. On Trail. Most services located on or near Janesville St. in Milton and south of STH-59 and at the old railroad depot area at Capman St. and Vincent St. Lodging on Trail at Goodrich Hall Guest house (414-574-1915, airbnb.com/rooms/35131146) and Northleaf Winery Guest House (608-580-0575, airbnb.com/rooms/3263222). Area info available from the Milton Chamber of Commerce (608-868-6222, visitmilton.com). Camping at Blackhawk Camping Resort, 2 mi north of Milton (877-570-2167, blackhawkcampingresort.com) and at Lakeland Camping Resort, 3.3 mi north of Milton (877-570-2267, lakelandcampingresort.com) and Milton KOA, 4.7 mi north of Milton (800-469-5515, hiddenvalleymilton.com).

Janesville: See Janesville Segment, p. 256. From the Storrs Lake Rd. Trail access go south ~5 mi. Also see Trail Access and Parking directions, above.

Walworth & Jefferson Counties

Atlas Maps 77f–80f; Databook pages 76–78
Total miles: 25.2 (Trail 20.3; Connecting Route 4.9)

In 1846, famed early scientist and conservationist Increase Lapham wrote of Walworth County: "It is one of the richest and most important agricultural counties in the Territory; possessing a rich soil, with about the proper proportion of timber and prairie land to suit the convenience and fancy of the first settlers of a new country."

The Kettle Moraine reaches its southern end near Whitewater Lake in Walworth County. Here, the Green Bay and Lake Michigan lobes parted to extend west and south. The Ice Age Trail in this section is mostly in the Kettle Moraine State Forest—Southern Unit (KMSF-SU). It features many forests of white, black and bur oak, oak savannas, prairies, lakes, eskers and kettles. One highlight is the trip to the top of Bald Bluff, which showcases a thriving prairie and offers panoramic views to the west. Controlled burns by the Wisconsin Department of Natural Resources have rejuvenated the original prairie landscape and have encouraged the return of native prairie flowers. See the Waukesha County section for further information about the KMSF-SU. Windows into cultural history can be visited at various sites on and off the Ice Age Trail, including the Whitewater Effigy Mounds Preserve located within the city limits of Whitewater, on the city's west side, and at different locations in Jefferson County, particularly Aztalan State Park, an offshoot of the pre-Columbian city of Cahokia across the Mississippi from present-day St. Louis. The University of Wisconsin-Whitewater is the state's first Ice Age Trail Campus. A Dispersed Camping Area (DCA) is located on the Clover Valley Segment.

CHAPTER INFORMATION

Since 1993, the Walworth/Jefferson County Chapter has reached out to residents of communities such as Whitewater, Elkhorn, Lake Geneva, East Troy and Palmyra. Chapter leaders conduct popular weekly walks, along with special-interest hikes such as full moon, prairie flower, National Trails Day and Fall Colors. Other chapter activities include an Adopt-a-Segment program, monthly Trail maintenance days, family events and potlucks. Contact the chapter for details on their "Kettle Trekkers" hiking program.

COUNTY INFORMATION

Kettle Moraine State Forest—Southern Unit (KMSF-SU): 262-594-6200, dnr.wi.gov/topic/parks/name/kms/

Jefferson County Tourism Council: enjoyjeffersoncounty.com

Walworth County Visitors Bureau: 800-395-8687, visitwalworthcounty.com

A distant view of Lake La Grange on the Blackhawk Segment.

Clover Valley Segment (Atlas Map 77f; Databook page 76)

SNAPSHOT

1.6 miles: County Line Rd. to Island Rd.

 This short and quiet segment crossing the Clover Valley State Wildlife Area features wet meadow habitat and Spring Brook.

From Spring Brook.

At a Dispersed Camping Area.

 Dogs should be leashed (8-ft max) and under control at all times. By law, dogs **must** be leashed April 15 to July 31 in the State Wildlife Area.

TRAIL ACCESS AND PARKING

County Line Rd.: From the south edge of Whitewater at the intersection of USH-12, STH-59 and STH-89, take STH-59 west for 2.6 mi. At County Line Rd. turn left and go south 1.5 mi. The segment starts at a tree line on the east side of the road. No parking. Instead, park at the Island Rd. parking area.

Island Rd.: From the south edge of Whitewater at the intersection of USH-12, STH-59 and STH-89, take STH-89 south 2.0 mi. At Island Rd., turn right and go west 0.9 mi to the parking area on the south side of the road.

THE HIKE

The Clover Valley State Wildlife Area is a part of a vast wetland that was previously drained for agricultural use. It has been managed as hunting and trapping areas for waterfowl, deer, pheasant, woodcock and small game. Other recreational activities available are hiking, berry picking, fishing and bird and wildlife viewing. Sandhill cranes frequent the area. Portions of this segment can be seasonally flooded or extremely wet after heavy rainfall.

The segment starts at a Trail access point just west of the Rock/Walworth county line. It begins by following a tree line of silver maple, box elder, willow

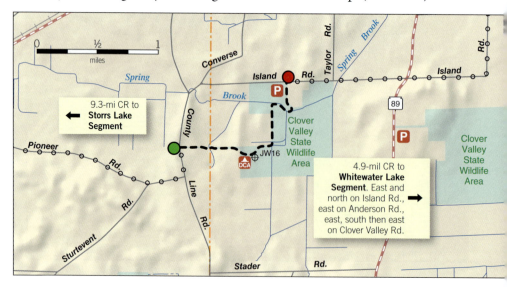

and hackberry, crosses a boardwalk and then a bridge over a small stream as it enters Walworth County. The segment continues through mixed grasses, shrubs and small trees including nannyberry viburnum and hawthorn. After crossing another boardwalk, the segment passes through an area of native grasses, small oaks, box elder, honeysuckle and buckthorn.

After passing through this area, the segment enters a slightly elevated mature hardwood woodland and soon intersects (**JW16**) a short spur trail that leads to a Dispersed Camping Area (DCA) for long-distance, multiday hikers. The Trail exits the woods, crosses a short grassland and enters a lower wet woodland consisting of large aspen and smaller invasive species that tolerate seasonal highwater levels. A large white oak on the southeastern edge of the woods marks the beginning of a 350-foot elevated curving boardwalk that carries hikers over exposed tree roots and slippery wet areas. The segment exits the woods and continues east through a field with summer-blooming bottle gentians. Here hikers can glimpse, on the right, one of the ditches dug to drain the wetland and former glacial lakebed for agriculture use.

The segment turns north, crosses over another drainage ditch and passes through an area of shrub carr (a wetland community of red-osier dogwood, willow, silky dogwood, nannyberry and other large shrub species adapted to saturated soils). Upon reaching Spring Brook, the Trail turns east and follows the stream for a quarter mile before crossing the brook on a wooden bridge.

From the bridge, the segment winds 0.2 miles north through shrub carr, meadow and prairie to the its terminus at the Island Road parking area.

Mobile Skills Crew project site, 2017

POINTS OF INTEREST

Whitewater Effigy Mounds Preserve: From the south edge of Whitewater at the intersection of USH-12, STH-59 and STH-89, take USH-12 west 1.6 mi. At Walworth Ave. turn right and go east 0.4 mi. At Indian Mound Parkway, turn left and go north 0.3 mi to the Preserve on the left side of the road. Roadside parking (288 S. Indian Mound Pkwy, Whitewater).

The Whitewater Effigy Mounds Preserve protects and preserves 13 American Indian mounds. The mounds in the preserve are either geometric in shape (conical or linear) or mimic the shape of an animal, such as the Turtle Mound. Most mounds in Wisconsin were built by American Indians during the Woodland Period, stretching from 500 BC (Early Woodland Period) up to 1200 AD (Late Woodland Period). The mounds are considered to be culturally significant sites and contain special or sacred objects or human remains. A level walking path of less than 1 mi—passing through an oak savanna, a stand of silver maples and bur oak and a meadow wetland—provides access to the 13 mounds. The preserve is listed on the National Register of Historical Places. Please respect the area; American Indian mounds are considered to be burial sites.

AREA SERVICES

Whitewater: See Whitewater Lake Segment, p. 268. From the Island Rd. Trail access go east then north ~3 mi. Also see Trail Access and Parking directions, above.

Whitewater Lake Segment (Atlas Map 78f; Databook pages 76–77)

SNAPSHOT

4.6 miles: Clover Valley Rd. to USH-12

This hilly segment features wooded moraines, kettles and outstanding views of Rice and Whitewater lakes from atop a steep rise.

 At the Kettle Moraine State Forest—Southern Unit (KMSF-SU) Rice Lake Nature Trail, DNR Contact Station and Whitewater Lake Campground.

 From Whitewater Creek.

 At KMSF-SU Whitewater Lake Campground (on Trail) and at a private campground ▲ (see Area Services).

 At KMSF-SU Rice Lake Nature Trail area and at Whitewater Lake Campground.

 At the KMSF-SU Rice Lake Nature Trail area, Whitewater Lake Campground and USH-12 Trail access parking area.

 Dogs should be leashed (8-ft max) and under control at all times.

 A small portion of the Trail overlaps a bridle/snowmobile trail.

 Connects with KMSF-SU Rice Lake Nature Trail and Whitewater Lake Recreation Area and DNR Contact Station spur trails.

TRAIL ACCESS AND PARKING

Clover Valley Rd.: From the south edge of Whitewater at the bypass intersection of USH-12, STH-59 and STH-89, take STH-89 south 1.5 mi. At Anderson Rd. turn left and go east. After 0.8 mi Anderson Rd. becomes Clover Valley Rd. Continue straight and follow Clover Valley Rd. east, south, then east for 2.6 mi. Access the Trail on the northeast side of the road. Roadside parking. Park with tires off pavement.

USH-12: *From LaGrange* take USH-12 west 2.7 mi to the Ice Age Trail parking area. *From Whitewater* at the intersection of USH-12 and STH-89, take USH-12 east 5.0 mi. to the Ice Age Trail parking area.

Additional Parking: (i) Kettle Moraine State Forest—Southern Unit (KMSF-SU) Rice Lake Nature Trail parking area on State Park Rd. To access the Ice Age Trail from the parking area, take the Rice Lake Nature Trail loop northwest for 0.4 mi. Continue on the blue-blazed spur trail 0.1 mi across Kettle Moraine Dr. to its junction with the Ice Age Trail near Hi-Lo Rd. (ii) KMSF-SU Whitewater Lake DNR Contact Station parking area on Kettle Moraine Dr. A 0.2-mi spur trail leads from the parking area to the Ice Age Trail. (iii) Esterly Rd. Trail access parking area.

THE HIKE

From the Trail access on Clover Valley Road, the segment starts off by passing through a shady pine plantation before crossing Whitewater Creek, the outlet stream from Rice Lake, on a series of puncheons and a 30-foot bridge. These structures protect the sensitive wetland bordering Whitewater Creek and offer tranquil views of the surrounding wetlands and valley. Many spring wildflowers, such as blue-flag iris and marsh marigold, along with skunk cabbage, line the creek valley.

After crossing Whitewater Creek the segment then skirts the Kettle Moraine State Forest—Southern Unit (KMSF-SU) Whitewater Lake Campground's walk-in campsites before reaching a junction (**JW6**) with a blue-blazed spur trail. The spur trail heads south across Kettle Moraine Drive to a self-guided 0.6-mile nature trail loop along the shore of Rice Lake. A large parking area is located off the loop trail.

From the junction with the spur trail the segment continues east, crossing Hi-Lo Road before reaching another spur trail, this one labeled "Office," which heads southeast 0.2 miles to the KMSF-SU Whitewater Lake DNR Contact Station parking area. After the path to the office, the segment encounters yet another side trail (**JW5**), this one to the entrance of the KMSF-SU Whitewater Lake Campground.

The segment continues east through rugged, rolling terrain past many trailside kettles. After passing behind several KMSF-SU Whitewater Lake Campground drive-in campsites the segment climbs a steep rise to a bench and lookout offering views of Rice and Whitewater lakes. The segment crosses CTH-P and rises steeply to another secluded pine plantation before crossing Esterly Road. The segment briefly joins a bridle/snowmobile trail before branching off and eventually crossing a cleared area beneath a power line. The headwaters of Bluff Creek lie below to the west and can be viewed off the segment by hiking north in the cleared area to the utility poles on top of the hill. A bench is located to the west of these poles. Just beyond the power line the segment passes through Bluff Creek State Natural Area. Here the segment travels across cavernous kettles with ancient oaks providing the canopy. This area is particularly beautiful after a wet-heavy snowfall. Shortly before the segment's end at USH-12, a clearing offers views to the west of the glacial outwash plain and the city of Whitewater from a trailside bench.

Mobile Skills Crew project site, 2007

AREA SERVICES

Kettle Moraine State Forest—Southern Unit (KMSF-SU) Whitewater Lake Campground (seasonal): Camping May through October. On Trail. (262-473-7501, dnr.wi.gov/topic/parks/name/kms/camping.html; reservations: 888-947-2757, wisconsin.goingtocamp.com).

LaGrange: Restaurant. From the USH-12 Trail access parking area go 3.0 mi east on STH-12 to CTH-H (Kettle Moraine Scenic Dr.) intersection..

Elkhorn: INN Style program lodging at Ye Olde Manor House B&B (262-742-2450, yeoldemanorhouse.com). From the USH-12 Trail access go east and south 7.0 mi.

Whitewater: Restaurant, grocery store, convenience store, general shopping, lodging, camping, library, medical service. From the USH-12 Trail access parking area, go 5.0 mi west on USH-12 and follow Business USH-12. INN Style program lodging at the Hamilton House B&B (262-473-1900, bandbhamiltonhouse.com). Lodging at the Super 8 Motel (262-472-0400) and Baymont Inn and Suites (262-472-9400). Camping at Scenic Ridge Campground, (608-883-2920, scenicridgecampground.com). Area info available from the Whitewater Chamber of Commerce (262-473-4005, whitewaterchamber.com).

Blackhawk Segment (Atlas Map 79f; Databook page 77)

SNAPSHOT

7.0 miles: USH-12 to Young Rd.

This segment highlights scenic Lake La Grange, hardwood forests and the historic Ole Oleson Homestead.

 At nearby Kettle Moraine State Forest—Southern Unit (KMSF-SU) Nordic Trails parking area south of CTH-H Trail access.

 From Lake La Grange and a pond along Duffin Rd. near KMSF-SU Backpack Shelter 3.

 At KMSF-SU Backpack Shelter 3 (reservations required).

 At the USH-12 Trail access parking area and KMSF-SU Backpack Shelter 3 (please respect those who have reserved the shelter) and parking areas for nearby KMSF-SU John Muir and Nordic trails.

 One ColdCache site on segment.

 Dogs should be leashed (8-ft max) and under control at all times.

 A small portion overlaps a snowmobile trail.

 White-blazed loop trail and several spur trails, including one (**JW3**) to KMSF-SU Backpack Shelter 3.

TRAIL ACCESS AND PARKING

USH-12: *From LaGrange* take USH-12 west 3.0 mi to the Ice Age Trail parking area. *From Whitewater* at the intersection of USH-12 and STH-89, take USH-12 east 5.0 mi.

Young Rd.: From the intersection of STH-59 and CTH-H in Palmyra take CTH-H southwest 3.0 mi. At Young Rd. turn left and go east 0.1 mi. Roadside parking.

Additional Parking: (i) Duffin Rd. Trail access (**JW12**) 0.4 mi south of the Oleson Cabin; roadside parking. (ii) Oleson Cabin Historic site on Duffin Rd.; roadside parking.

THE HIKE

The segment begins at the USH-12 Trail access information kiosk and parking area, a popular meeting point for events sponsored by the Ice Age Trail Alliance's local Walworth/Jefferson County Chapter. The segment crosses through excellent bird habitat and many species can be seen.

From the USH-12 parking area, the segment briefly climbs a hill, offering long views of deciduous forests and a nice view toward Whitewater from a bench. The Trail descends on a serpentine course and then meanders north and east around Lake La Grange past marshes bordering the lake and through woods and open tall-grass prairies. Along the way a couple of benches offer scenic views of Lake La Grange.

The segment intersects (**JW4**) a white-blazed path that heads south along the eastern shore of Lake La Grange back toward the USH-12 Trail access. From this intersection, the Ice Age Trail continues south, then eastward, passing through hardwood forest before descending 200 feet to Duffin Road (**JW12**).

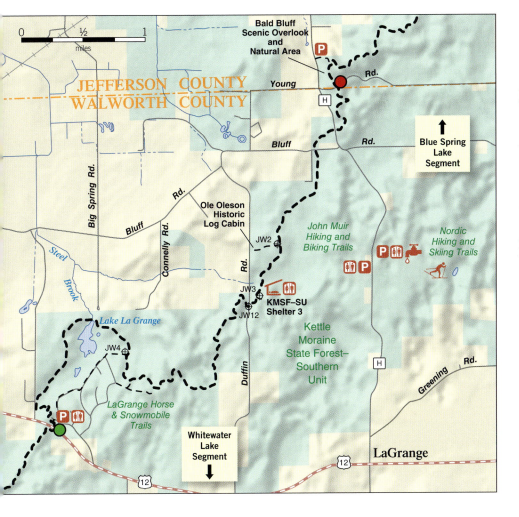

Walworth & Jefferson Counties

Shortly after the Duffin Road crossing the segment intersects (**JW3**) a spur trail that leads 0.1 miles to Kettle Moraine State Forest—Southern Unit (KMSF-SU) Backpack Shelter 3, situated atop a steep hill surrounded by dense forest.

A bit farther north from the shelter spur, the segment intersects a spur trail that heads east 0.6 miles to a pioneer lime kiln with a descriptive plaque. Continuing 150 feet north, the segment intersects (**JW2**) another spur trail leading west 0.2 miles to the historic Ole Oleson Homestead, where an early Norwegian pioneer built a two-story tamarack log cabin. On display outside the cabin is an old sleigh similar to the one used by Ole Oleson to transport the logs for the house.

Continuing from the Ole Oleson spur trail, the segment leads north through dense forest, passing along the rims of large kettle depressions, among a diverse and undisturbed quantity of flora and fauna. The Trail passes a small lake and then enters dense pine plantations.

After crossing Bluff Road, the segment goes through a section of red, black and jack pine before crossing CTH-H and climbing steeply through a savanna-like open forest of hardwoods, pockmarked by kettle depressions and scattered boulders. At the top there is a beautiful view to the horizon overlooking forests and the surrounding terrain. A short downhill trek takes hikers to the segment terminus on Young Road.

AREA SERVICES

Kettle Moraine State Forest—Southern Unit (KMSF-SU) Backpack Shelter 3: Camping. On Trail. Reservations required: 888-947-2757, wisconsin.goingtocamp.com. Only one group (up to 10) per shelter per night is allowed.

LaGrange: See Whitewater Lake Segment, p. 268. From the USH-12 Trail access go east 2.7 mi. Also see Trail Access and Parking directions, above.

Whitewater: See Whitewater Lake Segment, p. 268. From the USH-12 Trail access go west ~5 mi. Also see Trail Access and Parking directions, above.

Palmyra: See Blue Spring Lake Segment, p. 273. From the Young Rd. Trail access go west then north ~3 mi. Also see Trail Access and Parking directions, above.

Blue Spring Lake Segment (Atlas Map 79f, 80f; Databook pages 77–78)

SNAPSHOT

7.1 miles: Young Rd. to CTH-Z

 This up-and-down segment features panoramic views from the top of Bald Bluff and the Stone Elephant, a massive granite erratic.

At Kettle Moraine State Forest—Southern Unit (KMSF-SU) Horseriders' Camp on Little Prairie Rd. and KMSF-SU Emma Carlin Trails parking area.

From small ponds and springs near the segment.

Two ColdCache sites on segment.

Dogs should be leashed (8-ft max) and under control at all times.

Bald Bluff trails, Stone Elephant spur trail and KMSF-SU Emma Carlin bike/hike trail system.

TRAIL ACCESS AND PARKING

Young Rd.: From the intersection of STH-59 and CTH-H in Palmyra take CTH-H southwest 3.0 mi. At Young Rd. turn left and go east 0.1 mi. Roadside parking.

CTH-Z: From the intersection of STH-59 and STH-67 in Eagle, take STH-59 west 3.7 mi. At CTH-Z turn left and go south 0.6 mi. No parking. Instead, use nearby Kettle Moraine State Forest—Southern Unit (KMSF-SU) Emma Carlin Trails parking area on CTH-Z south of the Ice Age Trail access. A short blue-blazed spur trail leads to the Ice Age Trail.

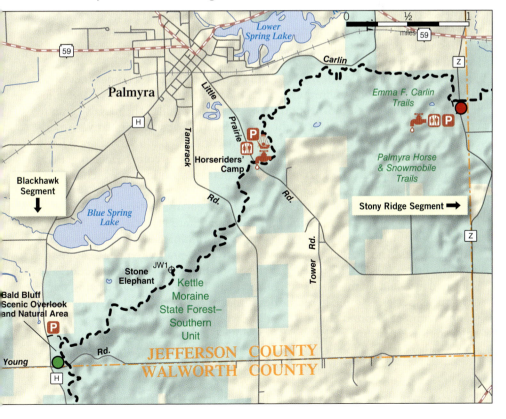

Walworth & Jefferson Counties

Additional Parking: (i) Bald Bluff Scenic Overlook parking area. From the intersection of STH-59 and CTH-H in Palmyra, take CTH-H southwest 2.8 mi. Parking area on east side of road. The trail to Bald Bluff serves as a spur to the Ice Age Trail. (ii) Tamarack Rd. Trail access. Roadside parking. (iii) KMSF-SU Horseriders' Camp parking area on Little Prairie Rd.

THE HIKE

From the trail access point on Young Road the segment heads north and quickly intersects (0.2 miles) a spur trail that leads west to the CTH-H Bald Bluff parking area. From this intersection the segment makes its way up Bald Bluff on a series of switchbacks. Bald Bluff is the largest and most diverse of the area's dry native prairie openings, which are often found on gravel knobs and steep south- and west-facing ridges. Here grow prairie flowers and grasses such as little bluestem, sideoats grama, prairie dropseed, silky aster, pasqueflower, grooved yellow flax and rough blazing star. Trailside benches encourage hikers to soak in the panoramic view. Bald Bluff is one of the highest points in Jefferson County at 1,050 feet above sea level and 200 feet above the surrounding area. Native Americans used the prominence as a lookout and for ceremonial dancing. Twice in July 1832, General Henry Atkinson camped with troops to the northwest of the bluff as he pursued the Sauk Chief Black Hawk in the Black Hawk War. A brochure for the self-guided nature trail is available at the Kettle Moraine State Forest—Southern Unit (KMSF-SU) headquarters or at the Bald Bluff trailhead on CTH-H.

The section of Trail from Bald Bluff to the KMSF-SU Horseriders' Camp provides hikers with outstanding views of glacial moraines, eskers, kettles and erratics, including spectacular long views of the surrounding topography during leaf-off seasons.

The segment descends down Bald Bluff and after 0.6 miles comes to a small clearing on the left with an impressive stand of white pines. In another 0.8 miles the segment intersects a short spur trail that leads downhill to the massive granite erratic known as the Stone Elephant (**JW1**). Prairie Potawatomi Native Americans visited the rock frequently and probably considered it a sacred area. Early settlers named the rock the Stone Elephant because of its color, size and general elephant-like shape. In the 1920s it was a popular day outing, in which tourists traveled to the site by horse-drawn surrey.

Almost all of the portion of this segment between Young Road and Tamarack Road traverses the Kettle Moraine Oak Opening State Natural Area. This area is a mixture of oak openings and oak woodland dominated by open-grown bur and black oaks. The Trail also passes a few native dry prairie remnants along the way. The first is located 0.2 miles past the Stone Elephant spur intersection and is located in a field on the north side of the Trail. The showy rough blazing star, a dry prairie species, is found here; the best time to see this plant is late August. The second remnant is found about 0.4 miles east of the first remnant (or about 0.5 miles southwest of Tamarack Road) on a south-facing slope. Here are found flora such as silky aster, leadplant, goldenrod, purple prairie clover, flowering spurge, sunflowers, arrow-leaf aster and a number of prairie grasses. A trailside bench provides a rest stop with a view.

The segment leaves the State Natural Area and crosses Tamarack Road. Three trails (horse, hiking and biking) converge/diverge near the Tamarack Road crossing, so pay close attention to signage. The Trail continues through the woods and eventually climbs and follows a steep ridge offering impressive views. Crossing Little Prairie Road, the segment again climbs for 0.2 miles to the top of a ridge where a short side trail leads to a clearing with a bench and views to the northwest. From the bench, the KMSF-SU Horseriders' Camp is 0.2 miles farther on. Horseriders' Camp is for equestrian camping only. However, showers are available for hikers who have reservations in one of the three KMSF-SU backpack shelters.

The segment crosses through the Horseriders' Camp and 0.2 miles east of the camp passes a small trailside pond. The segment continues east on level terrain past a few more small ponds and small springs. It eventually comes to an opening with a trailside map and a view of a barn across Carlin Trail (a road). From here hikers will travel up and down some hills and be rewarded with nice views down into the forest on both sides of the segment. In early spring hikers should watch for fields of mayapples in this area.

In the final mile a careful observer may notice a rock seat embedded in a tree and discover an old foundation with day lilies. Just south of the segment's endpoint on CTH-Z a short spur trail leads to the KMSF-SU Emma Carlin Trails parking area. *Note: As hikers approach the end of the segment they may hear gunfire; a public shooting range can be heard from the Trail.*

Mobile Skills Crew project site, 2003

AREA SERVICES

Palmyra: Restaurant, grocery store, convenience store, library. From the Little Prairie Rd. Trail access go 1.0 mi northwest on Little Prairie Rd. The library has limited hours.

Eagle: See Eagle Segment, p. 282. From the CTH-Z Trail access go north then east ~4 mi. Also see Trail Access and Parking directions, above.

Hikers explore the Blackhawk Segment.

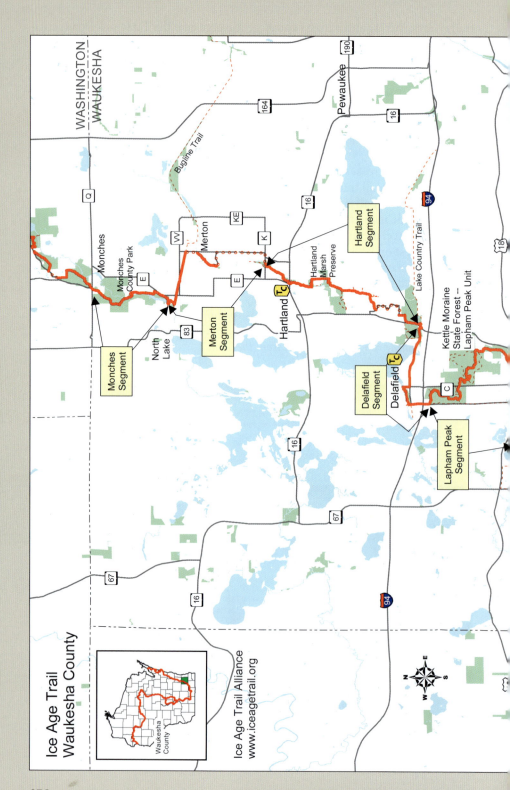

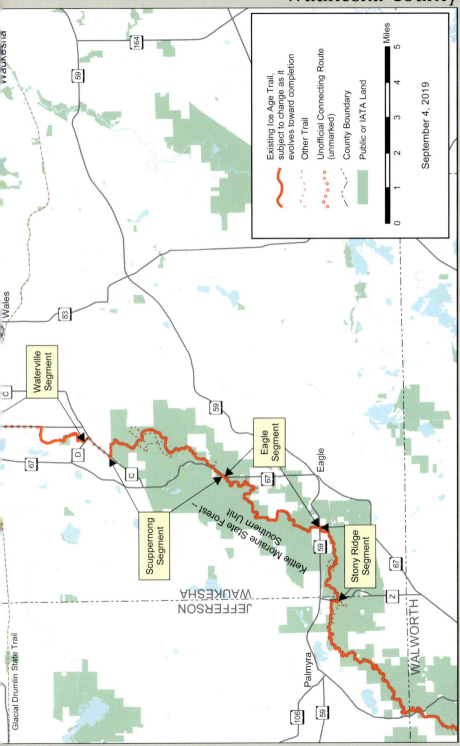

Waukesha County

Atlas Maps 80f–83f; Databook pages 79–84
Total miles: 45.3 (Trail 39.3; Connecting Route 6.0)

The Ice Age Trail is within the Kettle Moraine for most of Waukesha County but does occasionally veer to the west onto an outwash plain where small areas of the Niagara Escarpment protrude from the soil. The Ice Age Trail crosses major glacial meltwater spillways near the villages of Wales and Hartland. Many types of glacial landforms can be seen along the Trail such as kettles, eskers, drained lake plains, drumlins and kames. Erratics are abundant. Vegetation includes oak forest, oak openings and wet and dry prairie.

Seasonal wildflowers punctuate all these areas. The Trail highlights area city and county parks, multiuse recreation trails and the Kettle Moraine State Forest's Southern Unit(KMSF-SU) and Lapham Peak Unit (KMSF-LPU). The Trail also travels through two Ice Age Trail Communities, Delafield and Hartland.

The KMSF-SU contains 20,000 undeveloped acres of forest. It has numerous hiking, nature, mountain biking, equestrian, snowmobile and cross-country ski trails. Also within the unit are recreational sites for camping, picnicking, boating and swimming. The KMSF-SU headquarters in the Stony Ridge Segment features natural and historical exhibits about the surrounding area.

CHAPTER INFORMATION

The Waukesha/Milwaukee County Chapter was established in 1984 and has one of the largest chapter memberships. The chapter regularly sponsors trail improvement days, hikes and campouts. The chapter's "Walk the Wauk" program rewards hikers who have walked all Ice Age Trail segments in the chapter's territory.

COUNTY INFORMATION

Waukesha Area Convention and Visitors Bureau: 262-542-0330, visitwaukesha.org

Waukesha County Parks and Land Use Department: 262-548-7801, waukeshacounty.gov

Kettle Moraine State Forest—Southern Unit (KMSF-SU): 262-594-6200, dnr.wi.gov/topic/parks/name/kms

Kettle Moraine State Forest—Lapham Peak Unit (KMSF-LPU): 262-646-3025, dnr.wi.gov/topic/parks/name/lapham

Wisconsin Conservationists' Hall of Fame: Several of our country's foremost conservationists called Wisconsin home. The Ice Age Trail Alliance formally recognized these environmental immortals by creating the Wisconsin Conservationists' Hall of Fame. Conceived and funded by former U.S. Congressman Henry S. Reuss, five sites within Waukesha County honor Increase Lapham, Aldo Leopold, John Muir, John Wesley Powell and Carl Schurz. Each site is marked with an informative sign. Visitors have the opportunity to learn about the history of conservation in Wisconsin while enjoying a hike through the woods and wetlands of the Kettle Moraine.

Summer blooms on the Lapham Peak Segment.

Washington County

Atlas Maps 83f–87f; Databook pages 85–90
Total miles: 44.9 (Trail 35.4; Connecting Route 9.5)

The Ice Age Trail's entire route through the county is within the margins of the Kettle Moraine. These ridges formed from sand and gravel deposited where the Green Bay and Lake Michigan lobes butted up against each other, often atop the Niagara Escarpment. To either side of the Kettle Moraine are drumlins and till plains left behind by each of the lobes. Wisconsin's most distinctive geological landform is the glacier-formed moulin kame. Kames are the result of glacial streams that flowed down through cracks or shafts (moulins) in the ice sheets that rose thousands of feet above our modern landscape. Several prominent kames, such as Holy Hill, Powder Hill and a cluster known as the Polk Kames, dominate the narrow Kettle Moraine and offer panoramic hilltop views.

The Trail route in Washington County winds through the Kettle Moraine State Forest—Loew Lake Unit (KMSF-LLU) and Pike Lake Unit (KMSF-PLU), with a trek to Holy Hill sandwiched between. Farther north the route highlights the village of Slinger and the city of West Bend, both Ice Age Trail Communities, as well as Ridge Run Park and Glacial Blue Hills Recreation Area. Toward the northern end of the county the Trail begins its traverse of the Kettle Moraine State Forest—Northern Unit (KMSF-NU) near the Milwaukee River. Two county parks near West Bend maintain effigy mounds. Lizard Mound County Park, with over two dozen existing mounds, is listed in the National Register of Historic Places. Camping locations include a Dispersed Camping Area (DCA) in the Otten Preserve in the Kewaskum Segment and sites in the Kettle Moraine State Forest.

CHAPTER INFORMATION

Volunteers formed the Washington/Ozaukee County Chapter in 1987, though they had developed the first Washington County segment of the Ice Age Trail ten years prior. The chapter works to permanently protect Ice Age Trail segments in its territory and seeks routes to connect the existing Trail segments. The chapter promotes the Ice Age Trail with local news articles and service club memberships and sponsors regular hikes and trail improvement days. The chapter hosts annual events for National Trails Day and a Fall Colors Hike. The chapter's "Meander the Mid-Moraine" hiking program recognizes hikers who have walked all 45 miles of the chapter's Ice Age Trail segments and connecting routes.

COUNTY INFORMATION

Kettle Moraine State Forest—Pike Lake Unit (KMSF-PLU): 262-670-3400, dnr.wi.gov/topic/parks/name/pikelake

Kettle Moraine State Forest—Northern Unit (KMSF-NU): 262-626-2116, dnr.wi.gov/topic/parks/name/kmn

Washington County Convention & Visitors Bureau: 888-974-8687 or 262-677-5069, visitwashingtoncounty.com

"Glacier B" is enthralled by the sights and sounds on the Kewaskum Segment.

Loew Lake Segment (Atlas Maps 83f, 84f; Databook page 86)

SNAPSHOT

4.9 miles (4.3 IAT, 0.5 CR): CTH-Q to Emerald Dr. Northern Trail Access.

  This segment highlights the Oconomowoc River valley while passing through wooded terrain and a large, scenic meadow.

- From the Oconomowoc River.
- At the Emerald Dr. DNR parking area (**WA18**).
- One ColdCache site on segment.

- Dogs should be leashed (8-ft max) and under control at all times. By law, dogs **must** be leashed April 15 to July 31 when crossing the Loew Lake Unit (KMSF-LLU).
- Two short spur trails.
- Segment includes connecting-route roadwalks.

TRAIL ACCESS AND PARKING

CTH-Q: From Menomonee Falls take USH-41/45 north. Exit onto County Line Rd. (CTH-Q) and go west 11.5 mi, then turn right on CTH-K and go 0.1 mi to a parking area on the right with a spur trail to Ice Age Trail.

Emerald Dr. Northern Trail Access: From Hartford at the intersection of STH-83 and STH-60, take STH-83 south 4.7 mi. At STH-167 turn left and go east 1.5 mi. At CTH-K turn right and go south 1.0 mi. At Donegal Rd. turn left and go east 1.5 mi. At Emerald Dr. turn right and go south 0.3 mi. No parking. Instead, park at the Emerald Dr. parking area (**WA18**) 0.5 mi south of segment's northern terminus. A blue-blazed spur trail from the parking area leads to the Ice Age Trail.

Additional Parking: DNR parking lot on the north side of County Line Rd. (CTH-Q) 0.5 mi east of CTH-Q trail access.

THE HIKE

This segment is a key link in the green belt between Washington and Waukesha counties and generally follows the rim of the Oconomowoc River valley winding along the Oconomowoc River and 23-acre Loew Lake. The valley served as a glacial spillway where meltwater flowed south between the Green Bay and Lake Michigan glacial lobes. The segment highlights the Kettle Moraine State Forest—Loew Lake Unit (KMSF-LLU), an area that offers a variety of habitats for wildlife and is extremely popular with hunters and fishermen in all seasons.

From its starting point near the CTH-K and CTH-Q intersection at the Washington/Waukesha county line, the segment passes through a conifer plantation before dropping down to briefly parallel the Oconomowoc River. The segment departs from the riverbank and continues north to a boardwalk at the edge of a marsh filled with skunk cabbage and tall cow parsnip. The segment follows several hedgerows adjacent to an open field and cuts through another conifer plantation before intersecting Emerald Drive.

Upon reaching Emerald Drive hikers should turn right and head northeast along the road for 0.4 miles before heading east onto a short off-road section that features distant views of the Holy Hill Shrine to the north. Just before reentering Emerald Drive is a spring that forms a small stream. It flows southeastward and empties into the Oconomowoc River. The local chapter built a large wooden

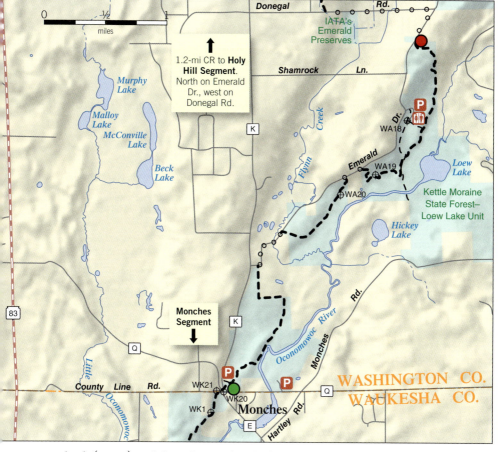

overlook (**WA20**) with benches and a platform overlooking the spring.

After an additional 0.1-mile walk along Emerald Drive, the segment again departs the road heading east and weaves in and out of woods, alongside meadows and atop a steep-sided esker (**WA19**). The segment intersects a horse trail and a short distance later you can see Loew Lake off to the right. Farther on, the segment intersects a blue-blazed spur trail that heads west to the DNR's Emerald Drive parking area (**WA18**). From this last junction, the segment continues north through a large meadow before climbing out of the river valley on a series of switchbacks to reach the its endpoint on Emerald Drive.

AREA SERVICES

Monches: See Merton Segment and Monches Segment, p. 295. From the CTH-K at CTH-Q Trail access go south 0.1 mi on CTH-E.

Hartland: See Hartland Segment, p. 292. From the CTH-K at CTH-Q Trail access go south ~7 mi.

Kettle Moraine State Forest—Loew Lake Unit (KMSF-LLU): On Trail. Access on Emerald Dr. (262-670-3400, dnr.wi.gov/topic/parks/name/loewlake).

Hartford: See Pike Lake Segment, Slinger Segment and Cedar Lakes Segment, p. 360. From the Emerald Dr. northern Trail access go west and north ~9 mi. Also see Trail Access and Parking directions, above.

Holy Hill Segment (Atlas Map 84f; Databook pages 86–87)

SNAPSHOT

6.9 miles: Donegal Rd. to CTH-E

 Especially popular during fall color season, this segment showcases the Holy Hill kame, wooded, hilly terrain and deep kettles.

Note: *A short reroute is planned between Pleasant Hill Rd. and Waterford Rd. Check with the Ice Age Trail Alliance (800-227-0046, iceagetrail.org) for details.*

	At the Basilica complex.		One ColdCache site on segment.
	At the Station Way Rd. picnic area.		Dogs should be leashed (8-ft max) and under control at all times and not stray from the Trail.
	At the Station Way Rd. picnic area and Basilica complex.		
	Portion of segment crossing private land between Pleasant Hill Rd. and CTH-E is closed during gun deer season.		Portions of the segment overlap Pleasant Hill Rd. and Glassgo Dr.
			Several short spur trails.

TRAIL ACCESS AND PARKING

Donegal Rd.: From the Menomonee Falls area take I-41/USH-45 north. Exit onto STH-167 and go west 6.0 mi. At CTH-CC turn left onto St. Augustine Rd. and go south 0.8 mi. At Emerald Dr. turn right and go west, curving south 0.7 mi. At Donegal Rd. turn right and go west 0.8 mi. No parking. Instead, park at one of the Holy Hill Shrine parking areas. See Additional Parking, below.

CTH-E: From I-41 exit onto STH-60 and go west 2.3 mi. At CTH-CC turn left and go south 2.0 mi. At CTH-E turn right and go west 1.4 mi to the Trail access just west of Glassgo Dr. Roadside parking on Glassgo Dr.

Additional Parking: (i) Carmel Rd. parking area near St. Mary of the Hill Parish. A blue-blazed spur trail leads to the Ice Age Trail. From Donegal Rd. Trail access, go west 0.1 mi on Donegal Rd. At Carmel Dr. turn right and go north 0.5 mi to parking area. (ii) Station Way Rd. picnic area. From the Menomonee Falls area take I-41/USH-45 north. Exit onto STH-167 and go west 7.3 mi. At Station Way Rd. turn left and go south 0.1 mi to the picnic and parking area. The Ice Age Trail follows the north edge of the picnic area. (iii) STH-167. Roadside parking with spur trail to Ice Age Trail. (iv) Shannon Rd. parking area, 0.5 mi east of CTH-K. A blue-blazed spur trail leads to the Ice Age Trail.

THE HIKE

From Donegal Road to the STH-167 Trail access, the segment passes through a mostly forested landscape across the glacial terrain that surrounds Holy Hill. The segment route offers just a few openings with views of glacial kame Holy Hill and the shrine and monastery that sit atop it, 1,350 feet above sea level. Glacial geologists estimate that at the time of the Wisconsin Glaciation, the thickness of the glacial ice extended another 1,000 feet above Holy Hill. Glacial erratics are a common trailside sight in this area and several spur trails offer vistas of the surrounding landscape. A blue-blazed spur trail (**WA16**) north of Holy Hill leads to both a parking area near St. Mary of the Hill Parish and a large glacial erratic perched at the top of a kame.

At STH-167 (**WA15**) the segment continues north, crossing an intermittent stream on a board bridge built as an Eagle Scout project and then winding through grasslands of a previous agricultural era with multiple stone fence remnants along the way.

Just south of the Shannon Road Trail access (**WA14**), a blue-blazed spur trail leads west to a DNR parking area on Shannon Road. Along this section of Trail several types of trees are identified by informational signs.

North of Shannon Road, the segment passes through a pine plantation and then continues north along the edges of two fields. At Pleasant Hill Road, hikers should turn right and follow the blazed telephone poles east for 0.5 miles. The segment departs north from Pleasant Hill Road (**WA13**), crosses a field along the edge of a small wetland, climbs two hills with a kettle pond in between, passes through a large wetland on a long, elevated boardwalk and then emerges onto Waterford Road after passing a farm field and house.

North of Waterford Road, the segment passes several deep kettles in a mature mixed forest, then follows along the edge of farm fields and then through a field before reaching an intersection (**WA12**) with Glassgo Drive. The segment follows the road northeast for 0.3 miles before departing off-road to the northwest on a short section that leads to the segment's terminus on CTH-E.

Mobile Skills Crew project site, 2006

AREA SERVICES

Holy Hill Shrine and Monastery: Restaurant (seasonal), lodging (call ahead). On Trail (262-628-1838, holyhill.com).

Glacial Blue Hills County Park cabins: Take STH-167 east 2.2 mi. At Friess Lake Rd. go 0.3 mi south to park's entrance drive. Cabin rentals through Washington County Parks Department. See the county website for VRBO cabin reservation link (1664 Friess Lake Rd., 262-335-4445, washcoparks.com/parks/shelters/).

Kettle Moraine State Forest—Pike Lake Unit (KMSF-PLU): See Pike Lake Segment, Slinger Segment and Cedar Lakes Segment, p. 306. From the STH-167 Trail access go west and north ~6 mi.

Hartford: See Pike Lake Segment, Slinger Segment and Cedar Lakes Segment, p. 306. From the STH-167 Trail access go west and north ~7 mi.

Pike Lake Segment, Slinger Segment and Cedar Lakes Segment (Atlas Maps 84f, 85f; Databook pages 87–88)

SNAPSHOT

Pike Lake Segment—3.3 miles: CTH-E to STH-60
Slinger Segment—1.5 miles: STH-60 to Kettle Moraine Dr.
Cedar Lakes Segment—2.8 miles: Kettle Moraine Dr. to CTH-NN

 The **Pike Lake Segment** passes through the family-friendly Kettle Moraine State Forest—Pike Lake Unit (KMSF-PLU) and offers outstanding views from the top of the nearby Powder Hill observation tower.

At KMSF-PLU facilities.

From Pike Lake.

Three walk-in campsites at KMSF-PLU (see Area Services).

 KMSF-PLU campground .

Dogs are not permitted at park facilities.

KMSF-PLU trail network loops and spurs. A spur trail (**WA34**) to three walk-in campsites.

 The short **Slinger Segment** mostly follows roads and sidewalks.

Note: A reroute is planned for the eastern portion of the segment. Check with the Ice Age Trail Alliance (800-227-0046, iceagetrail.org) for details.

At Community Park.

Dogs should be leashed (8-ft max) and under control at all times.

Portions of this segment may be suitable for those using wheelchairs or similar devices.

 The **Cedar Lakes Segment** features the Polk Kames, the second largest cluster of kames in the state.

 No reliable sources of water.

One ColdCache site on segment.

 Dogs should be leashed (8-ft max) and under control at all times.

 A white-blazed loop trail and blue-blazed connecting trail.

306 Ice Age Trail Guidebook 2020 – 2022 Edition

TRAIL ACCESS AND PARKING

CTH-E: From I-41 exit onto STH-60 and go west 2.3 mi. At CTH-CC turn left and go south 2.0 mi. At CTH-E turn right and go west 1.4 mi to the Trail access just west of Glassgo Dr. Roadside parking on Glassgo Dr.

CTH-NN: From I-41 take Exit 66 onto STH-144 and go north 0.4 mi. At CTH-NN turn right and go east 0.4 mi to the parking area on the south side of the road.

Additional Parking: (i) Kettle Moraine State Forest—Pike Lake Unit (KMSF-PLU) Swim Area on Kettle Moraine Rd. (ii) KMSF-PLU Black Forest Nature Trail parking area on Powder Hill Rd. The Ice Age Trail passes through the east end of the parking area. (iii) Roadside parking in Slinger. No parking along Cedar Creek Rd.

THE HIKE

The Pike Lake Segment heads north from its starting point on CTH-E, paralleling and then following quiet Glassgo Drive 0.3 miles to the southern property boundary (**WA10**) of the 446-acre Kettle Moraine State Forest—Pike Lake Unit (KMSF-PLU). Most of the segment here follows the edge of a glacial ridge through heavily forested maple and beech woods. Pike Lake is a spring-fed kettle with a very popular sandy beach; the segment reaches the swimming area parking lot 0.5 miles after entering the unit.

The segment crosses Kettle Moraine Road and makes its way uphill for 0.8 miles to an intersection with a spur trail that climbs 0.3 miles to the top of 1,350-foot Powder Hill, one of the larger kames in the area. A lookout tower on top offers spectacular 360-degree views. From the intersection with the spur trail the segment continues another 0.3 miles to Powder Hill Road, joining the Black Forest Nature Trail along the way.

East of Powder Hill Road the segment passes a spur trail to the Pike Lake Unit campground and turns north to pass through the east end of the Black Forest Nature Trail parking area. From here, the segment travels north and east through a heavily wooded area and intersects (**WA34**) a short spur trail that leads to three walk-in backpack campsites. The segment continues east to CTH-CC at a spot (**WA9**) marked with an Ice Age Trail signpost on the west side of the road. At this point, hikers should turn left and head north on CTH-CC for 0.3 miles to the segment's endpoint at the CTH-CC and STH-60 intersection.

Washington County

The **Slinger Segment** starts from the CTH-CC and STH-60 intersection by heading northeast on an abandoned road that leads to Howard Avenue. Hikers should head east and then north on Howard Avenue to Hartford Road, where the segment heads east to Kettle Moraine Drive (STH-144).

At Kettle Moraine Drive (STH-144) the segment heads northeast and takes hikers through the village of Slinger. Slinger was an important trading center for Native Americans. Over the years, it has been at the crossroads for many trails and roads such as the Winnebago Trail, which was the easiest route through the Kettle Moraine, and the Yellowstone Trail, America's first coast-to-coast automobile highway. Along Kettle Moraine Drive (STH-144) the segment passes Community Park before reaching its endpoint at the Cedar Creek Road intersection.

The **Cedar Lakes Segment** highlights several of the Polk Kames while traversing agricultural fields, wetlands and mixed forest of old oaks, sugar maple, white birch and beech. During the winter, the north and east sides of the kames retain snow later than the surrounding landscape. The spring months present a scattered display of woodland and prairie wildflowers, including trillium, wood anemone, mayapple, violets, jack-in-the-pulpit and many ferns. The fall colors here are not to be missed. A few Ice Age Trail informational signs are placed along the segment.

From the intersection of Kettle Moraine Drive (STH-144) and Cedar Creek Road the segment follows Cedar Creek Road east for 0.7 miles. The segment departs the road and heads north along the edge of a farm field and enters the woods, soon arriving at a junction with the 0.8-mile white-blazed Kame Loop trail, which curves around a prominent kame and allows hikers to see the west side of the kame; in spring look for a large area of shooting stars on a hilltop north of the kame. From this junction the segment heads east and then north, passing a bench and informational sign on the east side of the kame. The segment then reaches the north junction with the white-blazed loop trail and skirts the eastern sides of a second kame. Volunteer-built puncheons and rock-lined water drainage structures highlight this portion of the segment.

The segment bends west and passes the north side of the northern kame and then comes to a junction with a blue-blazed trail, which connects to the white-blazed Kame Loop. The segment continues west and then north, passing through a mix of forest and farm fields before reaching its endpoint at the Trail access on CTH-NN.

Mobile Skills Crew project site, 2004, 2009

AREA SERVICES

Kettle Moraine State Forest—Pike Lake Unit (KMSF-PLU): Camping. On Trail. (262-670-3400, dnr.wi.gov/topic/parks/name/pikelake). General camping and three walk-in backpack campsites available. Reservations required (888-947-2757, wisconsin.goingtocamp.com).

[TC] **Slinger:** Restaurant, grocery store, convenience store, library. From the STH-60 Trail access go 1.5 mi east on STH-60 or on Trail along Kettle Moraine Dr.

Hartford: Restaurant, grocery store, convenience store, lodging, camping, library, medical service. From the STH-60 Trail access go 2.5 mi west on STH-60. INN Style program lodging at the Jordan House B&B (262-673-5289, jordanhousebandb.com) and at Westphal Mansion Inn B&B (262-673-7938, westphalmansioninn.com). Area info available from the Hartford Chamber of Commerce (262-673-7002, hartfordchamber.org).

West Bend Segment and Southern Kewaskum Segment

(Atlas Maps 85f, 86f; Databook pages 88–89)

SNAPSHOT

West Bend Segment—6.7 miles: Paradise Dr. to CTH-D

Southern Kewaskum Segment—1.1 miles: CTH-D to Wildwood Rd.

The rolling **West Bend Segment** highlights scenic suburban parks with many additional hiking options.

> **Note:** A reroute is planned south of Washington St. (STH-33/144). Check with the Ice Age Trail Alliance (800-227-0046, iceagetrail.org) for details.

 At Ridge Run Park.

 From Lucas Lake and Silver Creek.

 Five ColdCache sites on segment.

 Dogs must be restrained on a leash no longer than 6 ft in Ridge Run Park and on portions between Washington St. (STH-33/144) and CTH-D.

 Portions overlap a gravel driveway and sidewalks. A small portion in Glacial Blue Hills Recreation Area is open to mountain biking.

 Several spur trails and three white-blazed loop trails.

Largely passing under a power transmission line, the **Southern Kewaskum Segment** highlights a beech-maple forest.

 No reliable sources of water.

 At nearby Timber Trail Campground (see Area Services).

 Dogs should be leashed (8-ft max) and under control at all times.

 Portion overlaps Friendly Dr.

 A short white-blazed loop trail.

TRAIL ACCESS AND PARKING

Paradise Dr.: From West Bend take USH-45 south. Take Exit 68 onto Paradise Dr. and go west 1.0 mi to the parking area on the north side of the road. No overnight parking.

Wildwood Rd.: From West Bend take USH-45 north. Take Exit 73 onto CTH-D and go west 0.9 mi. At Wildwood Rd., turn right and go north 0.2 mi to the parking area on the east side of the road.

Additional Parking: (i) Ridge Run Park, both north and south entrances. (ii) Washington St. (STH-33/144) commercial parking area near Culver's. (iii) Glacial Blue Hills Recreation Area off Beaver Dam Rd. (iv) CTH-D Trail access. Roadside parking on the south side of the road. (v) Friendly Dr. Trail access (**WA4**). Roadside parking.

THE HIKE

From its starting point on Paradise Drive the **West Bend Segment** meanders north and soon intersects a short white-blazed loop trail that bubbles off to the east of the main segment. The segment bends west and enters the heavily wooded property of the Girl Scouts' Camp Silver Brook at the south end of Lucas Lake. It continues past an esker and then drops to a marshy area with a bridge over Silver Creek, which flows northward from Paradise Valley Lake into Lucas Lake.

From here, the segment makes its way up a steep ridge and bends north, passing over lands protected by the Cedar Lakes Conservation Foundation. The segment then meanders back onto Girl Scout property offering hikers glimpses of Lucas Lake to the right.

The segment enters Ridge Run Park and curves past an artesian well and small pond near a picnic area, crosses over a water-filled kettle/wetland on a boardwalk (**WA6**) and soon heads north along picturesque Silver Creek and its chain of lily filled ponds and lakes. Continuing on, the Trail partially circles a ridge, then climbs the ridge, turns east and exits Ridge Run Park, briefly following a driveway to connect with University Drive near its intersection with Chestnut Street. The segment heads north and follows sidewalks along University Drive for half a mile. The segment then heads west on busy Washington Street (STH-33/STH-144), crosses at a stop light and then heads back east to a Trail access area (**WA35**) on the north side of the road, passing a large commercial area with most services. From here, the segment heads north ascending a forested ridge.

The segment passes through the scenic Glacial Blue Hills Recreation Area traversing rugged terrain as it goes along a moraine and dips between ridges on its way toward the segment terminus at CTH-D. Shortly after crossing Park Avenue, the segment skirts a kettle and climbs to the top of an esker (**WA5**), following the crest of the esker to Beaver Dam Road. The Recreation Area features a network of hiking and biking trails, including two white-blazed loop trails.

The **Southern Kewaskum Segment** begins by crossing CTH-D and following

Friendly Drive north for 0.3 miles. The segment departs (**WA4**) Friendly Drive and heads west, following a power line right-of-way over rolling hills while highlighting agricultural fields and mature beech–maple woods where hikers will find many spring and summer wildflowers. At about the midpoint of the segment, a portion of the Trail tends to have standing water in the spring and be wet and muddy at other times of the year. Climbing out of this low area, the segment briefly leaves the right-of-way and enters the beech–maple woods to connect with a short white-blazed loop trail. Continuing west there is a small footbridge over a small ephemeral stream before reaching the segment terminus at Wildwood Road.

POINTS OF INTEREST

Quaas Creek Park: From the Ice Age Trail parking area near the intersection of University Dr. and Washington St. (STH-33), drive east on Washington St. (STH-33) for 2.4 mi, turn right on S. River Rd., turn left on E. Decorah Rd. and turn left on County Creek Cir. (2500 Country Creek Cir., West Bend).

Quaas Creek Park has two bird mounds and possibly two water-spirits.

Lizard Mound County Park: From the Glacial Blue Hills Recreation Area on Beaver Dam Rd., continue onto Jefferson St., turn right onto N. Main St., turn left onto Barton Ave. (STH-144) and travel 2.9 mi, turn right onto CTH-A (2121 CTH-A, West Bend, 262-335-4445, co.washington.wi.us/departments.iml?Detail=1023).

The park, which is listed on the National Register of Historic Places, contains 28 effigy mounds in an excellent state of preservation. The variety of mound shapes found here is considered unusual. Two are large bird effigy mounds and seven are long-tailed animal forms, referred to as "panther" effigies. One of the 28 mounds is named "Lizard Mound" and may represent the same animal; it is in a spread-eagle posture that shows all four limbs.

AREA SERVICES

West Bend: Restaurant, grocery store, convenience store, general shopping, lodging, camping, library, medical service. On Trail. Most services are located either 0.7 mi east from the Paradise Dr. Trail access parking area or along Washington St. (STH-33/144). INN Style lodging at Wellspring Farm B&B & Hostel (262-675-6755, wellspringinc.org/bb-and-hostel.html). Camping at Timber Trail Campground (262-338-8561, timbertrailcampground.com; call ahead for availability, ask to speak with the manager if full). For West Bend area info contact the West Bend Park, Recreation and Forestry Department (262-335-5080, ci.west-bend.wi.us/departments/parks_recreation___forestry/)

A scenic overlook at the Otten Preserve along the Kewaskum Segment.

Kewaskum Segment and Milwaukee River Segment

(Washington County) (Atlas Map 86f, 87f; Databook page 89–90)

SNAPSHOT

Kewaskum Segment—2.1 miles: Ridge Rd. to Eisenbahn State Trail

Milwaukee River Segment (Washington County)—6.9 miles (6.8 IAT, 0.1 CR): Eisenbahn State Trail to Kettle Moraine Dr.

  *The **Kewaskum Segment** features the Otten Preserve and its scenic overlooks.*

- No reliable sources of water.
- At a Dispersed Camping Area on the Otten Preserve.
- Portion of segment crossing private land between Ridge Rd. and STH-45 is closed during gun deer season.
- Dogs should be leashed (8-ft max) and under control at all times.
- Portion overlaps Prospect Dr. and briefly overlaps the multiuse Eisenbahn State Trail.
- Loop trails at the Otten Preserve. A blue-blazed spur trail (**WA32**) to a DCA. The Eisenbahn State Trail extends north and south from the segment.

  *The hilly **Milwaukee River Segment (Washington County)** highlights forested woodlands and sunny meadows.*

- From a hand-pump water well (**WA24**) near Kettle Moraine State Forest—Northern Unit (KMSF-NU) Backpack Shelter 1 and at the nearby KMSF-NU New Fane Trails parking area.
- From the Milwaukee River.
- At KMSF-NU Backpack Shelter 1 (reservations required).
- At nearby KMSF-NU New Fane Trails parking area.
- At KMSF-NU Backpack Shelter 1 (please respect those who have reserved the shelter) and nearby KMSF-NU New Fane Trails parking area.
- One ColdCache site on segment.
- Dogs should be leashed (8-ft max) and under control at all times.
- Segment includes a brief connecting route roadwalk.
- Spur trail (**WA1**) to KMSF-NU Backpack Shelter 1.

TRAIL ACCESS AND PARKING

Ridge Rd.: From Kewaskum at the intersection of USH-45 and STH-28, take USH-45 south 1.8 mi. At the stoplight for Badger Rd. turn right and go west 0.3 mi. At Prospect Dr. turn left and go south 1.0 mi. The road curves west and changes to Ridge Rd. Continue on Ridge Rd. west 0.6 mi to the parking area.

Kettle Moraine Dr.: From Kewaskum at the intersection of STH-28 and USH-45, take STH-28 east 2.5 mi. At Kettle Moraine Dr. turn left and go north 2.0 mi. No parking at the Trail access on Kettle Moraine Dr. Instead, park at the Kettle Moraine State Forest—Northern Unit (KMSF-NU) New Fane Trails parking area 0.2 mi south on Kettle Moraine Dr. and 0.3 mi east on County Line Dr. A spur trail leads from the northwest corner of the parking area to the Ice Age Trail (**SF8**).

Additional Parking: (i) Sunburst Ski Area parking area (**WA2**). (ii) CTH-H parking area on the south side of the road. (iii) KMSF-NU Backpack Shelter 1 parking area on the north side of CTH-H. (iv) STH-28 parking area. (v) East Moraine Dr. parking area.

THE HIKE

The area traversed by the **Kewaskum Segment** has a rich Native American history. The word Kewaskum means "crooked river" in Algonquin, the language of the Potawatomi who once inhabited the area. The Potawatomi claim to the land ended with a treaty in 1833 and the Nation was resettled to Oklahoma. Years

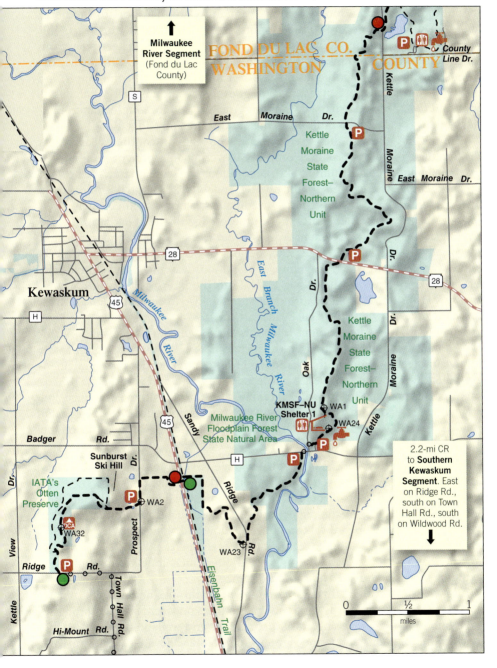

later, only a few returned.

The Kewaskum Segment heads north from its starting point on Ridge Road through the Ice Age Trail Alliance's 125-acre Roman and Mercedes Otten Preserve, home to not only the main segment route but also an additional 2.5 miles of loop trails. The main segment route features light forests and upland fields with spectacular views of the Otten Preserve and the surrounding areas. From the hilltops, hikers can look for Kewaskum and Campbellsport to the north and the Dundee Kame and Kettle Moraine State Forest to the northeast. This portion of the segment is a magnet for birds and hikers should keep an eye out for meadowlarks, bobolinks, turkeys and several birds of prey. In spring, the woods are filled with a gorgeous display of trillium and jack-in-the-pulpit, and in late summer, there are many areas of gooseberry and raspberry patches. A spur trail (**WA32**) to a Dispersed Camping Area (DCA) for long-distance, multiday hikers is located 0.5 miles from the parking area on Ridge Road.

After passing through the Otten Preserve, the segment continues east across the Sunburst Winter Sports Park property (covering a prominent kame) on an easement granted by the Summit Ski Corporation. The segment intersects (**WA2**) Prospect Drive, where hikers should turn left and follow the road 0.3 miles north. The segment departs Prospect Drive heading east along a field edge, crosses a series of boardwalks, then skirts the southern edge of the "tank farm" before arriving at USH-45. The segment crosses under USH-45 via an underpass built specifically for the Ice Age Trail. After periods of heavy rains, the underpass is often swamped with water. Therefore, as conditions warrant, hikers should turn left and hike north 0.1 miles along USH-45 to the intersection with CTH-H. Cross USH-45 at the stoplight, turn right onto the Eisenbahn State Trail and hike south 0.1 miles to where the Trail heads east.

East of USH-45, the segment intersects the Eisenbahn State Trail, a state-owned multiuse recreation trail on the former C & NW Railroad right-of-way. Twelve of the 24.0 miles of the abandoned former rail corridor are maintained, extending from the city of West Bend to Eden in Fond du Lac County. "Eisenbahn" is German for "iron road," harkening back to this rail line's heritage and original construction in 1871. The segment very briefly follows the Eisenbahn State Trail north to the segment's terminus where the Ice Age Trail heads off the Eisenbahn State Trail to the east.

From the Eisenbahn State Trail, the **Milwaukee River Segment (Washington County)** heads east then south, skirting a wetland mitigation site. The Trail crosses a boardwalk, cuts through woods and along the edge of a field and then enters a forested area. As the segment meanders through the forest it crosses a wet area on a curving boardwalk and travels below and alongside a ridge, gradually climbing the ridge until the segment reaches an open field (**WA23**) just before crossing Sandy Ridge Road. The open field offers nice, long views of the surrounding fields and forested hills in the distance.

After crossing the road, the Trail continues north through an open field and up the side of a hill, then shortly drops down into the woods and courses through a more hummocky area passing grassy depressions and wetland openings. Along the way, the segment enters the Kettle Moraine State Forest—Northern Unit

(KMSF-NU). Continuing on, the segment primarily cuts across agricultural areas until it reaches the CTH-H parking area.

Hikers should turn east on CTH-H and cross the Milwaukee River using extreme caution on the bridge, then head north on Oak Drive until the segment heads off-road to the east.

The segment continues into the dense forest and hummocky area of the south end of the KMSF-NU. The Kettle Moraine landscape dates back to the last Ice Age when the Green Bay Lobe and the Lake Michigan Lobe flowed into the area. As these lobes sideswiped each other and retreated, they created the rugged but beautiful high relief hummocky topography that makes up the landscape today, including numerous ridges, valleys, outwash plains, kettles, eskers and kames.

After leaving Oak Drive, the Trail quickly crosses the KMSF-NU Backpack Shelter 1 parking area, then comes to a trailside hand-pump water well (**WA24**), shortly followed by an intersection (**WA1**) with a short spur trail that leads to Backpack Shelter 1. Dedicated to Raymond T. Zillmer, founder of the Ice Age Trail Alliance, the shelter has a pleasant, lofty perch.

The segment continues northward through the high-relief hummocky topography landscape highlighting many trailside kettles and kames in a beautiful blend of deep forest and sunny meadows. The forest offers quiet solitude with a wide diversity of plants and fungal life along the Trail; the meadows offer great bird watching opportunities. The segment ends when it reaches Kettle Moraine Drive, just north of the Washington/Fond du Lac county line.

Mobile Skills Crew project site, 2013

AREA SERVICES

West Bend: See West Bend Segment and Southern Kewaskum Segment, p. 309. From the USH-45 Trail access go south ~6 mi.

USH-45 Local Area: Restaurant, convenience store. At USH-45 Trail crossing go north 0.2 mi.

Eisenbahn State Trail: On Trail (262-335-4445, dnr.wi.gov/topic/parks/name/eisenbahn).

Kettle Moraine State Forest—Northern Unit (KMSF-NU) Backpack Shelter 1: Camping. On Trail. Reservations required (888-947-2757, wisconsin.goingtocamp.com). Only one group (up to 10) per shelter per night is allowed.

Kewaskum: Restaurant, grocery store, convenience store, general shopping, lodging, camping, library, medical service. From the STH-28 Trail access go west 2.0 mi on STH-28. Most services on USH-45. Lodging at Bonne Belle Motel (262-626-8414, bonnebellemotel.com). Area info available from the Kewaskum Area Chamber of Commerce (262-626-3336, kewaskum.org).

> *The people are perhaps my favorite aspect of hiking the trail. I was just blown away by the kindness (and curiosity) of strangers during my hike.*
>
> JASON PURSELL (AKA "HALFWAY"), ICE AGE TRAIL THOUSAND-MILER

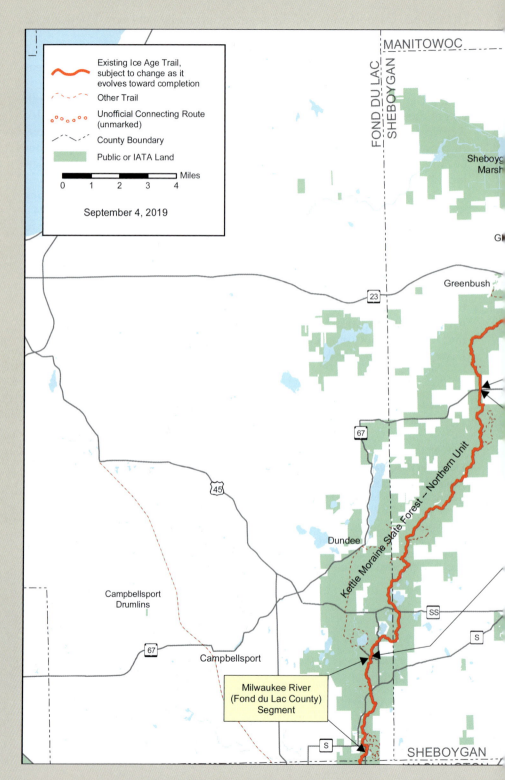

Fond du Lac & Sheboygan Counties

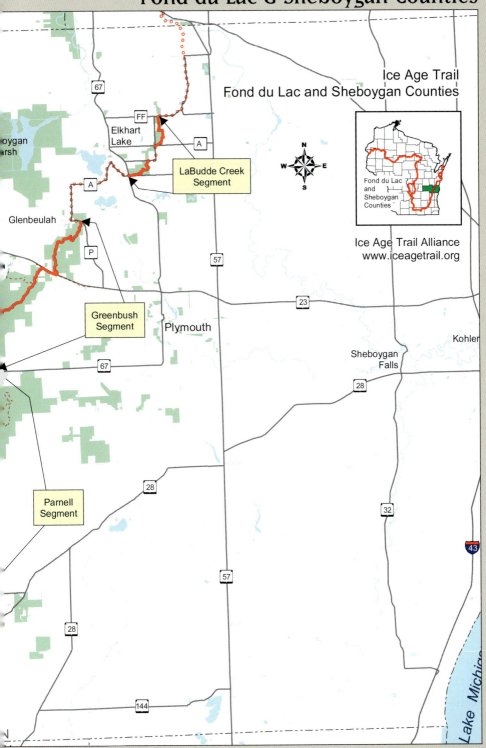

Fond du Lac & Sheboygan Counties

Atlas Maps 87f–91f; Databook pages 91–94
Total miles: 38.7 (Trail 29.6; Connecting Route 9.1)

The Interlobate Moraine (more commonly known as the Kettle Moraine) was formed when the Green Bay and Lake Michigan tongue-shaped glacial lobes met and formed a valley on the ice surface. South-flowing meltwater cascaded into crevasses and carried sand, gravel and erratics, leaving a 120-mile-long series of kettles and ridges. The last remaining ice blocks eventually melted, creating kettles, many of which filled with water resulting in kettle lakes. The Ice Age Trail meanders within the Kettle Moraine topography through Fond du Lac and Sheboygan counties. Large and small wetlands intersperse the many forested uplands.

The Ice Age Trail in the Kettle Moraine State Forest—Northern Unit (KMSF-NU) highlights the formation of glacial features such as kettles, kames and eskers. This State Forest unit contains 29,000 acres of rolling, wooded hills dotted with serene lakes. It offers year-round nature programs and hiking, biking, equestrian and cross-country ski trails. Developed campgrounds and backpack shelters are available for camping along the Ice Age Trail. It is this area that inspired Ray Zillmer to conceive of the Ice Age Trail. During the mid-1950s, he pursued government officials at all levels to recognize, preserve and establish a 1,000-mile national park. He envisioned this national park to be a conservation and recreation area featuring the glacial landscape that tells the story of the Ice Age.

CHAPTER INFORMATION

The Lakeshore Chapter was formed when volunteers from the old Door/Kewaunee County, Manitowoc County and North Kettle Moraine chapters of the IATA merged the three chapters into one. Chapter members actively work together on Ice Age Trail promotion, planning and maintenance in addition to sponsored hikes held at various locations throughout the year. Hikers can become members of the "Hall of Kamers" by hiking the Northern Unit of the Kettle Moraine State Forest Ice Age Trail segments. See the IATA website or contact the chapter for more information.

COUNTY INFORMATION

Fond du Lac Area Convention and Visitor Bureau: 920-923-3010, fdl.com

Sheboygan County Chamber: 920-457-9491, sheboygan.org

Kettle Moraine State Forest—Northern Unit (KMSF-NU): 262-626-2116, dnr.wi.gov/topic/parks/name/kmn

A mother-daughter pair hike the Trail through the Kettle Moraine State Forest—Northern Unit.

Milwaukee River Segment
(Fond du Lac County) (Atlas Map 87f; Databook page 92)

SNAPSHOT

4.3 miles: Kettle Moraine Dr. to Kettle Moraine State Forest—Northern Unit (KMSF-NU) Mauthe Lake Recreation Area

This segment parallels the Milwaukee River through densely wooded hillsides.

 At the KMSF-NU New Fane Trails and Mauthe Lake Recreation Area.

 At KMSF-NU Backpack Shelter 2 (reservations required).

 At KMSF-NU Mauthe Lake Recreation Area.

 At KMSF-NU New Fane Trails, Mauthe Lake Recreation Area and Backpack Shelter 2 (please respect those who have reserved the shelter).

 Dogs should be leashed (8-ft max) and under control at all times.

 Portion briefly overlaps a snowmobile trail.

 Spur trail to the KMSF-NU New Fane Trails parking area and spur trail (**SF7**) to KMSF-NU Backpack Shelter 2.

TRAIL ACCESS AND PARKING

Kettle Moraine Dr.: From Kewaskum at the intersection of STH-28 and USH-45, take STH-28 east 2.5 mi. At Kettle Moraine Dr. turn left and go north 2.0 mi. No parking at the Trail access on Kettle Moraine Dr. Instead, park at the Kettle Moraine State Forest—Northern Unit (KMSF-NU) New Fane Trails parking area 0.2 mi south on Kettle Moraine Dr. and 0.3 mi east on County Line Dr. A spur trail leads from the northwest corner of the parking area to the Ice Age Trail (**SF8**).

Kettle Moraine State Forest—Northern Unit (KMSF-NU) Mauthe Lake Recreation Area: From Kewaskum at the intersection of STH-28 and STH-45, take STH-28 east 0.4 mi. At CTH-S turn left and go north 6.1 mi. At CTH-GGG turn left (north) and go 1.0 mi to Mauthe Lake Rd. Turn left and go a short distance to a parking area at the entrance station. The Trail access is just west of the entrance station.

Additional Parking: KMSF-NU parking area just north of CTH-S on Gross Rd.

THE HIKE

This segment follows an irregular hummocky sand and gravel ridge for most of its length, crossing through densely forested terrain with some open prairie-like areas. The segment offers quiet passage through the forests, distant views from a ridge and opportunities to observe a variety of wildlife, including birds, plants and woodland flowers.

The segment starts where the Ice Age Trail crosses Kettle Moraine Drive at a point about a quarter mile north of the Fond du Lac/Washington county line. A short distance (~0.3 miles) from the start, after passing over rolling hills and prairie grasses, the segment intersects (**SF8**) a spur trail that leads to the Kettle Moraine State Forest—Northern Unit (KMSF-NU) New Fane Trails parking area. The segment continues through hardwood forests with some prairie clearings that contain an abundance of wildflowers like pinnate prairie coneflower, Queen Anne's lace and more. Just before reaching CTH-DD, the segment parallels a well-worn bike path.

After crossing CTH-DD, the segment climbs uphill and soon reaches a bench (**SF10**) in a clearing with views of kames to the west. The Trail continues on a mostly forested, hummocky ridge and crosses a snowmobile trail twice; at the second crossing, the segment and the snowmobile trail briefly overlap for about 50 feet. A short distance farther, a path to the snowmobile trail running parallel to the segment is visible. Hikers should pay close attention to blazes to avoid wandering off the Ice Age Trail.

The segment crosses CTH-S and soon reaches the southern end (**SF7**) of a loop trail that leads to KMSF-NU Backpack Shelter 2. Before reaching the loop trail there is a bench in a shady section where hikers can enjoy a rest. As the Trail continues, it courses through hummocky, forested topography and intersects the northern end of the loop trail. Eventually, it drops down to cross over wetland areas that can be muddy during rainy periods. After crossing a bridge over a small stream, the segment follows a wide, grassy tread before reaching its terminus at the Mauthe Lake Recreation Area entrance road, just west of the Recreation Area entrance station. Just before the terminus the segment passes a field of milkweed; be on the lookout for monarch butterflies.

AREA SERVICES

Kewaskum: See Kewaskum Segment and Milwaukee River Segment (Washington County), p. 312. From Kettle Moraine Dr.

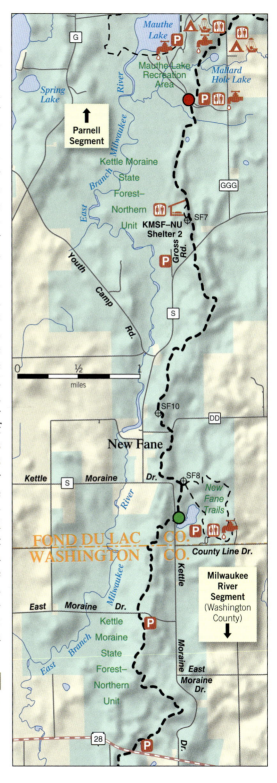

Trail access go south and west 4.5 mi or from Mauthe Lake Recreation Area go south and west ~8 mi. See Trail Access and Parking, above.

Kettle Moraine State Forest—Northern Unit (KMSF-NU) Backpack Shelter 2: Camping. On Trail. Reservations required: (888-947-2757, wisconsin.goingtocamp.com). Only one group (up to 10) per shelter per night is allowed. No water.

KMSF-NU Mauthe Lake Recreation Area: Camping. On Trail (262-626-4305; reservations: 888-947-2757, wisconsin.goingtocamp.com).

KMSF-NU Long Lake Recreation Area: See Parnell Segment, p. 323. From the Mauthe Lake Recreation Area go north and west ~8 mi.

Late summer tread on the Greenbush Segment.

Parnell Segment (Atlas Maps 87f, 88f, 89f; Databook pages 92–93)

SNAPSHOT

13.9 miles: Kettle Moraine State Forest—Northern Unit (KMSF-NU) Mauthe Lake Recreation Area to STH-67

This long segment highlights remarkable glacial formations including the world-famous Parnell Esker.

 At the KMSF-NU Mauthe Lake Recreation Area, Butler Lake, the Parnell Observation Tower and nearby Long Lake Recreational Area.

 From numerous lakes and streams.

 At KMSF-NU Backpack Shelters 3 and 4 (reservations required).

 At KMSF-NU Mauthe Lake Recreation Area and nearby Long Lake Recreational Area and private campground on Crooked Lake (see Area Services).

 At KMSF-NU Mauthe Lake Recreation Area and nearby Long Lake Recreation Area.

 At KMSF-NU Mauthe Lake Recreation Area, Parnell Observation Tower parking area, KMSF-NU Backpack Shelters 3 and 4 (please respect those who have reserved the shelter) and nearby Long Lake Recreational Area.

 Three ColdCache sites on segment.

 Dogs should be leashed (8-ft max) and under control at all times.

 Spur trail (**SF6**) to KMSF-NU Backpack Shelter 3, spur trail (**SF4**) to Backpack Shelter 4, Butler Lake Loop Trail and Parnell Tower Loop Trail.

TRAIL ACCESS AND PARKING

Kettle Moraine State Forest—Northern Unit (KMSF-NU) Mauthe Lake Recreation Area: From Kewaskum at the intersection of STH-28 and STH-45, take STH-28 east 0.4 mi. At CTH-S turn left and go north 6.1 mi. At CTH-GGG turn left (north) and go 1.0 mi to Mauthe Lake Rd. Turn left and go a short distance to a parking area at the entrance station. The Trail access is just west of the entrance station.

STH-67: From Plymouth at intersection of STH-23 and STH-67, take STH-67 south then west 8.3 mi. Park in the grassy parking area on the south side of STH-67 next to the Trail.

Additional Parking: (i) CTH-SS parking area north of Little Mud Lake. (ii) Butler Lake Trail parking area on Butler Lake Rd. (iii) Parnell Observation Tower parking area on CTH-U.

THE HIKE

The segment starts at the Kettle Moraine State Forest—Northern Unit (KMSF-NU) Mauthe Lake Recreation Area entrance road Trail access, just west of the Recreation Area entrance station. In 1926, the Milwaukee Chapter of the Izaak Walton League protected Mauthe Lake, known as Moon Lake at the time. This initiative was a precursor to the development of the Kettle Moraine State Forest and the Ice Age Trail. Ray Zillmer, founder of the Ice Age Trail Alliance, was a long-time member and president of the League.

The segment heads north from the entrance road and skirts along the eastern edge of the Mauthe Lake campground. Be careful not to get confused by the frequent side trails that connect the campground to the Ice Age Trail. The segment cuts by Forest Lake with scenic views from the southern shore. As the Trail makes its way to CTH-SS it drops down for a couple of stream crossings, climbs up a hummock then again drops down to follow the crest of a small esker.

North of CTH-SS, the segment skirts the western side of Crooked Lake Wetlands State Natural Area, which provides habitat for various forest and plant communities and diverse nesting bird and waterfowl populations. The segment passes west of the three small Kellings Lakes. Parts of the Trail in this area can be steep and a rocky tread can lead to unsure footing. The segment soon intersects (**SF6**) a spur trail that leads 0.6 miles west to KMSF-NU Backpack Shelter 3. The segment continues through forests that include maple, birch, hickory, pine and oak trees.

The segment crosses CTH-F and soon meets up with the Butler Lake Loop Trail and then crosses a bridle trail as the segment makes its way to Butler Lake, which lies between two prominent eskers and is part of the Butler Lake and Flynn's Springs State Natural Area. Fed from nearby Flynn's spring, Butler Lake is surrounded on three sides by a bog. A wide variety of flora and fauna are present here including

324 Ice Age Trail Guidebook 2020 – 2022 Edition

rare species such as the unicorn clubtail dragonfly and the swamp spreadwing. The Butler Lake Trail traverses the SNA and shares portions of the Ice Age Trail route.

Before reaching Butler Lake, the Ice Age Trail climbs to the crest of the Parnell Esker and follows it through the Butler Lake area. The Parnell Esker is a four-mile esker which ranges from 5 to 30 feet in height and runs southwest–northeast. The esker is described on a geologic marker near the Butler Lake Trail parking area. At a high point on the esker (SF5) hikers will find a bench overlooking scenic Butler Lake.

From the Butler Lake area, the Trail travels across an open prairie-like area and then continues to the northeast through beautiful forested terrain going up, down and around kettles, ridges and hummocks. The area westward between the Trail and STH-67 contains one of the most striking and world-famous collections of kames in the world. Hills on the western horizon are drumlins. Hikers may catch an occasional glimpse of some of these kames and hills through the forest.

From the intersection with the Parnell Tower Loop, the segment and the loop trail head north together. Just before the northern split of the Ice Age Trail and the Parnell Tower loop trail, the segment intersects (SF4) a short spur trail that leads to KMSF-NU Backpack Shelter 4, which is visible from the Trail.

Continuing on, the segment

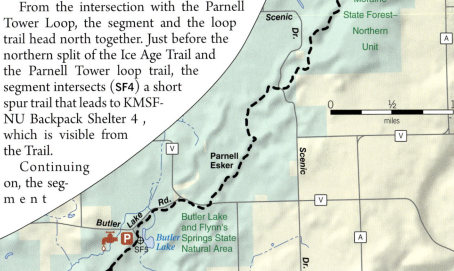

passes through progressively less hummocky forested terrain, part of which is strewn with rocks and boulders. Along the way to its terminus on STH-67, the Trail crosses a snowmobile/bridle trail twice and a power line right-of-way. Hikers should pay attention to Trail signage in these areas. Toward the end of the segment the Trail follows a wide grassy path in a more open area and reaches its terminus in a clearing at STH-67.

POINTS OF INTEREST

Henry S. Reuss Ice Age Visitor Center: From the Ice Age Trail at CTH-F go 2.5 mi west on CTH-F then south on STH-67 (920-533-8322, http://dnr.wi.gov/topic/parks/name/kmn/naturecenter.html).

At the Center hikers can view exhibits to learn about the frozen history of Wisconsin and the gifts of the glacier. There is a great view of the landscape from the Center and a naturalist is available to answer questions. The Center is open April through October, weekdays (8:30 am–4 pm) and weekends (9:30 am–5 pm). Hours vary November through March.

AREA SERVICES

Kettle Moraine State Forest—Northern Unit (KMSF-NU) Mauthe Lake Recreation Area: See Milwaukee River Segment (Fond du Lac County), p. 320.

CTH-GGG Local Area: Convenience store. Seasonal. (Pizza but no gasoline pumps). Restaurant and camping at Mike's Bar and Grill near the CTH-GGG Trail crossing (920-447-9244).

Hoeft's Resort and Campground: Camping. From Division Rd., go east 1.0 mi, south on Maple Tree Rd. 0.5 mi then west on Crooked Lake Dr. (262-626-2221, hoeftsresort.com).

KMSF-NU Backpack Shelters 3 and 4: Camping. On Trail. Reservations required (888-947-2757, wisconsin.goingtocamp.com). Only one group (up to 10) per shelter per night is allowed.

Dundee: Restaurant, convenience store. From the CTH-F Trail crossing go 2.0 mi west on CTH-F.

KMSF-NU Long Lake Recreation Area: Camping. From the Butler Lake Trail parking area go 1.2 mi west on Butler Lake Rd. (920-533-8612; reservations: 888-947-2757, wisconsin.goingtocamp.com).

Plymouth: See Greenbush Segment, p. 327. From the STH-67 Trail access go east and south 8.3 mi. Also see Trail Access and Parking directions, above.

The Trail shrouded in fog on the Greenbush Segment.

Greenbush Segment (Atlas Map 89f; Databook pages 93–94)

SNAPSHOT

8.7 miles: STH-67 to CTH-P

This segment dips into deep valleys and traverses ridges through forests of basswood, oak, maple and pine.

Note: A reroute is planned immediately south of Highway 23. Check with the Ice Age Trail Alliance (800-227-0046, iceagetrail.org) for details.

 From hand-pumped well 0.2 mi north of Kettle Moraine State Forest—Northern Unit (KMSF-NU) Backpack Shelter 5, at Greenbush Trails and Old Plank Road Trail parking area.

 At KMSF-NU Backpack Shelter 5 (reservations required).

 At KMSF-NU Backpack Shelter 5 (please respect those who have reserved the shelter), Greenbush Trails/Picnic Area and Old Plank Road Trail parking area.

 Dogs should be leashed (8-ft max) and under control at all times.

 The Old Plank Road Trail is open to biking, horseback riding and snowmobiling.

 KMSF-NU Greenbush Trails network, blue-blazed spur trail to Greenbush and other short spur trails, including a spur trail (**SF16**) to KMSF-NU Backpack Shelter 5. The Old Plank Road Trail extends east and west from the segment.

TRAIL ACCESS AND PARKING

STH-67: From Plymouth at intersection of STH-23 and STH-67, take STH-67 south then west 8.3 mi. Park in the grassy parking area on the south side of STH-67 next to the Trail.

CTH-P: From Plymouth at the intersection of STH-23 and STH-67, take STH-23 west 2.0 mi. At CTH-P turn right and go north 2.3 mi to the parking area.

Additional Parking: (i) Kettle Moraine State Forest—Northern Unit (KMSF-NU) Greenbush picnic area on Kettle Moraine Dr. 1.3 mi north of STH-67. (ii) KMSF-NU Greenbush Trails on Kettle Moraine Dr. 2.5 mi north of STH-67. (iii) Old Plank Road Trail parking area on Plank Rd. 0.3 mi west of the Ice Age Trail.

THE HIKE

Heading north from STH-67 initially on relatively flat outwash, the segment reaches the Greenbush Kettle area (**SF1**) after about a mile. The kettle, just a short hike from the Trail, is one of the most symmetrical deep depressions in the area. A short distance from the kettle is a spur trail (**SF16**) to Kettle Moraine State Forest—Northern Unit (KMSF-NU) Backpack Shelter 5, with a hand-pumped well 0.2 miles north. The Trail passes through a picnic area and continues north through hummocky topography toward Kettle Moraine Drive.

Just south of its crossing of Kettle Moraine Drive, the segment passes Greenbush Outdoor Group Camp. Right before the campground, a short unsigned spur trail leads off to the campground's parking area. This area is also a jumping-off point for the Greenbush Trails, a system of loops for mountain biking, hiking and cross-country skiing. Deep forests near the Greenbush Trails are a good place to see the hooded warbler, a rare migratory bird.

After crossing Kettle Moraine Drive, the segment travels through forested high-relief hummocky topography going up, down and around kettles and ridges

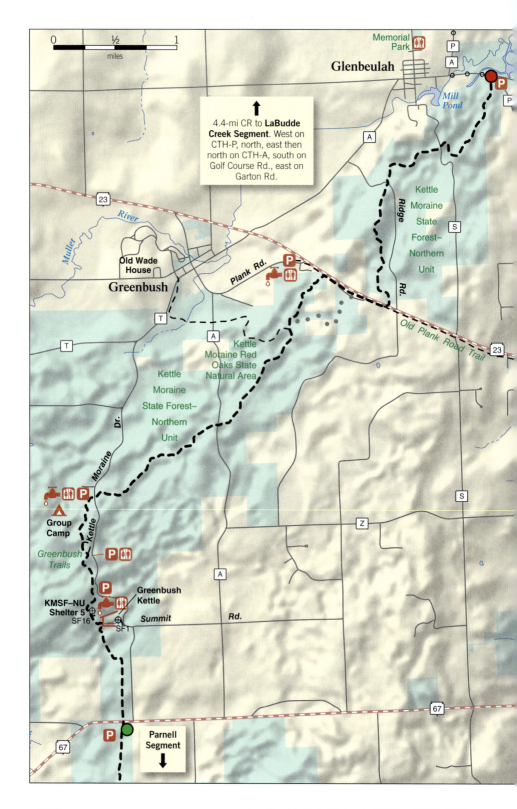

as it makes its way to STH-23. The region is marked by its rich domination of red oak and shagbark hickory, which as currently preserved will evolve to an old growth forest.

In addition to the red oak and shagbark hickory, the dry-mesic forest canopy also consists of basswood, sugar maple, white ash, white oak and black cherry trees. The understory attracts rare birds such as Acadian flycatcher, red-shouldered hawk and cerulean warbler. A variety of plant species thrive in the shady area such as ferns, orchids, trillium and mayapples. The segment enters the Kettle Moraine Red Oaks State Natural Area at CTH-A.

As the segment nears STH-23, it intersects a blue-blazed spur trail that leads 1.6 miles to the village of Greenbush and the Wade House Historic Site (see Points of Interest, below). Just south of STH-23, the segment intersects a snowmobile/equestrian trail before connecting with the Old Plank Road Trail. This 19th century historic stagecoach route linked Sheboygan and Fond du Lac. The segment follows the Old Plank Road Trail 0.6 miles east along a paved and partially grass-covered route paralleling STH-23, then separates at the point where the Trail crosses busy STH-23; use caution when crossing the highway.

From STH-23, the segment heads north through a mature red pine woods then again into forested high-relief hummocky topography with oak, maple and hickory trees being dominant. The Trail follows a roller coaster serpentine course as it ascends and descends and curves around kettles and ridges, crosses two quieter roads and makes it ways to the segment's terminus at the Trail access kiosk and parking area at CTH-P.

POINTS OF INTEREST

Wade House: In Greenbush south of STH-23 and accessible from the Ice Age Trail via a 1.6-mi spur trail (W7965 WI-23, Greenbush, 920-526-3271, wadehouse.wisconsinhistory.org).

The Wade House, an 1860s New England–style stagecoach inn, served travelers of the Civil War era. From the Wade House, a short walk will take you to the Wesley Jung Carriage Museum, which houses the state's largest collection of fine carriages and pioneer wagons. Also on site is the reconstructed historic Herrling Sawmill. The working water-powered mill portrays a vital component of the 19th century frontier settlement. There is a fee and hours vary by season.

AREA SERVICES

Kettle Moraine State Forest—Northern Unit (KMSF-NU) Long Lake Recreation Area: See Parnell Segment, p. 323. From the STH-67 Trail access go west and south 7.0 mi.

Plymouth: Restaurant, grocery store, convenience store, lodging, camping, medical service. From the STH-67 Trail access go 8.3 mi east then north on STH-67. Or from the STH-23 Trail access go east ~4 mi on STH-23 and CTH-C. Area info available from the Plymouth Chamber of Commerce (888-693-8263, plymouthwisconsin.com).

KMSF-NU Backpack Shelter 5: Camping. On Trail. Reservations required (888-947-2757, wisconsin.goingtocamp.com). Only one group (up to 10) per shelter per night is allowed.

KMSF-NU Greenbush Outdoor Group Camp: Camping (group camping only). Within the Greenbush Trails Area on Kettle Moraine Dr. Reservations required (888-947-2757, wisconsin.goingtocamp.com).

Glenbeulah: Restaurant, convenience store, camping. From CTH-P Trail access go 0.5 mi west on CTH-P (Glen Rd.).

Elkhart Lake: See LaBudde Creek Segment, p. 330. From the CTH-P Trail access go west and north 4.0 mi.

LaBudde Creek Segment (Atlas Map 90f; Databook page 94)

SNAPSHOT

3.5 miles (2.8 IAT, 0.8 CR): Garton Rd. at STH-67 to CTH-FF

 This segment features a wetland complex, undulating grassland and forested upland.

	From LaBudde Creek.		One ColdCache site on segment.
	At nearby Plymouth Rock and Broughton Sheboygan Marsh campgrounds (see Area Services).		Dogs should be leashed (8-ft max) and under control at all times.
			Portions overlap roads.
	At nearby Fireman's Park and Beach in Elkhart Lake.		Side trail to LaBudde Creek Channel.

TRAIL ACCESS AND PARKING

Garton Rd. at STH-67: From Elkhart Lake at STH-67 and CTH-A, take STH-67 south 1.3 mi to the Garton Rd. intersection. No parking. Instead, park at the Garton Rd. parking area 0.4 mi east of STH-67.

CTH-FF: From Elkhart Lake at the intersection of STH-67 and CTH-A, go east on CTH-A 1.6 mi. At Little Elkhart Lake Rd. turn left and go north 1.0 mi. At CTH-FF turn right and go 0.1 mi. No parking. Instead, park at the Keystone Rd. parking area 0.3 mi east of Little Elkhart Lake Rd.

Additional Parking: CTH-A parking area 0.1 mi east of Little Elkhart Lake Rd.

THE HIKE

This segment passes through the 426-acre LaBudde Creek Fishery Area. The LaBudde Creek area is home to several species of game birds including ruffed grouse, ring-necked pheasants and woodcock, as well as a variety of songbirds such as the yellow-throated and yellow warblers, catbirds, woodpeckers and brown thrashers.

The segment starts at the intersection of STH-67 and Garton Road with a 1,000-foot road walk east on the shoulder of Garton Road. Leaving the road, the segment heads east and north through upland brush and grasslands/wetlands with cedars, colorful sumacs and nice views, crossing a short boardwalk along the way.

Just north of the Garton Road parking area the segment intersects a side trail that leads to the LaBudde Channel (**SF9**), a glacial meltwater channel that was formed along the eastern edge of the Kettle Moraine and the western edge of the Lake Michigan Lobe. Continuing on its way to Badger Road, after crossing a second boardwalk (80 feet long) the segment enters a forest containing aspen, pine and cedar trees followed by mature hardwoods.

Once on Badger Road hikers will take a connecting route 0.3 miles east on Badger Road then 0.5 miles north on Little Elkhart Lake Road before the Ice Age Trail resumes again northeast of the intersection of Little Elkhart Lake Road and CTH-A.

From here the segment crosses an open grassland, skirts along the edge of a mature hardwood forest and cuts through another upland brush area. At Keystone Road, hikers should follow the road west 0.2 miles then turn north, heading

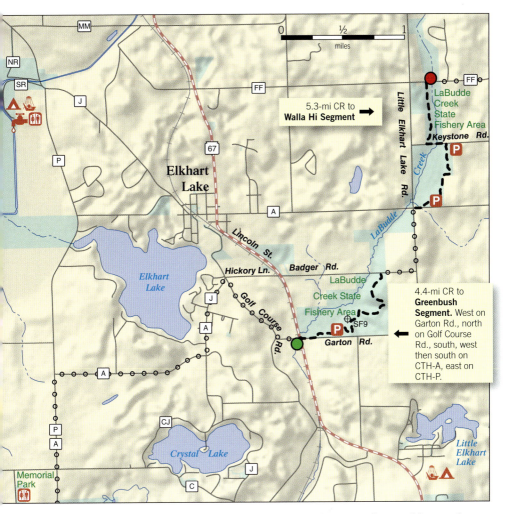

through a wetland and along a row of pine trees with views of LaBudde Creek to the east before reaching the segment terminus at CTH-FF.

Mobile Skills Crew project site 2008, 2009

AREA SERVICES

Plymouth Rock Campground: Camping. From the Garton Rd. at STH-67 Trail access go 1.6 mi south on STH-67, then left on Lando St. for 0.1 mi (877-570-2267, plymouthrock-resort.com).

Elkhart Lake: Restaurant, grocery store, convenience store, lodging, camping, library. From the Garton Rd. at STH-67 Trail access go 1.5 mi north on STH-67. INN Style program lodging at Tauschek's Pine Lodge Country Inn (920-876-5087, pinelodgecountryinn.com). Area info available from the Elkhart Lake Chamber Area Chamber of Commerce (920-876-2922).

Broughton Sheboygan Marsh County Park: Restaurant, camping. From the Garton Rd. at STH-67 Trail access go 1.3 mi north on STH-67. At CTH-J turn left and go 1.8 mi northwest to CTH-SR. Park entrance is on the left (920-876-2535, park vendor website: threeguysandagrill.com/pages/our-marsh -campground).

Plymouth: See Greenbush Segment, p. 327. From the Garton Rd. at STH-67 Trail access go south ~6 mi.

Fond du Lac & Sheboygan Counties

Manitowoc County

Manitowoc County

Atlas Maps 91f–98f; Databook pages 95–102
Total miles: 72.8 (Trail 31.3; Connecting Route 41.5)

During the Wisconsin Glaciation, Manitowoc County was covered by both the Green Bay Lobe and the Lake Michigan Lobe. The Niagara Escarpment divided the two lobes. In the southwestern corner of the county lies the Kettle Moraine, with its hummocky terrain. Drumlins near Valders have a north–south trend giving evidence of the direction the ice sheets flowed. The soils here are reddish brown and rich in silt and clay from the Lake Michigan Lobe advancements. In the northern part of the county, the East Twin River valley occupies a channel that formed along the ice margin. The West Twin River is part of an early drainage outlet of Glacial Lake Oshkosh. Shoreline remnants of ancient Lake Nipissing, a higher-level postglacial ancestor of Lake Michigan that existed 5,000 years ago, can be seen in Manitowoc County on the Point Beach Segment. Glacial debris was deposited in the form of eskers, erratics, kettles and drumlins now scattered throughout the county. Exposed dolomite, scraped of soil by glaciers, dots the countryside. The Two Creeks Buried Forest, a 14,000-year-old spruce forest knocked down by the glacier, is a unit of the Ice Age National Scientific Reserve not far from the Trail.

Hikes through the cities of Manitowoc and Two Rivers, together serving as an Ice Age Trail Community, highlight rich maritime histories and provide an opportunity to walk along the shore of Lake Michigan. The county is considered a premier birding area because of its position on the lakeshore migratory bird route. Dispersed Camping Areas (DCAs) may be found along the East Twin River and Tisch Mills Segments.

CHAPTER INFORMATION

Lakeshore Chapter volunteers actively work on Ice Age Trail promotion, planning and maintenance in addition to sponsoring hikes held at various locations throughout the year.

COUNTY INFORMATION

Manitowoc Area Visitor and Convention Bureau: 800-627-4896, manitowoc.info

An elegant stone staircase leads the way up to the Trail along the Walla Hi Segment.

Walla Hi Segment (Atlas Map 91f; Databook page 96)

SNAPSHOT

2.3 miles (2.0 IAT, 0.3 CR): Lax Chapel Road to Mueller Road at S. Cedar Lake Road.

 This segment highlights Walla Hi County Park, which showcases a glacial landscape's best features of kettles, moraines and erratics, and boasts a magnificent, hand-crafted stone staircase.

	From Lake Michigan and Molash Creek.		Dogs remaining on a leash are permitted in county parks per Manitowoc Co.
	At Walla Hi County Park.		Portions overlap Walla Hi hiking trails and small portions overlap equestrian trails.
			Walla Hi County Park hiking and equestrian trail network.
	At nearby Manitowoc County Expo Center grounds (see Area Services).		Portions of this segment may be suitable for those using wheelchairs or similar devices.
	Hikers will not have any interaction with hunting on this segment.		

TRAIL ACCESS AND PARKING

Lax Chapel Rd.: From Elkhart Lake at STH-67 and CTH-A, take STH-67 north 5.5 mi to STH-32/57. At STH-32/57 turn right and go east 2.6 mi. At Lax Chapel Rd. turn left and go north 0.4 mi to the Trail access on the east side of the road. No parking. Instead, park at Walla Hi County Park.

Mueller Rd. at S. Cedar Lake Rd.: From Elkhart Lake at STH-67 and CTH-A, take STH-67 north 5.5 mi to STH-32/57. At STH-32/57 turn right and go east (stay on STH-32) 4.2 mi to S. Cedar Lake Rd. At S. Lake Cedar Rd., turn left and go north 1.0 mi to Mueller Rd. No parking. Instead, go west 0.3 mi on Mueller Rd. to the Trail access near the Walla Hi County Park entrance sign. Roadside parking.

Additional Parking: Walla Hi County Park has three parking areas. (i) Parking near the barn; designated for horse trailers and winter use. (ii) Main parking area is located 0.2 mi south of barn. A wide grassy area leads 200 yards to the Ice Age Trail near the covered bridge. (iii) Walla Hi County Park picnic area.

THE HIKE

This segment travels along an easement and through the 160-acre Walla Hi County Park. It packs in both beauty and challenge over a short distance as the Trail navigates almost 200 feet in elevation change. From the Trail access on Lax Chapel Road, the segment heads east along an easement that overlooks farm fields. To the south of the Trail is a sand and gravel pit, and hikers may hear equipment operating during work hours. After 0.2 miles, the segment reaches a magnificent, hand-crafted stone staircase (**MN32**) built by volunteers as part of a Mobile Skills Crew project. The segment then descends 80 feet down "Slab Hill" as it makes its way toward Walla Hi County Park.

Shortly after the stairs, the segment makes a sharp serpentine trek up a wooded hillside, entering Walla Hi County Park along the way. The segment intersects several other hiking and horse trails throughout the park, but the intersections are well marked with signs and park maps. The first such intersection, a horse trail, appears almost immediately after reaching the top of the hill, quickly followed by a second. However, frequent yellow blazes make it easy to follow the Trail. The segment then intersects the western end of a white-blazed loop trail that allows hikers to explore other parts of the park and provides an alternate route to the park's main parking area.

Reminiscent of Northern Kettle Moraine topography, the segment begins a delightful, and sometimes challenging, series of ups and downs as it meanders through heavily forested oak and beech trees. The ground cover is thick and diverse with wildflowers as well as large moss-covered erratics. In the spring, hikers may find morel mushrooms. At a high point on the segment, hikers can rest on a bench and enjoy the quiet and stillness of the woods. Continuing on, the Trail quickly descends over rocky terrain, where it intersects the eastern end of the white-blazed loop trail. It crosses a covered bridge (**MN33**) over a small, clear stream, another gem in the delightful landscape. Just after the bridge, a wide grassy area leads 200 yards to the Walla Hi County Park main parking area.

From this junction, the Trail progresses through a more open area, then returns to the woods. It briefly overlaps a park service road as the segment winds its way to Mueller Road near the Walla Hi County Park entrance sign. The segment continues as a connecting route 0.3 miles to its terminus at South. Cedar Lake Road.

Mobile Skills Crew project site 2017, 2018

AREA SERVICES

Kiel: Restaurant, grocery store, convenience store, medical service. From Walla Hi County Park go east on Mueller Rd. 0.3 mi, south on S. Cedar Lake Rd. 1.0 mi and west on STH-32 (becomes STH-32/57) 4.6 mi. Restaurant on Lax Chapel Rd south of STH-32/57.

Elkhart Lake: See LaBudde Creek Segment, p. 330. From Walla Hi County Park go east, south, west and south ~12 mi. Also see Trail Access and Parking directions, above.

> *A fond moment was Memorial Day... We hiked from Manitowoc to Two Rivers and were hiking right through town when the Memorial Day parade was going on. It was special to see the crowds and hear the bands pass by, while we hiked. I would guess this is a very rare sight on the Ice Age Trail. Not only do you need to be in a town in which the parade route crosses the Trail, but you also need to be hiking on the perfect day, during the perfect hour.*
>
> DAWN THAYER, ICE AGE TRAIL THOUSAND-MILER

City of Manitowoc Segment (Atlas Map 95f; Databook pages 97–98)

SNAPSHOT

7.5 miles: Rapids Rd. (CTH-R) at Broadway St. to STH-42 at Taylor St.

 This urban segment highlights the city of Manitowoc and its rich maritime history and includes a lengthy stretch along the shores of Lake Michigan.

	At Henry Schuette Park (upper parking area), Union Park, the Manitowoc Chamber of Commerce and the Mariners Trail wayside south of Memorial Drive (STH-42) between Woodland Drive and Taylor Street.	Hikers will not have any interaction with hunting on this segment.
	At Henry Schuette Park (upper parking area).	Dogs should be leashed (8-ft max) and under control at all times.
		Much of the segment is on sidewalks and multiuse recreation trails.
		The Mariners Trail extends north from the segment.
	At nearby Manitowoc County Expo Center grounds (see Area Services).	Portions of this segment may be suitable for those using wheelchairs or similar devices.

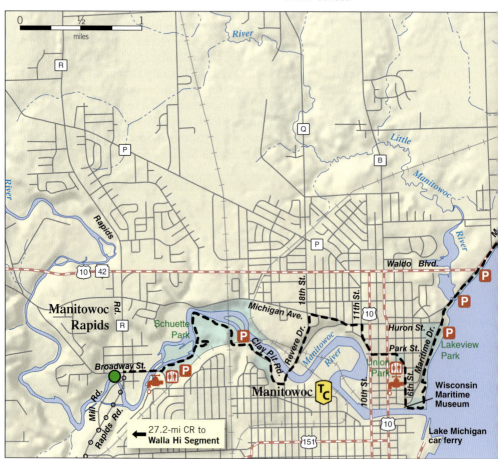

TRAIL ACCESS AND PARKING

Rapids Rd. (CTH-R) at Broadway St.: From I-43 take Exit 149 onto USH-151 and head east toward Manitowoc. At S. Rapids Rd. (CTH-R) turn left and go north 1.8 mi to Broadway St. Roadside parking on Broadway St.

STH-42 at Taylor St.: From I-43 take Exit 152 onto STH-42/USH-10 and head east then north 6.2 mi. No parking at the Taylor St. intersection. Instead, park at the Aurora Medical Center complex access from Taylor St. and Lake View Ave. in the hospital or clinic parking area. An Ice Age Trail sign is on the northeast corner of the clinic parking area.

Additional Parking: (i) Henry Schuette Park. (ii) Mariners Trail parking areas along Maritime Dr. and Memorial Dr. (STH-42). (iii) West of the Lake Gardens, 915 Memorial Dr. (STH-42).

THE HIKE

From the segment's starting point at the intersection of Rapids Road (CTH-R) and Broadway Street, the route heads east on Broadway Street for 0.3 miles. At Clay Pit Road (the access road for Henry Schuette Park encountered shortly after crossing the Manitowoc River bridge), hikers should turn left and head north along the road for 0.2 miles to the park's lower parking area. Here the segment departs Clay Pit Road and meanders through the park for 1.5 miles, mostly along the Manitowoc River, on the park's gravel roads and footpaths. Along the way hikers can rest at a deck and benches overlooking the Manitowoc River. *Note: Most of the facilities for Schuette Park are in the upper parking area, which is slightly off the segment route. The upper parking area is on Broadway Street just southeast of the intersection of Broadway Street and Clay Pit Road.*

The segment connects again with Clay Pit Road and heads southeast to its intersection with South 21st Street (Revere Drive). From here, hikers should take the following route through the city of Manitowoc: Head north on Revere Drive (which changes to North 18th Street as it crosses the river) past the Eternal Light Veterans Memorial to Michigan Avenue. Turn right and head east on Michigan Avenue (which turns into Huron Street). Turn right and head south on 11th Street (which turns into North Water Street). Turn left and head east on Park Street, passing the Rahr-West Art Museum at the intersection with North 8th Street. At the Park Street and North 7th Street intersection, turn right and walk southeast through Union Park to the North 6th Street and State Street intersection. Head south on North 6th Street for 4 blocks.

The segment departs North 6th Street and heads south across Maritime Drive in the area of the Wisconsin Maritime Museum, which is near the outlet of the Manitowoc River into Lake Michigan. The museum offers interactive educational exhibits that explore the maritime history of Wisconsin and the Great Lakes and includes a tour of the World War II submarine the USS *Cobia*. Manitowoc residents are proud of the fact that the Manitowoc Shipbuilding Company holds the unique distinction of being the only inland shipyard to build submarines for the U.S. Navy in World War II.

Near the museum south of Maritime Drive, the segment picks up a paved path and heads east along the river a short distance, offering views of the Manitowoc Breakwater Light situated on the north breakwater. The light has a 165-year history of guiding ships in and out of Manitowoc Harbor. During the summer months, hikers may catch a view of the SS *Badger* as it sets out across the lake, ferrying cars and people to Ludington, Michigan.

The segment then turns north along the shore of Lake Michigan to the Manitowoc Marina. This is the official southern terminus of the Mariners Trail (**marinerstrail.net**). The Mariners Trail connects the cities of Manitowoc and Two Rivers on sidewalks and paved blacktop along Memorial Drive (STH-42). With the waves and shoreline of Lake Michigan to the east, the Mariners Trail boasts the longest continuous scenic view of Lake Michigan in Wisconsin. Along the way, several waysides offer parking areas and trailside benches, and some even have free telescopes to gaze at ships passing.

Along the route of the Mariners Trail the segment passes West of the Lake Gardens, which are open seasonally to the public with free admission. Situated on 6 acres next to Lake Michigan, the area offers a peaceful respite featuring ornate gardens and lovely fountains.

The segment continues northeast on the Mariners Trail past the Manitowoc Chamber of Commerce building. Between the chamber building and the next wayside hikers are welcome to leave the Mariners Trail and explore the Lake Michigan beach. The segment ends a short distance northeast of the wayside at the stoplight at the Taylor Street and Memorial Drive (STH-42) intersection.

AREA SERVICES

Manitowoc: Restaurant, grocery store, convenience store, general shopping, lodging, camping, library, medical service. On Trail. Most services on USH-151, USH-10 and STH-42. INN Style program lodging at the Westport B&B (920-686-0465, thewestport.com). For area info, contact the Manitowoc Chamber of Commerce (920-684-5575, chambermanitowoccounty.org).

Manitowoc County Expo Center: Camping. From the Rapids Rd./Broadway St. Trail access, take Rapids Rd. south 1.0 mi. At Custer St. go west. At Vista Rd. go south 0.4 mi to the grounds (920-683 4378, co.manitowoc.wi.us/expo). Public camping available nonevent weekends and weekdays. RV with electric/water sites and tent gravel pads. Contact the main office for details.

A hiker follows the cordwalk through fragile dunes on the Point Beach Segment.

Dunes Segment and City of Two Rivers Segment

(Atlas Maps 95f, 96f; Databook pages 98–99)

SNAPSHOT

Dunes Segment—2.7 miles: STH-42 at Taylor St. to Columbus St.
City of Two Rivers Segment—3.0 miles: Columbus St. to Park Rd.

 The **Dunes Segment** highlights Woodland Dunes Nature Center and Preserve, an oasis of marshland, swamps, sandy meadows and wooded ridges.

At Aurora Medical Center.	A short portion is on sidewalks and follows paved surfaces on the Aurora Medical Center complex property.
All trails in Woodland Dunes Preserve are closed during gun deer hunting season.	Woodland Dunes Preserve trail network.
By law, dogs are required to be on leash. Dogs are permitted on the Ice Age Trail through Woodland Dunes but are not permitted on other trails through the preserve.	

 On the **City of Two Rivers Segment**, hikers can experience the city's claims to fame—home of the original ice cream sundae and maritime history at the Historic Rogers Street Fishing Village.

At nearby Zander Park, Harbor Park and Neshotah Park.

 At nearby Zander Park and at Neshotah Park.

 At a nearby private campground (see Area Services for Two Rivers).

 Hikers will not have any interaction with hunting on this segment.

 Dogs should be leashed (8-ft max) and under control at all times.

Much of the segment is on sidewalks.

 Portions of this segment may be suitable for those using wheelchairs or similar devices.

TRAIL ACCESS AND PARKING

STH-42 at Taylor St.: From I-43 take Exit 152 onto STH-42/USH-10 and head east then north 6.2 mi.

No parking at the Taylor St. intersection. Instead, park at the Aurora Medical Center complex access from Taylor St. and Lake View Ave. in the hospital or clinic parking area. An Ice Age Trail sign is on the northeast corner of the clinic parking area.

Park Rd.: From Two Rivers at the intersection of Washington St. and 22nd St., take 22nd St. east until it ends. *Note: 22nd St. turns right at Neshotah Park across from the water tower.* At Neshotah Rd. turn left and go north 0.1 mi. At Park Rd. turn right and go north 0.3 mi to the end of the road. Roadside parking.

Additional Parking: (i) Woodland Dunes Preserve parking area at the east end of Goodwin Rd. (ii) Columbus St. Roadside parking. (iii) Neshotah Park parking area on Zlatnik Dr.

THE HIKE

From the starting point of the **Dunes Segment** at the intersection of Taylor Street and Memorial Drive (STH-42), hikers should cross cautiously at the stoplight and head north on Taylor Street. The segment heads west at Lake View Avenue to the Aurora Medical Center complex then veers left between the Aurora Medical Center hospital and a small stream. Quickly reaching a bridge, the segment crosses the bridge then turns right toward an Ice Age Trail sign at the northeast corner of the Aurora Medical Center clinic parking area.

North of the clinic parking area the segment enters a wooded area and soon crosses a utility corridor (former railroad right-of-way) and enters 1,200-acre Woodland Dunes Nature Center and Preserve. The preserve represents a "tension zone" between two distinct areas of natural growth; found here are a tremendous number of both northern and southern species of plants and birds. The resulting habitat makes it one of the premier birding areas in the country. Within the preserve is the Woodland Dunes State Natural Area. It has shoreline remnants of postglacial Lake Nipissing, seen as ridges and swales. Many of these ridges have white birch, aspen, beech and hemlock trees.

The nature center at Woodland Dunes offers educational nature programs and the preserve has miles of hiking and nature trails. The Ice Age Trail route shares the preserve's Trillium Trail for much of its length within the property.

Shortly before the segment ends, the Trail crosses 10th Street bearing slightly to the left. The segment soon exits the preserve and reaches its endpoint at the intersection of 12th Street and Columbus Street.

Continuing along the **City of Two Rivers Segment**, the Trail takes the following route through the city: From the Columbus Street and 12th Street intersection, it heads east for 1.0 mile on 12th Street. At Monroe Street it passes the free Historic Farm Museum that is part of the Two Rivers Historical Society. At Washington Street (STH-42), it turns left and heads north for 0.1 miles, crossing the West Twin River. At East River Street, it turns right and goes northeast for 0.2 miles. At Jefferson Street, it turns left and goes north 0.2 miles to 17th Street. At this intersection is the historic Washington House (free admission, donations welcomed), home of the original ice cream sundae. This old hotel has beautiful murals and a ballroom on the second floor; antiques, restored period rooms and interesting collections are also on display.

At 17th Street, the Trail turns right and goes east across the East Twin River. At the intersection of 17th Street and East Street, it turns right and continues to Harbor Street. Here it turns left and continues to 16th Street, where it turns right and heads east on 16th Street. 16th Street turns into Zlatnik Drive, where the road turns to the northeast and continues into Neshotah Park. At the intersection of Zlatnik Drive and 22nd Street, the segment turns right and goes east 100 feet, then turns left onto Neshotah Road and goes north 0.1 miles where it turns right on Park Road and continues 0.3 miles to the segment endpoint.

POINTS OF INTEREST

Rogers Street Fishing Village: From the intersection of 17th St. and East St., go northeast on East St. then north on Jackson St. (2102 Jackson St., Two Rivers, 920-793-5905, rogersstreet.com).

The historic Rogers Street Fishing Village is listed on the National Register of Historic Places. The museum village and historic park showcase over 170 years of commercial fishing with the Great Lakes Coast Guard Shipwreck Exhibit and many other historic artifacts, including the climbable and symbolic 1886 North Pier Lighthouse.

AREA SERVICES

Manitowoc: See City of Manitowoc Segment, p. 338. From the STH-42 Trail access go south ~4 mi.

Two Rivers: Restaurant, grocery store, convenience store, lodging, camping, library, medical service. On Trail. Most services on Washington St. (STH-42). INN Style program lodging at Red Forest B&B (920-793-1794, redforestbb.com). Camping at Seagull Marina (920-794-7533). Area info available from the City of Two Rivers (920-793-5523, two-rivers.org).

> *I was overwhelmed with the utter kindness of people along my trip. I had no idea how I would be received walking into towns carrying my life on my back. After the initial glares and odd glances people seemed to naturally want to do something to make my life easier.*
>
> ADAM HINZ, ICE AGE TRAIL THOUSAND-MILER

Point Beach Segment (Atlas Map 96f; Databook pages 99–100)

SNAPSHOT

10.0 miles: Park Rd. to Lake Shore Rd.

This segment highlights both the ancient and current shorelines of Lake Michigan.

 At Point Beach State Forest (PBSF) entrance station, campground/nature center and outdoor group campground. Pit toilet (no water) is also available near the PBSF Ice Age walk-in campsite (please respect those who have reserved the campsite).

 From Lake Michigan and Molash Creek.

 At PBSF walk-in Ice Age campsite.

 At PBSF campground and nearby private campground (see Area Services).

 At PBSF campground/nature center area.

 Four ColdCache sites on segment.

 By law, dogs are required to be on leash and not permitted within PBSF facilities.

 Portions overlap park road, bike and XC trails. Hike off to the side of ski trails when groomed.

 PBSF and School Forest trail networks.

TRAIL ACCESS AND PARKING

Park Rd.: From Two Rivers at the intersection of Washington St. and 22nd St., take 22nd St. east until it ends. *Note: 22nd St. turns right at Neshotah Park across from the water tower.* At Neshotah Rd. turn left and go north 0.1 mi. At Park Rd. turn right and go north 0.3 mi to the end of the road. Roadside parking.

Lake Shore Rd.: From Two Rivers take STH-42 and follow it north out of town for ~ 6 mi. At CTH-V turn right and go east 1.8 mi. At Lake Shore Rd. turn left and go north 0.2 mi. Roadside parking on the east side of the road.

Additional Parking: (i) Viceroy Rd. (CTH-VV) parking area on the north side of the road, near its junction with Sandy Bay Road (CTH-O). (ii) Within Point Beach State Forest (PBSF), east and north of the entrance station. (iii) PBSF Red Pine Trail parking area on the west side of Sandy Bay Road (CTH-O) across from the main entrance road.

THE HIKE

From its starting point at the end of Park Road, the segment travels through a wooded area and across sand dunes atop a cordwalk installed to help protect the fragile environment to the beach along Lake Michigan. Hikers may encounter standing water between the cordwalk and the beach, especially during rainy periods. Expect to find smaller beaches and a possible new water run-off. Hikers should hike as close as possible to the shoreline. At an Ice Age Trail marker at the top of the beach, the segment turns north and follows the shoreline for 2.0 miles to another Trail marker (**MN14**) at the top of the beach. *Note: There are no other Trail markers or signage along the beach walk.* This Trail marker can be difficult to spot; a sure sign hikers have gone too far along the beach is if they reach the mouth of Molash Creek, which always requires a ford.

From the Trail marker, the segment heads west (inland), crosses sand dunes atop another cordwalk and then heads briefly north where it connects with Point

Beach State Forest's (PBSF) scenic Molash Creek Trail. It continues southwest, crosses a marshy area on a short boardwalk, then heads northwest. Along the way, the segment offers nice views of Molash Creek and surrounding wetlands.

As the segment nears Sandy Bay Road (CTH-O), it intersects (**MN13**) PBSF's Rawley Point Bike Trail. The segment follows the bike path north across a bridge over Molash Creek, then in about 0.4 miles departs the bike path and heads east in a mixed conifer/hardwoods forest to an intersection (**MN12**) with the Yellow Loop of PBSF's Ridges Trail.

From this point, the segment follows a series of PBSF's trails as it traverses over ancient beach ridges and swales left behind from Lake Nipissing, the predecessor of Lake Michigan. The Trail travels generally north in this unique area through mixed forests, with occasional glimpses of and openings to the dunes at the top of the

beach, and cuts across ridges and marshy swales. Hikers should pay attention to Ice Age Trail signage.

From the intersection with the Yellow Loop, the segment continues briefly south then north on the Yellow Loop, which then transitions (**MN11**) onto the Blue Loop. Farther on, the segment reaches a junction (**MN28**) with a spur trail that leads to a walk-in campsite with a bench, fire ring and a picnic table. A pit toilet and a kayak campsite are nearby. From here the Trail turns left away from Lake Michigan and soon reaches a junction (**MN10**) where the segment switches onto the Red Loop and follows it north. The segment eventually leaves (**MN9**) the Red Loop to follow a narrow, winding tread on a ridge between marshy swales under a red-pine canopy to PBSF's entrance road (**MN8**).

For a short side trip, hikers can head east on the entrance road to a trail leading to the working Rawley Point Lighthouse. At 113 feet, it is the tallest octagonal skeletal light tower and the only one of its kind on the Great Lakes. At the northern end of PBSF off Rawley Point lies Lake Michigan's most famous shipwreck, the *Rouse Simmons* "Christmas Tree Ship." In 1912, the ship, bound for Chicago with a cargo of evergreens, sank in a storm.

The segment continues west on the entrance road, crosses Sandy Bay Road (CTH-O) and heads for the northeast corner of the Trail access parking area for PBSF's Red Pine Trail. From here it travels through the woods where it intersects trails of the Red Pine Trail system at several unsigned junctions. At one of these trail junctions (**MN7**), about 0.5 miles from the Red Pine Trail parking area, an unsigned wide, grassy trail leads 0.2 miles east to the PBSF group campsite.

Continuing north, at a signed boundary the segment leaves PBSF and enters the Manitowoc Public School District's Rahr Memorial School Forest, a 300-acre parcel with a network of hiking trails. Hikers should watch carefully for Ice Age Trail signage to navigate through the network of trails as the segment makes its way across CTH-V and meanders to its endpoint on Lake Shore Road. Of particular interest north and west of the CTH-V Trail access is the School Forest's boardwalk, a 0.3 mile curving walkway that crosses a swamp/wetland full of trees, wildflowers, frogs, turtles, salamanders, ducks and other wildlife. A boardwalk donor board (**MN18**) marks the beginning of the boardwalk, which was designed to preserve the delicate swamp/wetland ecosystem.

Mobile Skills Crew project site, 2006

AREA SERVICES

Point Beach State Forest (PBSF): Camping, summer concession stand. On Trail. (920-794-7480, dnr.wi.gov/topic/parks/name/pointbeach; reservations: 888-947-2757, wisconsin.goingtocamp.com). The remote walk-in Ice Age backpack and kayak campsites are reservable through wisconsin .goingtocamp.com. If not reserved, they are first come, first served, with check-in at PBSF office (please respect those who have reserved the campsite). Pit toilets on site. *Note: For large groups, there is an outdoor group camp and group cabins available for rent.*

Scheffel's Hideaway Campground: Camping. On CTH-O just south of its intersection with Viceroy Rd. (920-657-1270, scheffelshideawaycampground.net).

Two Rivers: See Dunes Segment and City of Two Rivers Segment, p. 342. From the Point Beach State Forest entrance road go south ~5 mi. Also see Trail Access and Parking directions, above.

Mishicot: See Mishicot Segment and East Twin River Segment, p. 348. From Point Beach State Forest Trail entrance road go north and west 8.5 mi.

Rahr Memorial School Forest: On Trail (11617 Sandy Bay Rd., Two Rivers, 920-686-4777, manitowocpublicschools.org/services/school_forest). An outdoor education facility for the Manitowoc Public School District and area community. Buildings can be rented by organized groups. The School Forest has 4.5 mi of trails accessing a variety of habitats and is open to the public during daylight hours.

Mishicot Segment and East Twin River Segment (Atlas Map 97f; Databook pages 100–101)

SNAPSHOT

Mishicot Segment – 2.9 miles: CTH-V at Woodlawn Dr. to Princl Rd.

0.7-mile Connecting Route

East Twin River Segment—1.4 miles: Rockledge Rd. to Hillview Rd.

The **Mishicot Segment** travels through the village of Mishicot, highlighting the village Riverwalk and a covered bridge over the East Twin River.

 From the East Twin River.

 At Mishicot Village Park.

 One ColdCache site on segment.

 Portion of segment crossing private land between CTH-B and Princl Rd. is closed during gun deer season.

 Dogs should be leashed (8-ft max) and under control at all times.

 About one-third of the segment is on sidewalks, roads or urban paths.

The **East Twin River Segment** courses through the river's riparian zone and highlights towering northern white cedars and scenic views of the river.

 From the East Twin River.

 At a Dispersed Camping Area.

 One ColdCache site on segment.

 Dogs should be leashed (8-ft max) and under control at all times.

 Portions overlap farm access roads.

 A blue-blazed spur trail (**MN26**) to the DCA.

TRAIL ACCESS AND PARKING

CTH-V at Woodlawn Dr.: From I-43 take Exit 164 and follow STH-147 south 8.0 mi to the village of Mishicot. At CTH-V (Randolph St.) turn left and go east 0.6 mi to Woodlawn Dr. Roadside parking.

Hillview Rd.: From Mishicot at STH-147/CTH-V and CTH-B, take CTH-B north 2.4 mi. At Hillview Rd. turn left and go west 1.1 mi to a small parking area on the north side of the road, west of the river (second driveway after bridge). The segment begins on the east side of the river, south of Hillview Rd.

Additional Parking: Princl Rd., just west of the village of Mishicot on STH-147, take Princl Rd. north 0.5 mi. Roadside parking.

THE HIKE

The **Mishicot Segment** begins in Mishicot at the intersection of Woodlawn Drive and CTH-V (Randolph Street). The segment heads south on Woodlawn Drive for 0.1 miles, then turns and heads west on Washington Street for 0.5 miles. Hikers should cross Main Street (STH-147) and head south across a bridge to the Mishicot Village Park. A path to the right curves down to the Mishicot Riverwalk along the south side of the East Twin River.

At Rockway Street the segment turns right and heads north 0.2 miles, crossing the East Twin River on a picturesque covered bridge. At CTH-V (Randolph Street) the segment heads east briefly before turning north onto Oak Street. The segment splits off Oak Street and heads northwest on Pit Road (gravel road). Look for Trail signage

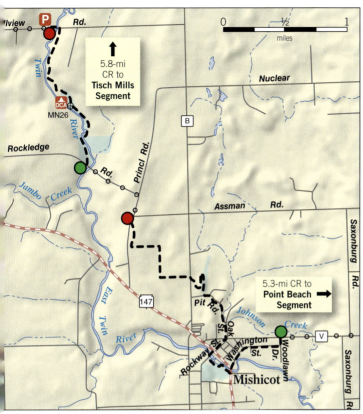

after about 0.5 miles on the right where the segment leaves the road and climbs and traces along the top of a thirty-foot esker. A Leopold bench offers hikers a woodsy rest stop. The segment then crosses CTH-B and zigzags along the edges of farm fields. The segment passes a wooded area and reaches its endpoint on Princl Road.

To reach the East Twin River Segment, hikers should follow a 0.7-mile connecting route by heading north on Princl Road 0.2 miles then turning left on Rockledge Road and going west 0.5 miles.

The **East Twin River Segment** heads north from Rockledge Road in a corridor of pine, oak and silver maple forest. Feet stay dry on this segment thanks to five boardwalks that elevate the Trail over seasonally wet areas of the floodplain. The segment soon intersects a farm road and crosses to the east side of the river on an old bridge. A bench sits close to the bridge where hikers can relax and enjoy the river. The Trail continues to meander north near the edge of a farm field in the forest corridor. Hikers will reach a split-log cedar bench that overlooks a giant silver maple (Thompson Family Maple) standing near the East Twin River. Shortly after passing the bench, the Trail intersects (**MN26**) a blue-blazed trail that leads to a Dispersed Camping Area (DCA) for long-distance, multiday hikers. The segment soon leaves the field edge and continues through the pine, oak and silver maple forest, crossing the last elevated boardwalk as it reaches its endpoint on Hillview Road. Along the way hikers can enjoy several scenic views of the river.

Mobile Skills Crew project site, 2014

AREA SERVICES

Two Rivers: See Dunes Segment and City of Two Rivers Segment, p. 342. From the CTH-V at Woodlawn Dr. Trail access go south and east ~8 mi.

Mishicot: Restaurant, convenience store, lodging, medical service. On Trail. Most services located on STH-147 (Main St.) and CTH-V (Randolph St.). Lodging at Fox Hills Resort (800-950-7615, foxhillsresort.com). For additional information visit the Village of Mishicot website (mishicot.org).

Tisch Mills Segment (Atlas Map 98f; Databook pages 101–102)

SNAPSHOT

2.6 miles (1.7 IAT, 0.9 CR): CTH-B to Nuclear Rd.

 This charming segment ducks into a white cedar forest and highlights both Tisch Mills Creek and the East Twin River.

 From Tisch Mills Creek and the East Twin River.

 At a Dispersed Camping Area (DCA) east of the Tisch Mills Creek crossing.

 At nearby Maple View campground.

🌐 One ColdCache site on segment.

 Portion of segment crossing private land between Mill Ln. and Nuclear Rd. is closed during gun deer season.

 Dogs should be leashed (8-ft max) and under control at all times.

 A blue-blazed spur trail (**MN24**) west of Tisch Mills Creek and a blue-blazed spur trail (**MN17**) to the DCA.

TRAIL ACCESS AND PARKING

CTH-B: From Two Rivers at the intersection of Washington St. (STH-42) and 22nd St. (STH-147), take STH-42 north 12.5 mi. At CTH-BB turn left and go west 5.0 mi through the village of Tisch Mills. At CTH-B turn left and go south 0.2 mi. No parking. Instead, park roadside at the CTH-BB western Trail access (**MN1**).

Nuclear Rd.: From Kewaunee at the intersection of STH-42 and STH-29, take STH-42 south 9.3 mi. At Nuclear Rd. turn right and go west 3.5 mi. Trail access is 100 ft west of the East Twin River. No parking. Instead, park roadside at the north end of Mill Ln. in Tisch Mills.

THE HIKE

The portion of the Tisch Mills Segment in Manitowoc County starts on CTH-B at an access point marked with a brown Carsonite post (on an elevation above the road) with the Ice Age Trail logo and blaze. The segment enters the IATA's Weber's Woods property, heading east along an agricultural field property line into a densely wooded area where the route makes good use of boardwalks that span wet areas. Wildflowers grow under the wooded canopy in this small oasis from the surrounding farmland.

Just west of its crossing of Tisch Mills Creek the segment reaches a junction (**MN24**) with a blue-blazed spur trail that veers left and leads north following an old fence line to CTH-BB. The blue blazes may be sparse but the spur trail is fairly well defined and easy to follow. Farther along on the main segment the route crosses the creek at a spot where there's no bridge but a wooden sign reading "Wading would be safer than walking on rocks." Hikers may want to use the blue-blazed spur during times of high water as it avoids the creek altogether. East of the segment's creek crossing the segment intersects (**MN17**) a spur trail leading to a Dispersed Camping Area (DCA) for long-distance, multiday hikers. The segment continues uphill and soon passes a memorial to the Weber family before emerging onto CTH-BB (**MN1**).

At CTH-BB, hikers should turn right and head east 0.7 miles through the village of Tisch Mills on a connecting route, then head north 0.2 miles on Mill Lane, which parallels the East Twin River.

Prior to hiking the Kewaunee County portion of the segment, hikers are advised

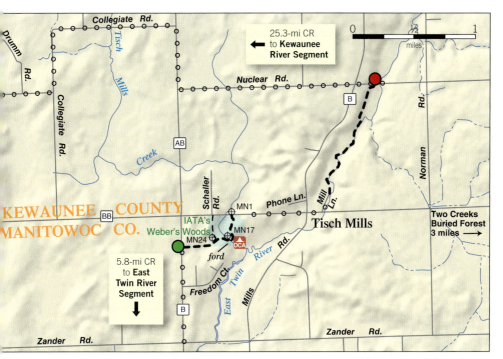

to check with the IATA for current conditions. At times of heavy rainfall and in spring this portion of the segment tends to be very wet and occasionally flooded.

From Mill Lane the segment heads north along the west bank of the East Twin River, which in this area represents the front of the Two Rivers Moraine. The riverside walk offers hikers an opportunity to observe many types of waterfowl and wildflowers in this vast wetland. The segment departs from the riverbank about a quarter mile south of the segment's endpoint and follows a fence line across a field until it reaches Nuclear Road.

POINTS OF INTEREST

Two Creeks Buried Forest: From Kewaunee, take STH-42 south 10.5 mi to the junction with CTH-BB at the Kewaunee County line. Park in the lot immediately east of the intersection and south of the restaurant. Walk southeast into the natural area (dnr.wi.gov/topic/Lands/naturalareas/index.asp?SNA=50).

Two Creeks Buried Forest is a unit of the Ice Age National Scientific Reserve. It is world-famous among geologists because it provides a unique, precise record of glacial advances and retreats during the Wisconsin Glaciation. The layers of glacial till and buried forest can be seen on the side of the steep bluff along the lakeshore due to wave erosion. Some features may be harder to see during the summer months because of ground cover. Wood from the forest has been radiocarbon-dated to 11,850 years ago. Removal of any material is strictly prohibited.

AREA SERVICES

Mishicot: See Mishicot Segment and East Twin River Segment, p. 348 . From the Tisch Mills Trail access on CTH-B go west and south ~6 mi.

Tisch Mills: Restaurant, convenience store. Store is at the intersection of CTH-B/CTH-AB/CTH-BB.

Maple View Campground: Camping. From Nuclear Rd. Trail access, go 0.4 mi east on Nuclear Rd., then left (north) on Norman Rd. for 2.0 mi (920-776-1588 or 920-388-2910 [reservations], mapleviewcampground.com).

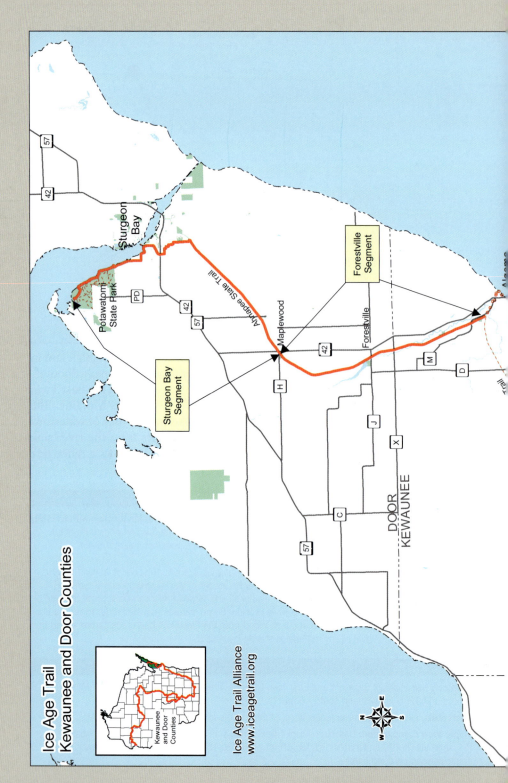

Kewaunee & Door Counties

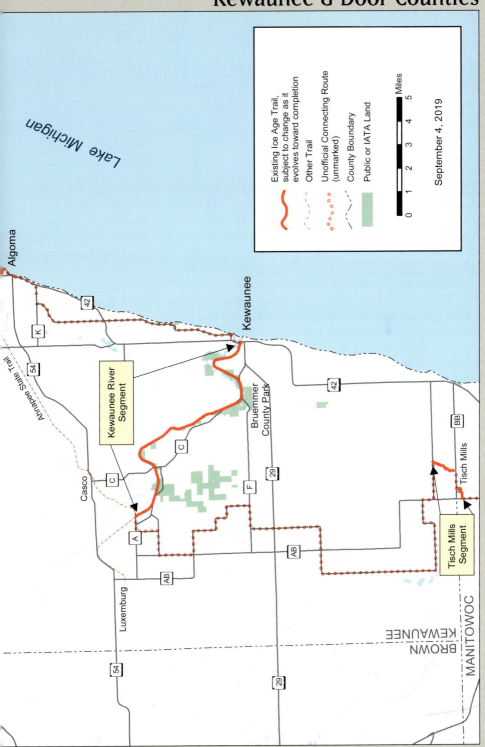

Kewaunee & Door Counties

Atlas Maps 98f–105f; Databook pages 103–106
Total miles: 75.0 (Trail 36.0; Connecting Route 39.1)

Door County's shape is due to the 400-million-year-old dolomite rock at its base, known as the Niagara Escarpment. The erosion-resistant rock extends in a broad arc from the east side of Horicon Marsh and Lake Winnebago through Door County, Michigan and Ontario and forms the crest of Niagara Falls. Blocks of Niagara dolomite, carried by glacial ice, are scattered through the counties to the south.

Door County is the location of the most recent Ice Age event along the Ice Age Trail. As the front of the Green Bay Lobe slowly melted northward, Glacial Lake Oshkosh formed in a large area of today's Fox River Valley. The Niagara Escarpment bound its waters on the east. As the Green Bay Lobe melted back, successively lower outlets of the lake opened (what are now the Manitowoc River, West Twin River, Kewaunee River, Ahnapee River and finally Sturgeon Bay). In what is today Potawatomi State Park, beaches made during higher levels of Lake Michigan can be seen along the Trail. These ancient shorelines of Lake Algonquin, from 11,000 years ago, and Lake Nipissing, from 5,000 years ago, rise as much as 20 to 60 feet above modern-day Lake Michigan.

The Ice Age Trail shares the route of the multiuse Ahnapee State Trail in Kewaunee and Door counties. The route passes through drumlins, farmlands, wetlands and forests and follows parts of the Kewaunee River Valley and Ahnapee River Valley. After making its way through the city of Sturgeon Bay the Ice Age Trail reaches its eastern terminus at the official terminus marker in Potawatomi State Park.

These counties have significant maritime history as told in the towns the Trail visits along the shores of Lake Michigan.

CHAPTER INFORMATION

Lakeshore Chapter volunteers actively work on Ice Age Trail promotion, planning and maintenance in addition to sponsoring hikes held at various locations throughout the year.

COUNTY INFORMATION

Door County Visitor Bureau: 920-743-4456 or 800-527-3529, doorcounty.com

Kewaunee County Promotions & Recreation Department: 920-338-0444, co.kewaunee.wi.gov

Tisch Mills Segment

This segment is located in both Kewaunee and Manitowoc counties and is described in the Manitowoc County section of this book (see pp. 350–351).

A view from the Ahnapee State Trail on the Kewaunee River Segment.

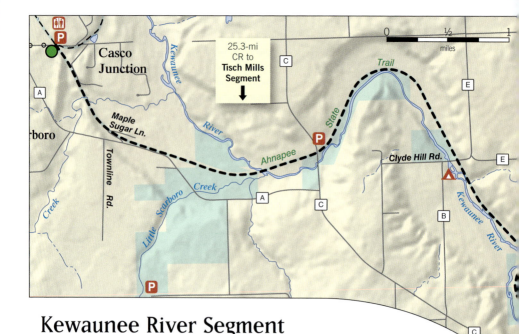

Kewaunee River Segment

(Atlas Maps 100f, 101f; Databook pages 104–105)

SNAPSHOT

12.5: Ahnapee State Trail at Sunset Rd. to Miller St. (CTH-E) at Milwaukee St. (STH-42)

 This segment follows the Kewaunee River section of the Ahnapee State Trail (AST), a crushed limestone rail-trail.

- At Bruemmer County Park and Zoo and nearby Harbor Park and Father Marquette Memorial Park.
- From the Kewaunee River.
- At nearby private campgrounds (see Area Services).
- At Sunset Rd. Trail access, Bruemmer County Park and Zoo, Harbor Park and Father Marquette Memorial Park.

- By law, dogs must be on leash on the Ahnapee State Trail.
- The AST is open to horseback riding, snowmobiling and biking.
- The AST extends west from the segment.
- Portions of this segment may be suitable for those using wheelchairs or similar devices.

TRAIL ACCESS AND PARKING

Ahnapee State Trail at Sunset Rd.: From Kewaunee at the intersection of Milwaukee St. (STH-42) and Ellis St. (STH-29), take Ellis St. (STH-29) west 1.0 mi. At the CTH-C/STH-29 fork, veer right onto CTH-C (Ellis St.) and continue northwest 1.4 mi to CTH-F. Turn right and go northwest 4.8 mi. At CTH-A turn left and go west 3.1 mi. At Sunset Rd., turn right and go east 0.4 mi. Park at Harold Reckelberg Park on the north side of Sunset Rd.

Miller St. (CTH-E) at Milwaukee St. (STH-42): In Kewaunee at the intersection of Milwaukee St. (STH-42) and Ellis St. (STH-29), take Milwaukee St. (STH-42) north 0.1 mi. Park at Clock Corner Park and the Ahnapee State Trail parking area on the southwest corner of Miller St. (CTH-E) and Milwaukee St. (STH-42).

Additional Parking: (i) CTH-C western Trail access parking area on the northeast side of CTH-C. (ii) Bruemmer County Park and Zoo parking area. (iii) CTH-C eastern Trail access parking area on the north side of CTH-C. (iv) Harbor Park.

THE HIKE

The Ahnapee State Trail (AST) is a multiuse rail-trail that was converted for recreational use in 1975. The trail was named for the Ahnapee & Western Railway (A & W), which served major industries in Algoma, Sturgeon Bay and Casco Junction dating back to its origin in 1892. It connected to Green Bay

and Kewaunee at Casco Junction via the Green Bay & Western Railroad. Steam and diesel powered locomotives hauled lumber, shipbuilding materials, dairy products, petroleum products and other commodities. During World War II, the A&W transported German prisoners of war to Door County to work the fruit harvest season. In the early 1970s, costs and alternative routes of shipping forced the A&W to abandon the line. The portion of the AST along the Kewaunee River is fairly new to the state's rail-trail network and has been described as one of the most scenic sections of rail-trail in Wisconsin.

The segment starts at the gravel parking lot of Harold Reckelberg Park located on Sunset Road. Heading southeast toward Kewaunee on the AST, the segment passes through mostly wooded, rolling terrain and follows the Kewaunee River, although the river is not always visible from the Trail. The Trail crosses the Kewaunee River and Scarboro Creek on three refurbished wooden trestle bridges and passes by and through the various tracts of the C.D. "Buzz" Besadny State Fish and Wildlife Area.

On the outskirts of Kewaunee the segment passes Bruemmer Park & Zoo. Hikers looking for an off-trail adventure can explore the C.D. "Buzz" Besadny Anadromous Fish Facility (details below in the Points of Interest section). Back on the segment route, the Trail follows a low area along the river through wetland and wooded areas. At mile 0.9 of the rail-trail the segment reaches a junction. Hikers should follow the Ice Age Trail as it angles south along the AST and leads 1.4 miles to the AST trailhead in Kewaunee (featuring the world's tallest grandfather clock) at the southwest corner of the intersection of Miller Street (CTH-E) and Milwaukee Street (STH-42).

POINTS OF INTEREST

C.D. "Buzz" Besadny Anadromous Fish Facility: From the Ice Age Trail at the intersection with CTH-F head west on CTH-F for 0.5 mi then north a short distance on Ransom Moore Ln. (N3884 Ransom Moore Ln., Kewaunee, 920-388-1025, dnr.wi.gov/topic/fishing/hatcheries/cdbesadny.html).

The Fish Facility is a spawning trout and salmon egg collection and harvesting facility. Following informational and educational displays, visitors can take a self-guided tour and obtain basic information on trout and salmon life history, facility operations and other related subjects. During spawning, visitors can watch trout and salmon swim up the Kewaunee River. Underwater windows offer views of the fish jumping and splashing their way up a fish ladder to large holding ponds. The Fish Facility grounds are open spring, summer and fall during daylight hours. The Facility building is open March 15 to December 15, M–F; hours vary. Call ahead to determine what fish are at the facility; fish are not always present.

AREA SERVICES

Ahnapee State Trail (AST): On Trail (920-388-0444 or 920-746-9959, dnr.wi.gov/topic/parks/name/ahnapee/).

Kewaunee: Restaurant, grocery store, convenience store, lodging, camping, library, medical service. On Trail. Most services on Milwaukee St. (STH-42), downtown at Milwaukee St. (STH-42) and Ellis St. (STH-29) or north of the Kewaunee River Bridge on Main St. (STH-42). Camping at Cedar Valley Campground (920-388-4983, cedarvalleycampground.com) and Kewaunee Village RV Park and Campground (920-388-4851, kewauneerv.com). Area information available from the Kewaunee Chamber of Commerce (920-388-4822, Kewaunee.org)

The Trail as it winds through Potawatomi State Park on the Sturgeon Bay Segment.

Kewaunee & Door Counties

Forestville Segment (Atlas Maps 102f, 103f, 104f; Databook pages 105–106)

SNAPSHOT

9.8 miles: BIrch St. (CTH-S) to CTH-H

This segment follows the multiuse Ahnapee State Trail (AST) through an area that is part of the Great Wisconsin Birding and Nature Trail.

 From the Ahnapee River and Forestville Flowage/Mill Pond.

 At nearby Timber Trails and Ahnapee River Trails campgrounds ▲ (see Area Services).

 At Blahnik Heritage Park, Forestville Dam County Park and town hall in Maplewood.

 At Forestville Dam County Park.

 On the AST just north of CTH-M, at Blahnik County Park, at Forestville Dam County Park and on STH-42 just north of the CTH-H Trail access.

 By law, dogs must be on leash on the Ahnapee State Trail.

 The AST is open to horseback riding, snowmobiling and biking.

 Trail network at Blahnik Heritage Park.

 Portions of this segment may be suitable for those using wheelchairs or similar devices.

TRAIL ACCESS AND PARKING

Birch St. (CTH-S): From Algoma take STH-42 north. At Navarino St. (CTH-S), turn left and continue west/northwest on CTH-S 0.8 mi. Roadside parking on Birch St (STH-S).

CTH-H: From Sturgeon Bay, take STH-42 south 9.0 mi to CTH-H in Maplewood. Park in the parking area just north of CTH-H on the west side of STH-42.

Additional Parking: (i) CTH-M parking area on the north side of the road. (ii) Blahnik Heritage Park parking area on Washington Rd. (iii) Forestville Dam County Park parking area on Main St. (CTH-J).

THE HIKE

The Ahnapee State Trail (AST), a wide, hardpacked limestone multiuse trail, got its start in the 1890s as the Ahnapee & Western Railway, transporting lumber and dairy products. Due to financial problems, most of the rail line was abandoned in the early 1970s. A number of years later it was converted to a recreational trail. It is a

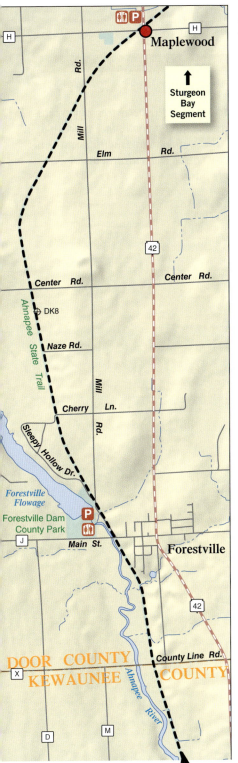

well used trail with good signage and a number of benches placed along the way.

From its starting point on Birch Road (CTH-S) the segment heads north and in 0.6 miles reaches CTH-M, the site of Timber Trail Campground just to the west. It continues north on the west side of the Ahnapee River and soon skirts the end of Wilson Road. Farther north, at the intersection with Washington Road, the segment passes Blahnik Heritage Park and crosses the Ahnapee River.

West of Forestville the segment crosses Main Street and briefly overlaps West Avenue (Mill Road) before it passes Forestville Dam County Park. Continuing north, the segment passes through an area (**DK8**) burned by the Great Peshtigo Fire, the most devastating forest fire in American history. On October 8, 1871, the fire destroyed more than 1.25 million acres and killed more than a thousand people. Today, mature hardwood stands erase all signs of the conflagration in the Ahnapee River Valley.

The segment reaches its endpoint in the village of Maplewood near its intersection with STH-42.

AREA SERVICES

Algoma: Restaurant, grocery store, convenience store, lodging, camping, library, medical service. Camping at Timber Trail Campground (920-487-3707, timbertrailcampgrounds.com), Big Lake Campground (920-487-2726, biglakecampground.com) and Ahnapee River Trails Campground (920-487-5777, ahnapee.com). Area info available from the Algoma Area Chamber of Commerce (920-487-2041, algomachamber.org). Also see Trail Access and Parking directions, above.

Ahnapee State Trail (AST): See Kewaunee River Segment, p. 356.

Forestville: Restaurant, convenience store, library. From the CTH-J (Main St.) Trail access take CTH-J east 0.3 mi. The library has limited hours.

Maplewood: See Sturgeon Bay Segment, p. 362.

Sturgeon Bay: See Sturgeon Bay Segment, p. 362. From CTH-H/STH-42 go north ~9 mi. Also see Trail Access and Parking directions, above.

Sturgeon Bay Segment (Atlas Maps 104f, 105f; Databook pages 106–107)

SNAPSHOT

13.7 miles: CTH-H to Ice Age Trail Eastern Terminus in Potawatomi State Park

This segment offers hikers three widely varying experiences representative of the overall Ice Age Trail experience and is therefore a good place to wrap up or start a thousand-mile journey on the Trail. The segment starts with a rail-trail hike, transitions into an urban hike through a city with a rich cultural history, then finishes with a quiet, forested trek through a state park.

- At Cherry Blossom Park and various locations in Potawatomi State Park (PSP).
- From Sturgeon Bay.
- At PSP and nearby private campground (see Area Services).
- On STH-42 just north of the CTH-H Trail access, at the S. Neenah Ave. Trail access (**DK6**), Cherry Blossom Park, Otumba Park and PSP.
- Two ColdCache sites on segment.
- By law, dogs are required to be on leash on the Ahnapee State Trail and in PSP. Dogs are not permitted in PSP facilities or on groomed ski trails.
- Portions overlap the multiuse Ahnapee State Trail. Other portions overlap sidewalks and roads and with PSP trails open to biking and skiing. Hike off to the side of ski trails when groomed.
- PSP trail network.
- Portions of this segment may be suitable for those using wheelchairs or similar devices.

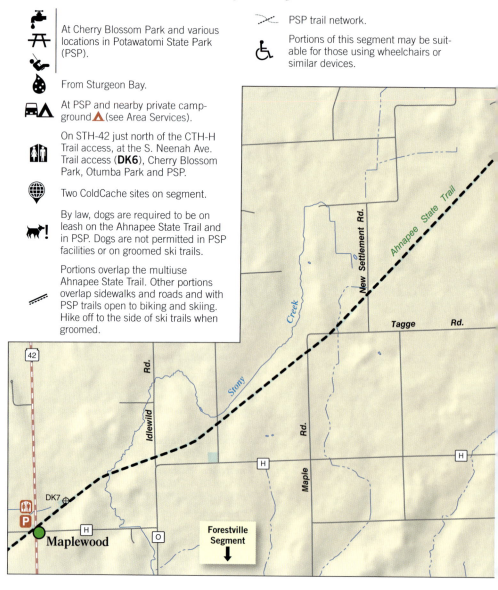

362   Ice Age Trail Guidebook 2020 – 2022 Edition

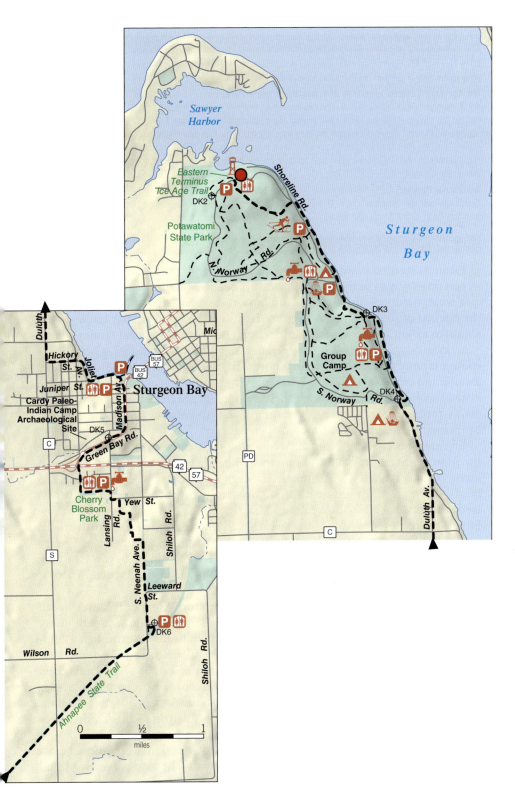

Kewaunee & Door Counties

TRAIL ACCESS AND PARKING

CTH-H: From Sturgeon Bay, take STH-42 south 9.0 mi to CTH-H in Maplewood. Park in the parking area just north of CTH-H on the west side of STH-42.

Ice Age Trail Eastern Terminus in Potawatomi State Park: From Sturgeon Bay take STH-57/42 southwest to CTH-PD (Park Dr.). Turn right and go north 2.4 mi to Potawatomi State Park (PSP). Follow the park's entrance drive (N. Norway Rd.) 3.5 mi to the Ice Age Trail eastern terminus at the observation tower. Short-term parking for tower access only. For day-hiking and overnight parking, park at the Ice Age Trail long-term parking area at the old ski hill (**DK2**), located 3.3 mi from the main entrance. An un-blazed spur trail leads from the parking area to the Ice Age Trail at the observation tower.

Additional Parking: (i) S. Neenah Ave. Ahnapee/Ice Age Trail access parking area (**DK6**). (ii) Cherry Blossom Park. (iii) Bayview Park. (iv) Otumba Park. (v) Duluth Ave. Roadside parking. (vi) PSP parking areas along Shoreline Road.

THE HIKE

From its starting point on CTH-H in Maplewood, the segment heads northeast on its way to Sturgeon Bay, sharing the route with the Ahnapee State Trail, a wide, hardpacked limestone multiuse recreational trail that was formerly the rail bed of the Ahnapee & Western Railway. The route quickly traverses the southern extent of the Maplewood Swamp (**DK7**), a unique peat swamp where waterlogged soil prevents dead vegetation from fully decomposing, creating a spongy layer of peat. As it continues northeast, the segment passes Stoney Creek Swamp and crosses the creek itself. Dark swamp water creeps within a foot of the raised trail bed as it cuts through these swamps. From here, the segment bends gently through forests, orchards and farmland, sometimes under the cover of overhanging trees and sometimes in openings.

Shortly after crossing Neenah Avenue, the segment arrives at a trailhead for the Ahnapee State Trail (**DK6**). From the trailhead area the segment heads north along Neenah Avenue for 0.7 miles. The segment departs Neenah Avenue and heads west and north on a path that skirts and weaves through an industrialized area between Neenah Avenue and Lansing Road, eventually arriving at Yew Street. The route follows Yew Street west briefly, then Lansing Road north briefly, before heading west off-road and following the southern perimeter of Cherry Blossom Park, a grassy neighborhood park. The Trail continues beyond the park and through the adjoining neighborhood to South Hudson Avenue, where it turns north.

After crossing West Walnut Drive, South Hudson Avenue becomes South Hudson Court. From South Hudson Court, the segment follows a path under STH-42/STH-57 to Green Bay Road, where it then heads east through a commercial area. On the southwest corner of the Green Bay Road and Lansing Road intersection the segment arrives at an Ahnapee State Trail/Ice Age Trail access area (**DK5**) marked with an Ice Age Trail sign and a brown-and-white Ahnapee Trail sign. This is where the City Trail Extension of the Ahnapee State Trail ends. From here, hikers may wish to take an interesting side trip to the Cardy Paleo-Indian Camp archaeological site (see Points of Interest, below).

From the Green Bay Road and Lansing Road intersection hikers should cross to the north side of Green Bay Road and continue east. The road curves north and becomes Madison Avenue. Downhill, over the roofs of stores and restaurants, hikers can see shipyards, dry docks, towering cranes and the city's old steel bridge. At the intersection of Madison Avenue and Larch Street the segment angles northwest through Bayview Park, which highlights the Sturgeon Bay Canal. Since 1882, Great Lakes freighters from Green Bay have bypassed the tip of the Door County peninsula, through a passage known as "Death's Door," and have instead traveled through the canal to Lake Michigan. Not only is it a safer passage, it reduces the travel distance from Green Bay to Milwaukee and Chicago by 150 miles.

The segment exits the park and follows Juniper Street west, Joliet Avenue north and Hickory Street west to Duluth Avenue. It follows Duluth Avenue north to the end of the road (**DK4**), where there is a large Ice Age Trail sign as the Trail continues north into Potawatomi State Park. A nearby informational sign shows a map of the park with marked trails.

Potawatomi State Park (PSP) is named after the Native Americans who inhabited Green Bay's shores and islands. Potawatomi means "keepers of the fire," a reference to the Council of Three Fires, a Potawatomi alliance with the Ojibwe and Ottawa. Bedrock outcrops of the Niagara Escarpment can be found throughout the area among cedar, birch, maple and pine forests. In the southern portion of PSP, the segment route overlaps the park's Hemlock Loop; in the northern portion, the segment shares the park's Tower Loop. A highlight of the segment's route through the park is a set of rock steps in Niagara dolomite (**DK3**) constructed by Ice Age Trail Alliance volunteers.

From the end of Duluth Avenue, the segment heads east briefly toward Sturgeon Bay before resuming a northward course along the shoreline. Near Picnic Area 4, the segment joins the Hemlock Loop and continues north between Shoreline Road and Sturgeon Bay. The segment crosses Shoreline Road and angles west toward the park campground. The Trail then departs from the Hemlock Loop and turns north, crossing Shoreline Road again and continuing along between the road and the bay, passing near the campground's South Camp Area and then the North Camp Area. Hikers can enjoy several bay vistas along the way. The segment joins the Tower Loop near the North Camp Area. A little farther on, hikers should skip a Tower Loop cutoff trail and continue north.

The segment crosses Shoreline Road a final time and heads inland climbing steeply into a forested area, eventually emerging onto Norway Road and the park's observation tower. From the tower, an unblazed spur trail leads to the Ice Age Trail long-term parking area (**DK2**) at the old ski hill. Situated atop a 150-foot dolomite bluff, the park's 75-foot tower, built in 1932, is permanently closed due to structural issues. At the base of the tower the Ice Age Trail eastern terminus is marked with an official terminus marker (similar to that found at the western terminus) affixed to a large rock.

Mobile Skills Crew project site, 2002

POINTS OF INTEREST

Cardy Paleo-Indian Camp Archaeological Site: From the Ice Age Trail at the intersection of Green Bay Rd. and Lansing Rd., head north on Lansing Rd. then turn left at Spruce St. and walk west 0.2 mi. (near 322 W. Spruce St., Sturgeon Bay).

The Cardy Paleo-Indian Camp archaeological site, listed on the National Register of Historic Places, is considered one of the most important archaeological finds in Wisconsin. The Cardy Site, marked by a kiosk and plaque, preserves the remains of a campsite used by Native Americans at the end of the Ice Age. An extensive dig in 2003 unearthed spear points, tools, a fire pit and other artifacts. Archeologists believe that Native Americans lived and worked in this area 11,000 years ago near the shore of Glacial Lake Algonquin and within walking distance of the receding continental ice sheet. This camp is unusual for its far north location. Glacial Lake Algonquin occupied the Lake Michigan and Lake Huron basins at the end of the Ice Age and would have been about 25 ft higher than Green Bay is today.

AREA SERVICES

Ahnapee State Trail (AST): See Kewaunee River Segment, p. 356.

Maplewood: Restaurant. On Trail. From the CTH-H Trail access go west 0.2 mi on CTH-H.

Sturgeon Bay: Restaurant, grocery store, convenience store, general shopping, lodging, camping, library, medical service. On Trail. Most services located on Green Bay Rd. (STH-45/57) and at Michigan St and 3rd Ave. INN Style program lodging at the White Lace Inn (877-948-5223, whitelaceinn.com). Camping at Tranquil Timbers Camping Resort (920-743-7115, tranquiltimbers.com). Area info available from the Sturgeon Bay Visitor Center (920-743-6246, sturgeonbay.net).

Potawatomi State Park (PSP): Camping. On Trail. (920-746-2890, dnr.wi.gov/topic/parks/name/Potawatomi; reservations: 888-947-2757, wisconsin.goingtocamp.com). There are several other state parks in Door County.

Each of the 105 segments of the Ice Age Trail rightly claims its own reserve of natural tranquility and remnants of immense glaciology. This trek, identified by simple yellow blazes and signs boasting the image of a woolly mammoth, offers an iconic cross-section of hiking topography for hikers of all abilities. For day-, section-, and thru-hikers alike, this is truly a unique experience that rewards everyone with pleasant memories to fondly recall in future years. On Wisconsin!

JAMES KING (AKA "J.J."), ICE AGE TRAIL THOUSAND-MILER

A hiker rejoices in the view, the adventure, and the accomplishment of a thousand-mile journey.

Glossary

Barrens Areas where pine and stunted oaks grow. Barrens made up 12% of the state's original landscape. Found in prairie-like areas with sandy, infertile soil. Animals that inhabit barrens include whitetail deer, grouse, prairie chicken, redheaded woodpecker and timber wolf.

Bog A wetland of spongy ground or peat, often with tamaracks and sphagnum moss.

Continental Glaciation The formation, movement, recession and related effects of colossal, nearly continent-sized ice sheets. Though common during the Pleistocene (or most recent) Ice Age, the only ice sheets that today approach the enormity of those existing during the Ice Age are in Antarctica and Greenland. Continental glaciation sculpted a quarter of the Earth's landmass and dramatically changed the Earth's climate, oceans, plants and animals.

Dells/Dalles A gorge cut by torrents of meltwater released by a melting glacier or draining of glacial lakes. Some dramatic examples: the Dells of the Eau Claire, the Wisconsin Dells and the Dalles of St. Croix.

Dispersed Camping Area (DCA) A minimally developed camping area for long-distance hikers. To help increase camping opportunities for Ice Age Trail long-distance hikers, the Ice Age Trail Alliance and its partners are working to establish DCAs, especially in areas (i.e., the southern two-thirds of the Trail) where convenient camping options are otherwise limited for long-distance hikers. DCAs are not "campgrounds" or even "campsites" in the traditional sense; instead, they are typically nothing more than a cleared area where hikers may legally camp for a night. Use of DCAs is restricted to those on long-distance, multiday hikes.

Dolomite A rock similar to limestone consisting largely of calcium magnesium carbonate.

Driftless Area The southwestern quarter of Wisconsin is unglaciated or shows no signs of past glacial activity. It is a landscape deeply cut by ancient streams into narrow, angular valleys and several-hundred-million-years-old ridges. The best place along the Trail to see the Driftless Area is Dane County between Mineral Point Rd. and Table Bluff Rd., west of the end moraine.

Drumlin An elongated, teardrop-shaped hill. These streamlined hills were sculpted in the direction of the glacial ice movement. They often occur in groups known as *swarms*. Because drumlins generally form miles behind, or up-ice, from an end moraine, they are rare along the Trail. The Farmington Drumlins, in Waupaca County, is the largest swarm of drumlins along the existing segments of the Trail. A small group of drumlins is in Door County between Maplewood and Sturgeon Bay. STH-60, between Columbus and Hartford, and I-94, between Madison and Sussex, cross one of the largest drumlin swarms in the world.

End Moraine A type of moraine formed at the outer edge of a glacier or glacial lobe where it paused or stopped. Prominent end moraines along the Trail can be witnessed at Prairie Moraine County Park in Dane County, Devil's Lake State Park in

Sauk County and the range of hills north and east of Antigo in Langlade County. End moraines define the general route of the Trail.

Ephemeral Ponds (*also* **Vernal Ponds**) Small isolated wetland depressions or pools of water that dry occasionally or are temporary. They can be deep or shallow with vegetation around them and occur in habitats such as sandhill, natural pinelands, dry prairies and other related communities. Lacking in fish, they are often home to insect species such as mosquitoes and mayflies and natal amphibians such as frogs and toads.

Erratics Boulders carried long distances by the glaciers and deposited when the glacier melted. They tend to be smooth and rounded. Erratics can be found along the entire Trail, except where it traverses parts of the Driftless Area. Large, famous erratics along the Trail are in Walworth, Waupaca and Langlade counties.

Esker A sinuous rounded ridge of sand and gravel deposited by the streams that flowed through tunnels at the base of the glacier. The Parnell Esker in the Kettle Moraine State Forest's Northern Unit is the most notable example along the Trail. Other excellent eskers are in Polk and Taylor counties.

Extinct Glacial Lake A glacial lake that drained, often catastrophically, when a glacier or glacial lobe melted back. Extinct Glacial Lake Wisconsin's lakebed remains visible in Adams and Juneau counties. Much of the Fox Valley was for a time under Glacial Lake Oshkosh.

Fen An area of low, flat marshy land where decomposing plants accumulate, forming peat.

Ford A shallow place in a river or stream where one can cross by wading.

Hummocky Describing hilly, knob-and-kettle topography.

Ice Age National Scientific Reserve Unit Areas administered by the Wisconsin Department of Natural Resources to protect, preserve and interpret the outstanding examples of glaciation in Wisconsin. There are nine units (Interstate State Park, Chippewa Moraine, Mill Bluff, Devil's Lake, Cross Plains, Horicon Marsh, Campbellsport Drumlins, Kettle Moraine and Two Creeks Buried Forest) and all but three (Mill Bluff, Horicon Marsh, Campbellsport Drumlins) are on or near established Ice Age Trail segments.

Ice Sheet A large, continental glacier that is not confined by underlying topography. The northeastern quarter of North America was covered over a dozen times by the Laurentide Ice Sheet during the Ice Age, between 10,000 and 2.5 million years ago. Today, ice sheets are found only in polar regions such as Greenland and Antarctica.

Ice-Walled Lake Plains Mesa-like hills that were once lakes on a melting glacier. Streams flowing on the glacier deposited loads of sediment into these lakes. When the surrounding glacier had completely melted, the lake bottoms became the hilltops. Ice-walled lake plains are showcased at the Chippewa Moraine National Scientific Reserve in Chippewa County.

Kame A conical hill composed primarily of water-rounded sand and cobbles that were deposited by streams that flowed downward through shafts in the glacial ice. The Kettle Moraine contains the largest and most important kame fields in the world, particularly between Dundee and the Parnell Tower, near Slinger and at Holy Hill. Kames are intriguing because of their shape and the way they were formed, not because of their size.

Karner Blue Butterfly (*Lycaeides melissa samuelis*) On the federal endangered species list. Wisconsin has the largest remaining population. It is slightly larger than a postage stamp with a wingspan of approximately 1 inch. It is seen in the beginning of June and again in August. This butterfly feeds exclusively on wild lupine, a bright blue flower, found in dry, sandy soil, partly shaded meadows and oak savannas in central and northwestern Wisconsin.

Kettle A surface depression formed by large, detached blocks of melting ice that were buried with sand and gravel. As the ice melted, the other material collapsed, leaving a crater-like depression. Some kettles are more than 100 feet deep. Kettles can be found in many places along the Trail.

Kettle Moraine Also called the Interlobate Moraine, the Kettle Moraine is a series of ridges, 120 miles long and only a few miles wide, in eastern Wisconsin. The combined action and deposits of the Green Bay and Lake Michigan lobes of the continental ice sheet formed the Kettle Moraine. The Kettle Moraine is the birthplace of the Ice Age Trail and the subject of the first published study of interlobate glaciation in 1878.

Leopold Bench A 33- or 48-inch-long bench seen along the Trail originally designed by conservationist Aldo Leopold. He built and used the bench when he lived in central Wisconsin while writing *A Sand County Almanac*. Design plans can be found by entering "Leopold Bench" into an internet search engine.

Lobe A tongue-like extension of an ice sheet. Six major lobes during the late Wisconsin Glaciation covered portions of Wisconsin. These lobes were the Superior, Chippewa, Wisconsin Valley, Langlade, Green Bay and Lake Michigan lobes. The Des Moines Lobe extended slightly into western Polk County.

Mammoth An extinct species of elephant with hairy skin and long tusks curving upward that roamed North America, Europe and Asia. It is the Ice Age Trail mascot.

Moraine A ridge formed by unsorted gravel, sand and boulders carried by the glacier and deposited at the outer edge, or front, of the glacier. Some are only 10 feet high, while others rise 250 to 300 feet. Moraines can be found in many places along the Trail.

Moulin A vertical shaft through a glacier that often extended all the way to the bed, occurring where the ice is relatively thin and where the glacier is at its melting point, so water could coexist with ice.

Outwash Plain A sandy plain formed when glacial meltwater streams in front of glaciers spread over a very wide, flat area. The water swept the sand into both glaciated and unglaciated areas. Between Hancock and Plover, I-39 crosses part of a vast outwash plain. Another example is the Antigo Flats of Langlade County, visible along the Trail from the Harrison Hills of Lincoln County.

Pitted Outwash An area of outwash that is dimpled with kettles. These areas were formed by meltwater-carried blocks of ice that were deposited with sand and gravel and later melted in place, leaving kettles.

Portage A route to carry a boat overland to get from one body of water to another or to avoid a water obstacle. Two well-known historic portage routes along the Trail are in the city of Portage on the land between the Fox and Wisconsin Rivers and at Grandfather Falls in Lincoln County.

Potable Water Water that is safe to drink or to use for food preparation.

Potholes A smooth bowl carved into bedrock by the grinding action of stones whirling around in a river eddy. Many potholes were formed by torrents of glacial meltwater during the Ice Age. The best place to see these along the Trail is near the western terminus in Interstate State Park. These potholes were formed when the St. Croix River was much deeper than today. Small potholes at Devil's Lake State Park formed before the Ice Age.

Riparian Zone The area of thick vegetation that runs along the bank of a river. It is characterized by shrubs, vines, trees and grasses. Important to a watershed, they help maintain streams and rivers in their natural state. During heavy rains they help prevent flooding by slowing the flow of water both into the river and along the river banks. In addition, by acting as a buffer between the land and the water, chemicals such as fertilizers and pesticides which are applied to the land, are absorb through many of the river area's plant roots.

Sedge Meadow A wetland that is dry in late summer and composed mostly of sedges. Sedges are plants that look like grasses but feel rough when stroked.

State Ice Age Trail Area (SIATA) A property owned by the Wisconsin Department of Natural Resources (DNR) and managed for the Ice Age Trail.

Swale A hollow or depression at the beginning of a valley that often has wet soils.

Terminal Moraine A type of end moraine where a glacier or glacial lobe reached its maximum extent and melted back.

Thru-Hike To hike an entire long-distance trail, such as the Ice Age Trail, end to end as a continuous journey.

Till Plain An extensive flat plain that forms when a sheet of ice becomes detached from the main body of a glacier and melts in place, depositing the sediments it carried.

Troad A former extraction route created for nontrail purposes that has been adopted as a recreational trail. Extraction activities include logging, agriculture and mining.

Tunnel Channel Created by a fast moving river under a glacier that carves a valley. After the glacier has melted, the valley often contains a series of lakes. Prominent tunnel channels can be seen along the Trail in the New Hope Segment in Portage County and the Straight River Segment in Polk County.

Wisconsin Glaciation A period of the Earth's history at the end of the Pleistocene Ice Age, between 10,000 and 75,000 years ago. All glacial lobes and landforms described in the Guide occurred or were created during the last part of the Wisconsin Glaciation, unless otherwise noted.

Bibliography

Birmingham, Robert A. and Rosebrough, Amy L. *Indian Mounds of Wisconsin*, 2nd Edition. Madison, WI: University of Wisconsin Press. 2000, 2017.

Bolles, Edmund Blair. *The Ice Finders: How a Poet, a Professor and a Politician Discovered the Ice Age*. Washington D.C.: Counterpoint. 1999.

DeLorme. *Wisconsin Atlas and Gazetteer*. Yarmouth, ME: DeLorme. 2011.

Dott, Robert H., Jr. and John W. Attig. *Roadside Geology of Wisconsin*. Missoula, MT: Mountain Press Publishing Company. 2004.

Hansen, Eric. *Hiking Wisconsin*. Guilford, CT: Globe Pequot Press. 2002.

Ice Age Trail Alliance. *Ice Age Trail Atlas*. Cross Plains, WI: Ice Age Trail Alliance. 2017.

Lapham, Increase A. *Wisconsin: Its Geography and Topography*. North Stratford, NH: Ayer Company Publishers. 1846 (reprint 1999).

Mickelson, David M., et al. *Geology of the Ice Age National Scenic Trail*. Madison, WI: University of Wisconsin Press. 2011.

Morgan, John and Ellen. *50 Hikes in Wisconsin*. Woodstock, VT: Backcountry Guides. 2004

Reuss, Henry S. *On the Trail of the Ice Age*. Sheboygan, WI: Ice Age Park & Trail Foundation, Inc. 1990.

Smith, Bart. *Along Wisconsin's Ice Age Trail*. Madison, WI: The University of Wisconsin Press. 2008.

Wisconsin Department of Natural Resources. *Wisconsin, Naturally, A Guide to 150 Great State Natural Areas*. Wisconsin Department of Natural Resources. 2003.

Useful Addresses & Phone Numbers

Ice Age Trail Alliance
PO Box 128, 2110 Main St.
Cross Plains, WI 53528
800-227-0046
info@iceagetrail.org
iceagetrail.org

Wisconsin Department of Natural Resources—Bureau of Parks and Recreation
PO Box 7921
Madison, WI 53707-7921
608-266-2181
DNRWisconsinParks@wisconsin.gov
dnr.wi.gov/topic/parks
For camping reservations at state parks:
888-WIPARKS [947-2757],
wisconsin.goingtocamp.com

**National Park Service—
Ice Age National Scenic Trail**
700 Rayovac Dr., Suite 100
Madison, WI 53711
608-441-5610
nps.gov/iatr

Wisconsin Department of Tourism
800-432-TRIP [8747]
travelwisconsin.com

Wisconsin road conditions:
511 (in Wisconsin) or 866-511-9472

Greyhound Bus Line
800-231-2222
greyhound.com

Badger Coaches
Milwaukee to Madison
877-292-8259
badgerbus.com

Van Galder Bus Co./Coach USA
Bus service to Madison, Janesville, Chicago, Milwaukee and Minneapolis.
800-747-0994
coachusa.com/vangalder

Jefferson Lines
Bus service to Midwest cities including Minneapolis, Rice Lake, Baraboo, Madison, Milwaukee, Manitowoc and Green Bay
800-451-5333
jeffersonlines.com

Megabus
Low-cost bus service to Midwest cities including Minneapolis, Madison, Milwaukee and Chicago
megabus.com

Amtrak
Empire Builder route includes Chicago, Milwaukee, Portage and the Twin Cities
800-USA-RAIL [872-7245]
amtrak.com

Index

Segment Names

ICE AGE TRAIL SEGMENT	COUNTY	GUIDEBOOK PAGE NO.	ATLAS MAP NO.	DATABOOK PAGE NO.
Albany Segment	Green	244	69f, 70f	68–69
Alta Junction Segment	Lincoln	105	30f	30
Arbor Ridge Segment	Rock	252	73f, 74f	72
Averill–Kelly Creek Wilderness Segment	Lincoln	99	27f, 28f	27–28
Baraboo Segment	Sauk	192	60f-W	112
Bear Lake Segment	Barron, Washburn	36	8f	9
Blackhawk Segment	Walworth	270	79f	77
Blue Spring Lake Segment	Jefferson	273	79f	77–78
Bohn Lake Segment	Waushara	168	51f	47–48
Brooklyn Wildlife Segment	Dane, Green	238	68f	67
Camp 27 Segment	Lincoln	96	26f, 27f	26–27
Cedar Lakes Segment	Washington	306	85f	88
Chaffee Creek Segment	Waushara, Marquette	175	52f, 53f-E	50
Chippewa Moraine Segment	Chippewa	54	15f	15–16
Chippewa River Segment	Chippewa	60	16f	17
City of Lodi Segment	Columbia	269	63f	59
City of Manitowoc Segment	Manitowoc	338	95f	97–98
City of Two Rivers Segment	Manitowoc	342	96f	99
Clover Valley Segment	Walworth, Rock	266	77f	76
Cross Plains Segment	Dane	223	65f	64
Deerfield Segment	Waushara	166	50f	47
Delafield Segment	Waukesha	288	82f	82
Dells of the Eau Claire Segment	Marathon	140	40f	38–39
Devil's Lake Segment	Sauk	197	61f	55–56
Devil's Staircase Segment	Rock	252	74f	72
Dunes Segment	Manitowoc	342	95f	98–99
Eagle Segment	Waukesha	282	80f	80
East Lake Segment	Taylor	80	24f, 25f	22–23
East Twin River Segment	Manitowoc	348	97f	101
Eastern Lodi Marsh Segment	Columbia, Dane	211	63f	59–60
Emmons Creek Segment	Portage	160	48f	44–45

ICE AGE TRAIL SEGMENT	COUNTY	GUIDEBOOK PAGE NO.	ATLAS MAP NO.	DATABOOK PAGE NO.
Fern Glen Segment	Columbia	209	62f, 63f	58–59
Firth Lake Segment	Chippewa	60	16f	16–17
Forestville Segment	Kewaunee, Door	360	103f, 104f	105–106
Gandy Dancer Segment	Polk	10	1f–3f	2–3
Gibraltar Rock Segment	Columbia	206	62f	58
Grandfather Falls Segment	Lincoln	101	28f	28–29
Grassy Lake Segment	Washburn	34	7f	8–9
Greenbush Segment	Sheboygan	327	89f	93–94
Greenwood Segment	Waushara	168	51f	48
Harrison Hills Segment	Lincoln	108	30f, 31f	30
Hartland Segment	Waukesha	292	82f	82–83
Hartman Creek Segment	Portage, Waupaca	158	48f	44
Harwood Lakes Segment	Chippewa	57	15f, 16f	16
Hemlock Creek Segment	Barron, Rusk	42	10f	10–11
Highland Lakes Segment	Langlade	120	32f, 33f	32–33
Holy Hill Segment	Washington	304	84f	86–87
Indian Creek Segment	Polk	22	5f	5
Indian Lake Segment	Dane	218	64f	62–63
Janesville Segment	Rock	256	74f	72–73
Janesville to Milton Segment	Rock	259	75f	73–74
Jerry Lake Segment	Taylor	71	22f, 23f	20–21
John Muir Park Segment	Marquette	180	56f-E	52
Kettlebowl Segment	Langlade	131	35f, 36f	35
Kewaskum Segment	Washington	312	86f	89–90
Kewaunee River Segment	Kewaunee	356	100f, 101f	104–105
LaBudde Creek Segment	Sheboygan	330	90f	94
Lake Eleven Segment	Taylor	68	21f, 22f	20
Lapham Peak Segment	Waukesha	288	81f, 82f	81–82
Lodi Marsh Segment	Dane	211	63f	60
Loew Lake Segment	Washington	302	83f, 84f	86
Lumbercamp Segment	Langlade	128	34f, 35f	34–35
Madison Segment	Dane	227	66f	65
McKenzie Creek Segment	Polk	20	4f, 5f	5
Mecan River Segment	Waushara	172	52f	48–49
Merrimac Segment	Sauk	202	61f	56–57
Merton Segment	Waukesha	295	83f	83
Milton Segment	Rock	261	75f	74

ICE AGE TRAIL SEGMENT	COUNTY	GUIDEBOOK PAGE NO.	ATLAS MAP NO.	DATABOOK PAGE NO.
Milwaukee River Segment (Fond du Lac County)	Fond du Lac	320	87f	92
Milwaukee River Segment (Washington County)	Washington, Fond du Lac	312	86f, 87f	90
Mishicot Segment	Manitowoc	348	97f	100–101
Monches Segment	Waukesha	295	83f	83–84
Mondeaux Esker Segment	Taylor	76	23f	21–22
Monticello Segment	Green	242	68f, 69f	68
Montrose Segment	Dane	235	67f	66–67
New Hope–Iola Ski Hill Segment	Portage, Waupaca	150	45f	42
Newwood Segment	Lincoln	96	26f, 27f	27
Northern Blue Hills Segment	Rusk	46	11f	12
Parnell Segment	Fond du Lac, Sheboygan	323	87f–89f	92–93
Parrish Hills Segment	Langlade	116	31f, 32f	32
Pike Lake Segment	Washington	306	84f, 85f	87
Pine Lake Segment	Polk	17	4f	4
Pine Line Segment	Taylor	80	24f	22
Plover River Segment	Marathon	138	39f	38
Point Beach Segment	Manitowoc	345	96f	99–100
Portage Canal Segment	Columbia	184	57f-E	54
Rib Lake Segment	Taylor	84	25f	23
Ringle Segment	Marathon	143	41f	39
Sand Creek Segment	Polk, Barron, Burnett	24	5f, 6f	5–6
Sauk Point Segment	Sauk	194	61f	55
Scuppernong Segment	Waukesha	284	80f, 81f	80–81
Skunk and Foster Lakes Segment	Waupaca	154	47f	43
Slinger Segment	Washington	296	85f	87–88
Southern Blue Hills Segment	Rusk	48	12f	12
Southern Kewaskum Segment	Washington	306	86f	89
Springfield Hill Segment	Dane	218	64f	62
St. Croix Falls Segment	Polk	6	1f	2
Stony Ridge Segment	Waukesha	280	80f	80
Storrs Lake Segment	Rock	261	75f, 76f	74–75
Straight Lake Segment	Polk	14	3f	3–4
Straight River Segment	Polk	17	3f, 4f	4

ICE AGE TRAIL SEGMENT	COUNTY	GUIDEBOOK PAGE NO.	ATLAS MAP NO.	DATABOOK PAGE NO.
Sturgeon Bay Segment	Door	362	104f, 105f	106–107
Summit Moraine Segment	Langlade	124	33f, 34f	33–34
Table Bluff Segment	Dane	221	65f	63
Thornapple Creek Sgment	Marathon	140	40f, 41f	39
Timberland Hills Segment	Barron, Burnett, Washburn	30	6f	8
Timberland Wilderness Segment	Lincoln	94	26f	26
Tisch Mills Segment	Manitowoc, Kewaunee	350	98f	101–102
Trade River Segment	Polk	14	3f	3
Turtle Rock Segment	Lincoln	101	28f	28
Tuscobia Segment	Barron, Washburn	38	8f–10f	9–10
Underdown Segment	Lincoln	105	29f, 30f	29
Valley View Segment	Dane	227	66f	64–65
Verona Segment	Dane	231	66f	65–66
Walla Hi Segment	Manitowoc	336	91f	96
Waterville Segment	Waukesha	286	81f	81
Waupaca River Segment	Portage, Waupaca	154	47f	44
Wedde Creek Segment	Waushara	175	52f	49
West Bend Segment	Washington	309	85f, 86f	88–89
Whitewater Lake Segment	Walworth	268	78f	76–77
Wood Lake Segment	Taylor, Lincoln	86	25f, 26f	23–24

> *I have a stubborn streak, and the more resistance I heard from people telling me that as a woman I should never hike alone, the more I wanted to prove that as a woman I was capable of completing the Ice Age Trail on my own, and that I could do it safely and intelligently. I never want a woman to feel so discouraged that she doesn't try.*
>
> AMY BAYER (AKA "ICE AGE AMY"), ICE AGE TRAIL THOUSAND-MILER

Places of Interest along the Trail

PLACE	COUNTY	GUIDEBOOK PAGE NO.	ATLAS MAP NO.	DATABOOK PAGE NO.
Ahnapee State Trail	Kewaunee, Door	356	102f–105f	104, 106
Aldo Leopold Legacy Center	Sauk	200	58f-E	55
Badger Prairie County Park	Dane	231	66f	66
Badger State Trail	Dane, Green	237	67f–69f	67
Broughton Sheboygan Marsh County Park	Sheboygan	331	90f	94
Brunet Island State Park	Chippewa	62	16f, 17f	18
CD "Buzz" Besadny Anadromous Fish Facility	Kewaunee	358	101f	105
Camp New Wood County Park	Lincoln	104	28f	28
Cardy Paleo-Indian Camp Archaeological Site	Door	365	105f	NA
Chequamegon National Forest	Taylor	70	20f–24f	20–22
Chippewa Lobe Interpretive Loop	Taylor	74	22f	21
Chippewa Moraine National Scientific Reserve and David R. Obey Ice Age Interpretive Center	Chippewa	56	15f	15
Circus World Museum	Sauk	193	60f-W	112
Cross Plains National Scientific Reserve	Dane	226	65f	NA
Cushing Memorial Park and Wisconsin Veterans Memorial Riverwalk	Waukesha	291	82f	82
Dells of the Eau Claire County Park	Marathon	142	40f	38
Devil's Lake State Park	Sauk	200	61f	56
Durward's Glen Retreat & Conference Center	Sauk	200	NA	55
Eisenbahn State Trail	Washington	315	86f, 87f	90
Emma Carlin Trails, Kettle Moraine State Forest—Southern Unit	Jefferson	273	79f, 80f	78
Fort Winnebago Surgeon's Quarters	Northern Columbia	187	57f-E	NA
Gandy Dancer State Trail	Polk	12	1f–3f	3
Gibraltar Rock	Southern Columbia	207	62f	58
Glacial Blue Hills Recreation Area	Washington	310	86f	89

PLACE	COUNTY	GUIDEBOOK PAGE NO.	ATLAS MAP NO.	DATABOOK PAGE NO.
Glacial Drumlin State Trail	Waukesha	291	81f	81
Grandfather Falls Dam and Hydroelectric Plant	Lincoln	101	28f	28
Greenbush Trails, Kettle Moraine State Forest—Northern Unit	Sheboygan	327	89f	93
Hartland Marsh, John Muir Overlook	Waukesha	292	82f	83
Hartman Creek State Park	Portage, Waupaca	159	48f	44
Henry S. Reuss Ice Age Visitor Center	Fond du Lac	326	88f	NA
Historic Rogers Street Fishing Village	Manitowoc	344	96f	99
Holy Hill Shrine and Monastery	Washington	305	84f	87
Ice Age Trail Alliance Headquarters	Dane	226	65f	64
Indian Agency House	Northern Columbia	187	57f-E	54
Indian Lake County Park	Dane	220	64f	62
Indian Mounds Park	Barron	41	NA	NA
International Crane Foundation (ICF)	Sauk	200	60f-W	NA
Interstate State Park	Polk	9	1f	2
Iola Winter Sports Club	Waupaca	150	45f	42
John Muir Memorial County Park	Marquette	180	56f-E	52
John Muir Trails, Kettle Moraine State Forest—Southern Unit	Walworth	270	79f	NA
Kettle Moraine State Forest—Northern Unit	Washington, Fond du Lac, Sheboygan	315	86f–90f	90, 92
Kettle Moraine State Forest—Southern Unit	Walworth, Jefferson, Waukesha	280	78f–81f	78, 80, 81
Lake Country Recreation Trail	Waukesha	288	82f	82, 83
Lake Emily County Park	Portage	157	NA	NA
Lapham Peak Unit, Kettle Moraine State Forest—Southern Unit	Waukesha	291	81f, 82f	82
Lincoln-Tallman House	Rock	258	74f	NA
Lizard Mound County Park	Washington	311	NA	NA

PLACE	COUNTY	GUIDEBOOK PAGE NO.	ATLAS MAP NO.	DATABOOK PAGE NO.
Loew Lake Unit, Kettle Moraine State Forest	Washington	303	83f, 84f	86
Long Lake Recreation Area	Fond du Lac	322	88f	93
Man Mound Park	Sauk	193	NA	NA
Mariners Trail	Manitowoc	340	95f	98
Mauthe Lake Recreation Area	Fond du Lac	322	87f	92
Merrimac Ferry (*Colsac III*)	Sauk	203	62f	57, 58
Merrimac Preserve	Sauk	202	61f, 62f	57
Military Ridge State Trail	Dane	234	66f	66
Milton House Museum	Rock	263	75f	74
Mondeaux Dam Recreation Area	Taylor	79	23f	22
Mountain-Bay State Trail	Marathon	145	41f, 42f	39
Murphy Flowage Recreation Area	Rusk	43	10f, 11f	11
Naga-Waukee County Park	Waukesha	292	82f	82
New Fane Trails, Kettle Moraine State Forest—Northern Unit	Washington	320	87f	92
New Glarus Woods State Park	Green	243	69f	68
New Hope Pines State Natural Area	Portage	150	45f	42
Observatory Hill State Natural Area	Marquette	178	56f-E	NA
Old World Wisconsin	Waukesha	281	80f	NA
Ottawa Lake Campground	Waukesha	285	80f, 81f	80
Parfrey's Glen State Natural Area	Sauk	195	61f	55
Pike Lake Unit, Kettle Moraine State Forest	Washington	305	84f, 85f	87
Point Beach State Forest	Manitowoc	347	96f	100
Potawatomi State Park	Door	366	105f	107
Prairie Moraine County Park	Dane	231	66f, 67f	66
Quaas Creek Park	Washington	311	NA	NA
Ridge Run Park	Washington	309	85f, 86f	89
Robert Cook Memorial Arboretum	Rock	252	73f, 74f	72
Rotary Botanical Gardens and Lions Beach	Rock	258	74f	73

PLACE	COUNTY	GUIDEBOOK PAGE NO.	ATLAS MAP NO.	DATABOOK PAGE NO.
Scuppernong Hiking and Skiing Trails, Kettle Moraine State Forest—Southern Unit	Waukesha	284	80f, 81f	81
St. Croix National Scenic Riverway	Polk	9	1f	2
Straight Lake State Park	Polk	16	3f	4
Sugar River State Trail	Green	246	69f–71f	68
Timm's Hill National Trail	Taylor	84	25f	23
Tuscobia State Trail	Barron, Washburn	41	8f–10f	10
Two Creeks Buried Forest	Manitowoc	351	98f	NA
Underdown Recreation Area	Lincoln	107	29f, 30f	29
University Ridge Golf Course	Dane	230	66f	65
UW-Madison Arboretum	Dane	230	NA	NA
UW-Waukesha Field Station	Waukesha	286	81f	81
Veterans Memorial Park	Langlade	127	34f	34
Wade House Historic Site	Sheboygan	329	89f	93
Walla Hi County Park	Manitowoc	366	91f	96
West of the Lake Gardens	Manitowoc	340	95f	98
Whistler Mounds Group & Enclosure	Waushara	171	51f	NA
Whitewater Effigy Mounds Preserve	Walworth	267	77f	NA
Whitewater Lake Campground	Walworth	259	78f	77
Wisconsin Conservationists' Hall of Fame	Waukesha	279	81f–83f	NA
Wisconsin Maritime Museum	Manitowoc	339	95f	98
Wood Lake County Park	Taylor	88	26f	24
Woodland Dunes Nature Center and Preserve	Manitowoc	342	95f, 96f	98
Yahara Heights County Park	Dane	230	NA	NA

How does one decide to hike the entire Ice Age Trail? I like to think there were many things in our lives that brought us to this quest: a love of the outdoors; a search for a low-cost activity that is also good for our health; a longing to do something epic.

DAWN THAYER, ICE AGE TRAIL THOUSAND-MILER

KEY TO MAP SYMBOLS (See also Segment Snapshot symbol key, opposite.)

Water

 Drinking Water Assume water source is unavailable early fall through late spring.

Camping

 Backpack Campsite A walk-in campsite (varying levels of development) established for backpackers.

 Primitive Camping Areas where hikers may practice Leave No Trace primitive camping. See p. xxi for Leave No Trace guidelines.

 Dispersed Camping Area (DCA) A minimally developed area where long-distance hikers may legally camp. DCAs are established by the Ice Age Trail Alliance and its partners in areas where convenient camping options are limited.

 Backpack Shelter A camping shelter. Those in the Kettle Moraine State Forest require reservations.

 Car Camping A traditional campground reachable by either car or foot.

Amenities

 Parking Area May not be plowed in winter.

 Cross-Country Ski Trails

 Toilet Assume facility is unavailable/closed early fall through late spring.

 Shower May be available only seasonally and/or for a fee.

Trail

 Ice Age Trail Marked with yellow blazes.

Unofficial Connecting Route Unmarked.

 Segment Endpoint The segment endpoint nearest the Ice Age Trail's western terminus.

 Future Ice Age Trail Approximate route.

Select Other Trails

 Segment Endpoint The segment endpoint nearest the Ice Age Trail's eastern terminus.

Other Map Features

Publicly Owned or IATA-Owned Areas Open to public access. Those labeled SIATA are State Ice Age Trail Areas, properties owned by the Wisconsin Department of Natural Resources and managed for the Ice Age Trail.

 Tower Includes fire towers with no public access.

 Gate A locked gate or berm that does not permit public motor vehicle access.

 Unreliable Water Source

 Trail Community A town or city with a formalized agreement with the Ice Age Trail Alliance to support the Ice Age National Scenic Trail and its users.

 GPS Waypoint

KEY TO SEGMENT SNAPSHOT SYMBOLS (See also map symbol key, opposite. See pages xxvii–xxix for more information about symbols.)

Elevation & Ruggedness

 This segment is: 1 (mostly flat) through 5 (very hilly).

 Factoring in signage, maintenance and/or layout challenges; water hazards or crossings; remoteness and logging, this segment is: 1 (not rugged) through 5 (very rugged).

Water

 Drinking water is available on this segment from a pump or spigot with potable water. Assume water source is unavailable early fall through late spring.

 Drinking water is available on this segment from a natural source; filtration required.

 Drinking water is NOT available on this segment.

Camping

 Backpack Camping—Segment has walk-in camping options further defined by map symbols. See map symbol key (opposite) for detailed descriptions.

 Car Camping—A traditional campground is located on or within a few miles of the segment.

Amenities and Activities

 Picnic areas are available on or near the segment.

 Child-friendly amenities like playgrounds and/or swim areas are available on or near the segment.

 Restrooms are available on or near the segment. Assume facility is unavailable/closed early fall through late spring.

 ColdCaching site is on the segment. ColdCaching is a family activity in which participants seek out natural features along the Ice Age Trail.

Hunting & Dogs

 Hikers will not have any interaction with hunting on this segment.

 Segment crosses private land and portions or the full segment may be closed to hikers during hunting season(s).

 In general (🐕), dogs are permitted but must be leashed and under control. Some segments (🐕!) have special regulations for hiking with dogs.

Shared, Spur & Accessible Trails

 Portions of the segment overlap biking, snowmobiling or groomed cross-country skiing trails or roads and/or sidewalks.

 Other hiking trails (spurs, loops or lollipops) are present off the main segment route.

 Portions of this segment may be suitable for those using wheelchairs or similar devices.

Hike Locator

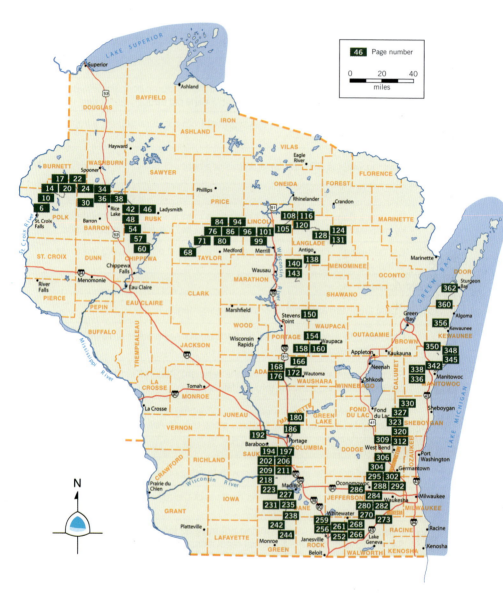

Note: All hike maps are oriented with north up and printed at the same scale.